BOOKS BY WILLIAM WARREN SWEET

BUST OF JOHN WESLEY
From the Model Made From Life by Enoch Wood, Burslem,
England, 1781

Reproduced by the courtesy of Dr. E. S. Tipple

Methodism in American History

WILLIAM WARREN SWEET

Revision of 1953

ABINGDON PRESS
New York • Nashville

METHODISM IN AMERICAN HISTORY

F
SET UP, PRINTED, AND BOUND BY THE
PARTHENON PRESS, AT NASHVILLE,
TENNESSEE, UNITED STATES OF AMERICA

CONTENTS

10-24-63/ Abingdon/ # 5.00

METHODISM IN AMERICAN HISTORY

ILLUSTRATIONS

PREFACE TO THE REVISION OF 1953

Methodism is a living and ever-growing phase of the history of the American people. As such, any account of it cannot be final and exhaustive. Each successive year's events must take their place in the story. The history of any on-going movement, such as American Methodism, must, therefore, periodically be brought down to date. During the past twenty years Methodism has undergone greater change and more far-reaching developments than in any other like period in its history. Its place in America and in the world has been greatly enlarged, as has the place the American nation occupies in the world. As the title of this book implies, the history of American Methodism is here considered as a phase of American history, and it is assumed that it can best be understood in relation to the history of the American people. In other words, it is taken for granted that American Methodism has never carried on its work in a vacuum.

The Revision of 1953 does not attempt to revise the original chapters. Rather, a new chapter and an appendix have been added which encompass the important developments in American Methodism during the twenty years which have elapsed since *Methodism in American History* first appeared.

WILLIAM WARREN SWEET

CHAPTER I

RELIGION IN MID-EIGHTEENTH CENTURY AMERICA

IN the middle of the eighteenth century when young evangelists who had shared John Wesley's heart-warming experience appeared in New York and Maryland and began to form classes and circuits of the people called Methodists, America presented a most complicated religious pattern. In nine of the thirteen colonies there were established churches; the Congregational Church being established by law in Massachusetts, Connecticut and New Hampshire; while in Maryland, Virginia, North and South Carolina, Georgia and in a section of New York around New York City the English Church was established. Only in Rhode Island and the Quaker colonies—New Jersey, Pennsylvania, and Delaware—were there no state churches, and here, naturally, the greatest variety of religious sects developed, and here also were to be found the most heterogeneous racial groups. But it must not be supposed that there was anything like complete uniformity in religion even in those colonies where there were established churches. New England presented the nearest approximation to uniformity, but by the middle of the eighteenth century, Baptist, Anglican, Quaker, and Presbyterian congregations were to be found here and there in New England communities. In none of the Church of England colonies were the members of that church in the majority, with the possible exception of Virginia, and in all the middle and Southern colonies the dissenting churches were making rapid progress from the middle of the century to the outbreak of the Revolution.

In New England the Congregational Church was dominant. Separatist Puritans had established the Plymouth colony in 1620, and though economically poor they have a place of importance in the history of America, in that their instruments of government in both church and state served as models for other Puritan colonies as they were established. The Puritans of Massachusetts Bay colony differed from the Plymouth Puritans both in their economic status and in their attitude toward the Established Church of England. Their leaders were men of wealth, station, and education, and they came to America not as separatists from the Church of England, but as Church of England men. It was the three thousand miles of ocean separating Massachusetts from England, together with the example of the church at Plymouth, which influenced them to become Congregationalists. In 1648, by the adoption of the *Cambridge Platform* the New England Congregationalists had become a church with a definitely established polity. Doctrinally they were strongly Calvinistic, though in the early years little was said of doctrine in their church covenants, not because they were not thoroughly indoctrinated, but because there was practically universal agreement among them.

The first generation of New England Puritans were devoutly religious, each professing a definite religious experience before admission into church membership. With the second generation a change was bound to take place, in that many of the children and grandchildren of the original American Puritan stock, though moral in life and attached to the church, did not have the religious experience required. This situation led to the adoption of the *Half-Way Covenant* (1662), by which the children of nonregenerate members might receive baptism, but were not permitted to receive the Lord's Supper, nor could they vote in church affairs. Thus there arose an increasing group of New England people who might be termed half-way members of the church, a situation that was bound to influence profoundly the cause of vital religion throughout New England.

Toward the close of the seventeenth century liberal tendencies began to make their appearance in some of the New England churches. This was particularly noticeable at Harvard College and in Cambridge, where the tutors at the college were leading a movement to make certain changes in the requirements for church membership and in the conduct of public worship. This liberal movement led to the calling of a convention in 1705 of Massachusetts ministers, where the conservatives, led by Increase Mather and his son Cotton Mather, made an attempt to create new machinery to check these tendencies. These changes, while partly rejected in Massachusetts, were three years later adopted in Connecticut under the title of the *Saybrook Platform*, which marks the beginning of a trend on the part of Connecticut Congregationalism in the direction of Presbyterian polity.

Connecticut Congregationalism had already manifested a tendency to go its own way independently of Massachusetts by the founding of Yale College in 1701; it was hoped the new seat of learning would offset the growing liberal tendencies developing at Harvard. Altogether this was a period of increasing aridity in New England Puritanism. Intercolonial wars, together with the uncertainty of political conditions, occupied the attention of New England leaders at the expense of moral and religious matters. By the end of the seventeenth century the New England Puritan had very largely divorced his religion from his everyday life. On Sundays, under the preaching of the well-trained Puritan divines, he lost himself in God and his conscience was satisfied; on Monday he devoted himself as wholeheartedly to business, and laid up things for his material well-being from "the abundant wealth of the Atlantic Ocean and the virgin forests and fields of a new continent."

Almost with the suddenness of a thunderclap on a sunny summer afternoon came the New England awakening. The heart and center of the revival at its beginning was Jonathan Edwards, the minister at Northampton. Edwards preached the doctrines of Calvinism, interpreted in the light of his own experience, with such tremendous effectiveness that soon the whole of central New England was in the throes of a great spiritual and emotional upheaval. A considerable proportion of the Congregational churches in the Connecticut valley were soon experiencing similar awakenings, and numerous ministers were engaged in promoting the revival. At least twenty-five thousand new members were added to the New England churches as a result of the awakening, though it also was the cause of a long and acrimonious controversy which lasted beyond the end of the century.

While the revival was still under way Jonathan Edwards wrote an account of its manifestations at Northampton which he called *A Narrative of the Surprising Work of God in the Conversion of many hundreds of souls in Northampton and the neighboring towns and villages of New Hampshire and New England.* Soon this account was being read on both sides of the Atlantic, and among the most interested of its English readers was John Wesley, who was just at the beginning of his career as the leader of the evangelical revival in England.

The Wesleyan revival may be said to have begun in 1737, when a little group of Oxford students, who had formed at that ancient University a "Holy Club," whose members were nicknamed Methodists, removed to London and began the work of carrying religion and morality to the submerged classes. Two years later John Wesley organized his first class in London and the same year the first Methodist congregations were formed in Bristol and London. These events mark the beginning of organized Methodism.

The connecting link between the revival movement in England and America was George Whitefield. A member of the "Holy Club" at Oxford, he graduated in 1736; and the same year he received ordination at the hands of the Bishop of Gloucester, who had been his friend and patron since boyhood. About the same time he offered himself to go to Georgia, there to take up the work which had proved too much for the Wesley brothers. It was while he was waiting to go out to America that Whitefield won his first great fame as a preacher, for he preached whenever and wherever opportunity offered. At Gloucester, Bristol, Bath, London, everywhere, crowds gathered to hear the "boy preacher." Wherever he spoke once he was called for again. He sailed for America on December 28, 1737. His first visit was short and was for the purpose of selecting a site for the orphanage, which was to be his principal interest in the New World until his death. His second visit (1739-1741) was an evangelistic tour. He landed at Lewes, Delaware, below Philadelphia. In Philadelphia he made the acquaintance of Benjamin Franklin, who became the American publisher of his sermons, and he was made welcome in all the pulpits of the city. Thence he visited New York, and later journeyed overland, southward to the new colony of Georgia, preaching as he went. The next year he came to New England, then in the very midst of the Great Awakening. Enthusiasm marked his progress. Newport and Boston gave him an immense hearing; Harvard and Yale colleges welcomed his appearance before their students. Journeying westward from Boston, he visited Jonathan Edwards at Northampton, and the four sermons he preached there were the cause of the breaking out of the revival anew. Whitefield made four subsequent tours of New England, and although he never lacked for admirers and friends in that section of the colonies, yet never again was he accorded such universal approval. On his second visit in 1744 enthusiasm for him had cooled, and both Harvard and Yale closed their doors against him. His last three visits were made in 1754, 1764, and

1770. He died in Newburyport the latter year, and his body lies buried there under the pulpit of Old South Presbyterian Church. Whatever limitations Whitefield may have had, he was one of the chief "human factors in the greatest religious overturning New England has ever experienced."

The New England awakening passed almost as quickly as it came. Even the Northampton church was utterly dead after 1744, and in 1750 Edwards was dismissed from his pulpit "amidst bitterness and slander" and from that time until the end of the century Congregationalism passed into a state of religious and moral indifference.

The middle colonies, especially the Quaker colonies, with New York and Rhode Island, were notable for the great variety of religious bodies to be found within their borders. Rhode Island, fathered by Roger Williams, had been established on the principle of complete religious liberty and separation of church and state, the first civil government in the world to be so established, while the well-known liberalism of the Quakers, who were in control in early New Jersey, Pennsylvania, and Delaware, attracted to these colonies a great variety of religious sects. In Pennsylvania, for instance, were to be found English Quakers, Welsh Baptists, and Scotch-Irish Presbyterians, besides Mennonites, Dunkers, German Reformed and German Lutherans. By the middle of the eighteenth century the Presbyterians were rapidly becoming the most numerous as well as the most aggressive religious body in the middle group of colonies. Most of them were Scotch-Irish and represented that immigration which came out of north Ireland in such overwhelming numbers in the first half of the eighteenth century. In 1706 the first American Presbytery was formed, and eleven years later the first Synod made up of four Presbyteries was organized. The Presbyterian Church grew in proportion to the migration from north Ireland, but the fact of greatest single importance to colonial Presbyterianism was the middle-colony awakening, which began about the same time as the New England revival and was responsible for making Presbyterianism the dominant religious force in that region.

William Tennent is for the middle-colony revival what Jonathan Edwards was for the New England awakening. The elder Tennent came to Pennsylvania from Ireland about 1716. He had been a priest in the Irish Established Church, but on coming to America joined the Presbyterians and became the minister of a small church on Neshaminy Creek in the vicinity of Philadelphia. To facilitate the education of his sons, he built a log cabin in his yard to serve as a school, and here his three younger sons, besides some twelve or fifteen other young men, received their training for the ministry; the elder son, Gilbert, had already been trained by his father for the ministry. The elder Tennent not only drilled his students in the languages, logic, and theology, but he imbued them with an evangelical passion which sent them out flaming evangelists. Eventually all of his sons became ministers of Presbyterian churches in central New Jersey, and associated with them were other graduates of the "Log College." Gilbert Tennent was the leader of the group and a revival movement was soon under way in these several churches. In 1738 the New Bruns-

From *The History of Methodism,* Hurst

THE HOLY CLUB: JOHN WESLEY AND HIS FRIENDS AT OXFORD

wick Presbytery, made up of five evangelistic ministers, was formed.

The enthusiasm of these young evangelicals aroused opposition among the more conservative ministers, which led to action by the Synod restraining the revivalists. Thus the Presbyterian ministers were divided into two groups, one favoring the revival, the other opposing it. Opposition came to a head in 1741 when the New Side party, as the revivalists were termed, were expelled from the Synod. Four years later the revivalists formed the New York Synod while the Philadelphia Synod remained the Old Side body. Such was the general situation among Presbyterians when George Whitefield arrived on his first preaching tour. Whitefield was one of the most catholic-spirited ministers of his time and readily co-operated with Quakers, Baptists, Lutherans, Moravians, Presbyterians, Congregationalists, and Reformed, and with all others as long as they advocated vital religion. On his first tour Whitefield spent some time in Philadelphia and New York. He met the elder Tennent, and Gilbert Tennent accompanied him to New York, where he preached in the Presbyterian Church. Jonathan Dickinson invited him to preach in his church at Elizabethtown; at New Brunswick he met the Dutch Reformed leader, Domine Frelinghuysen. Thus Whitefield was in full harmony with the revivalists among the Presbyterians and heartily co-operated with them.

For the next several years the New Side party forged ahead rapidly. At the time of the schism the two bodies were nearly equal in numbers, but by 1758 the New Side party were about three times as numerous as the Old Side. During this period also the New Side Synod organized the College of New Jersey (1747), which admirably served the purpose of its founders, in that for the next generation it poured a stream of zealous young men into the ministry of the Presbyterian Church. Fortunately for American Presbyterianism the schism created by differences over the revival was soon healed (1758), and from that time until the outbreak of the War for Independence the Presbyterian body continued to increase both in numbers and in prestige.

Of great significance to the growth of American Presbyterianism was the extension of the revival into Virginia and the South. The first Presbyterian revivalist to reach Virginia was William Robinson, a graduate of the "Log College." Others followed, and in 1748, Samuel Davies, of the New York Synod, was sent to Hanover County, Virginia, as the first settled Presbyterian minister in all that region. Davies succeeded so well that the Hanover Presbytery was formed in 1755; it was to be the "Mother" Presbytery for the South and the Southwest.

Ranking third in point of numbers among colonial churches was the Established Church of England. It was established by law in six colonies, but in only two—Maryland and Virginia—were the members of this church actually numerous and influential. Of great importance, not alone to the Anglican Church, but also to the colonies as a whole, was the *Society for the Propagation of the Gospel in Foreign Parts,* an Anglican missionary society formed in 1701. From the time of its origin until the War for Independence this great society maintained three hundred and ten ordained missionaries in America and expended more than two hundred thousand pounds. The society's work was carried on chiefly in those colonies where the Anglican Church was either not established or was weak. Thus its best work was done in New England, the middle colonies, and the Carolinas, and as a whole its missionaries were men of devotion and zeal. The Established Church had under its control two of the colonial colleges—William and Mary, which had been established in 1693; and Kings College in New York, chartered in 1754.

The Established Church had a particularly able group of ministers in New England, especially in Connecticut. This was due to the fact that in 1722 the whole teaching staff of Yale College, headed by President Timothy Cutler, had been converted to the Anglican Church, and with them went five other respected Congregational ministers, which proved as great a blow to Congregationalism as it was a boon to the Anglican Church in the colonies.

The Established Church was heavily handicapped throughout the colonial period by the fact that it had no bishop in America, and therefore all young men seeking to enter the Anglican ministry were compelled to journey to England for ordination, nor could the rite of confirmation be administered. In Virginia and Maryland the churches were under the control of lay vestries, and relatively few of the ministers were actually inducted into office, but were only temporarily employed. Nor was there any adequate clerical supervision, although commissaries representing the Bishop of London exercised a limited jurisdiction in some of the Anglican colonies. The Established Church was injured in its reputation among the people by the fact that it was the church of the royal governors; it therefore had little popular appeal, and as the eighteenth century wore on, it became increasingly easy for Presbyterians, Baptists, and Methodists to make converts from among its members.

It was not until the middle of the eighteenth century that the Baptists made large gains in the colonies. The first Baptist churches had been formed in Providence and Newport, Rhode Island, soon after the establishment of that colony. But Baptist principles made little progress in New England outside of Rhode Island: there were twenty-three Baptist churches in all New England in 1740. In the middle colonies the Baptists were relatively unimportant: a few congregations in eastern Pennsylvania, New York, Maryland, and Virginia—that was all. The great Baptist growth, beginning about 1740 and continuing until the outbreak of the War for Independence, was due largely though indirectly to the colonial awakening.

The New England Baptists took little part in the New England revival; they had been so harshly treated by Congregationalists that they were little inclined to join with them in the movement. But indirectly the Baptists reaped large benefits through the divisions and conflicts which appeared among the Congregational churches. Numerous congregations divided over the revival issues, and those favoring the revival, in some instances, formed separate churches which were known as *Separates*. Several of these separate congregations eventually became Baptist. Thus the number of Baptist churches in New England grew—in Massachusetts, from six to thirty; in Connecticut, from four to twelve; in Rhode Island, from eleven to thirty-six; while Baptist churches were established in New Hampshire, Maine, and what is now Vermont.

Of greater significance, however, was the Baptist revival in Virginia and North Carolina. Two New England Baptist preachers, Shubal Stearns and Daniel Marshall, with their families, settled on Sandy Creek, Guilford County, North Carolina, in the year 1755. Soon a church was formed, of which Stearns became the minister; and Marshall and Stearns began to travel through a wide region as evangelists. Other *Separate* Baptist churches were quickly formed and numerous other preachers were "raised up" to carry on the work. Sandy Creek Church grew into an association of Baptist churches, and this association became the mother of the great Baptist denomination throughout the South and Southwest.

The Baptists in Virginia made bitter attacks upon the Established Church and gave little attention to the law which required dissenting meeting houses to secure licenses. This disregard for regulation, and the fact that they were generally under suspicion for the way in which they conducted their meetings, brought upon them severe persecution, and the years just previous to the outbreak of the Revolution have been called the period of the great persecution. The patient manner in which their preachers bore these hardships gave them a great reputation for piety and increased their popularity among the common people. "Every year," to quote their chief historian in Virginia, "new places were found by the preachers whereon to plant the Re-

21

deemer's standard." Thus from a relatively small group the Baptists rapidly became a strong body, and when the Revolution came, their support was eagerly sought by the leaders of the patriot cause, which placed the Baptists in a most advantageous position.

By the end of the seventeenth century Quakers were to be found in every colony under British rule, for the early Quakers were imbued with a dauntless missionary spirit. The first Quaker missionaries in America were two women, Mary Fisher and Ann Austin, who came to Boston in 1656. They were imprisoned and sent away, only to be followed by eight other missionaries who were treated likewise. By the end of the century, however, Quaker Meetings or congregations had been formed in New England, as well as in every other colony. The great Quaker migration was to the middle colonies. Quaker ideas of government were flatly opposed to a state church, and outside the Quaker colonies, Rhode Island, and the Carolinas, the Quakers everywhere met opposition and persecution.

As is well known, the chief Quaker migration to America began when William Penn invited to his great colony of Pennsylvania the persecuted Quakers of England. Two years after Pennsylvania was opened to settlement more than four thousand had come; six years later the population numbered twelve thousand. This was but the beginning of the great flow of population into the Quaker colonies. Of course all who came were not Quakers, but the majority of the earliest settlers seem to have been either English or Welsh Quakers. Immediately Quaker meetings were formed in New Jersey,

Pennsylvania, and Delaware, and by 1700 there were forty congregations in Pennsylvania alone, and by 1760 it is estimated that there were thirty thousand Quakers, or Friends, in America.

The Quakers from the beginning were a loosely organized body, and they have never developed a rigid system of church government. At first spiritual life among them was warm and preachers were numerous and their meetings lively, but the introduction of "birthright membership" (1737) among them, in the words of a Quaker historian, "changed the Society of Friends from a church of believers, at least in theory, to a corporation or association of persons some of whom would be among the unconverted."

Besides the several English-speaking religious bodies, which have been noted, there were to be found in the colonies a considerable number of non-English groups. The oldest of these bodies was the Dutch Reformed, or the state Church of Holland, which was introduced by the Dutch West India Company during the period of its activity in North America. When the Dutch surrendered to the English (1664), there were thirteen Dutch congregations, and for many years the Dutch Reformed Church continued to be the strongest religious body in the colony of New York, though the Anglican Church was established in New York City by an act of the assembly in 1697. The Dutch churches, with few exceptions, used the Dutch language in their churches throughout the whole colonial period, and were dependent upon the "Classis" of Amsterdam, the Dutch Reformed ruling body in Holland, for their ministers. The Dutch Church remained more or less static until aroused through the activities of Theodore Frelinghuysen and the Great Awakening.

Of greater importance, at least from the standpoint of numbers, and geographical distribution, were the several German sects which began to appear in the colonies in the latter seventeenth and early eighteenth centuries. The first to arrive were the Mennonites and Dunkers, who came to Pennsylvania at the invitation of William Penn, from the lower Rhine region, where they had undergone terrible persecution for many years. Most of these industrious Germans settled in Pennsylvania, though several Dunker congregations were to be found in Maryland and Virginia. They settled in communities and were little interested in politics and other outside matters, but they were excellent farmers and their settlements were models of thrift and neatness.

Another small German sect to appear in Pennsylvania was the Moravian brotherhood, or the *Unitas Fratrum*. These interesting people trace their origin back to the Hussite movement in Bohemia, and in the sixteenth century they had grown rapidly. The Thirty-Years War had brought upon them severe persecution, and for almost a hundred years they were nearly extinct. They were kept alive, however, through the heroic leadership of John Amos Comenius (1592-1672), and were revived in the eighteenth century by a humble carpenter, Christian David. Again persecution broke out against them. They were invited by the devout Saxon nobleman, Count Zinzendorf, to take refuge on his great estate, where they were permitted to build a village called Herrnhut. Later Zinzendorf secured for them a refuge in America. They built their American center on the Delaware River above Philadelphia, which they called Bethlehem, and here they developed various industries, chiefly for the support of their missionary enterprises. The Moravians were primarily a missionary body and from the middle of the eighteenth century kept some fifty or more missionaries in the field working among the Indians. Of all the Protestant Indian missions of the colonial period, the Moravian missions were the most successful.

The prevailing religious complexion of German immigrants which swarmed into Pennsylvania, especially between the years 1727 and 1745, was either German Reformed or German Lutheran. In most instances they came without ministers or schoolmasters and were, as a rule, hopelessly poor. The most important name in the formative period of the German Reformed Church in America is Michael Schlatter, who came to Pennsylvania in 1746. Soon he was laying plans for the formation of the first American Coetus (Presbytery), which was organized in Philadelphia in the autumn of the following year. It is an interesting fact that much of the financial assistance which came to the German Reformed churches in the American colonies was contributed by the "Classis" of Amsterdam. In fact, for ten years following independence most of the German Reformed ministers in America were still receiving assistance from this source.

Henry M. Mühlenberg is the greatest Lutheran name in colonial history. He came to America in 1742, and his coming marks an epoch in the history of American Lutheranism. Mühlenberg was a pietist, and was as broad in his sympathies as he was zealous. After six years of labor, during which time he visited Lutheran congregations in all parts of the colonies, he led in the formation of the first Lutheran Synod in America, which took the name *Ministerium* of Pennsylvania. At this time there were perhaps seventy Lutheran congregations in the colonies, and at the outbreak of the Revolution it has been estimated that there were seventy-five thousand Lutherans in Pennsylvania alone, though doubtless a majority of these were to be found outside the churches.

A recent attempt to enumerate the religious organizations in America at the close of the colonial period has resulted in the following: The total number of congregations of all denominations is given as 3,105, with about one thousand each for New England, the middle colonies and the Southern colonies. Ranking first in number of congregations were the Congregationalists with 658; Presbyterians came next with 543; ranking third were the Baptists with 498; Anglicans came fourth with 480; the Quakers or Friends had 295; German and Dutch Reformed together had 251; Lutherans, 151; and Catholics, 50. Such was the religious complexion of the thirteen American colonies when the first Methodist lay preachers, coming out of Ireland in the last great wave of immigration previous to the War for Independence, found their way to America and began the laying of the foundation of the great American Methodist structure.

CHAPTER II

THE MESSAGE OF WESLEY TO HIS TIME

METHODISM arose out of two great urges: the first was the religious experience of John Wesley; the second was the vast spiritual destitution of eighteenth-century England.

Few careers have been so thoroughly studied as has that of John Wesley; few men of any time have left such an abundance of materials for an understanding of their life and work. Wesley began to keep a *Diary* at twenty-two years of age; the last entry was Wednesday, February 23, 1791, a week before his death. He began to keep a *Journal* when he embarked for Georgia on October 14, 1735; he wrote his last entry four months before his end, on October 24, 1790. All this has been gathered together, both *Diary* and *Journal* in eight admirable volumes, edited with consummate patience and skill.[1] Perhaps no man has ever left so revealing a document. Added to this we now have eight other volumes containing the letters of John Wesley edited with equal care.[2]

Thus we are able to trace the unfolding of the life of this remarkable man, who more than any other

---

[1] *The Journal of the Rev. John Wesley, A.M.*: enlarged from original manuscripts, with notes from unpublished diaries, annotations, maps, and illustrations. Edited by Nehemiah Curnock, assisted by experts. Eight volumes. London: Robert Cully, 1909-1916.

[2] *The Letters of the Rev. John Wesley, A.M.*, Sometime Fellow of Lincoln College, Oxford. Standard Edition. Edited by John Telford, B.A. London: The Epworth Press, 1931. 8 Volumes.

was to influence the spiritual well-being of eight-eenth-century England. And of the lives of Wesley there seems to be no end. Each generation desires to have him reinterpreted, and no generation has been more insistent in this respect than has our own.[3]

He who would understand American Methodism must begin by becoming acquainted with the life and experience of John Wesley. John Wesley was the son of Samuel and Susanna (Annesley) Wesley, and though both parents were loyal members of the Church of England, they came from sturdy and much-suffering nonconformist stock. Samuel Wesley for thirty-eight years was the rector of Epworth parish in Lincolnshire; he was the father of a numerous family; he was continually pressed by financial problems, and once was imprisoned for debt, but he had a passion for scholarship and was noted for his courage and independence. Susanna Wesley was brave and cheerful, and above everything else she was a devoted mother. Of the two parents John Wesley owes most to his mother, for she not only schemed and planned for the material well-being of her children, but she was forever concerned for their spiritual welfare.[4]

---

[3] Among the more recent books dealing with some phase of the life of John Wesley, the following may be mentioned: Four books by J. S. Simon, *John Wesley and the Religious Societies*, London, 1921; *John Wesley and the Methodist Societies*, London, 1923; *John Wesley and the Advance of Methodism*, London, ——; *John Wesley the Master Builder*, 1927. Lee, Umphrey, *The Lord's Horseman*, New York, 1928; Lunn, Arnold, *John Wesley*, New York, 1929; Piette, Maximin, *La Reaction de John Wesley dans l'Evolution Protestante, Etud d'Histoire Religieuse*. 2 Edition. Bruxelles, 1927.

[4] "John Wesley was his mother's son and it was from Susanna, rather than from Samuel Wesley, that Methodism received its imprint and traces its descent" (Lunn, Arnold, *John Wesley*, p. 13).

THE MESSAGE OF WESLEY TO HIS TIME

John Wesley was the fifteenth of nineteen children,[5] and was born at Epworth June 17 (O. S.), 1703. His early schooling was obtained in the rectory under his mother's instruction, but at ten and a half years of age he was sent to the famous Charterhouse school in London as a foundation scholar, where he spent six years. And Wesley never lost his love for Charterhouse; throughout his long and busy life we often find him seeking rest and refuge within the walls of this old school. In 1720 Wesley entered Christ Church College, Oxford, whither six years later his brother Charles followed. During his student days Wesley was not a religious zealot, as one might expect from his later career. He plays tennis, swims, reads plays, goes to the tavern, where he sometimes danced, sits in the coffee house and reads widely of all sorts of things, and as one might expect, has many friends. Toward the end of his Oxford career, however, a decided change began to come over him, which seems to have been due to the influence of some friends and the reading of four books—Thomas à Kempis' *Imitatio Christi*, Jeremy Taylor's *Holy Living and Dying*, and William Law's two books, *Serious Call*, and his *Christian Perfection*. Strange to say, the "religious" friend who seems to have had the greatest influence at this period was a young lady, Betty Kirkham, sister of a college friend, Robert Kirkham, and the daughter of the rector of Stanton, a parish near Oxford. By the beginning of 1725 Wesley had come to a definite decision to dedicate all his gifts and

---

[5] John Wesley was the fifteenth child. At the time of John's birth there were four living daughters and his elder brother Samuel, who was thirteen years old. Four children were as yet unborn.

time to God, and we find him adopting Jeremy Taylor's rules for regulating his life.

On September 19, 1725, Wesley was ordained deacon in the Church of England by the Bishop of Oxford, and the following March was elected a Fellow of Lincoln College. Very soon after this he obtained leave from the University to become his father's curate at Wroote, which was a part of his father's parish. Returning to Oxford in September, 1726, he became a lecturer in Greek at Lincoln College, and a year later was ordained a priest in the Church of England. Again he returned to Epworth to assist his father in the parish duties and did not return to Lincoln College until November, 1729. It was during this latter absence from Oxford that a little group of serious students, some undergraduates, others graduates, began to meet together to study the classics and for Bible reading and prayer.

On his return to Oxford John Wesley at once joined this group. Other members were Charles Wesley, Robert Kirkham, William Morgan; and later others united, including George Whitefield. Soon the club began to attract the attention and scorn of other students, for its members were so out of harmony both in their scholastic and spiritual life with the prevailing tone of the University. Soon the group were extending their activities by visiting near-by prisons and teaching poor children, while they continued their religious exercises most systematically. It was at this time that the term "Methodists" was applied to them by a cynical wit of Christ Church College. Other names were given them, such as "Bible Moths," "The Enthusiasts," the "Reforming Club." As we have seen, John Wesley was not the founder of the "Holy Club," but on his return to Oxford, in 1729, he found the club there and very soon was its recognized leader.

John Wesley never outlived his love for Oxford, and to the end of his days "Oxford was the standard by which he measured all other places." Nothing would have pleased him more than to have remained at Oxford all his days, but his father was nearing his end and was urging John to apply for the living at Epworth. After long hesitation, and after finding twenty-six reasons why he should remain at Oxford, Wesley finally made application for the place, but it was too late; the living had gone to another, and it seemed that John Wesley was destined to remain an Oxford Methodist.

The last days of Samuel Wesley were spent in seeing through the press a ponderous book called *Dissertationes in Librum Jobi,* a volume of six hundred pages. The book was dedicated, by her permission, to Queen Caroline, and after his father's death it was John's duty to present a copy of the book to the queen, and he made a trip to London to perform this duty. On its presentation the queen looked at the cover and pronounced it "prettily bound," and promptly laid it aside. But the *Dissertationes* produced a more far-reaching result than its author had ever dreamed, for it was on this trip to London that John Wesley met General James Oglethorpe, and this meeting was soon to bring both John and Charles Wesley to the far-away colony of Georgia.

The colony of Georgia had been founded as a refuge for English debtors and other unfortunates by a group of benevolently minded Englishmen, the leader of whom was James Oglethorpe. The colony was established in 1732, and Oglethorpe had then returned to England to further the interests of the project. He was at this time looking for a young priest who would minister to the English settlers, and at the same time work for the Christianization of the Indians. Wesley was introduced to Oglethorpe, who at once offered him the place. Wesley hesitated, and returning to Epworth left the decision to his mother. Her reply was: "If I had twenty sons, I should rejoice that they were all so employed, though I never saw them more."

On October 19, 1735, we find John Wesley, his younger brother Charles, together with Benjamin Ingham, on board ship bound for Georgia. John Wesley and Ingham were to be missionaries, while Charles Wesley went as secretary to General Oglethorpe. On board the same ship were twenty-six Moravians from Count Zinzendorf's estate in Saxony, also bound for Georgia as colonists, and with them was their Bishop Nitschmann. This little body of devout men and women greatly influenced the missionaries, and we find John Wesley beginning the study of German in order that he might converse with them. In the course of the long two-months' voyage the ship ran into three considerable storms, which were the cause of great anxiety to both passengers and crew. John Wesley himself was not entirely free from fear, for he records in his diary after one of the storms: "Prayed. Storm greater; afraid!" During a previous storm he had written: "Prayed, conversed; afraid to die; storm still." One evening while the waves were dashing

CAPTAIN WEBB PREACHING IN THE SAIL LOFT

against the side of the ship with such force "one would think" they would "dash the planks into a thousand pieces," Wesley went to the Moravians, who were holding their evening service on deck. About them people were screaming, while the sea broke over the ship, "split the mainsail in pieces, . . . and poured in between the decks." "The Germans," he says, simply looked up and, without intermission, "calmly sang on." Afterward he asked one of their number, "Was you not afraid?"

He answered, "I thank God, no."

He then asked, "But were not your women and children afraid?"

"No," was the reply; "our women and children are not afraid to die."

It was this evidence that convinced John Wesley that these simple-hearted Moravians possessed a secret which he had not yet discovered.

When John Wesley landed in Georgia, he was a rigid High-Churchman and a strict sacramentarian. He labored the best he knew how for the settlers—for he found little opportunity to work among the Indians—but he was tactless and overly severe in his attempt to enforce High Church regulations in a new and rude community. The most painful experience which came to him in Georgia was his love affair with Sophia Hopkey, an attractive eighteen-year-old young lady, a niece of the chief magistrate at Savannah. There can be no doubt that Wesley was deeply in love with Miss Sophia and that his love was returned. The idea of marriage he could not get from his mind, but he was strangely hesitant, always able to think up reasons why he should not marry at the very moment when most young men would have permitted their emotions to have swept them into matrimony. The result was that he hesitated too long, and Miss Sophia married another. After her marriage Wesley saw her interest in religion cool, which greatly distressed him, and finally he was led to repel her from the holy communion. The colonists naturally judged that he was actuated by the spirit of a disappointed lover, and charges were eventually lodged against him, one being that he had attempted to seduce Sophia Hopkey, and he was summoned to appear before the court at Savannah. He attended six sessions of the court, seeking to have his case decided, but evidently because of the lack of evidence, the case was purposely delayed. Sick at heart at the turn affairs had taken and thoroughly discouraged at the lack of good results from his work in Georgia, he decided to return to England, arriving in London February 3, 1738.[6]

Wesley returned from Georgia restless and discouraged. Of his Georgia experience he says in his *Journal:* "What have I learned myself in the meantime? Why (what I least expected), that I, who went to America to convert others, was never myself converted to God." Though Wesley later changed his views as to his spiritual condition while in Georgia, yet this reference, and others in his *Journal* like it, at this period, indicate clearly his depression of spirit. He craved some new and deeper experience. On his return he preached frequently

---

[6] For a sympathetic account of Wesley's first love affair read, Lunn, Arnold, *John Wesley*, Chapter V. See also Coulter, E. M., *When John Wesley Preached in Georgia*, Georgia Historical Quarterly, Vol. IX, No. 4, December, 1925.

in pulpits that were open to him, and attended the religious societies hoping to find light. He received much help from Peter Böhler, a Moravian temporarily in London on the way to America. In later years Wesley recognized in Böhler his best spiritual guide in these days of uncertainty. Among the things this wise Moravian said to Wesley, after patiently hearing the young man present his arguments—and Wesley was always full of them—was: "My brother, your philosophy must be purged away"; and he continually urged the acceptance of a simple faith. Böhler soon left England for America, but he had given Wesley sufficient guidance so that very soon he entered into that experience which marks the spiritual beginning of Methodism.

Charles Wesley had already (May 21, 1738) "found deeper rest for his soul"[7] through the guidance and prayers of a simple mechanic. We will let John Wesley tell what happened to him three days later: "In the evening I went very unwillingly to a society in Aldersgate Street, where one was reading Luther's preface to the *Epistle to the Romans*. About a quarter to nine, while he was describing the change which God works in the heart through faith in Christ, I felt my heart strangely warmed. I felt I did trust in Christ, Christ alone for salvation; and an assurance was given me that he hath taken away my sins, even mine, and saved me from the law of sin and death." After the service some friends brought John to Charles, and John cried

---

[7] George Whitefield was the first of the three to enter into a conversion experience, after a long period of physical and mental struggle. See Belden, *George Whitefield*, pp. 21-23.

METHODISM IN AMERICAN HISTORY

out when he saw his brother, "I believe." The two brothers were now united in a common experience, and no longer are the notes of uncertainty and despair to be found in the *Journal;* there is now the note of certainty and victory. Methodism is on its way!

Any adequate description of English society at this period must begin with an account of the agricultural and industrial revolution, which swept men, women and children from the countryside into the factories, mills, and mines, where they worked under conditions of indescribable cruelty. The factory system was the "new money-making, death-dealing Moloch" to whom the poor people of eighteenth-century England were thrown. A new moneyed class arose, imbued with a greedy materialism which swept away most if not all of the old restraints. The suffering and misery of the poorer classes, herded into the factory towns, caused them to seek temporary release in the new, cheap "tipples," such as rum and gin. Every sixth house in London was a saloon, and drunkenness became so universal throughout the whole land that the very nature of the people was changed. For the upper classes the court set an example of profligacy, which was all too generally followed by statesmen and social leaders. Crime was rampant among all classes, and so common was murder and robbery that no one thought of stirring out of his house at night without arms. At no period in all the history of the English people had morals sunk to such a low ebb.

And what was the religious situation in England at this time? The depth and apathy and shame to

36

which organized religion in eighteenth-century England had sunk beggars description. In 1731, Montesquieu reported, after a visit to England, that the people of England had no religion, and that not more than four or five of the members of the House of Commons attended church. The whole Church of England, from the Archbishop of Canterbury down, was honeycombed with indifference and complacency. Many of the clergy spent their time in gambling, fox-hunting, and drinking, and made little pretense of caring for the spiritual well-being of the perishing people about them. One day the Bishop of Chester, one of the "Working clergy," reproved a clergyman in his diocese for drunkenness.

"But, my lord," protested the surprised clergyman, "I was never drunk on duty!"

"On duty?" thundered the bishop. "Pray, sir, when is a clergyman not on duty?"

"True, my lord," stammered the culprit; "I never thought of that."

Who was to rescue religion "from the palsied hands of an institution moribund with respectability and complacency, and cursed with academic irrelevance?" This was the task to which John Wesley, his brother Charles, and George Whitefield, and their associates now set themselves; and as the eighteenth century wore on, any impartial observer would be compelled to say that the task was being done. In the remainder of this chapter we can only indicate in barest outline the steps by which this great transformation in the religious life of England was wrought.

Soon after his conversion experience, John Wesley made a visit to the Moravian community on the Zinzendorf estate at Herrnhut, and from them he learned much. Returning to England he met with the people in the religious societies,[8] but he did not often preach, as an increasing number of pulpits were now closed against him, for his preaching the doctrine of conversion marked him in the eyes of most of the clergy as an enthusiast. On the advice of Peter Böhler, Wesley had formed a society, differing somewhat from the usual societies of the period, and modeled after the Moravian system, and some of the original members of this society were Moravians. This society met in Fetter Lane, and this became the early headquarters of the work of the Wesleys. It was here that seven of the old Oxford Methodists and about sixty laymen met in a love feast on New Year's Day, 1739, and after its close a number continued in prayer until three in the morning. This meeting marks a high point in Wesley's religious experience, and from this time on he becomes increasingly active, "expounding" in the Fetter Lane society as well as in many others.

We must not lose sight of the fact that it was the new message which the Wesleys and Whitefield were now proclaiming with such effectiveness that created the movement. They began to work with the existing agencies already at hand, and when these were found insufficient, others were created or were adapted to carry on their activities. In some

---

[8] The Wesleys did not originate the religious societies. Such societies had existed in the Church of England for more than fifty years. See Woodward, Josiah, *Account of the Rise and Progress of the Religious Societies in the City of London, etc.* 4th Ed. London, 1712; also Simon, J. S., *John Wesley and the Religious Societies*, London, 1921, especially Chap. I.

instances Wesley was reluctant to adopt new methods. This is well illustrated by the manner in which field preaching came to be approved. When George Whitefield returned from his first American journey, he found that the London churches had closed their doors to the evangelists. Accordingly, he left London in more or less disgust and went down to Bristol. Here he found much the same opposition he had met in London; the churches were practically all closed against him, where but eighteen months before he had preached to throngs. But he refused to permit the stubborn Bristol clergymen to defeat him. Four miles from Bristol is Kingswood, formerly a park, but at that time a barren place, due to the discovery of coal in the vicinity, and occupied by lawless coal miners, most of whom had never been in a church. It was to these outcasts that Whitefield now went with his eloquent message. Taking his stand on a mound in Kingswood, he began field preaching.[9] It was immediately successful, and in a few weeks his outdoor congregations were numbered by the thousands. Soon many of the hardened miners were so visibly affected by Whitefield's moving appeals that "white gutters" were made by their tears as they rolled down their blackened cheeks.

America soon recalled Whitefield, but before leaving Bristol he wrote John Wesley, urging him to continue the work he had begun at Bristol. Wesley at once consented and immediately left London

---

[9] To those who lived on pew rents field preaching seemed dangerous; and because it had been practiced by the Quakers and Independents and other illegal religious groups, it seemed illegal to the strict churchman, though it had been a common practice in the Middle Ages.

for Bristol. Here he began to meet regularly the religious societies, and while expounding the Sermon on the Mount to one of them he was struck by the fact that here was a "remarkable precedent for field preaching." On April 2, 1739, he records in his *Journal:* "At four in the afternoon I submitted to be more vile, and proclaimed in the highways the glad tidings of salvation, speaking from a little eminence in the ground adjoining to the city, to about three thousand people." A few days before (March 31) Wesley had written that he scarce could reconcile himself to this strange way of preaching in the fields: "having been all my life (till very lately) so tenacious of every point relating to decency and order that I should have thought the saving of souls almost a sin if it had not been done in church." As has been well pointed out, the significant part of this statement is "till very lately." From now on Wesley ceases to be a slave to the past and the deciding factor from henceforth becomes: "How can we best serve the present age?"

Methodism had now two centers, Bristol and London, and from both the work spread rapidly. During the eleven weeks of Wesley's first sojourn at Bristol it became necessary to provide a room to accommodate the two classes of religious societies that had been formed there. This was done by leasing a piece of ground upon which a building was erected. Returning to London he continued his open-air campaign, preaching to vast crowds at Blackheath and Moorfields. In November of this year (1739) he began to preach at the Foundery near Moorfields. The Foundery, when purchased by Wesley, was a heap of ruins where the king's cannon had formerly been cast, but in 1716 had been wrecked by an explosion. Wesley purchased the lease, repaired the building, and it soon became the center of the Methodist societies in London.[10]

The Fetter Lane society had developed two parties, one dominated by tendencies the Wesleys could not approve; the other followed their leadership. Toward the end of 1739 the part of the society under the control of the Wesleys withdrew and began to hold its meetings at the Foundery, while, a little later, those remaining were formed into a Moravian church. These happenings in Bristol and London mark the beginning of organized Methodism.

There was but one condition of membership attached to the Wesley societies, which now began to be numerously formed—that of desiring to flee from the wrath to come. No doctrinal tests were ever laid down.[11] John Wesley was always very proud of this fact and often called attention to it. The following is a typical statement made by Wesley toward the end of his life: The Methodists "do not impose, in order to their admission, any opinions whatever. Let them hold particular or general redemption, absolute or conditional decrees; let them be churchmen, or dissenters, Presbyterians or Independents, it is no obstacle. Let them choose one

---

[10] The title to the Bristol building was at first placed in eleven trustees, but soon Wesley found that he would have to be responsible for the payment of the debt; accordingly, the people were called together, the instrument was canceled, and the property was placed in his name. This was the plan finally adopted in all his building operations.

[11] This does not mean that Wesley did not emphasize doctrine in his preaching. In fact, he was the great doctrinal preacher of the eighteenth century, but he did not insist that even his helpers share his views if they were peaceable. See Faulkner, *The Methodists*, pp. 23-30.

mode of baptism or another, it is no bar to their admission. The Presbyterian may be a Presbyterian still; the Independent and Anabaptist use his own mode of worship. So may the Quaker; and none will contend with him about it. They think and let think. One condition, and one only, is required—a real desire to save the soul. Where this is, it is enough; they desire no more; they lay stress upon nothing else; they only ask, 'Is thy heart herein as my heart? If it be, give me thy hand.'" And he proudly adds: "Is there any other society in Great Britain or Ireland that is so remote from bigotry? that is so truly of a catholic spirit? so ready to admit all serious persons without distinction? Where, then, is there such another society in Europe? in the habitable world? I know none. Let any man show me that can."

The two institutions which soon developed, and which more than any others account for the rapid spread of Methodism throughout Great Britain, and later in America, were the class meeting and lay preaching. In both cases Wesley stumbled upon them rather than deliberately planned them. The origin of the class meeting came about in this way: The question as to how the new preaching house in Bristol was to be paid for weighed heavily upon Wesley. In 1742 a meeting was held in Bristol, at which the question was asked, "How shall we pay the debt upon the preaching house?" Captain Foy, a captain of a seagoing ship, a member of the society, and accustomed to having the oversight of men, suggested: "Let every one in the society give a penny a week and it will be easily done." To the objection that some could not afford to give that much, the captain further suggested: "Put ten or twelve of them to me. Let each of these give what he can weekly, and I will supply what is wanting." Others made the same offer, and so it came about that all members of the society were placed in classes of about twelve each, and over each class a leader was appointed. Later reports began to come to Mr. Wesley from the leaders that in their visits among the members, one was found in drink; another was quarreling with his wife. Immediately it came to Wesley's mind: "This is the very thing I wanted. The leaders are the persons who may not only receive the contributions, but also watch over the souls of the brethren." From that time onward every society was so organized, and thus the key institution of early Methodism was born. Later smaller groups were instituted, made up of the more devout and trustworthy members of each society, which were called "bands." At the beginning Wesley depended upon the "bands" for advice in critical cases, and they were in general his counselors on affairs pertaining to the society.

The class meeting originated at Bristol; lay preaching began at about the same time in London. During one of Wesley's sojourns in Bristol, in the year 1742, word came to him that one Thomas Maxfield, a layman, was preaching to the London society, and he hurried over from Bristol to stop him. Fortunately, he saw his mother before he met Thomas Maxfield, and said to her, "Thomas Maxfield has turned preacher, I find." To this his mother replied: "John, you know what my sentiments have been, but take care what you do with that young man, for he is as surely called of God

43

to preach as you are. Examine what have been the fruits of his preaching, and hear him also yourself." Following his mother's wise advice, Wesley was convinced that she was right, and soon lay preaching was a regular and recognized feature of Methodism. Two years later the first Conference was held at the Foundery, which has met every year since that time. At first it was made up only of ordained ministers of the Church of England, but soon it came to include some of the lay itinerant preachers as well.

Wesley, throughout his whole life, was ever eagerly seeking new kingdoms to conquer. In 1739 he made his first preaching tour into Wales; in 1747 he first landed on the shores of Ireland, to be followed by forty-one other visits. The number of Irish Methodists was never large, yet Wesley received some of his best helpers from the Emerald Isle. In 1751 Wesley made his first preaching tour into Scotland, and although he made many subsequent visits, and Methodist societies were formed in many places, yet Methodist influence in Scotland was largely of an indirect kind. When in 1767 the first enumeration of the number in the Methodist societies was made, it was found that there were 22,410 members in England, 2,801 in Ireland, 468 in Scotland and 332 in Wales. But numbers were never emphasized by Wesley. He was always eager to admit anyone who expressed a desire to know the way of life, but he was equally swift to eject those who failed to come up to the high moral standards which were set by the Rules of the United Societies.

It must not be supposed that all this was accomplished by John Wesley alone. As a matter of fact, he had efficient helpers from the start. His brother Charles, though never sharing anything like equal authority with John, nevertheless worked in perfect harmony with him, and was the chief contributor to the hymnody of the revival. He wrote altogether more than six thousand hymns. Indeed, to a large extent, the revival sung its way into the hearts of the people. The range of Charles Wesley's hymns is astonishing. He wrote hymns for every occasion and to interpret every mood. There were, of course, other hymn writers of the period, Isaac Watts taking equal rank with Charles Wesley, but hymn singing in the churches was very largely a result of the Wesleyan Revival.

George Whitefield played an indispensable part in the revival movement, and although he and the Wesleys early separated over the question of doctrine, yet the work of each continued to supplement that of the other. Whitefield's patron was the Countess of Huntingdon, who was active in trying to evangelize her own class, and often invited lords and ladies to go with her to hear the evangelical preachers. Lord Dartmouth was one of her converts, later to become the secretary of state for the colonies and the patron of Indian missions in America. He and other noblemen like-minded did much to secure the appointment of evangelical clergymen to "livings" in various parts of the kingdom, and in many centers the evangelical influence became strong.

As time went on there gradually arose in the Church of England a group of clergymen who were sympathetic with the work carried on by the Methodists, and came finally to form a party known as the Evangelicals. These clergymen did not work as actual colleagues with Wesley, but were greatly influenced by him. Another group of Church of England clergymen were more closely associated with the revival, always gave the Wesleys access to their pulpits and in some instances organized their people into classes Methodist fashion. Two such clergymen were Charles Perronet, the vicar of Shoreham in Kent, who was called by Charles Wesley the "Archbishop of the Methodists," and John Berridge, who became the vicar of Everton, in Bedfordshire. The greatest of all Wesley's helpers, however, from among the clergy of the Church of England was John William Fletcher, the vicar of Madeley, whose beauty of life and deep devotion made a lasting impression upon his contemporaries. Often he defended Wesley when he could not defend himself. He wrote the chief defense of the doctrinal position of the Wesleys in their controversy with the Calvinists, called Fletcher's *Five Checks to Antinomianism,* which exerted a major influence on early Methodist theology.

Wesley's chief helpers, however, were his lay itinerants, and no movement has "ever called forth a nobler band of men."[12]

[12] Jackson, Thomas (Ed.), *The Lives of Early Methodist Preachers, chiefly written by themselves.* Fourth Edition, 6 Vols. London, 1872.

CHAPTER III

METHODISM IS PLANTED IN AMERICA

ON Friday, October 14, 1768, John Wesley had as his guest at Bristol one of the king of Sweden's chaplains, Dr. C. M. Wrangel, who had just returned from a sojourn of several years in the province of Pennsylvania, where he had served as provost of the Swedish Lutheran churches on the Delaware.[1] Four days later the Swedish chaplain preached in the new room at Bristol, to Wesley's entire satisfaction. We have every reason to suppose that the chief purpose of Doctor Wrangel's visit was to present to Mr. Wesley the needs of America and to urge upon him the necessity of sending some of his preachers to help the colonists, many of whom, he stated, "are as sheep without a shepherd." The following August, 1769, at the Conference at Leeds, John Wesley stated from the chair, "We have a pressing call from our brethren of New York (who have built a preaching

---

[1] Note: The Rev. Carl Magnus von Wrangel de Saga was the provost of the Swedish churches on the Delaware and the pastor of Gloria Dei congregation, now known as Old Swedes. He was educated partly in Sweden and at the University of Göttingen. He was sent to America to take charge of the Swedish churches in 1759, where he remained nine years. From 1751 to 1771 he was private chaplain to King Adolphus Frederick of Sweden. Wrangel was a sincere pietist and believed in the necessity of personal experience, and was in sympathy with Whitefield when he came to Philadelphia, and later assisted the Methodist preachers on their first visits to Philadelphia and vicinity. He also maintained cordial relations with Henry M. Mühlenberg, the great Lutheran leader. See Mann, William J., *Life and Times of Henry M. Mühlenberg* (Philadelphia, General Council Publication Board, 1911), pp. 342-348.

house) to come over and help them." He then asked "Who is willing to go?" and then and there two preachers offered themselves for this service—Richard Boardman and Joseph Pilmoor. A collection for the Americans was then proposed and taken, and of the seventy pounds secured, fifty were allotted toward the payment of the debt on the New York meetinghouse, and twenty pounds set aside to pay the expenses of the two missionaries. The next month the missionaries set sail from Bristol, and on October 24 arrived at Gloucester Point, a few miles below Philadelphia. A little group of Methodists were awaiting them, having been informed of their coming by a letter from Doctor Wrangel. Immediately the English preachers began their work, Pilmoor preaching from the steps of the Old State House, now known as Independence Hall, on Chestnut Street. This may be called the official beginning of American Methodism, but for its real beginning we will need to retrace our steps and recount an unusual story, even in this time of unusual happenings, of Irish immigration to America.

It is passing strange that Methodism should have been so long delayed in reaching America. English Methodism dates from 1739, when the first Methodist congregations were formed in London and Bristol and the first regular preaching places established. It was just thirty years from this date that the first official missionaries arrived in America. How may this long delay be explained? The principal reason, no doubt, is to be found in the type of immigration which was entering America during these years. At this period the English flow of population had largely ceased, but from 1708 on-

SAINT GEORGE'S CHURCH, PHILADELPHIA

ward to the American Revolution, German immigration from the lower Palatinate especially, and then immigration from Ireland, particularly from Ulster, was directed extensively toward America. Thus it becomes evident how it came about that the first Methodist immigrants to America were from Ireland.

The number of Irish Methodists on their native island, as has been noted, was never large, but they were to be found widely distributed. Altogether, John Wesley visited Ireland forty-two times, averaging one visit a year from 1747, the date of his first, to 1789, the date of his last visit. Tyerman has computed that he occupied altogether not less than six years in the Emerald Isle, and directly and indirectly these were among the most fruitful years of his long life. Lecky states[2] that Wesley found in Ireland "a soil pre-eminently suited for his seed." It is, of course, true that the great majority of the Irish people were Roman Catholic, and some of the Established Church clergy opposed him and his work bitterly, but on the whole Wesley met with comparatively little real opposition on his Irish pilgrimages. Writing from Dublin during the course of his first visit he says: "For natural sweetness of temper, for courtesy and hospitality, I have never seen a people like the Irish."[3] On his second tour he writes: "So general a drawing I have never known among any people, so that as yet none even seem to oppose the truth." Methodism's course in Ireland was not always so smooth as its founder has here

[2] *History of England in the Eighteenth Century*, Vol. III, p. 110.
[3] Telford, John, *The Letters of the Rev. John Wesley*, Vol. II, pp. 109-110.

indicated, but, from the first, persecution was the exception rather than the rule. Although the labors of Wesley and his preachers in Ireland resulted in the organization of a fairly numerous body of Irish Methodists, yet the greatest influences coming from Irish Methodism were indirect. One such influence was the rekindling of spiritual life in the Irish Established Church, indicated by the fact that by the end of the eighteenth century the Irish Church had become the most active evangelical section of the Anglican body. A second indirect result came about through Irish immigration; for the founders of American Methodism were none other than Irish immigrants. Still a third indirect influence flowed from the Irish activities of the early Methodists. The Scotch-Irish Presbyterians in America, familiar with Methodism in Ulster, welcomed the Methodists when they came to America; hailed them as spiritual kinsmen; and together they were responsible for the first great religious revival following Independence.

For more than a century there has been intermittent discussion as to whether American Methodism had its beginning in Maryland or in New York. In 1916 an official commission was created to investigate fully the whole matter, but when their report appeared[4] it gave satisfaction to but one side in the controversy; consequently the whole matter stands much as it did before. Since then the fruitless discussion has continued, furnishing considerable heat and some light upon the question. As a matter of plain fact, it is a type of controversy that can never be definitely settled, since the necessary documents

[4] *Report of the Joint Commission on the Origin of American Methodism,* 1916.

on both sides are lacking, and for that reason there can be no historical proof for either contention. This being the case, it would be folly to take definitely either one viewpoint or the other, and for that reason it is here proposed simply to set forth the known facts regarding the work of Robert Strawbridge in Maryland and Philip Embury in New York.

Robert Strawbridge was a native of County Leitrim, the southwestern county of Ulster, a region later made famous by one of the most successful of Wesley's early Irish preachers, Gideon Ouseley. As a local preacher Strawbridge soon won a reputation for zeal and courage. Persecution drove him from his native county to neighboring regions, where he continued his evangelical labors with success. In his personal traits Strawbridge seems to have been typically Irish, for he was fiery, generous, and energetic, "somewhat intractable to authority, and probably improvident." This latter characteristic, especially after his marriage, was probably one of the principal causes for his coming to America. Like many another Ulsterman of that day, he was attracted to America as a place where a competent livelihood might be more easily and surely secured. The exact date of his coming is uncertain. Some have placed it as early as 1760, others as late as 1766.[5] He settled with his family on Sam's Creek in Frederick County, Maryland, some thirty miles northwest of Baltimore. Here, after building his cabin, he began to hold meetings,

[5] For the arguments for the earlier date, see article in *Methodist Quarterly Review*, July, 1856, by W. Hamilton; also article by F. G. Porter, "Robert Strawbridge and American Methodism," *Methodist Review*, 1928.

gathering his neighbors first into his own cabin, and later erecting a log meetinghouse on Sam's Creek, about a mile from his home.

Strawbridge now began his career as, practically an independent itinerant, journeying over a large section of eastern Maryland, Delaware, Pennsylvania, and Virginia, gathering groups of his converts into classes, and calling forth a group of young men to assist him in his growing work. To Strawbridge belongs the high distinction of having called forth the first native Methodist preachers in America, and eventually a whole group came into the itineracy through his influence. Among these first native American preachers, spiritual sons of Strawbridge, were William Watters, Philip Gatch, and Freeborn Garrettson. Strawbridge himself, however, seems to have been a regular circuit preacher but two years, 1773 to 1775. When the American work was placed under such disciplinarians as Thomas Rankin and Francis Asbury, the independent-spirited Strawbridge was a thorn in their flesh. His Irish independence was too strong to bow to their authority, and for this reason, very probably, Strawbridge has failed to receive the credit he deserves, in the early accounts of the establishment of Methodism in America. This fact is fully borne out by the comment that Asbury makes in his *Journal*[6] on learning of the death of Strawbridge. He says: "He is no more; upon the whole, I am inclined to think the Lord took him away in judgment because he was in the way to do hurt to his cause. . . ."

While Strawbridge and his helpers were estab-

---

[6] September 3, 1781.

lishing the first Methodist preaching places in Maryland and the adjoining colonies, another group of Irish immigrants were founding the first Methodist class in New York. This little body of Methodists, consisting of five or six families, came to New York from County Limerick in 1760. Among their number was a local preacher and exhorter, Philip Embury, and his wife. These families were the descendants of German Palatinates who had settled in Ireland some fifty years before, having been driven from their homes in southern Germany by the armies of Louis XIV of France in his attempt to extend the northern boundary of France to the Rhine. Thousands of German farmers had fled before these terrible invaders, and more than six thousand had found refuge in London. Later (1710) three thousand had been sent to America at British expense, and were among the first German settlers to arrive in the colonies. A small group of these German refugees, about fifty families, emigrated to Ireland, where they found a home in County Limerick. There in 1758 Wesley found them on one of his Irish tours. The community, having been long without pastors, was completely demoralized, and was noted for profanity, drunkenness, and its utter disregard for religion. But Methodist preaching soon wrought a complete transformation, and they became a sober and devout community. Such is the background of the humble people who were to found the first Methodist society in New York.

It is now known that Philip Embury and his wife, with some of the others of their party, united with the Trinity Lutheran Church in New York, as no doubt this was the most congenial congregation in the town. The records of that church reveal the fact that Embury's children were there baptized, as was also the daughter of Barbara Heck, Embury's cousin, and that Embury in 1761 was teaching in a school under the direction of the pastor of that church.[7] It was not until 1766 that Embury began to exercise his gifts as an exhorter, and this was brought about through the concern felt by his cousin, Mrs. Barbara Heck, for the spiritual welfare of her family and their neighbors. Other Palatines had arrived in New York, most of whom were not Methodists, and their influence was creating a carelessness for religion among the whole group. Finding a party playing cards in the house of her brother, one of the later arrivals, Barbara Heck, after destroying the cards, went to the dwelling of her cousin Philip Embury, told him what she had done and appealed to him to begin to preach. She bore down his ready excuses and urged him to begin at once and in his own house. This he finally consented to do, and, once begun, he continued to meet the growing group weekly and enrolled them into a class in good Methodist fashion. Soon there were two classes, one of men, another of women. The groups were now too numerous to meet longer in Embury's house and a room in the neighborhood was rented, but soon even this larger room was crowded with eager listeners. Conversions became of frequent occurrence. Three musicians from the British regimental band, located at the neighboring barracks, joined the group, and soon became active helpers.

---

[7] See article, "Maryland and American Methodism," by Edward L. Watson, *Methodist Review*, 1929, pp. 409-425. In the above article Mrs. A. B. Bibbins contributes the materials regarding the relation of Philip Embury and Barbara Heck to Trinity Lutheran Church.

METHODISM IS PLANTED IN AMERICA

The superintendent of the almshouse invited Embury to preach there, and several of the inmates were enrolled as members of the society.

In the winter of 1767 as the society was gathered for worship there suddenly appeared among them a British officer, in full uniform with his sword at his side. What was his object in coming into this humble place? Had he come to put a stop to their religious gatherings? For a little while there was fearful apprehension among the gathered worshipers, until they saw this British officer join in their devotions. And at the close of the service apprehension was turned into joy when the officer introduced himself as Captain Thomas Webb, of Albany, an officer in the British army and one of John Wesley's own converts. Two years before he had joined a society in England, and soon afterward Wesley had licensed him to preach. Wesley described him as "a man of fire," and whenever he preached the common people flocked to hear him. John Adams, who heard him preach, has left his testimony as to his eloquence and described him as one who "reaches the imagination and touches the passions" and "expresses himself with great propriety."[8] Such was the man who now stepped into the leadership of the little Methodist society in New York. An aggressive leader was sorely needed and Webb was born to command. They needed financial help, and Captain Webb was well-to-do and generous.

Under the leadership and preaching of Captain

---

[8] There is an abundance of testimony as to the effectiveness of Captain Webb's preaching. See an excellent summary of this testimony in Stevens, Abel, *History of American Methodism*, Vol. I, pp. 58-62.

Webb the congregations soon outgrew the rented room where they had been meeting, and it became imperative to secure a larger room. To meet this demand a long narrow hall, eighteen by sixty, over a sail-maker's shop in William Street, was found, and the society even began to talk of building a meetinghouse, for even the rigging-loft could hold not more than half those who desired to hear the Captain. Embury, with his German caution, proposed a small wooden building on leased ground, but Barbara Heck, with her woman's faith, had a vision of better things, and the first permanent structure of Methodism in America is a monument to the faith of this devoted woman. After a day spent in prayer a subscription paper was started, with Captain Webb heading the list with thirty pounds, the largest single subscription obtained. The paper contains the names of nearly two hundred and fifty subscribers, and all classes are represented, from Negro servants to the Livingstons, Delanceys, and Stuyvesants. A site on John Street was first leased, and later (1770) purchased, and here a stone chapel was built, sixty by forty-two.[9] The Anglican Church was established in New York City and in a few neighboring counties and dissenters were not permitted to erect "regular churches." For this reason the new Methodist chapel had a fireplace and a chimney, to avoid any legal complications. Embury, who was a skillful carpenter, built the pulpit, and on October 30, 1768, he preached the dedicatory

---

[9] For details in regard to the building of the John Street Meetinghouse see Wakeley, J. B., *Lost Chapters Recovered From the Early History of American Methodism* (New York, 1858), Chaps. VI-XV; for the subscription list see pp. 69-72.

sermon. To the new meetinghouse was given the name Wesley Chapel, the first in a long list of churches and chapels to bear that name.

Meanwhile Captain Webb was also busy carrying the Methodist gospel into Philadelphia (1767 or 1768), where the way had been opened for him by the Swedish minister, Doctor Wrangel; he also preached on Long Island; formed societies in New Jersey, at Trenton, Burlington, and Pemberton, and was the first to carry the Methodist message into Delaware. Likewise it was largely due to Captain Webb's foresight and generosity that the little Methodist class in Philadelphia secured a large half-finished building (Saint George's), which they purchased from a German Reformed congregation in 1770. In 1772 he was in England and appeared before the Conference at Leeds, where he made a "spirited appeal" for missionaries for America. His urgent letters, together with Doctor Wrangel's direct appeal, were responsible for Boardman's and Pilmoor's coming. In fact, to this devoted and generous-hearted British soldier belongs a larger degree of credit for the founding of American Methodism than to any other single individual.

Captain Webb remained in America and continued active until the outbreak of the American Revolution, when he returned to England, where he took up his residence in Bristol. Here he died in 1796 in his seventy-second year. Embury continued to minister to the little flock in New York until the coming of Boardman and Pilmoor, when he, with several of the Palatinates, moved to Washington County, New York. Here he formed a society of Methodists to whom he ministered until his death in 1775, as a result of overexertion while mowing. Barbara Heck, with others of her family, moved to the vicinity of Montreal, later moving down the Saint Lawrence to Augusta and became the founders of Methodism in that far-away province.

Nor must we forget to note the arrival of two additional English local preachers who reached America about the same time the first two official missionaries arrived—Robert Williams and John King. Williams came to America with Wesley's consent, but on his own responsibility. He had no money to pay his passage, but he had great faith in an Irish friend who was also embarking for America. Selling his horse to pay his debts, he hastened to the port, where his friend did not disappoint him, and he arrived in New York some time before Boardman and Pilmoor arrived in Philadelphia. He helped Embury at Wesley Chapel until Boardman came, and then made his way southward. For a time he assisted Strawbridge in Maryland, then pushed on into Virginia and was the first to introduce Methodism into the Old Dominion. Under his preaching Jesse Lee, later to become the apostle of Methodism in New England, was converted. He also penetrated into North Carolina, and on this journey took with him William Watters, and thus ushered into the itineracy the first native American Methodist preacher. Williams also has the distinction of having published the first Methodist book in America; of being the first Methodist preacher who married; was the first to locate and the first to die. He died in Norfolk, Virginia, in 1775, and Asbury in preaching his funeral sermon stated that "perhaps no man in America has been an instrument of awakening so many souls as God has awakened by him."

John King, another English local preacher, landed in Philadelphia also in 1769 and at once offered his services to the Methodist society and asked them for a license to preach. Later he met Strawbridge and assisted him in his work, and was the first to introduce Methodism into Baltimore. His first sermon was preached in the town from a blacksmith's block; his next sermon was on a muster day when a drunken crowd upset the table on which he stood. Later he was invited to preach in the Established Church, but his excessive fervor doubtless precluded any further invitations, for it was this same John King to whom John Wesley gave the famous admonition, "Scream no more, at the peril of your soul."

The first Methodist work established in America was due to the devotion of men who had not come primarily to preach the gospel. Methodism owes much to the local preachers for the foundations they have laid in countless communities across this broad land, and Strawbridge, Embury, and Webb stand at the head of the long list. When the first official missionaries arrived in Philadelphia on that autumn day in 1769, Methodism had been planted in Maryland, Delaware, New Jersey, Pennsylvania, and New York, and as Richard Boardman and Joseph Pilmoor stepped ashore Captain Thomas Webb placed in their hands a plan of the American circuit.

CHAPTER IV

WESLEY'S AMERICAN MISSIONARIES AND THE VIRGINIA REVIVAL

"WHEN we got ashore, we joined in the Doxology, and gave praise to God for our deliverance, and all the mercies bestowed upon us during the passage. When we had rested a little while at a public house, Mr. Boardman and I walked up to the city. . . . In a little time Capt'n Webb, who had been in the city some days, came to us, and gave us a hearty welcome to America." Thus Joseph Pilmoor describes his and Boardman's arrival in America. Mr. Boardman, who had been in the itineracy about six years, was to act as Wesley's assistant in the colonies. He was thirty-one years of age and was pronounced by Mr. Wesley "a pious, good-natured, and sensible man." Pilmoor was a graduate of Wesley's Kingswood School and had been in the itineracy four years. He was a man of commanding presence and courage, though inclined to be critical of those over him.[1]

---

[1] This failing of Pilmoor's is well illustrated by the following criticism of Mr. Wesley which he wrote in his *Journal* near the end of his first stay in America: "Since I came to America I have had innumerable trials, and many of them from persons I least of all expected— For more than two years Mr. Wesley, who should have been as a compassionate father to us, has treated us in a manner, not to be mentioned—During that time we have not had so much as one single letter that we could read to the people; nothing but jealous reflections, unkind suspicions, and sharp reproofs came from under his hand, which greatly discouraged us in the work, and would certainly have driven us away if we had not regarded the work of the Lord above

MISSIONARIES AND VIRGINIA REVIVAL

Philadelphia and New York were the centers around which the activities of Wesley's first missionaries revolved. Boardman began his work in New York, Pilmoor in Philadelphia; but they exchanged frequently.[2] Pilmoor was restless under Boardman's management of affairs, and as soon as additional helpers arrived from England he made an extensive preaching tour into Pennsylvania, Maryland, Virginia, North and South Carolina, and even visited Whitefield's Orphan House in Georgia.[3] He left New York in May, 1772, crossed New Jersey, thence into Pennsylvania, through the German counties, where he met the great Lutheran leader, Henry M. Mühlenberg. Turning southward he entered Maryland, and there came in contact with the activities of King, Williams, and Strawbridge. In Baltimore he preached in the Dutch church, thence on into Virginia, where at Norfolk he formed a new society of twenty-six members. Everywhere great numbers attended his preaching, and he states "the more I stay in these parts the more I am desired to preach." Reaching Newbern, North Carolina, he is delighted with the people, and states: "In all my travels through the world I have met

---

everything this world can possibly give— . . . I was greatly amazed that Mr. Wesley should treat me as if I had been the foulest offender and an enemy to God and mankind!" (*Manuscript, Journal of Joseph Pilmoor*, entry of June 4, 1773.)

[2] Pilmoor objected strongly to these frequent changes: "Frequent changes amongst gospel preachers may keep up the spirits of some kinds of people but is never likely to promote the spirit of the Gospel nor increase true religion" (*Journal*, November 23, 1772).

[3] Stevens states (Vol. I, p. 108): "He spent nearly a year in this excursion, but left no record of its events." For some strange reason Pilmoor's *Journal* was not known to Stevens. The *Journal* contains 309 manuscript pages and is now in the possession of Philadelphia Methodist Historical Society.

with none like the people of Newbern," and when
he left some gentlemen of the town presented him
with several bills of North Carolina currency as a
token of their love and respect. Arriving in Charleston after a most distressing journey, he was admitted to the pulpit of the Baptist meetinghouse
and the two ministers who were present "behaved
very well."[4] Leaving his horse at Charleston to
rest for the return journey to Philadelphia, Pilmoor borrowed a "poor creature" to ride to Georgia. Reaching Savannah he is accompanied by a
young lawyer from Boston to Whitefield's Orphan
House twelve miles away. He finds the country
barren, though "the House itself is well enough."
Pilmoor continually speaks of the friendly relations
which he enjoyed on the journey with Presbyterians, Anglicans, the Dutch, and the Baptists.

Wesley's missionaries were all careful to attend
the services of the Established Church whenever
possible, and Pilmoor seemed especially concerned
that their coming to America be not misunderstood
by Church of England people. Soon after Boardman and Pilmoor arrived in America the Methodist people in Philadelphia, led by the generous
Webb, had purchased Saint George's Church.[5] This

[4] Stevens' statement that Pilmoor was compelled to preach in the
theater in Charleston does not agree with the statement of the *Journal*.
(See *Journal*, entries for January 18, 19, 22, 1773.)

[5] The following is Pilmoor's account of the way in which Saint
George's Church was secured by the Methodist society in Philadelphia:
"At length we came to an agreement to purchase a very large shell
of a church that was built by the Dutch Presbyterians, and left unfin-
ished for want of money—as the poor people had ruined themselves
and families by building it, they were obliged to sell it to pay their
creditors—It was put up at public oction, and sold for seven hundred
pounds, though it cost more than two thousand: The circumstances
that have attended this place are very remarkable. The Church was

seems to have aroused considerable comment and was the occasion for Pilmoor's reading a public statement setting forth their design in coming to America and the reason for the purchase of the building. In this statement he assures his hearers "that the Methodist society was never designed to make a separation from the Church of England or be looked upon as a church." He further states that they had not come to make divisions nor to promote schism, "but to rather gather together in one the people of God that are scattered abroad and revive spiritual religion."

In the year 1770 the name "America" made its first appearance in the list of Wesley's Conference appointments, with the names of four American preachers—Joseph Pilmoor, Richard Boardman, Robert Williams, and John King. The next year (1771) the English Minutes record three hundred and sixteen members in the American societies, while during the year appeals continued to reach Wesley, especially from Captain Webb, Boardman, and Pilmoor, asking that more preachers be sent to America. In the Conference of this year, though faced with a serious controversy between the Arminian and Calvinistic parties among his preachers, Wesley, to quote the words of Stevens, "turned from

built to support a *party*. They spent their fortunes and were thrown into goal for debt. The church was appointed to be sold by an act of the Assembly—A gentleman's son who was *non-compos-mentis* happened to step into the oction room and bought it—His father wanted to be off the bargin, but could not, without proving the insanity of his son—Rather than to attempt this, he was willing to lose fifty pounds by the job—Thus the Lord provided for us, our way was made plain and we resolved to purchase the place which we did for six hundred and fifty pounds. How wonderful the dispensations of Providence! Surely the very hairs of our heads are all numbered" (*Journal*, November 23, 1769).

the gathering storm and pointed the Conference again to the brightening light in the western sky." Arising before the Conference he stated: "Our brethren in America call aloud for help. Who are willing to go over and help them?" To this appeal five responded, and two were appointed—Francis Asbury and Richard Wright.

When Francis Asbury was appointed to America, he had been in the traveling ministry about five years and was about twenty-six years of age. The great qualities of leadership which he was later to display were little in evidence in this quiet, introspective young man, whose expression bore evidence of melancholy. His practical prudence, the sagacity with which he planned his work, his directness of purpose, his persistence and courage, only years of ceaseless toil could sufficiently express. Richard Wright, Asbury's traveling companion and fellow missionary, was a young man with but one year's traveling experience previous to his sailing. He remained in America but three years, spending much of his time in Maryland and Virginia. Asbury and Wright landed in Philadelphia in October, 1771, after a long voyage and were met by "a considerable congregation," who received them with affection. While on shipboard Asbury had written in his *Journal:* "Whither am I going? To the New World. What to do? To gain honor? No, if I know my own heart. To get money? No: I am going to live to God and to bring others so to do. If God does not acknowledge me in America, I will soon return to England. I know my views are upright now. May they never be otherwise."

The next year (1772), largely through Captain

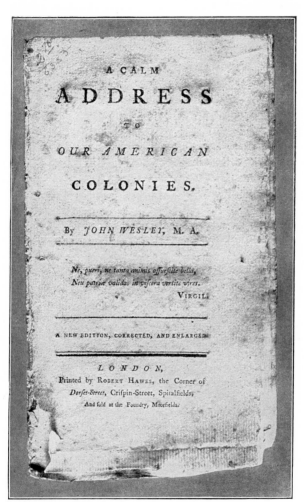

A CALM

ADDRESS

TO

OUR AMERICAN

COLONIES.

By *JOHN WESLEY*, M. A.

Ne, pueri, ne tanta animis affuescite bella,
Neu patriæ validas in viscera vertite vires.
VIRGIL.

A NEW EDITION, CORRECTED, AND ENLARGED.

LONDON,
Printed by ROBERT HAWES, the Corner of
Dorset-Street, Crispin-Street, Spitalfields;
And sold at the Foundry, Moorfields.

From *The History of Methodism*, Hurst
TITLE-PAGE OF WESLEY'S *CALM ADDRESS*

Webb's appeal before the English Conference of that year, Wesley sent out Thomas Rankin and George Shadford. Shadford became perhaps the most successful evangelist of all Wesley's missionaries to America, while Rankin was to play an important rôle as a strict disciplinarian. With Rankin and Shadford came Joseph Yearbry, a volunteer. Two years later (1774) James Dempster and Martin' Rodda were added to the number of Wesley's American missionaries, and with them came William Glendenning, who, like Yearbry, came on his own responsibility. Thus the complete list of Wesley's missionaries to America numbered eight: Boardman and Pilmoor, 1769; Asbury and Wright, 1771; Rankin and Shadford, 1772; Dempster and Rodda, 1774; while Williams, King, Yearbry, and Glendenning came as volunteers, but with Wesley's consent.

American Methodism in its beginnings was very largely a movement within the Southern colonies, and was strongest in Virginia and Maryland. This fact seems to have escaped the attention of most Methodist writers, who have given chief place to the development of early Methodism in the middle colonies. This emphasis is doubtless due to the fact that it was here that Wesley's missionaries spent much of their time, while the work in the Southern colonies was carried on largely by the irregulars, such as Strawbridge and Williams, or by the native American preachers. The numerical strength of American Methodism at the opening of the Revolution (1775) was 3,148, and of this number 2,384 were south of Mason and Dixon's line, with only 764 north of that line. In the midst of the Revolution (1780) there was a total of 8,540 Methodists in

America, and of this number 7,808 were to be found in the South. All this in spite of the fact that Wesley's missionaries gave most of their attention to the societies in New York, Pennsylvania, New Jersey, and Delaware.

The reasons for this more rapid extension of early Methodism in the South may be summarized as follows: (1) The Middle and New England colonies were better churched than were the Southern colonies, and in these colonies also Calvinistic theology was dominant. In New England Congregationalism prevailed; in the middle colonies the Presbyterians were the most numerous. Thus these regions were much less liable to be sympathetic with the doctrinal tenets of the Wesleyan preachers. (2) The South, on the other hand, presented a most inviting field for the spread of Methodist doctrine and organization. Here the Established Church of England was strongest, and it must be remembered that Methodism was a movement within the Established Church, and Wesley continually reminded his preachers of that fact and of their dependence upon the Established Church ministers for the sacraments. It is a most significant fact that Methodism had its first extensive growth in Virginia in the tidewater and valley sections, those regions where the Established Church had been strongest. The Baptists and Presbyterians, on the other hand, gained their largest successes in the Piedmont and back country sections of the colony. (3) A third cause for early Methodist expansion southward was the fact that the best Established Church co-operation came from the Rev. Devereux Jarratt, whose work and influence upon early Methodism in America has been given too little attention. The mere fact that the Methodist preachers were reputed to have some official connection with the Established Church would make them more acceptable to colonial Marylanders and Virginians. With these facts in mind let us now return to a recital of the happenings from the landing of Wesley's first missionaries to the outbreak of the American War for Independence.[6]

The new missionaries, Asbury and Wright, soon departed from Philadelphia for their fields of labor, Asbury going northward, Wright to the south. Asbury, soon after his arrival, expressed strong disapproval of the tendency among the American preachers of permitting themselves to be localized. "My brethren," he says, "seem unwilling to leave the cities, but I think I will show them the way." And he was as good as his word, for he soon had a large circuit organized around New York where he preached in log cabins, courthouses, prisons, and at executions. The importance of Asbury's influence in setting an example of tireless itineracy at the very beginning of his American ministry can hardly be overestimated. If Methodism had lost its itinerary feature at this early period, the whole movement could not have succeeded as it did in America.[7]

When Asbury made his first visit to Maryland in the late autumn of 1772, he found the Methodist cause spreading in all directions, carried on largely by native local preachers and exhorters. There were now ten or twelve of these native preachers,

[6] Batten, J. M. *Early Methodism in Virginia*, manuscript.
[7] Tipple, Ezra Squier, *Francis Asbury: The Prophet of the Long Road*. (New York: The Methodist Book Concern, 1916.) Chap. VIII.

including among them William Watters and Philip Gatch. The first American Quarterly Conference of which we have any record was held by Asbury in Maryland in Christmas week, 1772. The Maryland Circuit lay in six counties and included some twenty-four preaching places. The circuit was manned by six preachers besides the local preachers and exhorters. Asbury continued his work in Maryland until April, 1773, when he returned to the north. He had now become Wesley's assistant, succeeding Boardman in that capacity, and it was the duties which were involved in superintending the entire work that now called him northward.[8] On June 3 he met Captain Webb and his wife at Philadelphia, who had just returned two days before from England, bringing with them two additional helpers, Thomas Rankin and George Shadford.

About the middle of the following month the Methodist itinerants in America began to gather in Philadelphia for the first American Methodist Conference.[9] This conference was called by Rankin, who, by Wesley's appointment, had succeeded Asbury as his assistant in America. None of the native American preachers were present, with the possible exception of William Watters, and for that reason Maryland and Virginia were inadequately represented. Those present were Thomas Rankin, Richard Boardman, Joseph Pilmoor, Francis As-

---

[8] Wesley called his superintendents of circuits "assistants." For a full account of these early years see, Lednum, J. A., *History of the Rise of Methodism in America*, Chaps. X to XXII.

[9] The date of the first American Conference has been variously given. Bangs gives the date as July 4 (Vol. I, p. 78); Asbury's *Journal*, Vol. I, p. 80; Rankin's *Journal* in Jackson's *Early Methodist Preachers*, Vol. III, p. 62, fix the date as July 14-16. See also Wakeley's *Lost Chapters*, p. 240,

bury, Richard Wright, George Shadford, Thomas Webb, John King, Abraham Whitworth[10] and Joseph Yearbry. The reports brought to the Conference showed that up to that time Maryland was by far the most fruitful field. The total membership, as reported, was New York, 180; Philadelphia, 180; New Jersey, 200; Maryland, 500; and Virginia, 100.

Thomas Rankin presided at the Conference as Wesley's representative. He complained of the lack of discipline which prevailed outside New York and Philadelphia, and the principal work of the Conference was to adopt rules for the enforcement of a more rigid order. The first rule warned the preachers not to administer baptism or the Lord's Supper, while the second exhorted the people to attend the Established Church and there to receive the ordinances, and especially were the people in Maryland and Virginia urged to observe this "minute." We have here another indication of the influence of the native and more or less irregular preachers. It was undoubtedly the growing independence of these native colonial leaders which disturbed Wesley's assistants. At the close of the Conference the preachers were stationed as follows: New York, Thomas Rankin; Philadelphia, George Shadford, to change in four months; New Jersey, John King, William Watters; Baltimore, Francis Asbury, Robert Strawbridge, Abraham Whitworth, Joseph Yearbry; Norfolk, Richard Wright; Petersburg, Robert Williams.

---

[10]Abraham Whitworth was an Englishman who was received into the Conference in 1773. He was the first conspicuous apostate among American Methodists. He fell into intemperance and other vices.

For the next number of years the greatest Methodist increase was to take place in Virginia, and for that reason it is important that we understand the factors responsible for this first great Methodist revival in America. The chief influence undoubtedly was Devereux Jarratt, who was the outstanding evangelical leader in the Established Church in the colonies.

Devereux Jarratt was a native of Virginia and came of a nominally Church of England family, but like many another youth of that time he received practically no religious instruction and grew up almost completely ignorant of and indifferent to all religion. When about nineteen years of age he became a teacher in one of the western counties of Virginia, and there a book of Whitefield's sermons fell into his hands, the first religious book which he had ever tried to read. His second school was in Albemarle County, where he "boarded around" in the homes of his pupils, and thus came under the influence of a Presbyterian family, the mistress of which was the first person whom he had ever known who was "experimentally acquainted with vital religion." Here also he was able to attend Presbyterian preaching in an adjoining county and soon accepted their Calvinistic tenets and began himself to hold meetings when the regular preacher was absent. He now determined to enter the Presbyterian ministry, and although he was twenty-five years of age he entered a school to prepare himself to meet the educational requirements. He finally decided, however, that he could do more good in the Established Church than in the Presbyterian, and accordingly took steps to enter its ministry. As there was no Anglican bishop in the colonies, he was compelled to seek ordination in England. He crossed the Atlantic in 1762 and was ordained deacon by the Bishop of London on Christmas day of that year, and a week later was ordained priest by the Bishop of Chester. For three months he was detained in London, where he heard both John Wesley and Whitefield preach and also had the opportunity of preaching in several of the London churches.

Returning to Virginia in the summer of 1763, Jarratt learned of a vacant parish in Dinwiddie County in the south central section of the colony, and was received as the minister of Bath parish in August. Jarratt was thirty-one years of age when he began to work as a clergyman. He had wholly accepted evangelical doctrines and was determined to preach them. He says, "I endeavored to expose, in the most alarming colors, the guilt of sin, the entire depravity of human nature," etc. This sort of preaching soon aroused "religious concern" in his parish, and he now began to go out among the people during the week, visiting them in their homes, and convening them in private houses for prayer, singing, and preaching. More good, he thinks, was done by these means than at the churches. His church, however, was soon crowded by a great "concourse of strangers, both far and near." The clergy of the Established Church were generally opposed to Jarratt, and were unwilling to open their churches to him, which soon brought him to the necessity of preaching "under trees, arbors, or booths." Sometimes his congregations were so numerous that the extremities of the audience stood at the distance of sixty or eighty yards on the right and left and in front. By 1772 the revival under Jarratt had "extended itself in some places for fifty or sixty miles around."

Jarratt was frequently threatened with "writs and prosecutions" because of his breach of canonical order. He says that "no man was ever more cordially abhorred than I was by the clergy in general." In a few years, however, a neighboring clergyman, the Rev. Mr. McRoberts, joined Jarratt in his evangelical labors, and these two were a great "comfort and support to each other." McRoberts, however, left the Anglican Church in 1779 and joined the Presbyterians. Eventually Jarratt extended his labors over many counties in both Virginia and North Carolina.[11] Such was the preparation that Devereux Jarratt was making for the coming of the first Methodist itinerants to Virginia.

Robert Williams was the first Methodist preacher with whom Jarratt came in contact; he describes him as a "plain, simple-hearted, pious man." Williams came to Jarratt's house in 1773 and remained with him a week, preaching several times in his parish. Jarratt liked Williams' preaching "in the main,

[11] In Carolina he visited the counties of Northampton, Halifax, Warren, Franklin, and Granville. In Virginia, the counties of Brunswick, Greenville, and Southampton, on the south; Lunenburg, Mecklenburgh, Charlotte, Bedford, Prince Edward, Nottoway, and Amelia, on the west; Cumberland, Powhattan, Chesterfield, Henrico, Hanover, Caroline, King and Queen, and King William on the north and Kent, James City, Charles City, Surrey and Sussex on the east—in all twenty-eight counties. (*The Life of Devereux Jarratt*, Rector of Bath Parish, Dinwiddie County, Virginia. Written by Himself in a series of letters addressed to the Rev. John Coleman, one of the ministers *of the Protestant Episcopal Church in Maryland*. Baltimore; printed by Warber and Hanna, 1806, p. 97.)

very well, and especially the affectionate and animated manner in which his discourses were delivered." Williams worked during his first year in the vicinity of Norfolk and Portsmouth, and the same year Pilmoor and William Watters were also in Virginia. In 1774 Williams formed the Brunswick Circuit, which extended from Petersburg to beyond the Roanoke in North Carolina. The territory covered by the Brunswick Circuit was the exact area in which the Jarratt revival was most pronounced. Two years later (1776) the Brunswick Circuit numbered sixteen hundred and eleven members, nearly one third of the total Methodist membership in the colonies. Jarratt tells us: "In the counties of Sussex and Brunswick the work from the year 1773 was chiefly carried on by the labors of the people called Methodists."

Jarratt clearly sets forth his attitude toward the Methodist itinerants in his autobiography. He states that Williams informed him that the Methodists were true members of the Church of England, and that their design was to build up, and not divide the Church; that the Methodist preachers did not assume the office of priests, but, rather, depended wholly upon parish ministers for baptism and the Lord's Supper. He states that he "concurred in and encouraged Christian societies," and in different parts of Virginia and North Carolina exhorted his hearers to join these societies and accept the assistance of Methodist preachers. There were some who objected to joining the Methodist societies for fear of being led away from the church, but the Methodists, Jarratt says, were sincere in their professions of attachment to the church. Often he "rode many a mile, and endeavored to quiet the minds of the people by showing them that the Methodists were members of the church."

Jarratt continued to work with the Methodists throughout the Revolution though his cordial relationship with them was somewhat disturbed[12] by the movement in Virginia among the native preachers to ordain ministers. Asbury's success in heading off this movement restored his confidence. Later he bitterly condemned the formation of the Methodist Episcopal Church in 1784, and accused the Methodists of attempting to "defame and depreciate" his "character, preachings, and writing."

The Virginia revival reached its culmination in the very year the American Revolution began, 1775-1776. George Shadford had been sent to travel the Brunswick Circuit at the Conference of 1775, and he remained eighteen months—an unprecedented length of time—and he undoubtedly was the chief immediate instrument in promoting the revival. Williams carried the news of the revival to Asbury, who records in his *Journal:*[13] "I met with Brother

---

[12] At the meeting of the Conference of 1782 a special resolution was passed thanking Jarratt for his services to the Methodist preachers and people and the Southern preachers were advised to consult with him in the absence of Asbury (*Minutes of Conferences*, p. 17. New York, 1840).

[13] Asbury, Francis, *Journal*, April 28, 1775. Of the number of circuits Brunswick was the largest and embraced fourteen counties in Virginia and two counties in North Carolina; Fairfax Circuit appeared first in the *Minutes* in 1776 and included the territory along the Potomac; Hanover Circuit covered originally six counties on both sides of the James, later the circuit included territory north of the river only; Pittsylvania Circuit appeared first in the *Minutes* in 1776 with 100 members reported. In the *Minutes* for 1777 two more Virginia circuits appear, Amelia and Sussex, both formed from territory formerly included in the Brunswick. In 1777 the Virginia and North Carolina Circuits reported the following membership: Fairfax, 320; Hanover,

Williams from Virginia, who gave me a great account of the work of God in those parts—five or six hundred souls justified by faith, and five or six circuits formed." For the best account of the Virginia revival we are dependent upon Devereux Jarratt, who wrote *A Brief Narrative of the Revival of Religion in Virginia. In a Letter to a Friend*,[14] to which he appended several contemporary letters, either written by himself or written to him by others who were actively engaged in revival labors.

The revival, Jarratt states, broke out nearly at the same time in three places. Two of the centers were in Jarratt's parish, the third in Amelia County at a place notorious for "carelessness, profaneness, and immoralities of all kinds." The revival began under the preaching of a local preacher when "many sinners were powerfully converted." Throughout the winter the revival continued and "many old stout-hearted sinners felt the force of truth," and there was a great "shaking among the dry bones." The people now flocked to hear the preachers, not alone Jarratt and the traveling preachers, "but the exhorters and leaders" also. The region covered by the revival took "in a circumference of between four and five hundred miles,"

262; Amelia, 620; Brunswick, 1,360; Sussex, 727; Pittsylvania, 150; North Carolina, 930, or a total membership in the territory cultivated by Devereux Jarratt and the Methodist preachers associated with him of 3,369, which was about half the total Methodist membership. The three Maryland circuits, Baltimore, Annapolis and Frederick, had a membership of 1,381; Kent Circuit in Delaware had 720 members, while the four circuits in Pennsylvania and New York had but 489 members.

[14] Jarratt's *Narrative* is printed in full in Bangs, Nathan, *A History of the Methodist Episcopal Church.* (New York: 1839, 3rd ed., Vol. I, pp. 90-108). Also found in Asbury's *Journal* (Vol. I, pp. 157ff.). The *Narrative* was published separately; 4th ed., London, 1779.

and the work continued until May. One local preacher, writing to Jarratt, stated (July 29, 1776), "It is common with us for men and women to fall down as dead under an exhortation; but many more under prayer: perhaps twenty at a time." Lee states that "I have been at meetings where the whole congregation would be bathed in tears; and sometimes their cries would be so loud that the preacher's voice could not be heard. Some would be seized with trembling, and in a few moments drop on the floor as if they were dead; while others were embracing each other with streaming eyes, and all were lost in wonder, love, and praise." Jarratt did not like these extreme displays of emotion. He observes that there was "some wild fire mixed with the sacred flame" and in some of the meetings "there was not that decency and order observed" which he desired. As a whole, however, Jarratt did not doubt the genuineness of the work and was somewhat comforted when he read "President Edwards on that head," who observed that "wherever these most appear, there is always the greatest and deepest work."[15]

This was the first great Methodist revival in America and it made a most profound impression upon all those who have left accounts of it. Jesse Lee, Jarratt, Rankin, and Asbury are all in agreement in their descriptions. Lee states that he could not "describe the one half of what I saw, heard, and felt. I might have written a volume on the subject and then leave the greater part untold."[16] Jarratt

---

[15] See letter dated May 7, 1776. Bangs, Vol. I, pp. 99ff.
[16] Lee, Jesse, *A Short History of the Methodists in the United States of America*, p. 59.

was convinced of the greatness and permanency of the influence of the revival, and states that although the zeal of many soon flagged, still many profligates had been "effectively and lastingly changed into pious, uniform Christians."

From 1773 onward regular Conferences of the American preachers were held, the first three meeting in Philadelphia. Thereafter the center of Methodism moved southward and Baltimore became the most frequent meeting place, the fourth Conference convening there in May, 1776. At this Conference twelve circuits were reported with a membership of 4,921, and twenty-four preachers. The preachers having the rank of assistants were Thomas Rankin, Francis Asbury, Martin Rodda, George Shadford, Philip Gatch, William Watters, Daniel Ruff, Edward Dromgoole, and Samuel Spragg. Nine preachers were this year admitted on trial, among them Francis Poythress and Freeborn Garrettson. Boardman and Pilmoor had gone back to England, though Pilmoor later returned to America, and took orders in the Protestant Episcopal Church. He was first rector of a church in Philadelphia, later removed to New York, where he served a church on Ann Street, and from 1809 to his death in 1825 was the Rector of Saint Paul's Church in Philadelphia. He never lost his evangelical zeal and was a friend of Methodism as long as he lived. Boardman, on his return to England, traveled as an itinerant in Ireland, but died suddenly a few years later of apoplexy. Such, in brief, was the status of Methodism in the American colonies at the opening of the War for Independence.

CHAPTER V

DURING THE WAR FOR INDEPENDENCE

ONLY within recent years has there been any serious attempt to evaluate the influence of organized religion upon the American Revolution. In a recent volume, *The New England Clergy and the American Revolution*,[1] the author, Miss Baldwin, has admirably summarized the close relationship between the doctrines of civil liberty, as taught by the Congregational ministers, and that of the Revolutionary leaders. Recent studies of the great colonial awakening in the middle[2] and Southern colonies especially have pointed out the political significance of these movements. The awakening brought religion for the first time to the masses of the people, and the evangelical doctrines preached created among the converts an enlarged degree of self-respect, as well as inculcated ideas of self-government. The dissenting churches were great leveling forces, for they taught that all men were on an exact equality, at least as far as their souls were concerned, and social rank counted for little among the preachers of the revival. The awakening also gave to the common people their first leadership, a leadership which sprang from their own ranks.

[1] *The New England Clergy and the American Revolution.* By Alice M. Baldwin. Duke University Press, Durham, N. C., 1929.

[2] *The Great Awakening in the Middle Colonies.* By C. H. Maxson. Chicago: University of Chicago Press, 1920. *The Great Awakening in Virginia.* By W. M. Gewehr. Durham: Duke University Press, 1929.

The revival likewise furnished to the masses of the people their first common emotional and intellectual interest; and for the first time intercolonial leaders emerged, who broke over political as well as sectarian lines. Whitefield, for instance, was a great intercolonial figure, known from New Hampshire to Georgia, from 1740 to his death in 1770; he was an advocate of co-operation and union, and was a foe of denominational and racial prejudice. The movement of revivalists from one colony to another created a larger intercolonial interest and helped to form a common American spirit.

The American Methodists were greatly embarrassed during the earlier years of the War for Independence by the fact that John Wesley was a Tory in politics and a stanch supporter of King George and his policies. In a pamphlet written in 1768 Wesley had stated, speaking of the colonies: "I do not defend the measures which have been taken with regard to America; I doubt whether any man can defend them either on the foot of law, equity, or prudence." But by 1775 Wesley seems to have completely changed his mind, for in that year there appeared his *Calm Address to the American Colonies*,[3] in which he comes over completely to the side of the king's policies and roundly condemns the measures taken by the colonists. As a matter of fact, the *Calm Address* was nothing more nor less than an abridgement of Samuel Johnson's famous tract, *Taxation no Tyranny*, the reading of which

[3] See Wesley's *Journal* (Curnock Edition), Vol. VI, pp. 66, 67; Trevelyan, *The America Revolution* (New York, 1915), Vol. II, pp. 5-8, Vol. III, pp. 265-271; Tyerman, Vol. III, p. 191; *Methodist Quarterly Review*, Vol. LXXI, pp. 255-268 (article on "John Wesley: Tory," by W. W. Sweet).

seems to have completely converted Wesley to Johnson's views.

Wesley's *Calm Address* created a sensation, and
within three weeks forty thousand copies were sold;
and altogether it is estimated that the sale reached
a hundred thousand. Trevelyan states that Wesley's *Calm Address* was far more influential in shaping English public opinion than was Johnson's pamphlet, and the government was evidently pleased to
have Wesley's support, for an edition was purchased
and distributed at all the church doors in London.
It is also stated that one of the officials of state waited
upon him and asked whether there was anything
the government could do to assist either Wesley or
his people. To this Wesley replied that "he looked
for no favors, and only desired the continuance of
civil and religious privileges." He did, however,
finally accept fifty pounds from the privy purse to
apply toward some of his charities. Later, Wesley
expressed himself "as sorry that he had not requested to be made a royal missionary, and to have
the privilege of preaching in every church." (See
Everett, James, *Life of Adam Clarke Portrayed*. 3
vols. London, 1843-1849.)

But if the government was pleased with the *Calm
Address,* many others were not, and a storm of
stinging criticism soon broke over the head of the
author. Among the most able of Wesley's critics
was a Baptist minister of Bristol, who accused him
of grave inconsistencies, in that he had previously
recommended to the Bristol Methodists that they
vote for the American candidate and had recommended a book favoring the American cause. Wesley at first denied this, but later admitted that he

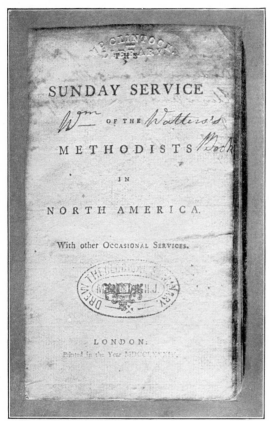

From *The History of Methodism*, Hurst.

THE METHODIST PRAYER BOOK

Wesley's Sunday Service for the Methodists in North America

had done so, though for the time he had forgotten it, so that "even when it [the book] was brought" to his attention, he could not recollect that he had seen it.[4] Another critic attacked Wesley in a pamphlet called *A Cool Reply to a Calm Address,* in which the author of the *Calm Address* is accused of being in quest of a "miter," though instead "he ought to sit in sackcloth and pour dust upon his head." Again the Baptist clergyman from Bristol issued a new attack and calls attention to the "shameful versatility and disingenuity of this artful man."

The attacks of his enemies did not discourage Mr. Wesley from reprinting his *Calm Address,* though in the second printing he acknowledges that he had borrowed from Johnson's *Taxation no Tyranny,* and states that he had spoken according to the light he had. In the meantime Johnson had written Wesley thanking him for his "important suffrage" to his "argument on the American question," and states that to have gained such a man as Wesley confirmed him in his own opinion. Wesley's explanations, however, did not appease his enemies, for replies continued to pour in upon the leader of the Methodists. One entitled *"A Wolf in Sheep's Clothing; or an old Jesuit Unmasked,"* concludes by stating that the father of the Methodists "deserves to be presented, not with lawn sleeves, but with a hempen neckcloth; and instead of a miter, ought to have his head adorned with a white nightcap drawn over his eyes." It remained, however, for Wesley's bitter

---

[4] For a discussion of Wesley's forgetfulness, see Buckley, *A History of Methodists in the United States,* pp. 160-161. The Christian Literature Co., New York, 1896.

doctrinal opponent, Toplady, the author of "Rock of Ages," to make the most scurrilous attack. His pamphlet, entitled *An Old Fox Tarr'd and Feathered,* had on the cover the head of a fox in clerical robes, and the opening sentence read: "Whereupon shall I liken Mr. Wesley? and with what shall I compare him? I will liken him to a low and puny tadpole in divinity, which proudly seeks to disembowel a high and mighty whale in politics." He accuses Wesley of plagiarizing Johnson's tract, of stealing a "bundle of Lilliputian shafts out of Dr. Johnson's pincushion." Another writer in the *Gentlemen's Magazine* (1775, p. 561) has his fling at Wesley, stating: "You have forgot the precepts of your Master, that God and mammon cannot be served together. You have one eye upon a pension and the other upon heaven—one hand stretched out to the king, and the other raised up to God. I pray that the first may reward you and the last forgive you."

At about the time of the appearance of the *Calm Address* Wesley wrote two letters, one addressed to Lord North, the prime minister, and the other to Lord Dartmouth, at the time secretary of state for the colonies.[5] The letters were almost identical. In them Wesley points out to the ministers that he has excellent means of learning the temper of both the people in America and England, which is the reason for his addressing them. All his prejudices, he says, are against the Americans, as he is a High Churchman and the son of a High Churchman, and

[5] See *John Wesley's Letters,* Vol. VI, pp. 155-164. The letter to Lord Dartmouth contains a final paragraph of a personal nature, as Lord Dartmouth was an Evangelical and sympathetic with Wesley's religious activities.

notions of nonresistance and passive obedience have been bred into him; and yet, in spite of this prejudice, he thinks that the Americans are asking for no more than their legal rights. But, waiving all this, he asks, "Is it common sense to use force against the Americans?" The Americans, he points out, are evidently not easily frightened, as the news of the first fighting of the Revolution testifies. The Americans, he reminds the ministers, are fighting for their wives, children, and liberty, which gives them vast advantage over those who fight only for pay. He doubts whether England can subdue the colonists, especially if England's neighbors come to their help. Nor are France and Spain the only enemies to be feared. The people of England and Scotland he knows to be "exasperated almost to madness," and the bulk of the people are cured of all love and reverence for the king and are ripe for rebellion.[6]

There can be no doubt that John Wesley was a loyal supporter of the king throughout the entire Revolution. In the autumn of 1775, in a letter to his brother Charles he says: "I find a danger now of a new kind—a danger of losing my love for the Americans; I mean for their miserable leaders; for the poor sheep are more sinned against than sin-

---

[6] Stevens, in *History of American Methodism* (Vol. I, pp. 283-285), wrongly assumes that Wesley had written his *Calm Address* previous to the battle of Lexington and Concord, and the news of these battles caused him to change his views regarding the Americans, and he then wrote these letters to the two ministers. As a matter of proven fact, Wesley wrote the letters to the ministers while he still sympathized with the Americans, and later was convinced by Johnson's tract that the American cause was not just, and his *Calm Address* followed. Stevens convinced George Bancroft that his view of the matter was correct, and Bancroft changed his statement regarding Wesley accordingly. See Bancroft, George, *History of the United States*, Vol. IV, pp. 187-188 (the Author's last revision).

ning."[7]   Later Wesley wrote other political pamphlets.   One appeared in 1776, entitled *A Seasonable Address to the More Serious Part of the Inhabitants of Great Britain Respecting the Unhappy Contest Between Us and Our American Brethren.* This is a plea for a united England, for it is a kingdom divided against itself which he beholds and deplores.   In 1777 appeared from his pen a *Calm Address to the Inhabitants of England,* in which he reviews events leading up to the war and the chief military happenings since the war began.   He tells of the smuggling, so common in America, in which "the celebrated John Hancock" was among the most successful, and how England's attempts to suppress this illegal practice were laughed to scorn, "for the people were too good patriots to condemn their countrymen."   In Washington's retreat across New Jersey, flying before the victorious British, he sees the hand of Providence, giving final victory to the English, especially after the king had proclaimed a general fast.   In America, he says there has been a huge outcry for liberty, but the Americans have destroyed liberty, for a clergyman cannot even pray for the king in America; nor is there any civil liberty: indeed, "Wherever these brawlers for liberty govern, there is the vilest slavery."   In closing he addresses his followers: "Do any of you blaspheme God or the king?   None of you, I trust, who are in connection with me.   I would no more continue in fellowship with those who continued in such practices than with whoremongers, or Sabbath breakers, or thieves, or drunkards, or common swearers."

---

[7] See *Wesley's Letters,* VI, pp. 179-180.   This letter is dated October 17, not 19, as *Buckley* has it.

The year 1778 saw two other political utterances of John Wesley's, one addressed to the people of England on the status of the nation, the other to the inhabitants of Ireland. In this latter pamphlet he assures the Irish people that England is not in such bad shape as it might appear, for Washington's army is melting away, day by day, through desertions and disease, while Howe's army is in perfect health. Nor are the French such a great menace, since the British fleet is in better condition than ever before. Nor is there as much danger from Spain and Portugal, as from "those intestine vipers, who are always ready to tear out their mother's bowels." And the last reason for his assurance that the Governor of the universe will not give the three kingdoms up to destruction is the fact that religion is on the increase.

During the course of the war we find Wesley frequently preaching on war texts. In November, 1775, he preached a charity sermon for the widows and orphans of the soldiers killed in America.[8] He says: "Knowing how many would seek occasion to offense, I wrote down my sermon." In the course of this sermon he speaks of the many who are "mad with party zeal, foaming with rage against their quiet neighbors, ready to tear out each other's throats." Toplady, in his *Gospel Magazine*, describes this sermon as being: "as dry as an old piece of leather that has been tanned five thousand times over," and the preacher as "a tiptop perfectionist in the art of lying." In February Wesley hurries down to Bristol, having heard of disturbances "oc-

---

[8] See *Journal*, Vol. VI, November 12, 1775.

casioned by men whose tongues are set on fire against the government," and on arriving he preaches on the text: "Put them in mind to be subject to principalities and powers, to speak evil of no man." During these years a favorite text is: "Render unto Cæsar the things that are Cæsar's," which he used especially in the west of England and in Wales and Ireland, where there was much disaffection with the government. The day before the Conference in 1777 he desires as many as possible to join together in fasting and prayer: "that God would restore the spirit of love and of a sound mind to the poor deluded rebels in America."[9]

Charles Wesley was as stanch a Tory as was his brother, and characteristically gave expression to his political sentiments in some of his hymns of the period. His *Hymns for the Nation in 1782* went through many editions, and among the various titles of the hymns are: "For His Majesty King George," "A Paper for the Congress," and a "Hymn for Loyal Americans." An extract from one of these hymns reads:

> "Surely thou wilt vengence take
>   On rebels 'gainst their king and God,
> And strict inquisition make
>   For rivers spilt of guiltless blood,
> For men who take thy name in vain,
>   By fiends in sanctity's disguise;
> As thou wert served with nation's slain,
>   Or pleased with human sacrifice."

One stanza of the Hymn, "To Loyal Americans," reads:

---

[9] *Journal,* Vol. VI, p. 167.

"The men who dare their king revere,
  And faithful to their oaths abide,
Midst perjured hypocrites, sincere,
  Harassed, oppressed on every side;
Galled by the tyrant's iron yoke,
By Briton's faithless sons forsook."

Some American Methodists have been chagrined because of John Wesley's loyalty to his king and government during the American Revolution, and have felt that this somehow reflected adversely upon him and the American Methodists. But any student of Wesley would know on what side he would have been found in such a disturbance, and his motives are not difficult to explain. First of all, he was a patriot and as he says in explaining his *Calm Address*, he saw England in a flame, "a flame of malice and rage against the king, and almost all in authority under him." "I labor," he says, "to put out that flame. Ought not every true patriot do the same?" Then, as he explains in his letters to Lords North and Dartmouth, he was born and bred a Tory; he believed in the divine right of kings and repudiated the idea of the sovereignty of the people, and he was always a supporter of kingly authority, as is evidenced not alone by his support of King George III, but also by the type of government he devised to govern his Methodist societies. Then he was drawn to King George also because the king was a decent man in his personal life; he believed in the Bible; he feared God and "he loves the queen." The king's character, he says, in spite of all that has been done to render him odious, remains unimpeached. "His whole conduct, both in public and private, ever since he began his reign, the uniform

tenor of his behavior, the general course both of his
words and actions, have been worthy of an Englishman, worthy of a Christian and worthy of a king."
Then, too, the king had shown favor to the Methodists, and Lord Dartmouth, an important member
of the king's government, was an Evangelical. These
influences were certainly among those responsible
for Wesley's attitude toward the American War.

The effect of Wesley's actions upon Methodism in
America, during the Revolution, is obvious. In 1775
he had written Rankin, his assistant in America, advising him and the American preachers to remain
free of all party: "And say not one word against one
or the other side." But Wesley set a poor example,
and his own partisan position soon became known
in America and American Methodists were made to
suffer for their leader's attitude, Asbury observing
in his *Journal*:[10] "Some inconsiderate persons have
taken occasion to censure the Methodists in America on account of Mr. Wesley's political sentiments."
In the same entry he remarks, I "am truly sorry that
the venerable man ever dipped into the politics of
America," but if he "had been a subject of America,
no doubt he would have been as zealous an advocate
of the American cause."

As a result of their leader's strong Toryism and
his partisan activity, it was not long until the American Methodists were almost universally considered
as Tories. In Maryland test oaths were required,
pledging the taking up of arms if called upon by
the authorities to do so. Asbury, as a minister, was
unwilling to bear arms, and was unwilling to take
such an oath. Accordingly, he retired into Dela-

---

[10] Vol. I, p. 132, March 13, 1776.

ware in 1778, where he remained for more than two years. Much of this time he was a guest in the home of Judge White,[11] though during the latter months of his stay in Delaware he moved about among societies near at hand, and carried on correspondence with the Methodists. During his stay in Delaware Asbury made the acquaintance of Judge Barrett and Richard Bassett, both of whom became stanch friends and influential Methodists. In the spring of 1780 Asbury left his refuge in Delaware and from that time to the end of the war was permitted to carry on his work without interference.

In April, 1778, a patrol came to the house of Judge White, seized the judge on a charge of being a Methodist, and although he was finally freed, he was detained five weeks. This occurrence led Asbury to leave Judge White's house and after traveling on back roads far into the night he finally found shelter. Once, due to alarming rumors, he took refuge in a swamp until sunset. After a month of concealment among strangers he returned to Judge White's home. Martin Rodda's partisan activity in distributing the royal proclamation in his circuit, and the forming of a company of Royalists by an ex-Methodist, Chauncey Clowe, were among the causes for the suspicion in which Methodists were held. The Maryland authorities were especially active in persecution of the Methodists.[12] In

---

[11] Judge White and his wife were devout members of the English Church. Both were friendly to the Methodists and their home was a frequent stopping place for the preachers as well as a regular preaching place.

[12] There seems to have been little persecution of Methodists in Virginia. Gatch says the "Baptists had preceded the Methodists in all this region, and had rolled back the wave of persecution." M'Lean, John, *Sketch of Rev. Philip Gatch* (Cincinnati, 1854), pp. 50-51.

the spring of 1778 Joseph Hartley, the preacher on the Kent Circuit on the Eastern shore, was confined by the authorities, accused of Toryism, and on his release the court prohibited him from preaching. Hartley, however, went on his rounds singing and praying, and would remain on his knees and exhort. Finally his accusers stated that they were as willing to have him preach on his feet as on his knees. Freeborn Garrettson was especially active during the years of the Revolution, and in 1778 was threatened with imprisonment and beaten and finally fell from his horse unconscious. When the magistrate came to commit him to prison, Garrettson exhorted him, showing him how sinful it was to stop the gospel thus, and we are told the magistrate "dropped the pen without finishing the *mittimus.*" In the latter part of this year Garrettson was surrounded by a mob in Dover, Delaware, which cried out: "He is a Tory! *He is one* of Clowe's men; hang him, hang him!" He was finally rescued by some friendly gentlemen, one of whom stood by him on the steps of the academy while he preached. Later (1780) Garrettson was confined in the Cambridge jail in Maryland, for a fortnight, where he says "I had a dirty floor for my bed, my saddlebags for my pillow." Here he occupied his time in reading, writing, praying, and in meditation.

Philip Gatch was one of the most active Methodist preachers during these years of persecution. His most distressing experience occurred on the Frederick Circuit in Maryland, where on one occasion he was waylaid by a mob on the road to his appointment, who gave him a coat of tar, and in its application one of his eyes was permanently injured.

Gatch, with Dromgoole, Glendenning, and Watters, had been appointed by the Conference of 1777[13] as a committee to have general superintendence of the societies, during Asbury's retirement, and Gatch continued his leadership until Asbury was able to venture again into the open field, and even afterward remained the recognized leader of the Southern brethren in their struggle for the ordinances. At the Conference of 1778 Philip Gatch gave up the traveling ministry, due to broken health, and his name no longer appears in the records.[14] He, however, continued to preach in the vicinity of his home in Powhatan County, Virginia, and continued to be recognized as a leader among the Southern preachers.

Meanwhile the last of Wesley's missionaries had departed for England, leaving only Asbury of the English preachers. Thomas Rankin left Maryland in the fall of 1777 and spent the winter in Philadelphia, then in the possession of the British, after the battles of Brandywine and Germantown. In the spring he sailed for England, and during the remainder of his life was active as a preacher in the Wesleyan chapels in and about London, and was one of the little group gathered about the deathbed of John Wesley. Martin Rodda was the most partisan of Wesley's American missionaries, and was soon in trouble for distributing the king's proclamation in his Delaware circuit. He was forced to flee, and aided by slaves, made his way to the coast

---

[13] The Conference *Minutes* has no record of this appointment. See McLean, *Philip Gatch,* p. 59.

[14] In those days there were no *superannuates* or *supernumeraries,* and a man without a circuit was a man without a record.

and took refuge on a British ship. The last of the missionaries to depart was George Shadford. Shadford and Asbury were close friends, and in the early part of 1778 they agreed to spend a day together in fasting and prayer to determine what should be their course. At the end of that day Asbury said, "My convictions are as clear and strong as ever that it is my duty to remain." Shadford said, "My work in America is done; I feel with as much certainty that it is my duty to return now as I felt it to be my duty to come hither four years ago." "One of us must be in error," said Asbury. Shadford replied, "Not necessarily so; I may have a call to go and you to stay." And so Shadford left America, leaving Asbury homesick and lonesome, "considered by some as an enemy of the country, every day liable to be seized by violence and abused."[15] Of all Wesley's missionaries who returned to England, Shadford had been the most successful in his American labors, and was the greatest revivalist of the times.

With all the English preachers departed, except Asbury, and he largely confined to a small area in the little state of Delaware, the native preachers now took things very largely into their own hands. The Conference of 1777 met in Harford County, Maryland, and reported 36 preachers and 6,968 members. Of the total membership, less than five hundred were in the states north of Delaware and Maryland, while Virginia still had, by far, the largest number. The Conference of 1778 met in May at Leesburg, Virginia, and the records show a loss of 873 members

---

[15] For Shadford's life after his return to England, see Stevens, Vol. I, pp. 339-343; for the parting with Asbury, see Asbury's *Journal*, Vol. I, p. 268.

and 7 preachers. Neither New York[16] nor Philadelphia is in the list of circuits, for the reason, of course, that both were in possession of the British, but several new Virginia and North Carolina circuits appear, though Chester, Frederick, and Norfolk Circuits were also omitted.

The year 1779 was a critical one in the history of American Methodism, for it was only by a narrow margin that a serious schism was avoided. There were two Conferences held this year; one, for the Northern circuits, meeting at the home of Judge White, in Kent Circuit, Delaware, on April 28, was attended by sixteen preachers from New Jersey, Delaware, and the eastern shore of Maryland. The Conference at Judge White's was considered as preparatory to the Conference which was to convene at Fluvanna, Virginia, on May 18. The preachers meeting with Asbury were deeply concerned about the tendency of the Southern brethren to go their own way, and the most important action taken at Judge White's was the answer to the question: "Ought not Brother Asbury to act as General Assistant in America?" Answer: "He ought: first, on account of his age; second, because originally appointed by Mr. Wesley; third, being joined with Messrs. Rankin and Shadford by express order from Mr. Wesley." As to the extent of Asbury's power,

---

[16] New York appeared in the *Minutes* in 1777 for the last time until 1783. We now know that the Methodist society in New York continued during the Revolutionary War under the ministry of Samuel Spragg, who served the society for five consecutive years. At the Conference of 1783 Asbury sent John Dickins to New York, and shortly after Dickins arrived Spraggs withdrew and joined the Church of England and became pastor of the church at Elizabeth, New Jersey. (For an account of the New York Society during the Revolution, see Wakeley, J. B., *Lost Chapters,* etc. Chaps. XXIX and XXXI.)

it was agreed that: "On hearing every preacher for and against what is in debate, the right of determination shall rest with him." This was giving Asbury full power to decide every issue. In other words, he was to have the same power in America that Wesley had in England. But would the Southern brethren abide by the decision of the smaller group gathered about Asbury? That was the great issue at the Fluvanna Conference.

The year had been especially successful for the Virginia and Carolina preachers and circuits. Revivals had taken place in many places which were not directly affected by the war, and the total membership reported for all the societies was 8,577, and the number of preachers was given as 49. During Asbury's retirement the work had gone forward as well or better than before; the war likewise separated them from Wesley, while most of the Established Church clergymen had fled the country, and the few who were left had little interest in vital religion. Therefore, why not form a Presbytery of their own, ordain preachers, and thus provide the people with the sacraments? Such were the arguments of the Southern preachers.

Accordingly, they proceeded to appoint a committee made up of the oldest brethren who first ordained themselves, then ordained other preachers,[17]

---

[17] Nelson Reed, one of the preachers present at the Fluvanna Conference, thus describes what happened:

"Tuesday 18, in the morning rising before the day appear'd many prayers were made to god and early we went into conference & endeavour'd to go on with business as usual but could not for there was a division in appinions about the Ordinances so enquiry was made amongst all concerning the matter and there was a great majority for it O what a soul rending time it was many herts did Tremble many tears was shead and many prayers made to god my and throughout the year the preachers administered the sacraments wherever they had opportunity. Lee tells us that most of the people "fell in with their measures. However, some of the old Methodists would not commune with them; but steadily adhered to their former customs." As a whole, however, the work in the South greatly prospered during the year.[18]

Was there to be a permanent division between Asbury and the preachers north of Virginia and the Southern preachers? Upon the Conferences to be held in 1780 lay the burden of determining this momentous question. The Northern brethren met at Baltimore on April 24, and among the important questions asked and answered were: "Shall we continue in close connection with the [English] church, and press our people to a closer communion with her?" *"Yes";* "Does this whole Conference disapprove the step our brethren have taken in Virginia?" "Yes"; "Do we look *upon them* no longer as Methodists in connection with Mr. Wesley and us till they come back?" "Agreed." "Shall Brothers Asbury, Garrettson, and Watters attend the Virginia Conference, and inform them of our proceedings in this, and receive their answer?" "Yes"; "What must be the conditions of our union with

---

very soul was made to tremble so, we spent the first day & little was done." (*Diary of Rev. Nelson Reed,* manuscript.) Reed was a close friend of Philip Gatch, the prime mover in the Fluvanna Conference.

[18] Nelson Reed, in his Diary, speaks of receiving the Lord's Supper at the hands of "bro. Gatch" on August 1 (1779), and states that his "soul was refresht," and that the people seem glad "to partake of the blessed Ord." Again he speaks of the Ordinance of the Lord's Supper being administered by "bro. poythress" at a Quarterly Meeting held at Ellis's Meetinghouse in Hanover on May 7, 1779.

our Virginia brethren?" "To suspend all their administrations for one year, and all meet together in Baltimore?" The preachers favorable to the administration of the ordinances were undoubtedly in the majority, and the action of the minority Conference at Baltimore appears more or less presumptuous. Fortunately, the peremptory tone which one detects in the action of the Conference at Baltimore was not carried to Virginia by the committee appointed to meet with the Southern preachers.

The Southern preachers met at Manakintown, in Virginia, and were in session when Asbury, Watters, and Garrettson arrived. The committee did not enter the Conference room until they were invited to do so, and Asbury then addressed them; read letters from Wesley and the letters that had passed between the Southern and Northern brethren. The three Northern brethren then withdrew, and after an hour's deliberation the Conference decided that they could not give up the ordinances, nor submit to the terms of union. Asbury states that he was "under the heaviest cloud I ever felt in America." The next day (May 10) he was planning to leave for the North, and with Watters and Garrettson was praying, when the Conference reached an agreement, much to the surprise and delight of all.[19] Asbury naturally concluded that

---

[19] For Asbury's account of what happened at the Conference in Virginia, see his *Journal*, Vol. I, pp. 366-367; Nelson Reed, one of the Southern preachers, gives this brief account of the meeting (*Diary* manuscript): "Mund 8. rode from bro. Ellises to bro. Smiths at the Manacan town with several more fellow labouerers and in the evening we had public preaching. the q. conference began early in the morning. the Lord was with us and gave us a spirit of humility and gentleness so that in all the debates there was not a hasty or tart expression many were much distrest with the thoughts of a

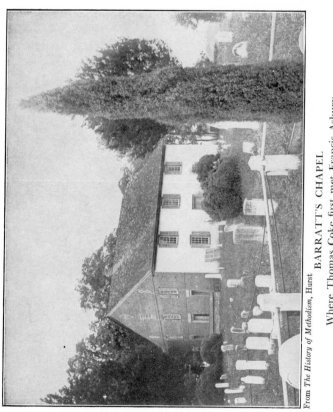

From *The History of Methodism*, Hurst   BARRATT'S CHAPEL

Where Thomas Coke first met Francis Asbury

"the hand of God has been greatly seen in all this." The Conference in Virginia was considered as a part of the Baltimore Conference, and no separate record of the Virginia meeting is found in the general *Minutes*.

For the next six months Asbury remained in Virginia and North Carolina "endeavoring to reconcile the preachers and people to be content without the ordinances administered by Methodist preachers." In this he seems to have been successful, and the year as a whole was a prosperous one for the Methodist societies. The Conference of 1781 was held in two places, beginning at Choptank, Delaware, on April 16, adjourning to Baltimore on April 24. Devereux Jarratt, pleased at the giving up of the ordinances the year before, attended this Conference, and delivered several discourses, and administered the Lord's Supper and baptism. The work was beginning to revive in Pennsylvania and New Jersey, while revivals had been reported in Delaware and the southern shore of Maryland. This year the membership was 10,539 and the number of preachers 54.

The center of the operations of the war was now in the South, and throughout 1781 there was much fighting in Virginia, and numbers of Methodists were drafted, among them Jesse Lee, who was just entering upon his career as a minister. His conscience revolted against bearing arms and killing his fellows, and when he was brought to the camp and was given a gun he refused to take it. His case was

---

separation but when it seem'd as if all hope of a union was gone God who art a lover of unity and peace brought in peace and terms of reconciliation——"

reported to the colonel, who attempted to remonstrate with him, but to no avail. It was not long until Lee, although a prisoner under guard, was preaching to the soldiers. When the colonel heard of his preaching, he again came to Lee, who told the officer that he could not bear arms with a good conscience, but that he was a friend to his country and would be willing to do anything while in the army, except fight. Finally the colonel asked him if he was willing to drive the baggage wagon, and to this Lee consented. He continued to preach as long as he was in the army and became practically a chaplain as well as teamster.

With the surrender of Cornwallis at Yorktown on October 19, 1781, the fighting of the Revolution was over, though peace was not signed until September 3, 1783. During these two years, while the country was waiting for peace to be signed, the Methodists gained steadily. It had now become necessary, on account of the rapid expansion of the work, to have two Conferences, one at the North and the other at the South. The Northern Conference, however, was recognized as the more authoritative body, since it could annul the acts of the Virginia body, but the Virginia body could not veto theirs. This year (1782) the membership was reported as 11,785.

The last two Conferences to convene previous to the organization of The Methodist Episcopal Church were those of 1783 and 1784, both of which assembled at Ellis' Preaching-house in Virginia and adjourned to Baltimore in the month of May. Again increases are reported both in membership and preachers, there being 13,740 members in 1783, and

14,988 in 1784. For the first time the term "United States" appears in the *Minutes* (1783), while two days of thanksgiving are set aside "for our public peace, temporal and spiritual prosperity, and for the glorious work of God." The question of caring for the wives of preachers also came up for the first time, and stringent rules were passed regarding both slavery and temperance. There were growing indications in these latter Conferences that the Methodists were becoming denominationally conscious. The largest proportion of membership was still south of Mason and Dixon's line, there being but eleven per cent north of that line and eighty-nine per cent south of it.

When Francis Asbury received the news that peace had finally been signed, and that the United States had become in fact a free and independent nation, he wrote in his *Journal:* "I had various exercises of mind on the occasion: it may cause great changes to take place amongst us; some for the better, and some for the worse. It may make against the work of God; our preachers will be more likely to settle in the world, and our people, by getting into trade and acquiring wealth, may drink into its spirit." There were, indeed, great changes ahead for American Methodism!

CHAPTER VI

ORGANIZES FOR A GREAT TASK

THE first religious body in America to work out an independent and national organization was the Methodist Episcopal Church. This may seem somewhat strange when we consider the following facts: The American Methodists at the close of the War for Independence numbered but fifteen thousand, and they were, therefore, one of the smaller religious bodies in the country; they lacked an educated leadership, such as had the Presbyterians and Congregationalists; and their first Conference in America had been held but eleven years previous. The Methodist congregations and circuits in America had never constituted a real church, since their ministers were not ordained clergymen. Their places of worship were called chapels or meetinghouses, never churches, and nominally they were what Wesley's societies in England were—groups of pious people within the Church of England, formed into societies for the promotion of holiness. As we have seen, both Wesley and Asbury were throughout the Revolution insistent that the American Methodists maintain their relationship to the Established Church.

At the opening of the Revolution the Methodists of Virginia presented a petition to the Virginia House of Delegates in opposition to a movement on the part of the Baptists and other dissenters to bring about the separation of church and state. The petition states that they wish to disassociate themselves from "common dissenters," and they want it to be understood that this name cannot be applied to them, since they are a "religious society in communion with the Church of England and do all in their power to support the said church." They conceive that very bad consequences will arise from abolishing the establishment, and they pray "that the Church of England, as it ever hath been, may continue to be, the Established Church."[1] After 1779, however, Virginia Methodists united their efforts to the Baptists in bringing about the separation of church and state.[2] Thus the Virginia Methodist preachers were no longer professing to be adherents of the Established Church, but were taking steps to form an independent organization, and had, in spite of all the influence Asbury could bring to bear, ordained several of their number, who went about the Southern circuits administering the sacraments. It was only with the greatest difficulty that Asbury in 1780 had persuaded the Virginia preachers to suspend their action and to await the conclusion of the war. The long years of war had wrought a transformation in the attitude of the American Methodists toward both the Anglican Church and their venerable founder, John Wesley, and the close of the struggle found them thoroughly imbued with the new American ideals. Their leaders, with the exception of Francis Asbury, were native Americans, most of them young men, all of them devoted to the great cause for which Methodism stood, but also determined to have things their

---

[1] *Journal of the House of Delegates* (Virginia), October 28, 1776.
[2] *Op. cit.* November 10, 1779.

own way, rather than blindly follow the Anglican traditions, which they considered unsuited to conditions which they confronted in America.

Just how fully Mr. Wesley sensed this change in attitude on the part of the American Methodists is difficult to determine, but he was undoubtedly partially aware of it, as his subsequent action indicated. When the war closed, Asbury found himself in a very difficult position. He was anxious to do Mr. Wesley's bidding as far as possible, but at the same time he knew full well that the preachers were more and more inclined to go their own way. Just as the war closed, Wesley wrote to the American Methodists, exhorting them to abide by the Methodist doctrine and discipline, and the larger minutes of the (British) Conference, and he exhorts them to be careful about receiving English preachers, especially any who may "make a difficulty of receiving Francis Asbury as the General Assistant." Wesley had been kept informed as to conditions among American Methodists. He knew that many of them had not partaken of the sacrament for years, while children of members were generally unbaptized. The possibility of the success and growth of American Methodism under such conditions would be slight, and this was doubtless the determining factor in the momentous step which John Wesley now took to provide the American Methodists with the sacraments. That Wesley did not intend to form an American Church, independent of his control, has been, I think, adequately proven.[3]

---

[3] See Faulkner, J. A., *Burning Questions in Historic Christianity* (New York, The Abingdon Press, 1930), Chap. XIII, "Did Wesley Intend to Found The Methodist Episcopal Church?"

The steps which the aged Wesley now took to meet the critical situation in America have been often described, and are well known to every student of Methodism. In February, 1784, Wesley invited Dr. Thomas Coke into his private room in London, where he informed him of the deplorable situation in America. He then set forth his plan to ordain preachers for America, stating that he had been convinced of his scriptural authority as a presbyter to ordain, since it had been the practice of the ancient church of Alexandria for presbyters to ordain bishops, never suffering the interference of a foreign bishop.[4] He then asked Doctor Coke to accept ordination at his hands. Coke was already a presbyter in the Church of England, but, of course, Coke would have no authority to ordain the American Methodist preachers unless Wesley gave him that authority. This had been suggested by Coke to Wesley in a letter written on August 9, 1784, in which he says, "The more maturely I consider the subject, the more expedient it appears to me that the power of ordaining others should be received by me from you by the imposition of your hands." Later in the same long letter he suggests that everything possible be done on "this side of the water," and further suggests that the ordination of Richard

---

[4] Drew, Samuel, *The Life of the Rev. Thomas Coke*, etc. (London, 1817), pp. 63-64; Wesley had been converted to this position by the reading of Lord King's *Enquiry into the Constitution, Discipline, Unity and Worship of the Primitive Church* in 1746. King had contended that *presbyters* were different from *bishops* in degree, but equal to them in *order*. Ten years later Wesley had been further convinced by the reading of Bishop Stillingfleet's *Irenicon*. After reading this latter book Wesley says that he still believed that the Episcopal form of church government is scriptural and apostolic, but that he did not believe that it was prescribed in Scripture.

Whatcoat, Thomas Vasey, and himself take place in private in Wesley's room at City Road Chapel. At the Conference at Leeds in July, 1784, Wesley appointed Coke, Whatcoat, and Vasey to go to America, and at the close of the Conference, after having received Coke's letter above referred to, in which the whole thing seems to have been carefully planned, Wesley sent for Whatcoat and Vasey to come to Bristol, and there on September 1 and 2 (1784), assisted by James Creighton, who was also a presbyter in the Church of England, these two Methodist preachers were ordained first as deacons and then as elders. On the latter day Wesley, assisted by Creighton, ordained Coke superintendent, and on September 18 the three, thus ordained, set sail for America.[5]

With Doctor Coke and his two companions, Wesley sent three documents; the first was a sketch of what he intended should be done in America. This document was destroyed, or, at least, it has disappeared. Professor Faulkner thinks that the reason it was suppressed, was because it ran counter to what actually took place in America. The second document was Wesley's letter of testimonial of Coke's ordination. This document has been many times printed, but since it is the basic document on which Methodist Episcopal orders rest, it deserves a place in every history of American Methodism.

To all to whom these presents shall come, John Wesley,

---

[5] The biographer of Coke, Samuel Drew, states that Wesley's proposal to ordain preachers for America at first startled Doctor Coke (p. 64), "and he expressed some doubts, as to the validity of Mr. Wesley's authority to constitute so important an appointment." Professor Faulkner, however, suggests that Doctor Coke supported Wesley to the utmost in this proposal, and prompted him when he seemed to waver. See Faulkner, *op. cit.*, p. 211.

late fellow of Lincoln College in Oxford, presbyter of the Church of England, sendeth greeting.

Whereas, many of the people in the Southern provinces of North America, who desire to continue under my care, and still adhere to the doctrines and discipline of the Church of England, are greatly distressed for want of ministers to administer the sacraments of baptism and the Lord's Supper, according to the usage of the said church; and, whereas, there does not appear to be any other way of supplying them with ministers;

Know all men, that I, *John Wesley*, think myself to be providentially called, at this time, to set apart some persons for the work of the ministry in America. And, therefore, under the protection of Almighty God, and with a single eye to his glory, I have this day set apart as a superintendent, by the imposition of my hands and prayer (being assisted by other ordained ministers), Thomas Coke,[6] Doctor of Civil Law, a presbyter in the Church of England, and a man, whom I judge to be well qualified for that great work. And I do hereby recommend him to all whom it may concern, as a fit person to preside over the flock of Christ. In testimony whereof, I have hereunto set my hand and seal, this second day of September, in the year of our Lord one thousand seven hundred and eighty-four.

JOHN WESLEY.[7]

The third document was a letter addressed "to Doctor Coke, Mr. Asbury, and our brethren in North America," in which after describing the situation in America following the Revolution, Wesley gives a brief account of the process by which he had come to believe that he, as a presbyter, had the right to or-

---

[6] See facsimile of Coke's ordination certificate, *Wesley's Journal* (Curnock), Vol. VII, facing p. 16.

[7] The Letter Testimonial of the Ordination of Coke, quoted in full above, was never published either by Coke or Asbury, but was found among Coke's papers by his biographer, Samuel Drew. The reasons for their failure to publish this letter seem perfectly clear, since it gives no support to the view that Wesley intended to establish a new church in America.

dain ministers, especially for America, since there were no bishops there, and none to baptize or administer the Lord's Supper "for some hundreds of miles together." Therefore he felt at full liberty to appoint and send laborers into the harvest. He then states that he has appointed Doctor Coke and Mr. Francis Asbury to be joint superintendents for America, and has also sent Richard Whatcoat and Thomas Vasey to "act as elders" by baptizing and administering the Lord's Supper. Along with these ordained preachers he sends a liturgy, "little differing from that of the Church of England," which he thinks the best constituted national church in the world, and he advises that all traveling preachers in America use this liturgy every Lord's Day, and also that the Lord's Supper be administered every Sunday.

These suggestions as to liturgy and the use of read prayers show how little Wesley understood the American Methodists. The documents also show that Wesley was not ordaining a bishop in the modern sense, but, rather, had in mind the primitive episcopacy. Nor did he intend to form a new church. Coke and Asbury are not to be joint superintendents over a church, but "over our brethren in America," "who desire to remain under my [Wesley's] care, and still adhere to the doctrines and discipline of the Church of England." There is no doubt in my mind that Wesley's plans for America in their entirety could not have been carried out, and Coke and Asbury were wise in departing from them.

Wesley's assumption of the ordaining power aroused great opposition in many quarters, and among his most severe critics was his brother, Charles. Of his brother's assumption of episcopal powers Charles writes: "I can scarcely believe it, that in his eighty-second year my brother, my old, intimate friend and companion, should have assumed the episcopal character, ordained elders, consecrated a bishop, and sent him to ordain our lay preachers in America. I was then in Bristol at his elbow; yet he never gave me the least hint of his intention. How was he surprised into so rash an action? He certainly persuaded himself that it was right."[8] On another occasion Charles Wesley summed up his views on his brother's action in this bitter quatrain:

> "How easy now are Bishops made
> At man or woman's whim!
> Wesley his hands on Coke hath laid,
> But who laid hands on him?"

On the third of November, 1784, Doctor Coke and his two companions landed in New York. There they immediately met the pastor of the John Street Church, John Dickins, who was delighted when he learned the purpose of their coming. For several successive days Coke preached at the John Street Church, and then journeyed to Philadelphia, where he was heartily received, not only by the Methodists, but also by Dr. William White, soon to be a bishop of the Protestant Episcopal Church, and at that time the leader in the movement to nationalize that body. About two weeks later Coke is in Delaware, the guest of that generous friend of the Methodists,

---

[8] For the correspondence between the Wesley brothers over the matter see, Lunn, *John Wesley*, pp. 342-347.

Judge Bassett. On Sunday, the 14th, he met Freeborn Garrettson and preached at a quarterly meeting at Barratt's Chapel, where he administered the
sacrament to more than five hundred people. When
the sermon was finished, Doctor Coke noticed "a
plainly dressed, robust, but venerable-looking man
moving through the congregation and making his
way to the pulpit; on ascending the pulpit, he
clasped the doctor in his arms, and without making
himself known by words, accosted him with the holy
salutation of primitive Christianity. This venerable man was Mr. Asbury."[9]

Asbury thus describes what took place at his first
meeting with the newly ordained representatives
from Mr. Wesley:

Having had no opportunity of conversing with them before public worship, I was greatly surprised to see Brother
Whatcoat assist by taking the cup in the administration of
the sacrament. I was shocked when first informed of the
intention of these, my brethren, in coming to this country; it may be of God. My answer then was, if the preachers unanimously choose me, I shall not act in the capacity
I have hitherto done by Mr. Wesley's appointment. The
design of organizing the Methodists into an Independent
Episcopal Church was opened to the preachers present, and
it was agreed to call a General Conference to meet at Baltimore the ensuing Christmas.[10]

The next two months were filled with activity for
Coke, Asbury, Whatcoat, and Vasey, but especially
for Freeborn Garrettson, for to him fell the task

[9] Drew, *Life of Coke*, p. 92. At this time Asbury was but forty
years of age, but evidently his appearance and manner made him
appear much older than his years.
[10] Asbury's *Journal*, Vol. I, p. 484. At this meeting there were
fifteen preachers present. On September 16 Asbury met Thomas
Vasey.

of summoning all the preachers to meet at Baltimore on December 24. We are told that he was "sent off like an arrow," but some of the preachers did not get the notice in time to be present at the Conference, among them Jesse Lee, who complained that Garrettson took too much time preaching by the way, and depended too much on writing. Asbury planned a preaching tour of a thousand miles for Coke, procured for him an "excellent horse" and sent a Negro preacher, Harry Hosier, to accompany him. Black Harry, as he was called, greatly impressed Coke with his power as a preacher, and Coke found Harry particularly useful in preaching to the black people. Whatcoat and Vasey accompanied Asbury on an extensive preaching tour into western Maryland.

The week preceding the Conference Asbury, Coke, Whatcoat, and Vasey, with a few of the older preachers, met at the elegant home of Mr. Gough, about twelve miles from Baltimore, a home always open to Methodist preachers, where the matters to be considered were prayerfully discussed. On Friday, December 24, the group rode from Perry Hall to Baltimore, where, about ten o'clock in the morning, the Conference convened at Lovely Lane chapel. For several days the preachers continued to arrive, until about sixty were present,[11] out of the eighty-one in active service at the time. The Conference was in session ten days, from Decem-

---

[11] The preachers known to be present were Thomas Coke, Francis Asbury, Richard Whatcoat, Thomas Vasey, Freeborn Garrettson, William Gill, Reuben Ellis, LeRoy Cole, Richard Ivy, James O'Kelley, John Hagarty, Nelson Reed, James Cromwell, Jeremiah Lambert, John Dickins, William Glendenning, Francis Poythress, Joseph Everett, William Black, William Phoebus, Thomas Ware, and Thomas Haskins.

ber 24 to Sunday, January 2. No journal of the proceedings of the Conference has been preserved, but several of the preachers have left brief accounts of what took place in their journals, and in 1785 the first *Discipline* was printed, which sets forth the official acts under the title—*A Form of Discipline for the Ministers, Preachers, and other members of the Methodist Episcopal Church in America.*

Asbury says in his *Journal:* "We spent the whole week in conference, debating freely, and determined all things by a majority vote. The Doctor preached every day at noon, and some one of the other preachers morning and evening. We were in great haste and did much business in a little time." After the reading of Wesley's letter, the first thing agreed upon was to form themselves into an Episcopal Church, John Dickins suggesting the name Methodist Episcopal Church. Asbury would not submit to be merely appointed superintendent by Wesley, and only consented to be ordained when he and Coke were unanimously elected by the Conference. The ordination of Asbury as deacon, elder, and superintendent took place consecutively on Saturday, Sunday, and Monday.[12] Asbury requested that his friend, Philip William Otterbein, a pietistic German Reformed minister in Baltimore, later to become the cofounder of the United Brethren Church, should assist in his ordination, and the famous picture of the ordination shows Otterbein in a white gown standing in the foreground.

[12] Lee, *History of the Methodists*, p. 107. A number of the older preachers were elected and ordained elders, among them Garrettson and Cromwell for work in Nova Scotia, and Lambert for work in Antiqua in the West Indies, while three were elected and ordained deacons.

The form of *Discipline* adopted was modeled after Wesley's *Large Minutes,* while the twenty-four Articles of Religion, adapted from the Thirty-nine Articles of the English Church, which Wesley had prepared, were also adopted, the Conference adding one article, the present Twenty-third, entitled *Of the Rulers of the United States of America.* The *Sunday Service* and *Hymns,* prepared by Wesley, were made a part of the liturgy of American Methodism. For a time the service was used in the larger churches, and gowns and bands were worn by the superintendents and elders, but a majority of the people disliked such formality, and the Prayer Book was soon laid aside. A stringent rule was passed prohibiting ministers and traveling preachers from drinking intoxicating liquors, except when used as a medicine, while Rule Forty-two comprised an elaborate plan "to extirpate the abomination of slavery." Each slaveholding member was to free every slave between the ages of forty and forty-five immediately, while younger slaves were to be freed within a given time. A note was added, however, making exceptions where state laws made it impossible to comply.

Among the things discussed by Coke and Asbury at the hospitable home of Mr. Gough during that week preceding the Christmas Conference was the advisability of establishing a literary institution for the education of the sons of the preachers and others. Asbury wanted a school; Coke, more ambitious, and with his university degree, urged the establishment of a college, and when the matter was presented to the Conference, they favored Doctor Coke's plan and voted that the college should be

called Cokesbury, in honor of the two superintendents. The college was to be located in Abingdon, Maryland, twenty-five miles from Baltimore,
and immediately on the adjournment of the Conference elaborate plans[13] were drawn up for its erection,
and a long list of rules was adopted for the *Economy
of the College and Students.* In 1785 the foundation
of the building was laid, and two years later the college was opened. In 1795, after having operated
with moderate success for eight years, the college
building was burned to the ground, which was to
Asbury an indication of Providence that it was not
the duty of the Methodist Episcopal Church to
found and operate colleges. It was not until a decade after the death of Asbury that the first permanent institutions of higher learning were established. In the last letter John Wesley wrote Francis
Asbury, dated September 20, 1788, he has this to
say concerning the founding of Cokesbury College:

> "But in one point, my dear brother, I am a little afraid
> both the Doctor and you differ from me. I study to be
> little: you study to be great. I creep, you strut along. I
> found a school: you a college! Nay, and call it after your
> own names! O beware, do not seek to be something! Let
> me be nothing, and 'Christ be all in all!' "[14]

William Watters states in his journal: "We became, instead of a religious society, a separate
church. This gave great satisfaction through all our

---

[13] *The Plan for erecting a College, intended to advance religion in
America, to be presented to the principal members and friends of the
Methodist Episcopal Church,* may be found in Bangs, *History of the
Methodist Episcopal Church.* Vol. I, pp. 330-340.

[14] Telford, *The Letters of John Wesley,* Vol. VIII, p. 91. Referring
to this letter in his *Journal* for March 15, 1789, Asbury says: "Here I
received a bitter pill from one of my greatest friends. Praise the Lord
for my trials also! May they all be sanctified!"

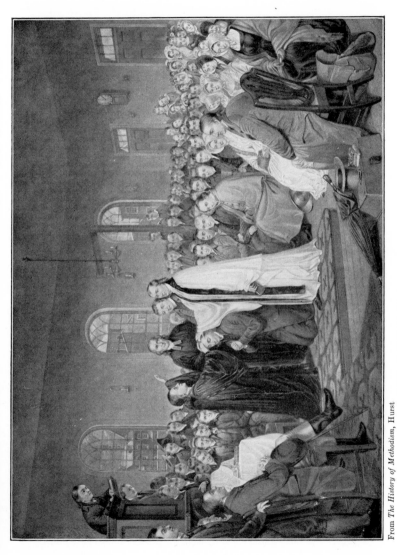

From *The History of Methodism*, Hurst   THE ORDINATION OF FRANCIS ASBURY

societies"; while Lee reports, "The Methodists were pretty generally pleased at our becoming a church, and heartily united in the plan, which the Conference had adopted, and from that time religion greatly revived." Naturally, such favorable comments upon the work of the Conference have received the largest publicity, but there is evidence that some of the preachers were seriously disturbed as to the wisdom of what had been done. Thomas Haskins, one of the preachers in attendance at the Conference, seriously questioned the "expediency of adopting such a plan immediately," and feared that "unhappy consequences" would follow. He acknowledged that Mr. Wesley was a great and good, judicious and sensible man, "but not infallible, particularly with respect to the political, civil, and religious affairs of America. This may be discovered in some of his later writings on these heads." He thinks that more consideration should have been given the opinion of the clergy of the mother church and suggests that they might have been invited to the next Conference, or perhaps some delegates from the Methodist Conference might have been sent to attend the next general Convention of the Episcopal Clergy at Philadelphia. He fears that such hasty action might give occasion for critics to accuse them of being "Hunters after power and disturbers of the peace and good order of the church and state." When the Conference is ended, he still feels uneasy and records in his *Journal,* "Oh how tottering I see Methodism now."[15]

[15] Thomas Haskins' *Journal* has seemingly escaped the knowledge of Methodist historians. It has recently been discovered in the Manuscript Division of the Library of Congress. It is contained in three

Fortunately, Haskins' fears for the future of American Methodism proved to be unfounded, though some communicants of the English Church did withdraw their sympathy and support. Devereaux Jarratt became hostile for a time and made some sharp criticisms of the action of the Methodists, but before his death in 1801 he had again become friendly.[16] The newly formed church was soon to prove the effectiveness of its organization in meeting the problems of the expanding new republic, especially the demands of the moving and restless population, as it pushed its way westward over the Allegheny Mountains into the great valley of the Mississippi.

For the next several years the Methodist Episcopal Church was gradually finding its way under its new organization. The expansion southward continued, seven new circuits being added in 1785, all of them south of Maryland, while among the new circuits were two in Nova Scotia, and one in the island of Antigua, for which elders had been ordained at the Christmas Conference. In 1786 five new circuits appear, two in South Carolina, one in North Carolina, one in New Jersey, and for the first time preachers are sent to Kentucky, forerunners of a great body soon to be found west of the mountains. At the Baltimore Conference, held in 1787, the preachers complained that Doctor Coke had altered the time and place of holding the Conferences with-

small manuscript volumes and covers the years 1782 to May 13, 1785. At the time of the Christmas Conference Haskins was twenty-four years of age. Haskins states that he "was nominated for the Deaconship but begged time for consideration."

[16] Bangs, *History of the Methodist Episcopal Church,* Vol. II, pp. 126-130.

out their consent, and in other ways had interfered with American affairs while out of the country. Coke saw that the preachers were united against him and accordingly consented to sign a paper, which was embodied in the *Minutes,* in which he promised to exercise no authority over the American churches while out of the country, and further engaged to limit his activities while in the country to those which belong to him as superintendent. It was evidently difficult for Doctor Coke to understand that he did not possess supreme authority over the American Methodists, since he had been sent as Mr. Wesley's representative.

The relationship of Mr. Wesley to the newly formed Methodist Episcopal Church is difficult to determine. In 1787 Wesley had written, directing that Freeborn Garrettson be ordained superintendent for Nova Scotia, and that Richard Whatcoat be ordained joint superintendent with Asbury. The Conference refused to carry out these directions, although Coke contended that since the Christmas Conference had agreed that "during the lifetime of the Rev. John Wesley, we acknowledge ourselves his sons in the gospel, ready in matters belonging to church government, to obey his commands" these appointments should be made. The preachers answered that they were not "ready *now* to obey his command." In 1800, however, Richard Whatcoat was elected a bishop. It was further argued that Mr. Wesley, while in England, was not qualified to govern the church in America. In a letter to Whatcoat, July 17, 1788, Wesley states: "It is truly probable the disavowing me will, as soon as my head is laid, occasion a total breach between the English and

American Methodists. They will naturally say, 'If they can do without *us*, we can do without *them*.' "

It was during this year (1787) that Asbury reprinted the *General Minutes* of the Christmas Conference and in the revision the title "bishop" appears for the first time. Some of the preachers objected to the change, but a majority approved it, and its use soon became established. Wesley did not approve the change of title and in a letter to Asbury (September 20, 1788), already referred to, states: "How can you, how dare you suffer yourself to be called Bishop? I shudder, I start, at the very thought! Men may call me a knave or a fool, a rascal, a scoundrel, and I am content: but they shall never by my consent call me Bishop! For my sake, for God's sake, for Christ's sake put a full end to this!" In the *Minutes* of the Conference for 1789 the question is asked: *"Who are the persons that exercise the episcopal office in the Methodist Church in Europe and America?"* The answer is, "John Wesley, Thomas Coke, Francis Asbury." For the next several years the question takes this form: *"Who have been elected by the unanimous suffrages of the General Conference to superintend the Methodist Episcopal Church in America?"* But in 1800 the title "bishop" again appears.

The relation of Doctor Thomas Coke to the beginnings of the Methodist Episcopal Church needs some clarification at this point. Coke was undoubtedly greatly desirous of office and honors, and because of his ambition he received many rebuffs, both in England and America, but these never soured his nature nor dampened his ardor. When he came to America he undoubtedly thought that he was to be

116

recognized as the undisputed head of American Methodists, but he soon found in Asbury and in the other leading preachers stronger wills and a wider experience than his own. Whenever he came up against the opposition of the Conference, he always gave way as gracefully as possible. At one of the General Conferences, probably that of 1796, he had introduced a matter which seemed dictatorial to some of the preachers, and an Irishman, a convert from Roman Catholicism, cried out "Popery, Popery, Popery!" Coke rebuked the disturber for his rudeness, and the Irishman sat down. Coke then seized the paper, containing his resolution, and tore it up, remarking as he glanced about the Conference, "Do you think yourself equal to me?" Nelson Reed, one of the leading preachers, then arose and turning to Bishop Asbury said: "Doctor Coke has asked whether we think ourselves equal to him—I answer, yes, we *do* think ourselves equal to him, notwithstanding he was educated at Oxford and has been honored with the degree of Doctor of Laws— and more than that, we think ourselves equal to Doctor Coke's king." Coke's anger was now completely cooled, and he remarked, "very blandly," "He is hard upon me." Asbury then replied, "I told you our preachers were not blockheads," whereupon Coke asked the pardon of the Conference.[17]

In the year 1791 Doctor Coke approached Bishop William White, the leading spirit in the new Protestant Episcopal Church in America, on the matter of bringing about a union between American Methodists and the Protestant Episcopal Church, sug-

---

[17] Sprague, W B., *Annals of the American Pulpit,* Vol. VIII, "Methodist," pp. 68-70. New York, Robert Carter & Brothers, 1865.

gesting the reordination of the Methodist preachers, and later in a letter to Bishop Seabury, suggested his own and Asbury's ordination as Episcopal bishops. In his letter to White, Coke states that Wesley "did not intend, I think, that an entire separation should take place," and he further says Wesley had not meant to establish a new denomination in America. Coke was anxious that this reunion should take place before Wesley's death, hoping that his approval would settle the matter. The scheme was undoubtedly purely a personal one and doubtless would not have met the general approval of the American Methodists. Asbury knew nothing of it, and Coke was careful to keep it from him, and very probably it would not have had his consent. On both sides there was "a lack of genuine interest in, or comprehension of, the subject of unity." But, as one of the Protestant Episcopalian historians has stated, "a century has developed sentiments then dormant or unknown. Time has added to the difficulties of a settlement; but it has also deepened a conviction and stirred a feeling, which may prove more than a match for the difficulties. In one respect the tables are turned. The church of Seabury and White now holds out the hand."[18]

The next few years following the organization of the Methodist Episcopal Church saw a number of changes introduced. At the Conference of 1789

[18] For a discussion of this whole question see Tiffany, C. C., *A History of the Protestant Episcopal Church* (American Church History Series, Vol. VII), pp. 405-408; White, William, *Memoirs of the Protestant Episcopal Church*, (Philadelphia, 1820), pp. 208-215, also Appendix, No. 21, for Coke's letter to White and White's reply, pp. 224-231; also an article by Hale, Charles R., "The American Church and Methodism," *Church Review*, January, 1891.

the bishops presented a scheme to form a "Council" to be composed of the bishops and presiding elders. There were no official "presiding elders" until the Conference of 1792, but the office had been gradually evolving from 1785 onward, and in that year certain elders were directed to take the oversight of several circuits. The Council thus composed was to consider all matters for the well-being of the church, but their action was not to be binding until it had been agreed upon by a majority of the Conference for that district. The first meeting of the Council met at Cokesbury College December 1, 1789, and the second convened at Baltimore the year following, while a third was appointed for 1792. But by this time so much opposition had developed among the preachers and people that it never again convened.

From 1784 to 1790 was a period of rapid growth. A great revival had swept over certain counties in Virginia in 1787, even greater, Lee states, than was that of 1776. The Brunswick circuit added 1,800 members, Amelia, 800, and Sussex more than 600. This year Virginia and Kentucky circuit added 4,761 new members, Maryland, 2,475; Georgia, 707; South Carolina, 704; Delaware and Pennsylvania, 544; New Jersey, 504, and New York, 861. The total increase for the year was 11,481. This year there were eighty-five circuits, and one hundred and sixty-five traveling preachers. The next year (1788) the increase of new members was 5,911, and the circuits now numbered ninety-seven. For the year 1790 the number of new members added was 14,-356, or almost the exact number in the entire church at its organization six years before, while the total for the later year numbered 45,949 whites, and 11,-862 colored members. Certainly, such rapid growth would seem to vindicate fully the action taken at the Christmas Conference in 1784 in the formation of an independent church.

In the years immediately following the formation of the Methodist Episcopal Church the two superintendents had two significant interviews with George Washington. The first was held in 1785, when Coke and Asbury met Washington at Mount Vernon, by appointment, to urge him to use his influence to bring about the emancipation of slaves in Virginia. He informed them that he agreed with their sentiments, but refused to sign their petition, stating that if the Assembly took the matter under consideration, he would send them a letter setting forth his sentiments. He then invited them to spend the night at Mount Vernon, but their engagements the following day would not permit acceptance.[19] The second interview took place on May 29, 1789, just a month after Washington's first inauguration. Asbury had presented a proposition to the Conference, meeting in New York, that they send a congratulatory address to George Washington, in which they should express their approbation of the Constitution and present their allegiance to the government. This was approved, an address was drawn up, and John Dickins and Thomas Morrell were appointed to present the address to Washington and request him to appoint a time to receive the bishops, one of whom would at that time read the address. The President appointed a day and

---

[19] Coke, Thomas, *Extracts of the Journals of the Rev. Dr. Coke's Five Visits to America.* London, 1793, p. 45.

at that time Asbury and Coke, with Dickins and Morrell, met the President. Asbury read the address, to which Washington read a response, the last paragraph of which reads:

"It always affords me satisfaction when I find a concurrence of sentiment and practice between conscientious men, in acknowledgments of homage to the great Governor of the universe, and in professions of support to a just civil government. After mentioning that, I trust the people of every denomination, who demean themselves as good citizens, will have occasion to be convinced that I shall always strive to prove a faithful and impartial patron of genuine, vital religion. I must assure you in particular that I take in kindest part the promise you make of presenting your prayers at the throne of grace for me, and that I likewise implore the divine benediction on yourselves and your religious community."

The Methodists pride themselves upon the fact that they were the first religious denomination to present such an address promising support to the head of the new civil government.

CHAPTER VII

INVADES NEW ENGLAND

WHILE Methodism was becoming well established in the middle states, and particularly in the regions south of Maryland, in the period immediately following the Revolution, it had not as yet succeeded in gaining a permanent foothold in New England. The fifty years following the great New England revival were a period of religious and moral indifference throughout New England. A bitter doctrinal controversy within Congregationalism was one of the causes for this slump in religious vitality. But there were other causes. New England took a leading part in the War for Independence, and the New England clergy were particularly active in preaching the political philosophy of the Revolution, and throughout the War Congregational people, as well as their ministers, were practically unanimous in their support of the patriot cause. For such support to the great cause of independence New England Congregationalism may well be proud, but at the same time such activity always reacts unfavorably to the cause of vital religion. Indeed, war is always hurtful to the cause of morality and religion, and such was the case in New England. A historian of that church has stated that "the two decades from the close of the War of Independence include the period of the lowest ebb tide of vitality in the history of American Christianity."[1]

These were the years also in which both English and French deism were exercising an increasing influence in America, especially in the colleges, while a blatant type of infidelity was rampant in every section of the country, but particularly in the newer regions. Conditions in New England, as well as on the frontiers, were calling loudly for a type of religion which would infuse new life into the dry bones.

On May 28, 1789, at the Methodist Conference, which met at the John Street Church in New York City, Jesse Lee was appointed to "Stamford Circuit" in Connecticut. This was the beginning of organized Methodism in New England. It is true that other representatives of Methodism had previously visited New England; Charles Wesley, on his way home from Georgia (1737), stopped for a month in Boston, where he preached in Christ Church and in King's Chapel, but he was not at that time a Methodist; Whitefield, as we have already seen, had made five visits to New England, and although many thousands had heard him, he created no organization; Richard Boardman came to Boston in 1772 and formed a small society there, but it soon disappeared; in 1785 William Black, the Methodist apostle to Nova Scotia, tarried several months in Boston, but nothing permanent came of his labors; two years later Cornelius Cook preached in Norwalk, Connecticut, and finally Freeborn Garrettson, returning from his mission in Nova Scotia in

[1] Bacon, L. W., *History of American Christianity*, American Church History Series, Vol. XIII, New York, 1897, p. 221.

1787, preached in Boston, where he found three Methodists, dating back to Boardman's visit. He determined to return to New England the next year, but Bishop Asbury sent him up the Hudson instead. Thus it remained for Jesse Lee, the tall, handsome, courageous Virginian, to become the founder of New England Methodism, and on June 17, 1789, he began his New England labors in a sermon at Norwalk, Connecticut, from the text, "Ye must be born again."

The first week of Lee's labors in Connecticut resulted in the formation of a circuit of twenty preaching places, and on the first round he preached at New Haven in the Courthouse, and in his audience were President Stiles and several students of Yale College. It was several months before Lee was able to form the first Methodist class, but by the beginning of the year 1790 three had been organized. Asbury now dispatched three additional preachers to assist Lee in his difficult field, and a second circuit was formed, centering at New Haven, while in the spring Lee made a preaching tour into Massachusetts and as far north as New Hampshire and Vermont, and on May 3 (1790) preached the first Methodist sermon at Wilbraham, Massachusetts. July found him in Boston, and on July 11 he preached his first sermon in the Puritan metropolis, on Boston Common, standing on a deal table as a pulpit. At the end of sixteen months' labor he reported at the Conference in New York in October, 1790, five circuits formed, two chapels erected, and two hundred souls gathered into classes. Lee states that "Methodist preaching was a strange thing in that part of the world."

Meanwhile Freeborn Garrettson, in charge of the territory along the Hudson, with his several preachers, had been attacking New England from the west, while Lee and his helpers were working in the central and eastern part. In 1790 Lee was named presiding elder of four circuits, his work centering in Boston. The outstanding event of this year was the establishment of the society at Lynn, the first to be formed in Massachusetts. Methodism at Lynn reaped the benefit of a controversy in the Congregational Church. Lee states that in May "upwards of seventy men, who paid tax, came together and took certificates shewing that they attended public worship with the Methodists, and paid to the support of their minister." This was done so they would not be compelled to pay toward the support of the Congregational minister, whom they did not like. So rapid was the progress of Methodism at Lynn that a meetinghouse was soon erected, and for a number of years it was the strongest society in New England, and had the honor in 1792 of entertaining the first Methodist Conference in New England. Boston Methodism, however, made slow progress, and it was not until July, 1792, that a few members were formed into a society. The Boston society was small and the members poor, and the first Methodist meetinghouse was not begun until 1795, when in August of that year they were able to begin a small frame building through the assistance of generous Methodists in New York, Pennsylvania, and Maryland. But even after the erection of their own place of worship it was a long time before it was filled.

While Methodism was making its feeble begin-

ning in Boston, preaching tours were made into
New Hampshire, Vermont, and into the province
of Maine, then a part of Massachusetts. In 1793
Lee was assigned to Lynn and the Province of
Maine, and that year formed the first Maine circuits. Lee states that he was the first Methodist
preacher "that ever went to that province to
preach." He made a long tour along the coast to
the mouth of the Penobscot, thence up that river
to the "upper settlements." The first circuit was
on the west side of the Kennebec and was two hundred miles beyond any other circuit in New England.

In spite of predictions to the contrary, Methodism had won notable successes in New England, and
by the time of the formation of the New England
Conference in 1796 the number of Methodists in
each of the New England states was as follows: Connecticut, 1,201; Massachusetts, 913; Maine, 606;
Rhode Island, 177; New Hampshire, 92. Naturally, Congregationalism, then the state church in
Massachusetts, Connecticut, and New Hampshire,
resented the invasion of their territory by this aggressive band of religious enthusiasts, and considerable opposition was experienced by the Methodist
preachers throughout Massachusetts and Connecticut particularly. Connecticut magistrates would
not recognize Methodist preachers as regular
ministers, and at least one was fined for performing
the marriage ceremony. Thomas Ware, who succeeded Garrettson on the Albany District in 1793,
received the following advice from a Congregational
deacon: "My advice to you and your itinerant
brethren is, to go home; or, at least, to desist from

disturbing the order of things among us. We want none of your instruction; and, indeed *you* are not competent to instruct *us*. You make people commit sin in the loss of so much precious time as is wasted in attending your meetings on week days, when they ought to be at labor; or on the Sabbath, in leaving the places where they ought to worship, to run after you. We have learned and able ministers, and all the necessary means of grace among us, and we do very well without you. Why, then, do you trouble yourselves about us?"[2] A Congregational minister, Nathan Williams, published a sermon against the Methodists, together with a letter from Doctor Huntington, of Coventry, Connecticut. This publication received the unanimous approval of the Congregational Association. In Doctor Huntington's letter Wesley is denounced as a "flaming enthusiast, given to wild singularities," among which are enumerated classes and class meetings.

In the *Congregational Catechism*,[3] published in 1844, the last three chapters are devoted to the constitutions of the Protestant Episcopal, the Methodist Episcopal, and the Presbyterian Churches, largely for the purpose of showing in what respects the Congregational polity is superior. The chief objections to the Methodist system are: (1) It divests the churches of power, vesting it in the hands of the clergy, "by whom, history informs us, it is extremely liable to be abused." (2) It overlooks the rules of

---

[2] *Sketches of the Life and Travels of Rev. Thomas Ware*, Written by Himself, p. 202. New York: T. Mason and G. Lane, 1839.
[3] *The Congregational Catechism containing a General Survey of the Organization, Government and Discipline of Christian Churches.* (New Haven, 1844.)

discipline given by Christ in Matthew 18. (3) It takes from the brethren the right of choosing their own religious teachers, which is the chief defense against incompetent teachers. (4) It deprives the church of resident pastors and teachers. As to whether the Methodist system has been productive of good, the answer is given that the system has undoubtedly led to rapid growth, but it is adapted to the early operations of a new sect and a sparse population, and does not result in the highest edification and improvement of the people.

Bishop Asbury seems never to have liked New England, for to him "it was socially and religiously inhospitable." On his visit there in 1794 he speaks of his "affliction of body and mind," of his "sad heart" and sinking spirits. The fact that three of the New England states "are fettered with ecclesiastical chains—taxed to support ministers, who are chosen by a small committee," gives him "great dejection of spirit," and he prophesies that "this must come to an end with the present century."[4] Here he felt the presence of "iron walls of prejudice" and exclaims, "O what a happy people these would be if they were not thus priest-ridden." The good bishop seems always to have been in bad health when visiting New England in these early years, and the state of his health may have influenced his opinion—or it may have been the state of the roads. In 1798, traveling in a carriage in Connecticut, he says, "We came on without touching the ground sometimes, as the carriage would frequently jump from rock to rock." A few days later he speaks of riding "through heat and over rocks twelve miles to

[4] *Journal*, Vol. II, p. 236.

THE FIRST MEETINGHOUSE IN BOSTON

Brother Lyon's, at Canterbury; this made me feel like Jonah. I was much outdone, having slept very little for two nights: but I was compensated for all in finding the life of religion amongst this people."[5]

At the General Conference of 1796 the country was divided into six portions, each of which was to have a yearly Conference of its own. The divisions were as follows: New England, Philadelphia, Baltimore, Virginia, South Carolina, and the Western. Previous to this time the Methodist circuits in America were considered as forming but one Conference, and the so-called Conferences held from time to time were simply sectional meetings of the one Conference. The boundaries of the New England Conference included, besides all of the New England states, that part of New York east of the Hudson, and also upper Canada.

As we have already noticed, the Christmas Conference ordained Garrettson and Cromwell as elders for Nova Scotia. This had been brought about through the earnest efforts of William Black, who visited the United States in 1784 to urge the Methodists of the United States to send helpers into eastern Canada. Black had been converted in 1779 under the influence of some Yorkshire Methodists, who had come out to Nova Scotia some years before. He at once dedicated his life to the ministry and without assistance or promise of support, went from place to place, holding services under trees, in barns or the homes of the people. After two years Garrettson and Cromwell returned to the United States (1787), but two years later Black, James and John Mann were ordained by Asbury and Coke at

[5] *Journal,* Vol. II, pp. 384, 385.

Philadelphia, and Black was appointed superintendent for New Brunswick, Nova Scotia, and Newfoundland. Up until 1799 the maritime provinces were supplied with preachers by the Methodist Episcopal Church, but thereafter the work there was connected with the Wesleyan Methodism of the old country.

Methodist work in Quebec and Upper Canada dates from the activities of lay preachers in Wolfe's army, in which there was a Methodist society, and it is quite probable that Captain Webb was influenced by this society since he fought with Wolfe at the siege of Quebec.[6] During the Revolution an Irish local preacher in a British regiment, Tuffy, began preaching among the English immigrants, and although he left no organization, his converts, who remained in Canada, were the first to open their doors to welcome the Methodist preachers, who later came to that region.[7] Other local preachers, some from England, others from among the American Loyalists, who went to Canada during and following the Revolution, were active in preaching to the scattered settlers. Finally in 1790 the first regular Methodist preacher, William Losee, was authorized by Freeborn Garrettson, his presiding elder, to visit Canada, and in 1791 Losee was sent to the Kingston Circuit. The work along the lower Saint Lawrence made progress, and in 1794 Canada appears as a separate district of the Methodist Episcopal Church, with two circuits, Upper Canada, lower

[6] Stephenson, Mrs. Frederick C., *One Hundred Years of Canadian Methodist Missions, 1824-1924*, Vol. I, pp. 29ff. Toronto, 1925.

[7] Sanderson, J. E., *The First Century of Methodism in Canada*, p. 23. Toronto, William Briggs, 1908.

circuit, and Upper Canada, upper circuit. At first
the Canada circuits were a part of the New England
Conference, but later became a part of the New
York Conference, until with the organization of the
Genesee Conference the more western Canadian
circuits were placed in that Conference. Thus at
the outbreak of the War of 1812 there were two districts in Canada, the Upper Canada District, in the
Genesee Conference, with seven circuits with a membership of 2,250, and the Lower Canada District, in
the New York Conference, consisting of four circuits, with a membership of 242.

The War of 1812, which was largely fought on
the Canadian frontier, greatly disturbed the relationship between the Canadian Methodists and their
brethren in the United States. At the close of the
war missionaries began to be sent to these regions
by the Wesleyan Methodists, and the Canadian government was naturally more favorably disposed to
the British Methodist preachers than to those from
the United States. Gradually the feeling developed
that Methodism in Canada should not be under the
control of authorities in the United States, and as
a result of the political and social unrest of the period it was thought advisable (1824) to organize the
Canadian circuits into a separate Conference, and
four years later an independent Methodist Episcopal Church in Canada was formed. Thus there
came to be three Methodist bodies in Canada: the
Canadian Wesleyan Methodist Church; the British
Wesleyan Methodist Church, and now the Canadian
Methodist Episcopal Church.

While Methodism was making its first impact
upon staid New England events of great importance

for the future of American Methodism were taking place elsewhere.

On March 2, 1791, John Wesley breathed his last, but the news did not reach Coke and Asbury until April 29. They were at that time traveling northward on separate routes from Georgia to hold a Conference in North Carolina. Asbury on this day records in his *Journal:* "The solemn news reached our ears that the public papers had announced the death of that dear man of God, John Wesley. . . . I conclude that his equal is not to be found among all the sons he hath brought up, nor his superior among all the sons of Adam he may have left behind. Brother Coke was sunk in spirit, and wished to hasten home immediately. . . . I feel the stroke most sensibly."

The last letter Wesley addressed to America was to Ezekiel Cooper and was written February 1, 1791: "Those that desire to write or say anything to me have no time to lose; for time has shaken me by the hand and death is not far behind." Such is the opening sentence. After mentioning his failing sight and strength, he urges that some of the American Methodists "give us a connected relation of what the Lord has been doing in America from the time that Richard Boardman accepted the invitation and left his country to serve you."[8] In 1798 Cooper was made general book steward, succeeding John Dickins to that office, and he was thus able to carry out Wesley's suggestion. It is of particular interest

---

[6] Wesley does not mention Joseph Pilmoor, who actually volunteered to go to America some time before Boardman, but by this time Pilmoor had left the Methodists. John Dickins, the founder of The Methodist Book Concern, had died of yellow fever in Philadelphia in 1798.

to American Methodists to note that the last letter
the aged Wesley wrote was to William Wilberforce,
dated February 24, 1791, encouraging him to go
forward with his courageous fight against slavery and
the slave trade, and in the letter are these words:
"Oh be not weary in well doing: Go on, in the name
of God, and in the power of his might, till even
American slavery (the vilest that ever saw the sun)
shall vanish away before it."

At the first General Conference, held in 1792 at
Baltimore, the first schism in American Methodism
took place.[9]   The leader in the discontent was James
O'Kelley, of Virginia, who had begun to preach in
1778 and was one of those receiving ordination at
the Christmas Conference.   He was a man of ability
and was popular in the region, where for eight years
he had been a presiding elder.   He objected to the
large authority and life-tenure of the superintendents, and at this Conference introduced an amendment to the *Discipline*, providing that a preacher
dissatisfied with his appointment shall have the
right to appeal to the Conference and state his objections, and if the Conference approve his objections, the bishop shall then appoint him to another
circuit.   The debate over this proposal lasted several days, and when it finally came to a vote a large
majority were found to be against the change.   Immediately O'Kelley and a few of his followers left
the Conference, stating, in a letter to that body, that
they could no longer sit with them, because of the
rejection of their proposal.   All attempts to per-

---

[9] There is no official record of this Conference extant, but Lee has
preserved a summary of the proceedings in his *History*, pp. 174-192.
See also the account by Thomas Ware in his *Life and Travels*, pp.
219-222.

suade the disaffected members proved unsuccessful, and a number of the preachers declined to accept their appointments, among them William McKendree. On the adjournment of the Conference Asbury hastened to the center of disaffection and succeeded in making a temporary compromise with O'Kelley, but later O'Kelley entirely withdrew and formed a church, which was called the Republican Methodists, some of whose members later merged with the followers of Barton W. Stone to form the Christian Church.[10]

From 1794 to 1797 there was a decrease in the membership of the church, especially in those regions of Virginia and North Carolina where the Republican Methodists were the most active. In the year 1795 the decrease was more than six thousand, and the following year nearly four thousand. There were other reasons for the decline, however, which have no connection with the O'Kelley schism. One of these was the spiritual and moral deadness which generally prevailed throughout the country. In the year 1798 the General Assembly of the Presbyterian Church, in their address to the church, thus describe moral and religious conditions:

We perceive with pain and fearful apprehension a general dereliction of religious principles and practice among our fellow citizens, a visible and prevailing impiety and contempt for the laws and institutions of religion, and an abounding infidelity, which in many instances tends to atheism itself. The profligacy and corruption of the public morals have advanced with a progress proportionate to

[10]A series of isolated movements, each emphasizing much the same tenets, arose about this time, most of which were finally merged into the Stone and Campbell movements. See Garrison, W. E., *Religion Follows the Frontier: A History of the Disciples of Christ*, pp. 59-68. New York, Harper, 1931.

declension in religion. Profaneness, pride, luxury, injustice, intemperance, lewdness, and every species of debauchery and loose indulgence greatly abound.

Deistic influences were particularly strong in the colleges, where Thomas Paine's writings were widely read and believed by the students. Lyman Beecher tells us that while he was a student at Yale during these years the students boasted of their infidelity, and addressed one another as Voltaire, Rousseau, etc., while profanity, intemperance, gambling and licentiousness were common among them. When Bishop Asbury visited Vermont in 1795 he preached in the woods near Bennington to a company in which were deists and Universalists. Conditions in the other colleges were similar to those at Yale. Few students made any profession of Christianity. A student at the new University of Georgia at Athens in 1803 states that "there was not at that time a single serious student in the college. Indeed, there were but very few who were not grossly immoral." It was, therefore, to quote a Baptist historian of the time, a "very wintry season" for religion generally, and for all the churches.

The General Conference of 1792 legalized the office of *presiding elder* and defined its duties. The office had actually been in existence for several years, but it had not received recognition in the *Discipline*. The status of a supernumerary preacher was also defined as one who could not preach constantly because of broken health, but was willing to do any work in the ministry which the Conference might direct or his strength allow. The salaries of all traveling preachers were fixed at sixty-four dollars and traveling expenses, which included ferriages, horse-shoeing and provisions for themselves and horses. To the question, "What shall be annually allowed the wives of the traveling preachers?" was the answer, "Sixty-four dollars if they be in want of it." Provision was also made that there should be another General Conference in four years in which all traveling preachers should have a seat.

The first five General Conferences from 1792 to 1808 were made up of all the traveling preachers, and all convened in the city of Baltimore. An important action of the General Conference of 1796 was the creation of the "Chartered Fund" for the relief of "distressed traveling preachers, their families, worn-out preachers, and the widows and orphans of preachers." The fund was to be supported by voluntary gifts, under the direction of a board of trustees. Incorporation was secured through the Legislature of Pennsylvania.

In all of the early General Conferences both slavery[11] and temperance came up for discussion. The General Conference of 1796 adopted a regulation providing that:

If any member of our society retail or give spirituous liquors, and anything disorderly be transacted under his roof on this account, the preacher, who has the oversight of the circuit shall proceed against him, as in the case of other immoralities, and the person accused shall be cleared, censured, suspended, or excluded, according to his conduct, as on other charges of immorality.

As already noticed, this General Conference also created the Annual Conferences with definite boundaries.

[11] The whole question of the relation of the church to slavery will be treated in a later chapter.

The great task of supervising the growing new church throughout the vast territory of the United States and Canada was largely upon the shoulders of Bishop Asbury. Bishop Coke was absent in England a part of every year, while there was some feeling of distrust among the preachers concerning his administration. At the General Conference of 1796 it was thought expedient to elect an assistant bishop. Bishop Coke, learning of this feeling among the preachers, offered to give himself entirely to the American work in assisting Asbury, promising not to station the preachers at any time when Asbury was present, but to exercise all episcopal duties when he presided at a Conference in Asbury's absence. This offer was accepted by the Conference, and Coke fulfilled his obligation until he was released by the General Conference of 1808, which gave him the right to remain in Europe "until called to the United States by the General Conference, or by all the American Conferences respectively." His name was retained in the *Minutes* as a bishop until his death (1814) with a note that he was not to exercise the office of superintendent in America until recalled.

Throughout the year 1799 Asbury suffered greatly from physical ailments, due to his excessive labors, and constant exposure to all kinds of weather. Though he had continued his annual tour of the Conferences, he was able to preach but seldom. Such entries as "I rode in great pain and heat, hungry and sick, twenty-five miles,"[12] "I have been greatly afflicted and dejected with pain and labor" (August 5, 1799), "I put a blister in the morning

[12]*Journal,* July 20, 1799.

to my breast, but I must go to meeting and preach"
(September 17), are of frequent occurrence in his
Journal. On October 26 of this year he observes:

> I tremble and faint under my burden; having to ride
> about six thousand miles annually; to preach from three to
> five hundred sermons a year; to write and read so many
> letters, and read many more: all this and more, besides
> the stationing of three hundred preachers; reading many
> hundred pages; and spending many hours in conversation
> by day and by night, with people and preachers of various
> characters, among whom are many distressing cases.

As the time for the General Conference approached, he began to entertain thoughts of resigning his office of superintendent and taking a "seat on
a level with his brethren in the Conference." When
the Conference convened, he informed them of his
intention.

In an unpublished letter to Thomas Haskins,
written October 17, 1807, from Hanging Rock,
twenty miles northwest of Camden, South Carolina,
Bishop Asbury makes this interesting comment on
the power of the Methodist bishop:

> I have only to say I sit on a joyless height, a pinacle
> of power, too high to sit secure and unenvied, too high to
> sit secure without divine aid. My bodily and mental
> powers fail, I have a charge too great for many men with
> minds like mine. I hope not to jump down, fall down, or
> be thrown down by haughty ambition, but I mean to step
> down as soon and safely and completely as I can; and not
> to stand alone, but break the fire by having more objects
> than one. I am happy, the ship is safe in harbor with an
> increase of 10,000 annually but how many more, if the
> dead, and removed and expelled were numbered. . . .
> In the year 66 I began my present line of labor, between
> 40 and 50 times I have X the alleghany mountains, swamps,
> and rivers, of the south going and returning. When a man

is in his 62 year it is not safe to trust a great work to his trembling hands. A president of a State or the states ought to know when to retire for fear of damages, and if heaven would insure my life bodily and mental powers, would heartily advise my brethren to provide immediately for such an important charge! and not to rest it with me, or any one man on earth. Only to think seven Conferences, 500 traveling, possibly two or three thousand local and official men, possible near ten million (in the land) . . . 100,000 membership. Lord be merciful to me. Amen.

(From the private Collection of Mr. Charles F. Eggleston, Philadelphia, Pennsylvania.)

Immediately the Conference took action, unanimously urging Asbury to continue as one of the general superintendents, and at the same time determined to choose another superintendent to assist Asbury, though it was decided that the bishops were to be equal in every particular. There were two ballots cast; on the first Richard Whatcoat and Jesse Lee received the same number of votes, but on the second Whatcoat received four more votes than Lee and was declared elected. Whatcoat was in his sixty-fifth year and is characterized as a man of meek and modest spirit. As a preacher he appealed mightily to the emotions and often moved congregations "as the leaves of a forest by the power of a mighty wind."

At this Conference the allowance of a traveling preacher was raised to eighty dollars, besides traveling expenses. The same allowance was made a preacher's wife or widow, besides sixteen dollars each for children under seven, and twenty-four dollars for each child between the years of seven and fourteen. The same provision was made for supernumerary and superannuated preachers, their wives, widows and orphans. At the General Conference of 1816 the salaries of preachers, their wives and widows were raised to one hundred dollars, while the allowance to children remained the same.

During the latter years of the eighteenth and the early years of the nineteenth centuries a great revival was sweeping over the country. Its most spectacular manifestations, however, were beyond the Alleghenies, and for that reason we will give consideration to it in connection with the expansion of Methodism westward.

At the General Conference of 1804 the question of the time limit came up for consideration, and a resolution was passed providing that a bishop should not allow any preacher to remain longer than two years in the same station or circuit, except presiding elders, superannuated and worn-out preachers. Asbury was greatly concerned over the tendency of preachers to remain several years in the same station, and probably his influence was largely responsible for the passage of the resolution.

Of outstanding significance in the development of American Methodism was the introduction of representative government by the General Conference of 1808. Up to that time every traveling preacher had the right to a seat in the General Conference. This meant, of course, that the Conferences nearest the place of meeting always had the largest representation, while those farthest away had little influence. The question of a delegated body had been under consideration since 1791, when Lee had made such a proposal to Asbury. In 1808 the Methodist Episcopal Church had about five hundred traveling preachers, ministering to about one hundred and forty thousand members scattered throughout the nation. The question of preserving the unity of the church was becoming a problem of increasing seriousness, and by this time many of the leaders in the church were urging the necessity of a delegated body on this ground, while several of the Annual Conferences had passed resolutions favoring such a change. When the General Conference met, a committee was formed to consider the matter, made up of two members from each of the seven Conferences, and a subcommittee of three was appointed to draft a report. As a result of the work of these committees, what is known as the Constitution of the Methodist Episcopal Church was formulated and adopted. It represented very largely a plan proposed by Joshua Soule,[13] of New England, who had been a member of the subcommittee.

The main features of the plan as adopted were: First, the General Conference shall be composed of one member for every five members of each Annual Conference, and each Conference shall have the power to choose their delegates either by seniority or choice. Two thirds of the representatives of all Annual Conferences shall be necessary for a quorum in the General Conference. Second, a series of Restrictive Rules were adopted as follows: The General Conference "shall not change or alter any part or rule of our government so as to do away with episcopacy, or to destroy the plan of our itinerant general superintendency." The General Conference shall have full powers to make rules and regu-

---

[13] Du Bose, H. M., *Life of Joshua Soule*. Nashville, Tennessee, Smith & Lamar, Agents, 1916. See Chap. V, "Writing the Constitution." Also Tigert, *Constitutional History of American Episcopal Methodism*, Chap. XII.

lations for our church under the following restrictions:

The Articles of Religion shall not be revoked or altered, nor shall there be any new standards or rules adopted contrary to the present standards of doctrine.

They shall not allow more than one representative for every five members of an Annual Conference, nor less than one for every seven.

The General Rules of the United Societies shall not be changed or revoked.

The right of ministers to be tried by a committee, and of an appeal shall not be done away; nor shall members be deprived of the right of trial before the Society, or by a committee, and of an appeal.

The incomes from the Book Concern or of the Chartered Fund shall be used only for the benefit of traveling, supernumerary, superannuated, and worn-out preachers, their wives, widows and children.

Provided, nevertheless, that upon the joint recommendation of the Annual Conferences, then a majority of two thirds of the General Conference succeeding shall suffice to alter any of the above restrictions.

It was further decided that a General Conference could be called at any time by the superintendent with the advice of all the Annual Conferences, but "that the General Conference shall meet regularly on the first day of May once in four years perpetually, and at such place or places as shall be fixed on by the General Conference from time to time."

The adoption of the Constitution marks the beginning of a new epoch in the Methodist Episcopal Church, for it meant the stabilization of the church government and regulations, and from this time forward Methodism becomes more and more "like a drilled army, ready for the charge."

CHAPTER VIII

CROSSES THE ALLEGHENIES

THE greatest accomplishment of America has been the conquest of the continent. The pushing of population westward from the Atlantic seaboard over the Allegheny Mountains into the valley of the Ohio; thence into the great Mississippi basin; on into the trans-Missouri region; then during the eighteen-forties and fifties to the Pacific and the far Northwest; gradually filling in the Rocky Mountain region, in the years following the Civil War; the carving of farms from the forest and the prairies; the building of roads, and bridges and fences; the erection of towns and cities; the founding of churches, schools, and colleges in the vast region between the Atlantic seaboard and the Pacific—this has been the greatest accomplishment of America. It is no exaggeration to say that the most significant single factor in the history of the United States has been the Western movement of population, and the churches which devised the best methods for following the population as it pushed westward were the ones destined to become the great American churches. The Methodist Episcopal Church is one of the two largest Protestant Churches in the United States to-day largely because it possessed, or developed, the best technique for following and ministering to a moving and restless population. "It alone was organized as to be able to follow step by step this movable population,

143

and to carry the gospel even to the most distant cabin. It alone could be present whenever a grave was opened, or an infant was found in its cradle."

The itinerant system was admirably suited to the spreading of the gospel in a new country. The Methodist system was highly centralized, with the power of sending the circuit riders to their circuits wholly in the hands of the superintendents. Such arbitrary power was bitterly assailed, as we have seen, by James O'Kelley and his followers, and later by a party within the church known as the "Reformers," which finally led to the formation of the Methodist Protestant Church; but, notwithstanding such criticism, it cannot "be gainsaid that for the infant church functioning in a sparsely settled, rapidly developing country, centralization was the best policy."[1] Undoubtedly Asbury fully realized this, which accounts for his stanch support of a system which seemed, to so many, to be both arbitrary and ruthless.

Circuits in newly settled regions were always large, sometimes covering territory so vast that it required from five to six weeks to make the rounds. Circuits were known as two-weeks, three-weeks, four-weeks or five-weeks circuits, according to the time required for the circuit rider to go the rounds once. Thus, in the year 1800, Henry Smith's circuit in southern Ohio covered the entire region along the Ohio from the Scioto eastward. Benjamin Lakin the same year traveled a circuit in northern Kentucky extending from Maysville to the

---

[1] Gewehr, W. M., *Some Factors in the Expansion of Frontier Methodism. 1800-1811. The Journal of Religion*, Vol. VIII, No. 1, January, 1928, pp. 98-120.

From *Old Redstone*, Joseph Smith

SACRAMENTAL SCENE IN A WESTERN FOREST

Licking River, while William Burke, the first secretary of the Western Conference, traveled a circuit
in Central Kentucky extending a hundred miles
in each direction. James B. Finley's first circuit,
called the Will's Creek, was four hundred and seventy-five miles around. At the Western Conference of
1803 a preacher was assigned simply to Illinois as
his circuit, while three years later another was assigned to Missouri. Tobias Gibson traveled up
and down the lower Mississippi for several hundreds
of miles, and Elisha W. Bowman, after the Louisiana
Purchase, covered a territory equally large. Neither
hardship nor distance deterred the preachers from
carrying on the work to which they were assigned.
The average circuit had from fifteen to twenty-five
preaching places. The early circuit rider generally preached every day in the week, except Monday, and this day was occupied in writing letters,
or in getting his meager wardrobe ready for the
remainder of the week.

Few of the first circuit riders in a new country
were married men, for the reason that most of the
early circuits were too poor to support a married
preacher. When a preacher married, it was usually
necessary for him to locate, that is, he stopped traveling a circuit and settled down on a farm, as did
William Watters and Philip Gatch, and although
most of them continued their interest in the church
and preached frequently in their vicinity, their
names disappeared from the list of active preachers
in the *Minutes,* and they then had the status of local
preachers.[2] All of the early bishops were unmar-

[2] Bangs, Nathan, *A History of the Methodist Episcopal Church,* Vol.
II, Appendix, pp. 421-454, gives a list of all the preachers received into

ried men, the first married bishop being Bishop
Robert R. Roberts, who was elected to the episcopacy in 1816. Bishop Asbury discouraged preachers from marrying, for he knew too well that in most
instances marriage meant the loss of the preacher
to the church. The idea prevailed that "a traveling
preacher has no business with a wife: let him locate
and take care of his wife." The few who in the
early days did marry and continue in the traveling
ministry met every form of discouragement, and
very little inclination on the part of the people to
pay for the support of his wife. William Burke
states that he was the first married preacher in the
Western Conference who continued to travel and he
states: "I shared equally with the single men when
they were on the circuit with me, in order to keep
the peace. . . . The presiding elder thought I
had better locate, for he said, 'The people would
not support a married man.' "[3]

The large circuits required constant activity and
movement on the part of the preachers, which
tended to develop a zealous, energetic ministry. The
time limit, imposed by the General Conference of
1804, made it impossible for a man to settle down
comfortably in one place; and if results were to be
obtained on a given circuit, it had to be done
quickly. This kept the preachers constantly on the
alert. Another factor, contributing to the success

full connection in the Methodist Episcopal Church to the year 1814,
with dates when received, date when located, died, withdrawn, or
expelled. Of the 1,616 preachers received during these thirty years
821 had located, most of them within a few years after their admission;
131 had died; 34 had been expelled and 25 had withdrawn.

[3] "As late as 1809, out of eighty-four preachers in Virginia Conference but three had wives" (*Central Methodist*, November 2, 1889,
p. 6).

of the circuit system, was the fact that a young preacher was not under the compulsion of preparing many new sermons, since on large circuits he constantly preached at different localities and, therefore, could use the same sermon again and again. This made for the development of effective oratorical preaching, the type particularly well adapted to the frontier.

Most of the preachers who followed the moving population westward were men of little education; but to say that they were ignorant men is far from the truth. They were uneducated in the same sense that Abraham Lincoln was uneducated; but, like Lincoln, they became educated men in the truest sense of the word. Both Wesley and Asbury set the Methodist preachers an example of reading as they traveled. Bishop Asbury always had his saddlebags filled with books, and the list of books which he found time to read as he went from place to place is a long one, and contains not only books on religious subjects but literature, biography, history, and even medicine. The average circuit preacher was a man of few books, but he thoroughly absorbed those few. The books with which he was most familiar were the Bible, the *Discipline,* Wesley's *Sermons,* and Fletcher's *Appeal.*

The local preacher was a factor of immense importance to the development of frontier Methodism. Frequently among the early settlers of a new region were to be found local preachers, and as soon as their cabins were built and a few acres cleared for a crop the next year, the local preacher invited his neighbors to his cabin for religious service. In many localities the first Methodist classes were formed by the local ministry, and when the regular circuit preacher came on the scene, he found Methodism already planted. In both Kentucky and Ohio the first classes were formed in this way, and in hundreds of communities across the land this story was repeated. When James Haw was sent as the first missionary to Kentucky in 1786, he found Francis Clark, a local preacher from Virginia, already on the ground, and a Methodist class under way. So, likewise, when John Kobler was sent as the first regular Methodist itinerant to the region north of the Ohio, he found classes formed by Francis McCormick, who had come to the same region three years before.

The Methodist Episcopal Church also had the most effective local organization from the standpoint of frontier needs. Besides the local preachers there were class leaders and exhorters. The first unit to be formed was a class, made up of a few "believers" in a given community, and over them was appointed a class leader, generally selected for his qualities of leadership. Each class leader should "carefully inquire how every soul in his class prospers; not only how each person observes the outward rules, but how he grows in the knowledge and love of God." The circuit preacher met the classes on his rounds, and at least once a quarter the leader was examined as to the care and faithfulness with which he looked after the religious life of the members. Thus was developed a system of supervision of every individual member admitted into church membership.

We have already noticed how a new official, the presiding elder, had developed (1792) soon after the formation of the Methodist Episcopal Church. The great extent of the country and the rapid expansion of the church had made such an official necessary. New preachers had to be added constantly to take charge of the growing work, and these needed the supervision of an older and more experienced man. His duties were to travel through his appointed district and in the absence of the bishop to supervise all elders, deacons, traveling and local preachers and exhorters. In other words, in the absence of the bishop he was to be in control of the affairs of his district, which was made up of a group of circuits.

The rapid expansion of early Methodism was likewise greatly aided by the type of theology which it preached. The great emphasis in the preaching of the circuit riders was upon individual responsibility, and the equality of all men in the sight of God. God had made provision for the salvation of all men, and it was man's responsibility simply to accept this provision so amply made. There was equal opportunity for all; no favored class whose salvation had been determined from the beginning of the world. In other words it was a democratic gospel. The men who preached this gospel were men of the people, plain and simple in their tastes, who were willing to accept whatever hospitality the humblest settler's cabin afforded. Even the bishops were humble men, who likewise traveled among the people, stayed in the crowded cabins and made their appearance at countless camp meetings and other frontier gatherings. It is very doubtful whether the highly centralized, autocratic system of church government which the Methodist Epis-

copal Church possessed, could have been successfully administered if the early bishops had not
moved about constantly among the people. As has
been well said, Methodism had an autocratic form
of church government and preached a democratic
gospel, while the Presbyterians had a democratic
form of church government and preached an autocratic gospel.

Methodism had another advantage over the other
churches working on the frontier, in that The Methodist Book Concern, established in 1789, furnished
suitable religious literature for its constituency.[4]
John Wesley was a prolific writer and editor, and to
him the press was a close ally of the pulpit, and in
this respect the American Methodists followed
closely in his footsteps. All Methodist traveling
preachers were book agents for the Book Concern.
In the year 1800 the General Conference passed the
ruling that "It shall be the duty of every presiding
elder, where no book steward is appointed, to see
that his district be fully supplied with books." The
presiding elder was to see that books were ordered
and then was to account to the superintendent for
them. It is further stated that "It shall be the duty
of every preacher who has charge of a circuit to see
that his circuit is duly supplied with books," while
he, in turn, is to account to the presiding elder for
all books sent to him for sale. And so the Methodist
preachers resolutely carried books to the people,
and frequently crowded them upon the settler,
while the settler paid for them often a few cents at
a time. These books were read in the household,

---

[4]Archibald, F. A., *Methodism and Literature*, New York, 1883. Has
considerable bibliographical material on American Methodism.

and were then loaned to the neighbors until they made the circuit of the settlement.

Still another influential factor in giving Methodism a larger frontier influence was its emphasis upon singing. Often religion sang its way into the hearts of the people, just as it had done in England. Methodists sang their hymns in their homes, about their work, at their family altars, as well as in their more formal religious meetings. The *Discipline* (1805) advised that "In every large society let them learn to sing, and let them always learn our tunes first." In the Christmas Conference to the question, "How shall we reform our singing?" the answer was, "Let all our preachers who have any knowledge in the notes improve by learning to sing true themselves, and keeping close to Mr. Wesley's tunes and hymns." The Methodist Episcopal Church began with a great musical tradition and possessed a hymnal from its organization, which Wesley had prepared. The hymns were so arranged as to make the hymn book a practical manual for the teaching of Christian truth, and the hymns were, of course, heavily freighted with Methodist theology. Frequently no one in the congregation possessed a hymn book except the preacher, who gave out the verses, two lines at a time, but many of the hymns became so well known to the people that they were able to sing them without the process of lining out.

On the frontier, and especially at camp meetings, there came to be a considerable number of crude religious songs which seem to have been improvised, some of which no doubt never got into print. At the beginning of the camp meetings the regular hymns would be sung; but as the meeting warmed up "spiritual songs," as they were called, many times improvised by some preacher present, were used. A typical example of a "spiritual song" is the following, "Shout Old Satan's Kingdom Down," which contains eighteen verses:

1. This day my soul has caught on fire, *Hallelujah,*
   I feel that Heaven is coming nigher,
   O glory Hallelujah!

   CHORUS

   Shout, shout we're gaining ground, Hallelujah!
   We'll shout old Satan's kingdom down, Hallelujah!

2. I long to quit this cumbrous clay, *Hallelujah!*
   And shout with saints in endless day,
   O glory Hallelujah!

3. When Christians pray, the Devil runs, *Hallelujah!*
   And leaves the field to Zion's sons,
   O glory Hallelujah!

4. One single saint can put to flight, *Hallelujah!*
   Ten thousand blust'ring sons of night,
   O glory Hallelujah!

5. Ye Little Sampsons, up and try, *Hallelujah!*
   To chase the Philistines 'till you die,
   O glory Hallelujah!

6. The troops of Hell are mustering round, *Hallelujah!*
   But Zion still is gaining ground,
   O glory Hallelujah!

7. The hottest fire is now begun, *Hallelujah!*
   Come stand the fire 'till it is won,
   O glory Hallelujah![5]

Methodist singing thus became an important factor in spreading the Methodist gospel on the frontier.

---

[5] *A General Selection of the Newest and most Admired Hymns and Spiritual Songs Now in Use,* by Steth Mead, preacher of the Gospel M. E. C. Note. . . . The profits of this Edition to be applied in diminishing the debt on the Lynchburg Meeting-House. Richmond: Printed by Seaton Grantland, opposite the Bell Tavern, 1807.

Such was the equipment with which Methodism now faced the problems presented by the great mass of moving people as they pushed westward over the Alleghenies.

Between the years 1790 and 1820 ten new states west of the Allegheny Mountains had been added to the Union, while at the latter date among the whole number of states in the Union, Ohio ranked fifth in population, and Kentucky sixth. So vast had been the movement of people westward during these thirty years that the older states were alarmed at their loss of population. From the beginning of the War of 1812 to 1820 occurred the greatest movement of population ever witnessed in America. The roads westward swarmed with wagons, cattle, sheep, and horses. Even throughout the winter months sleighs, loaded with women, children, and household goods, were to be seen on their way to Ohio and the West. New towns sprang up as if by magic along the rivers, and the southern shore of Lake Erie in the Connecticut Reserve. "All America," said a European observer in 1817, "seems to be breaking up and moving westward."

To a surprising degree the formation of new circuits kept pace with the establishment of new settlements. Thus in 1782 a circuit preacher was sent to the Yadkin Circuit in western North Carolina, and the next year the Holston Circuit appeared in what is now eastern Tennessee, while in 1784 a preacher was sent for the first time to the Redstone country in the southwest corner of Pennsylvania. Two years later (1786) the Kentucky Circuit appeared, and by 1789 there were four circuits in Tennessee, three in Kentucky, and three on the upper

Ohio. After the close of the Indian Wars and the signing of the Treaty of Greenville in 1795, the region north of the Ohio began to settle rapidly, and the first circuit in the state of Ohio was formed in 1798 by John Kobler, who had been appointed presiding elder of the Kentucky District. The same year Tobias Gibson was sent to the Southwest. Starting from the Cumberland settlements in Central Tennessee, he traveled on horseback some four to five hundred miles southward; then trading his horse for a canoe, he paddled down the Mississippi to the new settlements, which were springing up in that region. It was not until 1802 that he returned and reported to the Western Conference of that year.

The *Minutes* for 1800 show more than seven hundred members in Tennessee; more than seventeen hundred in Kentucky; two hundred and fifty-seven in the Northwest Territory, and sixty in the extreme southwest. By this time Bishop Asbury had made a number of trips across the mountains, and between 1788 and 1800 at least eighteen Conferences had been held in the trans-Allegheny region. In 1790 Asbury crossed the mountains into Tennessee, and speaks of swimming his horse across the Watauga, and of the dangers from the Indians. He found the "poor preachers indifferently clad with emaciated bodies." Later in the same year he crossed from Virginia to Kentucky, this time with a company of sixteen men and thirteen guns. At one place he speaks of seeing the graves of the slain, twenty-four in one camp. In 1793 Asbury visited Tennessee and Kentucky in the month of April. He finds "low times for religion on Holstein and

Watauga Rivers." But he meets some kind Presbyterians, and he remarks: "I must give the Presbyterians preference for respect to ministers." Passing into Kentucky he travels one hundred miles in two days, and when he finally reaches his destination, he is grateful for supper and bed, "having not slept in one for three nights."

Of outstanding importance from the standpoint of the progress of religion in the West, and of Methodism in particular, was the great Western or Kentucky revival, which swept like a flood over the entire Western country from about 1797 to 1805. During these same years a spirit of revival was manifest in the Eastern states, which quietly spread from place to place, influencing all the Protestant churches, while religious awakenings were experienced in all the colleges, particularly at Yale, Dartmouth, Williams, and Amherst. The Western phase of the revival was especially notable for the excitement which everywhere attended it, and for the appearance of such strange manifestations as were never before seen in America.

It may surprise many informed people to know that this great Western revival was in its inception a Presbyterian movement, and had its beginnings under the preaching of James McGready, a Presbyterian minister. McGready came to southern Kentucky from North Carolina in 1796, where he became the minister over three little Presbyterian churches in Logan County. Here, under his zealous and persuasive preachings, the great Western revival began, which came to be known as the Logan County, or Cumberland revival. In the year 1800 the Cumberland revival reached its culmination, when in June of that year a great meeting was held on Red River, attended by thousands of people. Great excitement attended this meeting, which was encouraged by a Methodist preacher, John McGee, who, overcome by his feeling, "shouted and exhorted with all possible energy."

People of all denominations came to these great outdoor meetings, some journeying great distances. They came, prepared to spend several days on the ground, bringing their provisions and their families with them, which is undoubtedly the origin of the camp meeting. The movement from its beginning was interdenominational in scope. Presbyterians, Methodists, and Baptists especially united their efforts. The outdoor sacramental meetings were the occasions for vast gatherings in the woods. Presbyterians and Methodists commonly united in these sacramental meetings; the Baptists, because of their advocacy of close communion, refused to join, but commonly joined in the preaching and exhortation.

During the summer of 1801 the revival spread to northern Kentucky, centering at Cane Ridge in Bourbon County. Here the Presbyterian minister was Barton W. Stone. He had visited McGready's meetings in Logan County and had become thoroughly convinced of the genuineness of the work there going on. Immediately a revival began under his preaching, and at a great sacramental meeting in August at Cane Ridge the most spectacular single phase of the whole revival movement occurred. A vast assembly, variously estimated at from ten thousand to twenty-five thousand, were present, and hundreds of people professed conversion. There are numerous contemporary accounts of this great meeting. Peter Cartwright, who began his ministry three years later, thus describes the Cane Ridge meeting:

Somewhere between 1800 and 1801, in the upper part of Kentucky, at a memorable place called "Cane Ridge," there was appointed a sacramental meeting by some of the Presbyterian ministers, at which meeting, seemingly unexpected by ministers or people, the mighty power of God was displayed in a very extraordinary manner; many were moved to tears, and bitter and loud crying for mercy. The meeting was protracted for weeks. Ministers of all denominations flocked in from far and near. The meeting was kept up day and night. Thousands heard of the mighty work, and came on foot, on horseback, in carriages, and wagons. It was supposed that there were in attendance at times during the meeting from twelve to twenty-five thousand people. Hundreds fell prostrate under the mighty power of God, as men slain in battle. Stands were erected in the woods, from which preachers of different churches proclaimed repentance toward God and faith in our Lord Jesus Christ, and it was supposed, by eye and ear witnesses, that between one and two thousand souls were happily and powerfully converted to God during the meeting. It was not unusual for one, two, three and four to seven preachers to be addressing the listening thousands at the same time from the different stands erected for the purpose. The heavenly fire spread in almost every direction. It was said by truthful witnesses that at times more than one thousand persons broke out into loud shouting all at once, and that the shouts could be heard for miles around.[6]

Another contemporary thus describes some of the scenes at Cane Ridge, which he witnessed:

I attended with 18 Presbyterian ministers; and Baptist

[6] *Autobiography of Peter Cartwright, the Backwoods Preacher.* Edited by W. P. Strickland, pp. 30-31. New York and Cincinnati: The Methodist Book Concern, 1856. Cartwright states that from the Cane Ridge meeting the camp meeting arose. As has been pointed out, the same thing had taken place in Logan County the previous year.

and Methodist preachers, I do not know how many; all being either preaching or exhorting the distressed with more harmony than could be expected. The governor of our state was with us and encouraging the work. The number of people computed from 10,000 to 21,000 and the communicants 828. The whole people were serious, all the conversation was of a religious nature, or calling in question the divinity of the work. Great numbers were on the ground from Friday until the Thursday following, night and day without intermission, engaged in some religious act of worship. They are commonly collected in small circles of 10 or 12, close adjoining another circle and all engaged in singing Watt's and Hart's hymns; and then a minister steps upon a stump or log, and begins an exhortation or sermon, when, as many as can hear collect around him. On Sunday I saw above 100 candles burning at once and I saw 100 persons at once on the ground crying for mercy, of all ages from 8 to 60 years. . . . When a person is struck down, he is carried by others out of the congregation, when some minister converses with and prays for him; afterwards a few gather around and sing a hymn suitable to the case. The whole number brought to the ground, under convictions, were about 1,000, not less. The sensible, the weak, etc., learned and unlearned, the rich and poor, are the subjects of it.

The revival in many instances was accompanied by certain peculiar bodily exercises, such as jerking, rolling, barking, dancing, and falling. The falling exercise was the most common, and frequently at these great meetings scores, and even hundreds, were on the ground, many lying for a considerable length of time either entirely unconscious or semi-conscious. The "jerks" were also common, though affecting different persons in different ways. Sometimes the head would be affected, twisting it rapidly to the right and left; sometimes it would seize the limbs, sometimes the whole body. Cartwright tells us that "No matter whether they were saints or sinners, they would be taken under a warm song or sermon, and seized with a convulsive jerking all over, which they could not by any possibility avoid, and the more they resisted the more they jerked."

It is quite the general conception that the early preachers, and especially the Methodist, desired to work the people up to a state of religious frenzy at every meeting, and that they took special delight in just such extravagances, which we have described, but this is an entire misconception. It is true that the preachers did not object to hearty shouts during the preaching, or in the testimony meetings, but wild extravagances they deplored and did their best to repress. Asbury, like Wesley, believed that everything should be done decently and in order. Indeed, order was his passion and this he communicated to his preachers. Of one presiding elder on the frontier it is said: "He would not suffer anything which was manifestly enthusiastic or extravagant in religious assemblies to pass without rebuke," while Cartwright states: "The Methodist preachers generally preached against this extravagant wildness. . . . I did it uniformly in my ministrations, and sometimes gave great offense."[7]

From the time of the great Western revival onward, for at least three generations, the camp meeting became an increasingly important factor in spreading Methodism throughout the land. Within a few years practically every presiding elder's district held such gatherings, usually in the fall of the year. Although originating among the Western

[7] Sweet, William Warren, *Rise of Methodism in the West*, pp. 60-62. New York: The Methodist Book Concern, 1920.

Presbyterians, the camp meeting soon fell under the condemnation of the strict Calvinists among them, and it was left for the Methodists and Cumberland Presbyterians to utilize it to the full. By 1812 at least four hundred Methodist camp meetings, large and small, were held annually in the United States. The Long-Calm Camp Meeting in Maryland, held from the 8th to the 14th of October, 1806, reported five hundred and eighty converts; in August, 1813, Asbury reports three thousand people on a camp-ground in Pennsylvania, among them "some drunkards" who were so "deeply laden" that they could do little mischief. In 1809 seventeen camp meetings were held on the Indiana district of the Western Conference; Muskingum district held four the same year; Miami district, seventeen; Scioto circuit, four; Hockhocking circuit, two; Deer Creek, two; Mad River, three; Whitewater, two; Cincinnati, two, and White, two. Asbury, recording these camp meetings, states:[8] "I hear and see the great effects produced by them, and this year there will be more than ever."

[8] Asbury's *Journal*, Vol. III, pp. 210, 240, 271, 286, 292, 294, 321, 420, 441.

From *The Illustrated History of Methodism*, Lee and Luccock

THE HOME OF GENERAL WILLIAM RUSSELL IN SALTVILLE, VIRGINIA

Where the first Holston Conference met

CHAPTER IX

THE CIRCUIT RIDER KEEPS PACE WITH THE WESTWARD MARCH

THE General Conference of 1796 made provision for the division of the territory of the United States into six Annual Conferences. The region west of the Allegheny Mountains formed the Western Conference, whose boundaries in 1804 included "the states of Tennessee, Kentucky, and Ohio, and that part of Virginia which lies west of the great river Kanawha, with the Illinois and the Natchez." The *General Minutes* continued to designate the Western circuits as the Kentucky District, however, until 1800, but from that date until 1812 the name "Western Conference" was applied to the vast region of trans-Appalachia.

The first meeting of the Western Conference in the new century met at Bethel Academy, Kentucky, on October 6, 1800, with Bishop Asbury presiding. Bishop Whatcoat was also present. Plans for the establishment of Bethel Academy, the first Methodist seat of learning west of the mountains, had been made ten years before, when a subscription of three hundred dollars had been obtained. The Kentucky Legislature thought well enough of the enterprise to grant it six thousand acres of land, but the poverty of the new frontier made it impossible for the institution to continue long. Asbury's comments concerning the Academy at this session of the Western Conference are interesting:

Here is Bethel-Cokesbury in miniature—eighty by thirty feet, three stories, with a high roof, and finished below. Now we want a fund and an income of three hundred per year to carry it on; without which it will be useless. But it is too distant from public places; its being surrounded by the river Kentucky in part, we now find to be no benefit: thus all our excellencies are turned into defeats.

In passing through Virginia on the way to the Western Conference the two bishops were joined by William McKendree, who for twelve years had traveled circuits in the East, but was now destined to become the major general of the Methodist forces in the West.

For several years past Francis Poythress had presided over the Western circuits, but exposure and excessive work had undermined his health, compelling his location. No better choice could have been made for his successor than William McKendree, who for eight successive years continued to preside over the frontier districts. There was but one district in the Western Conference until 1802, but in this year three were formed, the Holston in eastern Tennessee; the Kentucky, containing circuits in central Kentucky and southern Ohio, and the Cumberland, which covered the region in central Tennessee and southward along the Mississippi River.

As population pushed across the Ohio into southern Indiana and Illinois, the circuit preachers followed, and soon circuits were formed in these new settlements. The first circuit in Indiana was the Whitewater, which was located along the banks of

that stream in southeastern Indiana. Joseph Oglesby was sent by John Sale, presiding elder on the
Ohio district, to the Whitewater valley in 1806.
Oglesby has left us a description of the formation
of this new circuit. After opening several preaching places in southwestern Ohio, Oglesby struck
General Wayne's old road from Hamilton to Fort
Wayne, which he said "seemed still fresh and plain."
Branching off from this road he came to an Indian
trail, which led him into Indiana, and finally to one
of the settlements on the Whitewater River. He
followed the Whitewater to its mouth, establishing
preaching places in the cabins of the settlers along
the way. Arriving at the Ohio, he started up the
Miami, preaching on both sides of that stream
until he arrived at the place of beginning. In 1808
a second Indiana circuit, the Silver Creek, was organized, in what was known as Clark's Grant, and
by 1811 there were five circuits in what is now the
state of Indiana.[1]

In 1803 Benjamin Young was sent as circuit
preacher to Illinois. It may have been that Young
was sent on this far-away mission as a matter of discipline, for he is charged in the *Minutes* this year
"of having said that he composed a certain song,
when in truth he did not; that he had the misfor-
tain to get his horses thye broke, when it was not
so; and that he has baptized contrary to the order
of the M. E. Church." After "a plain talk, and
hopeful promises," Young was admitted to the Conference, and elected a deacon, and since he was ap-

---

[1] "Introduction and Progress of Methodism in Southeast Indiana,"
by Allen Wiley, a series of thirty-seven articles in the *Western Christian Advocate*, 1845-1846. See article for August 15, 1845.

pointed "a Mitionary to the Illinoies, he was ordained to the office of Elder." Young went to the settlements along the Mississippi, centering his work at Kaskaskia. Here he found two classes already formed by local preachers. In 1806 the Illinois Circuit reported 110 members, and in 1811 an Illinois District was formed with five circuits, on both sides of the Mississippi.

The father of Methodism in the territory south of the state of Tennessee, which was then known as Mississippi Territory, was Tobias Gibson, whose first journey (1798) into the lower Mississippi region has been noted. Gibson rode through all the settlements to the Florida line and died in 1804 in his twenty-eighth year.[2] Soon after the purchase of Louisiana, Bishop Asbury called for volunteers to carry the gospel into the new territory, and Elisha W. Bowman offered to go. Bowman rode on horseback from Kentucky to New Orleans, which, he states, he found as dirty as a pigsty and in almost as bad condition morally. The governor promised him the city hall as a preaching place, but when he attempted to avail himself of the promise, he found it locked against him. The few Americans in the region represented the dregs of society and knew "very little more about the nature of salvation than the untaught Indians," and he states "that some of them, after I had preached, asked me what I meant by the fall of man, and when it was that he fell."[3] By 1811 the Mississippi District, which had been

[2] Jones, John G., *Methodism in Mississippi*, Vol. I, pp. 23-113. Nashville, 1908.

[3] For a description of Bowman's experience in southern Louisiana, see his letter to William Burke, dated January 29, 1806, printed in Jones, *Methodism in Mississippi*, Vol. I, pp. 148-152.

formed in 1805, included nine circuits, and nearly eight hundred members.

While new circuits and districts were being formed on the edges of settlements, settlers in increasing numbers were moving into Kentucky, Tennessee, and Ohio, and church membership was increasing accordingly. In 1812 the two oldest Western states, Kentucky and Tennessee, contained a total Methodist membership of nearly 19,000, while Ohio had two districts, the Miami and the Muskingum, and a membership of more than ten thousand. The whole Western country was now covered with a network of circuits and districts, and the total membership west of the Allegheny Mountains was 30,741, and of this number 1,648 were colored. In 1800 Bishop Asbury had sent out fourteen preachers to take the gospel to the frontiersmen, scattered here and there along the creeks and rivers of the new West; in 1811 Bishop McKendree stationed just one hundred preachers at the last session of the Western Conference.

At the General Conference of 1808 William McKendree was chosen a bishop, Bishop Whatcoat having died two years previously. McKendree had now spent eight years in the West, and was probably little known among the Eastern brethren. On the first Sunday of the General Conference McKendree was appointed to preach in the Light Street Church in the city of Baltimore. A large congregation was present, among them many members of the General Conference. McKendree was clothed in coarse and homely garments; he appeared awkward and his manners were rustic. Nor did the first part of his sermon strike fire. But by the time the discourse was half finished his manner changed, and the "lion of the West" made the walls of the old Light Street Church, as he had often made the forests of Kentucky, ring with his powerful voice, while his eloquence overwhelmed the whole congregation. "Multitudes fell helpless from their seats as if shot with a rifle," and an "electric influence thrilled through every heart." The sermon closed and a "sweet and holy influence, like the mellow light of Indian summer . . . seemed to invest the assembly." The ministers said, "This is the man for a bishop." Accordingly, a few days later he was elected, the first native American to hold the office of bishop in the Methodist Episcopal Church. The choice was a most fortunate one, for there was not another man in the church better fitted to carry on the work of Asbury than this rugged pioneer, who had learned the ways of the wilderness in the school of experience.

The secretary of the Western Conference, from 1800 to 1811, was William Burke. He was one of the sturdy characters of the Conference, and though not an educated man, was evidently a clear-headed and capable secretary. The *Minutes,* which he kept during these years, are still extant. His penmanship is excellent, though his spelling followed no rule, nor had he any standard for capitalization or punctuation. Some years he was lavish with his commas and semicolons, while other years the *Minutes* lack punctuation almost entirely. Burke was one of the few married preachers in the West, and in 1813, worn out by his arduous labors in the ministry, he wrote a letter to the Ohio Conference asking for supernumerary relations. He had obtained

166

the appointment as postmaster of Cincinnati, evidently thinking that in a year or so his health would be sufficiently restored to resume his traveling connection.   Later, however, charges were brought against him for treating the elder with contempt, and he was suspended, and in 1820 was expelled from the church.   He was not restored to the church until near the end of his life.[4]

In the year 1804 two young preachers, later to become famous throughout the Western country, were admitted to the Western Conference on trial—Peter Cartwright and James Axley.   The entry in the *Minutes* admitting Cartwright reads: "Peter Cartwright, a native of Virginia, born September 1, 1785, has provesed religion about 4 years, has travilled a Circuit 9 months, was well received, and comes recommended from the Quarterly Meeting Conference of Wayne Circuit." The entry for Axley states that he "has been converted about two years, has travilled some months, was received as a man of undoubted piety, but small gifts."   These entries are typical descriptions of young preachers coming before the Conference for admission.   All came recommended from a Quarterly Meeting conference, and all had to show some evidence of usefulness.   Thus were the preachers obtained for carrying forward the work on the ever-expanding frontiers.

Such inexperienced young men were seldom sent to a circuit alone, but generally as junior preachers

---

[4] For the Autobiography of William Burke, see Finley, J. B., *Sketches of Western Methodism*, pp. 22-92.   Cincinnati: 1855.   Also Sweet, William Warren, *Circuit-Rider Days Along the Ohio*, pp. 53-54.   New York: The Methodist Book Concern, 1923.

under an older and more experienced man. Thus in this year Cartwright was assigned to the Salt River and Shelby Circuit in Kentucky with Benjamin Lakin, one of the ablest preachers in the Conference, as senior preacher, while James Axley is assigned to the Red River Circuit with Miles Harper. The senior preacher thus acted as both adviser and instructor to the younger preacher. At the General Conference of 1816 a course of study for candidates for the ministry was prescribed. The presiding elders were to supervise the young preachers in their studies and before their reception into full membership into the Conference the candidates were to give "satisfactory evidence respecting their knowledge of these particular subjects." Such was the meager formal training received by the early Methodist preachers.

At the General Conference of 1812 three new Conferences were formed—the Ohio, the Tennessee, and the Genesee. The Western Conference was divided into the Ohio and Tennessee Conferences, while the Genesee Conference covered western New York and Pennsylvania, northern Ohio, with upper and lower Canada. The Ohio Conference embraced the whole of the state of Ohio, southeastern Indiana, and eastern Kentucky, while the Tennessee Conference covered western Kentucky, the circuits southward along the Mississippi, with western Indiana, and the whole of Illinois. In 1800 the New York Conference had been formed, which in 1812 included all the state of New York which was not included in the Genesee and Philadelphia Conferences, together with that part of Connecticut and Massachusetts west of the Connecticut River, and that part of Vermont west of the Green Mountains. Four years later (1816) the continued westward flow of populations, together with the success achieved by the circuit preachers, made necessary the forming of two new Conferences, and the revising of Conference boundaries. The two new Conferences were the Missouri and the Mississippi. The Mississippi included all the state of Louisiana south of the Arkansas, and all the Mississippi Territory south of the Tennessee. The Missouri boundaries are described as the Ohio Conference on the north, the Ohio and Mississippi Rivers on the east, and the Arkansas River on the south. In 1820 the Kentucky Conference was formed, making twelve Conferences in all; in 1824 there were seventeen Conferences, the new ones being Maine, Canada, Pittsburgh, Holston, and the Illinois. There were no new Conferences created at the General Conference of 1828, but in 1832 there was expansion in every direction, the new Conferences being New Hampshire, Troy, Oneida to the northeast, the Indiana in the central West, and the Alabama and Georgia Conferences in the South. By 1840 there had come to be thirty-four Conferences, including the Liberia Mission Conference. Four years later, when the great slavery controversy divided the church, there were thirty-nine Conferences in the United States, and the Liberia Mission Conference, with a total membership of 985,698 whites; 145,409 colored, and 4,129 Indians.

As Methodism extended into the expanding frontiers in every direction the preachers were soon brought face to face with the distressing moral conditions common to new and rude communities.

Lawlessness, rowdyism, Sabbath-breaking, gambling, swearing, drinking, and fighting were common. Even some who had in the older sections of the country been members of the church, when they came to the backwoods threw off all restraint. People from the East, traveling in the West, were often "terrified at the drunkenness, the vice, the gambling, the brutal fights, the gouging, the needless duels they beheld on every hand." In the rough society of the frontier the amounts of liquor consumed were incredible. Everyone, with practically no exception, seemed to have indulged, including the women, and even the preachers. Those who objected to liquor as a common beverage often took it as a tonic, or as a preventive of the diseases common to the frontier, such as ague and fever, and large quantities were consumed avowedly for these purposes. Cartwright tells us that if a man would not have liquor in his family, his harvest, his house-raisings, log-rollings, and weddings, he would be "considered parsimonious and unsociable," and even professing Christians would not help a man at his log-rollings and in his harvest if he did not furnish liquor and treat the company. Whisky was considered one of the necessities, and in almost every frontier store there "was a whisky pail and cup, and all comers were at liberty to help themselves."

Some of the early Methodist preachers were themselves users of liquor. Among the recommendations to the preachers, made by the Christmas Conference, was: "After preaching, take a little lemonade, mild ale, or candied orange-peel. All spirituous liquors, at that time especially, are deadly poison." As early as 1743 Wesley had required all members of his societies to abstain from drinking, buying or selling spirituous liquors. Wesley's general rule forbidding "drunkenness, buying and selling spirituous liquors, or drinking them, unless in cases of necessity," was adopted by the Christmas Conference, but Cartwright tells us that the rule long remained a dead letter. In 1796 the following regulation was adopted: "If any member of our society retail or give spirituous liquors, and anything disorderly be transacted under his roof on this account, the preacher, who has the oversight of the circuit, shall proceed against him, as in the case of other immoralities, and the person accused shall be cleared, censured, suspended or excluded, according to his conduct, as on other charges of immorality." This rule, by implication, permitted Methodist members to sell liquor as long as nothing disorderly took place under their roof. This relaxation of the earlier rules against liquor evidently soon resulted in their increased use, among both local preachers and members. James Axley was the outstanding temperance leader in the church, and in the General Conference of 1812 and 1816 introduced resolutions providing that "No stationed or local preacher shall retail spirituous or malt liquors without forfeiting his ministerial standing." This motion was defeated in 1812, but was passed in 1816.

The manner in which these resolutions were carried out in the circuits depended upon the individual circuit preacher. Some of them, as James Axley, Peter Cartwright, and James B. Finley, were bitterly hostile to the use of liquor and took heroic measures to rid the church of the evil practice. Finley says that "I suffered no opportunity to pass that I did not improve in portraying the physical, social, and moral evils resulting from intemperance. . . . Frequently I pledged whole congregations, standing upon their feet, to the temperance cause." On one occasion Joseph Tarkington, a member of the Indiana Conference, was conducting a "speaking meeting" when a "well-to-do Methodist farmer and distiller arose to speak. He began by saying, 'I have been governed by two spirits; one is the good spirit, that prompts me to be good and do good. The other is——!' Here Tarkington called out 'Whisky!' at the top of his voice. 'No,' said the distiller, who was at the time under the influence of his own homemade goods, as he often was, 'nobody ever saw me drunk.' 'Some people never get drunk,' was Tarkington's reply, and the half-drunken Methodist took his seat." This rude treatment, we are told, was effective, for within a few months the distiller abandoned his trade and became a total abstainer. At one time James Axley was located in eastern Tennessee, a country noted for its production of peach brandy and for the free use of it. In opposition to this practice, he preached a famous temperance sermon, based on the text: "Alexander, the coppersmith, did me much evil; the Lord reward him according to his works," which was remembered in all that region for a generation.[5]

The General Conference of 1812 met in the city of New York, the first delegated General Conference as well as the first to convene outside the city of Baltimore. At this Conference a resolution was

---

[5] Finley, J. B., *Sketches of Western Methodism*, Chap. XVI, "James Axley," pp. 231-246.

introduced by John Sale, prohibiting both preachers and members from buying or holding lottery tickets, or having anything to do with them. Strange as it seems to us, the motion did not carry, for lotteries were still considered by many good people as legitimate means of raising money for churches, schools, and colleges. The most important question before this Conference was that of electing presiding elders by the Annual Conferences, a question that was to continue to agitate the church for years to come.

Soon after the adjournment of this General Conference, the War of 1812 began. Since the war was fought very largely upon the Canadian frontier, it was the Western section of the church which was most largely affected by it. The preachers of the Ohio Conference were urged to preach to the soldiers, wherever opportunity offered. At Uniontown, Pennsylvania, Bishop Asbury preached to a company of soldiers, who came to the camp meeting to hear him. One who heard the sermon pronounced it as admirable. He began by deploring the evils of war and stated that if Christian nations went to war at all, it ought to be on the defensive. Within a few months the frontier preachers began to feel the effects of war prices, with flour in Ohio at sixteen dollars per barrel, and other provisions in proportion. Preachers often had to pay fifty cents a peck for oats to feed their weary horses, while four dollars was the price of horse-shoeing. The prevalence of the war spirit among the people was found to be harmful to the work of the church. Finley complains: "This year [1812-1813] the war spirit unfortunately entered into many professors of religion, and as soon as they caught it they began to lose their religion. . . . Several who had been saved from drunkenness by the church returned to their evil habits." The decrease in membership in the year 1812-13, Cartwright states, was due to the war, and he says: "We felt the sad effects of war throughout the West."

A little more than a month previous to the convening of the next General Conference (1816), Bishop Asbury died at the house of Mr. Arnold, in Spottsylvania, Virginia. He preached his last sermon at Richmond on March 24, and his death occurred five days later. Thus passed the father of American Methodism, who during his American ministry had "preached sixteen thousand five hundred sermons, ordained more than four thousand preachers, traveled on horseback or in carriages two hundred and seventy thousand miles."

One of the first things to occupy the attention of the General Conference of 1816 was the funeral of Bishop Asbury, which was said to have been one of the largest ever held in the city of Baltimore. There was now but one bishop remaining, McKendree, and it was determined that two additional bishops should be chosen. When the ballot was taken, it was found that Enoch George and Robert R. Roberts were elected. Bishop George was a native of Virginia and became a traveling preacher in 1789. For several years before his election he had occupied important positions in the church and was a man of dignity, humility, and sound judgment. Roberts was a native of Maryland, and at the time of his election was thirty-eight years of age, and was the first married bishop of the church. He was a large man, of great dignity, and was noted for his effective preaching and great executive gifts. From 1819 to his death in 1843 Bishop Roberts lived on a farm in Lawrence County, Indiana, and was the first bishop to have his permanent residence in the West. At this Conference Joshua Soule, later to become a bishop of the church, and the senior bishop of the Methodist Episcopal Church, South, was elected editor and general book steward.

On Bishop Asbury's death it was learned that he had willed his horse, some books and clothes to Bishop McKendree, and Jacob Young, of the Ohio Conference, was commissioned by Bishop McKendree to take the articles from Baltimore to Wheeling, as Young returned to Ohio from the General Conference. Young has left us this description of an interesting incident of that journey:

The books and clothes were packed in two valises, buckled together by two leather straps, and laid across his [Asbury's] old packsaddle. There was another valise buckled behind the saddle, and all were handsomely covered by a large bearskin. I rode my own horse and led the bishop's. This equipment, he states, resembled that of those who carried silver from one part of the country to another, and after he got into the mountains he was overtaken by two men, who after inquiring his destination and where he had been, suggested that he seemed to have plenty of money in his packs. To this Young replied that his packages contained Bishop Asbury's books, papers, and some clothes willed to Bishop McKendree. One of the men then asked, "Is Bishop Asbury dead?" and on receiving a reply in the affirmative he remarked, "I have seen and heard him preach in my father's house," after which the men rode off looking much disappointed.[6]

---

[6] Young, Jacob, *Autobiography of a Pioneer*, pp. 326, 327. Cincinnati: 1857. Quoted in Sweet, William Warren, *Circuit-Rider Days Along the Ohio*, p. 41.

A few months after the passing of Asbury occurred the death of Jesse Lee, who was perhaps the most popular of all the early Methodist preachers. Large of size and courtly of manner, his preaching was simple and earnest, while his own integrity and goodness of heart created confidence on the part of his hearers. He introduced Methodism into New England; he was the first historian of the Methodist Episcopal Church, and for six years (1809-1815) he was the chaplain of the House of Representatives of the United States, finally resigning that position, when some of his brethren thought it "too near an approach to secular work for a man in the office of a Methodist preacher." His last station was Annapolis, where he died in September, 1816.[7]

From the close of the War of 1812 to 1835 was a period of rapid growth throughout the church. In the nation as a whole it was an age of restlessness and change; people moving westward; new manufacturing towns springing up in New England, and the seaboard states, and everywhere there was road building and canal digging. In the realm of politics the West was becoming increasingly important, and in 1828 the new democracy arising west of the Alleghenies was to manifest its power by electing Andrew Jackson to the Presidency of the United States. During the last year (1814) of the War of 1812 there had been an actual decrease of more than three thousand members in the Methodist Episcopal Church, and in 1815 the total increase was but thirty-six; but beginning with 1816, year by

---

[7] Lee, Leroy M., *The Life and Times of the Rev. Jesse Lee.* Louisville, Kentucky: 1848. The last chapter presents a good summary of the life and work of Lee.

FIRST DWELLING BUILT IN SALEM, CAPITAL OF
OREGON, 1842

THE OREGON INSTITUTE

year the membership mounted, until in 1833 the increase alone was 51,143, and the total membership had reached the astonishing number of 599,736.

With the church expanding so rapidly, influences began to be exerted for the establishment of new church institutions to meet the new needs. As yet there was no Methodist educational institution of college grade; no missionary society; no church periodical, but the next few years, from 1816 to 1840, was to witness the rise of many such organizations and institutions within the church.

Again in 1820 the General Conference convened in the city of Baltimore, which was still the capital of American Methodism. At this Conference it was recommended to the Annual Conferences that they establish, as far as practicable and as soon as possible, literary institutions under their control—an indication that Methodist young people were beginning to go to college in increasing numbers, and that the colleges in the country were largely under Calvinistic control. A sign that the church was beginning to be churchly conscious was the adoption of the hymn book, prepared by the Book Concern, while the spirit of the rising democracy was shown in the protest against the rental of pews in churches. This year (1820) Joshua Soule was the choice of the General Conference for bishop, receiving forty-seven of the eighty-eight votes cast. Later, however, when the Conference adopted a resolution providing for the election of presiding elders, Soule resigned as a protest against the measure,[8] which he thought unconstitutional, and even when the Con-

---

[8] At least two thirds of the General Conference was in favor of reform. After the passage of the reform measure, Bishop-elect Soule

ference reconsidered its action and suspended the resolution, he refused to withdraw his resignation, and the Conference passed without electing another superintendent. This year Nathan Bangs was chosen editor and book steward, and action was also taken to provide a book agent for the West, and Martin Ruter was chosen for that position.

For the next eight years the outstanding issue before the church gathered about certain reform measures, which were being agitated by a growing number of both laymen and ministers. The final defeat of the resolution to elect presiding elders in 1820, and the growth of the contention that the bishops were the supreme interpreters of the laws of the General Conference, but were themselves not amenable to them, created resentment among the more liberal minded. Added to the large number of laymen who were agitating for representation in the Annual Conferences, were the great host of local preachers, many of whom had themselves been active ministers and had been compelled to locate because of ill health, poverty, or marriage. They naturally desired to be represented in the General Conference. The General Conference of 1820 had created the District Conference to appease the demands of the local preachers, making them members of that body, and giving that body supervision over them. The reform movement came finally to stand for three measures—the election of presiding elders and the representation of laymen and local preachers in the General Conference.

"uttered his veto," and before adjournment had the Conference at his feet (Drinkhouse, E. J., *History of Methodist Reform*, 2 Vols., Baltimore, 1899, Vol. II., pp. 14-18).

The General Conference of 1824, meeting at Baltimore, again elected Joshua Soule a bishop, and this time he accepted the office. Soule looked upon himself as the author of the constitution of the church and was the outstanding advocate of episcopal prerogative. The other bishop elected at the same Conference was Elijah Hedding, who later on took strong ground against the "Reformers."

The rise of the reform movement may be considered as a continuation of the O'Kelley agitation of twenty or more years before, and it is not strange that it should have broken out again three decades later. The latter twenties and thirties was a period of growing agitation throughout the nation for a wider suffrage, and more liberal constitutions. The rising tide of democracy compelled the adoption of new state constitutions, or the amending of the old ones, widening the suffrage in Maryland and South Carolina in 1810, Connecticut in 1818, Massachusetts in 1821, New York in 1826, and Virginia in 1830. The same set of influences which brought about these reforms in the states was at work in the church. It was the period in which the common man was coming into his own.

In 1821 a pious layman, William S. Stockton, founded a paper at Trenton, New Jersey, called the *Wesleyan Repository*, to agitate the reform ideas. Through this paper a considerable influence was exercised in the direction of a wider democracy in the church, and its publication continued for three years. In 1823 a public meeting of the Reformers was held at Cincinnati and issued a powerful circular, setting forth their views, and to the General Conference of 1824 a great number of memorials were presented, asking for reform legislation. These memorials were referred to a committee every member of which was an enemy of the measures desired, and as a result no progressive legislation was passed. The agitation, following the triumph of the conservatives at the General Conference of 1824, grew in volume year by year, and the next four years were filled with disturbing developments.

The *Wesleyan Repository* suspended publication in 1824, when a new periodical with the title, *The Mutual Rights of the Ministers and Members of the Methodist Episcopal Church,* was launched at a convention of the Reformers at Baltimore, which met while the General Conference of 1824 was in session. This convention was attended by large numbers of laymen and ministers, including seventeen members of the General Conference. The Reformers were under the necessity of publishing their own periodical since the editors of the *Methodist Magazine* had announced that they could not admit to their pages "subjects of controversy, which act to disturb the peace and harmony of the church."

The reform movement centered largely in Baltimore and vicinity. Its two most prominent leaders were Nicholas Snethen, one of the strongest ministers of the day, who had been a friend and traveling companion of Asbury, and Alexander McCaine. McCaine, though no longer in the active ministry, produced the most effective arguments in favor of reform, setting forth his views in three able pamphlets: *The History and Mystery of Episcopal Methodism* (1827); *Defense of the Truth;* and *Letters on the Organization and Early History of the Methodist Episcopal Church.* Both Snethen and

McCaine were active correspondents of the *Repository* and *Mutual Rights*. McCaine declared that the Methodist Episcopal organization did not have the sanction of Mr. Wesley, and that episcopacy had been "foisted upon the Methodist societies." Such statements naturally aroused the forces of conservatism, and soon charges were brought against some of the agitators, and there were trials, suspensions, and expulsions from the church.

The outstanding case of this sort was that of the Rev. Dennis B. Dorsey, of the Baltimore Conference, who, in 1827, was arraigned before his Conference for circulating and commending *Mutual Rights*. The trial resulted in his conviction and suspension for one year. From this decision Dorsey took an appeal to the General Conference of 1828, which sustained the action of the Baltimore Conference, and Dorsey was expelled from the church. Meanwhile eleven other preachers had been suspended for sowing dissension, and for speaking evil of ministers. The Reformers now began to form local organizations known as *Union Societies,* and in November, 1827, the several expelled ministers and members, with their sympathizers, met at Baltimore and formed an organization called the *Associate Methodist Reformers*. Later petitions were drawn up to the next General Conference, asking for admission of laymen to the General Conference, and for other reforms.

The General Conference of 1828 convened in the city of Pittsburgh, and the great issue, overshadowing all others, was the question of the appeal for restoration of the expelled ministers, and the petition for lay representation. The petition for the restoration of the expelled ministers was signed by Asa Shinn and H. B. Bascom, while Shinn presented their case in an eloquent speech. Willbur Fisk and John Emory represented the Baltimore Conference, and when the vote was taken the following morning the decision of the Baltimore Conference was upheld.[9] The Conference went on record, however, stating that its decision could not be construed as denying to minister, or member, of the Methodist Episcopal Church any liberty of speech or the press consistent with moral obligations as Christians and the associate obligations as Methodists. From this distance, however, and looking at the whole matter with as nearly an unprejudiced eye as is humanly possible, free speech and the right of free press were denied the Reformers, in that the official press of the church was closed against them, and they were thus compelled to establish their own press in order to gain a hearing. If the official church press had been opened to a fair discussion of the whole issue, this itself would have influenced the Reformers to more moderate statement, and thus expulsion of members and ministers would not have taken place, and very probably some of the reforms would have been granted.

The action of the General Conference of 1828, in rejecting all their petitions, convinced the leaders among the Reformers that all chance at conciliation was past. Many churches were split over the questions involved, and in some instances ministers and

---

[9] For a detailed account of the debate in the General Conference, and the various activities on both sides, see Drinkwater, *History of Methodist Reform*, Vol. II, Chaps. IX-XII.

members were expelled for refusing to receive the overtures of the General Conference. Soon congregations of Reformers began to form, and Conferences were organized in several of the states. In 1830, November 2, a convention was called to meet in the city of Baltimore, composed of eighty-three ministerial and lay delegates, and proceeded to form the Methodist Protestant Church. A constitution was framed, providing for lay as well as ministerial representation in their General Conferences, while the title of bishop was dropped, the chief executive officer receiving the title of president. Within four years fourteen Conferences had been organized, which reported a total membership of 26,587.

Having disposed of the Reformers, the General Conference four years later (1832) assembled in the city of Philadelphia, and proceeded to elect one of the conservative leaders, John Emory, a bishop, while the second bishop chosen this year, James O. Andrew, of Georgia, was later to become an important actor in the slavery controversy which finally was to divide the church. Andrew had not incurred the enmity of the progressives, as had Emory, and accordingly received the larger vote. At this Conference the friends of William Capers, then the most popular preacher in the South, had urged him to permit his name to be presented for the office of bishop. He had refused on the ground that he was an unwilling slaveowner, and suggested that Andrew was a more suitable candidate from the South, since neither he nor his father had held slaves. Emory was a native of Maryland and was well educated, having studied law and been admitted to the bar. Previous to the General Conference of 1824 he had advocated the election of presiding elders and was known as a progressive, but by 1828 he had completely changed his views.

An important action at this Conference was the selection of John P. Durbin as editor of the *Christian Advocate and Zion's Herald*. American Methodism pioneered in the publication of weekly religious journals. In 1823 a society of the New England Conference began the publication of a small weekly paper called *Zion's Herald*. Two years later (1825) the *Wesleyan Journal* was established in Charleston, South Carolina, while on September 9, 1826, the first issue of *The Christian Advocate* made its appearance in New York. The next year (1827) the South Carolina paper was purchased by The Book Concern at New York, as was also the *Zion's Herald* the following year. The New York paper now appeared under the cumbersome name of *Christian Advocate and Journal and Zion's Herald*. In 1830 the New England Methodists resumed the publication of a paper, and in 1833 petitioned the Book Concern for the return of the name *Zion's Herald*. This was granted, and this part of the name was dropped from the New York paper, leaving it the *Christian Advocate and Journal*.

The New York paper was a great success from the start, and by 1828 it "had a weekly circulation of fifteen thousand copies, the largest, it was claimed, then reached by any newspaper in the world, the *London Times* not excepted." It was also one of the first papers in the United States to have a nation-wide circulation.[10]

[10] McMaster, J. B., *History of the People of the United States*. Vol. V, pp. 274-275. (New York, Appleton, 1904.) "Before 1826

KEEPING PACE WITH WESTWARD MARCH

By the opening of the Civil War eight other *Advocates* had been authorized by the General Conference as follows: *The Western Christian Advocate* at Cincinnati, 1834; the *Pittsburgh Christian Advocate* begun as a Pittsburgh Conference enterprise in 1833 and taken under General Conference control in 1844; the *Northern Christian Advocate,* the *California* and *Northwestern Advocates* authorized in 1852, to be followed four years later (1856) by the *Pacific* and *Central Christian Advocates.* In 1841 the Western Methodist Book Concern at Cincinnati began the publication of a literary and religious monthly, *The Ladies Repository and Gatherings of the West,* which in its earlier years exercised a marked influence upon the culture of the Middle West.

. . . *Zion's Herald,* the great Methodist weekly, had a circulation of five thousand copies. . . . In 1828 there were in the United States thirty-seven religious newspapers. . . ." A recent study of the periodicals received through the post office at Jacksonville, Illinois, in 1831-32, shows that the *Christian Advocate and Journal* was the most widely circulated paper in that region. See *Journal of the Illinois State Historical Society,* October, 1930, pp. 371-438, article by Heinl, F. J., "Newspapers and Periodicals in the Lincoln-Douglas Country, 1831-1832." *The Christian Advocate and Journal* had 58 subscribers; *The Louisville Public Advertiser,* a Jacksonian Democratic paper, had the largest circulation among the secular papers, with 22 subscribers. A quarterly charge of 19½ cents was made for *The Christian Advocate.*

CHAPTER X

SHARES IN THE MISSIONARY ENTERPRISE

A MONG the influences responsible for the missionary movement which began in the latter years of the eighteenth century and which led to the formation of missionary organizations in America were, first, the new humanitarianism growing out of the evangelical revival, causing a larger concern for the Indians and Negroes particularly; second, the western movement of population into new frontiers, and the establishment of communities cut off from church and school privileges. These were the two major influences, out of which came a rebirth of American missionary activities. Thus the first Congregational missionary societies, which were local and state organizations, were primarily concerned with bringing the gospel to frontier communities. Indian missions, since the days of John Eliot (d. 1690) had concerned the New England Congregationalists, but the great colonial awakening had greatly increased missionary interest, not only among Congregationalists but among Presbyterians, Baptists, and others, and missions were established in central New York and other sections of the frontier.

While interest in what might be termed home missions was thus increasing, at the same time there arose a large concern for the conversion of the so-called heathen in distant lands. In England the Baptists formed a society in 1792 and sent William

Carey to Calcutta. The London Missionary Society, organized three years later, was composed principally of Presbyterians and Congregationalists, while similar societies were springing up in Germany, the Netherlands, and in Scotland. Some of the missionaries, sent out by these early English societies to the Orient, came to America *en route* and their presence in the United States served further to arouse interest in foreign missions. Another influence was the numerous new maritime discoveries resulting in growing popular interest in new lands and strange peoples.

American Methodism lagged somewhat behind the other major American churches in the formation of a formal missionary society, first, because the church was very new and poor in material resources; second, because the whole organization of Methodism was missionary in purpose with no line of demarcation between missions and evangelism. From the beginning the Methodist itinerants gave attention to the evangelization of Negroes, and in 1810, the year of the formation of the American Board of Commissioners for Foreign Missions, a Negro Methodist membership of 34,724 was reported. The Methodists, it is true, did not undertake Indian work until 1819, but it was not because they were not concerned with their evangelization. For instance, Bishop Asbury records in his *Journal* (April 3, 1789), "I wish to send an extra preacher to the Waxsaws, to preach to the Catawba Indians: they have settled amongst the whites on a tract of country twelve miles square." Again in the same year he writes: "I wrote a letter to Cornplanter, chief of the Seneca nation of Indians. I hope God will shortly visit these outcasts of men, and send messengers to publish the glad tidings of salvation amongst them." Two years later[1] we find Coke and Asbury preaching to the Indians in South Carolina, and later holding a conversation with the chiefs "about keeping up the school we have been endeavoring to establish amongst them."

Nor must we forget the missionary influence exercised by Bishop Coke. Coke was thoroughly imbued with the missionary spirit and may truthfully be called the father of Methodist foreign missions. He was possessed with a large private fortune, and during his lifetime lavished upon Methodist missions practically the whole of it. Eighteen times he crossed the Atlantic, always defraying his own expenses. On his first voyage to America Coke read the lives of two great missionaries, Francis Xavier and David Brainerd, and from that time forward he was filled with a dauntless missionary zeal. At the Christmas Conference Coke took a collection at one of the noonday meetings to assist "our brethren who were going to Nova Scotia," which was the beginning of foreign missions in the Methodist Episcopal Church. In 1786, on his second voyage to America, the vessel on which he sailed for Nova Scotia was driven by adverse winds to the West Indies, where he remained from December 25 until February 10 (1787), visiting in that time the islands of Antigua, Dominica, Saint Vincent, and several other of the British sugar islands, where classes were formed and a permanent work begun. Coke was made the head of the first Wesleyan missionary committee in England in 1790, and in 1804 he became

[1] *Journal*, Vol. II, p. 112.

the president of the reorganized society. He was on his way to India with a company of missionaries to found a Methodist mission when he died at sea in 1814 (May 3). The American Methodists released Coke from his promises to them in order that he might carry on his missionary labors. Thus the American Methodists shared in the task of world evangelization, which Coke had begun.[2]

The first actual missionary work undertaken by the American Methodists was begun in 1819 among the Wyandot Indians, at that time living on a reservation in central Ohio. The first official missionary action was taken by the Ohio Conference at its session in Cincinnati in the above year, when

The Conference determined that a Missionary be sent to the northern Indians, and that James Montgomery, a Local Preacher, be employed. Moved by James Quinn and seconded by J. Collins that the mission be under the direction of the Presiding Elder of the Lebanon District and the Preachers of the Mad River circuit. John Strange, Moses Crume, and John Sale were appointed to wait on Brother Montgomery, to ascertain if he want any assistance to enable him to carry into effect his Mission; and also to open a subscription to raise supplies for that purpose.[3]

There was no missionary fund available, and in order to make Montgomery's mission possible a collection was taken among the preachers of the Conference. It amounted to seventy dollars. The missionary, James Montgomery, soon entered the

---

[2] For an excellent appraisal of the missionary influence of Thomas Coke, see Luccock, Halford E., and Hutchinson, Paul, *The Story of Methodism*, pp. 303-306, New York, 1926. See also Etheridge, J. W., *The Life of the Rev. Thomas Coke, D.C.L.* London, 1860.

[3] Sweet, William Warren, *Circuit-Rider Days Along the Ohio.* Chap. IV, "The Wyandot Mission." The above quotation is from the manuscript *Journal of the Ohio Conference, 1819.*

employ of the government as a subagent to the Senecas, and the presiding elder then employed Moses Henkle. The first regularly Quarterly Meeting held with the Indians met at the House of Ebenezer Zane, a half-white man, at Zanesville, where about sixty Indians were present, among them four chiefs, Between-the-Logs, Hicks, Mononcue, and Scuteash.

While the above was the official beginning of Methodist missions, the actual beginning was due to the efforts of a humble mulatto, John Stewart, whose story of how he was led to the Wyandot Indians is as strange a tale as may be found in the *Arabian Nights.*

Stewart was a free-born mulatto, a native of Virginia, who, during his youth, became addicted to intemperate habits. Wandering aimlessly about from place to place, he finally came to Marietta, Ohio, where on a Sunday in 1815, while he was probably in a half-drunken condition, he stumbled into a Methodist camp meeting and was converted. The next Sunday he joined the church and almost immediately felt the call to preach. He says that he heard voices calling him toward the Northwest and finally started off in the direction from which the voices came, traveling sometimes in the woods, sometimes on the road, until finally he came to a Moravian mission, established among the Delaware Indians. From them he learned of Indians further north, and traveling in that direction, finally came to the Wyandot Reservation, and to the home of the United States subagent, William Walker. Walker suspected that Stewart was a runaway slave, but when he heard the story of his conversion and his call to preach, he was convinced of Stewart's sincerity, and the agent and his wife became his stanch friends, and directed him to another mulatto, Jonathan Pointer, who had long lived among the Indians and understood their tongue. With Pointer as interpreter, Stewart began to preach, and during the course of the winter there was a religious awakening among the Indians.

Until 1818 Stewart's work among the Wyandots was entirely independent of any church, and there began to be rumors that he was an imposter. This led him to attend a Quarterly Conference near Urbana, Ohio, where he sought a local preacher's license. He was accompanied by several of his Indian converts, who bore recommendations that Stewart was a proper person to receive such a license. Bishop George was present at this Quarterly Conference and approved the granting of the license. Thus Stewart, and his work among the Indians, was brought to the attention of the Methodists, which resulted in the appointment of James Montgomery as a missionary at the session of the Ohio Conference in 1819. At the next session of the Ohio Conference (1820) the missionary committee was authorized to give "John Stewart and Jonathan Pointer, men of color, who were also employed in the mission, what support they think needful." In 1820 Stewart married a Negro woman, and Bishop McKendree collected money for the purchase of a small farm near the Wyandot Reservation, and there Stewart lived until his death in 1823.

While the first Methodist mission was getting under way within the bounds of the state of Ohio a missionary society was forming in New York City.

191

The reasons for the organization of a missionary society are thus stated by Nathan Bangs: First, other denominations had organized missionary societies and many Methodist people were making contributions to them; second, although the Methodist system is missionary in character, yet there were many places, such as new and destitute settlements, which had not been reached and could not support the gospel; third, work among the Indians was opening up in Ohio; fourth, it might become the duty of Methodists to help "others in extending the Redeemer's kingdom in foreign nations"; and, finally, it was evident that such an organization could raise much more money and, therefore, do more good than under the present arrangement.

The initiative in the formation of the Methodist Missionary Society was taken by the book agents and preachers resident in New York, who at a meeting in the year 1818 appointed a committee to draft a constitution. This committee consisted of Laban Clark, Freeborn Garrettson, and Nathan Bangs, each of whom drafted a constitution. The constitution prepared by Bangs, after some slight change, was adopted. On April 5, 1819, a meeting was called of all interested in such a society at the Forsyth Street Church in New York, and there the Missionary Society of the Methodist Episcopal Church was launched. The senior bishop, William McKendree, was made the president, while Bishops George and Roberts, with Nathan Bangs, were named vice-presidents. Besides the usual list of secretaries there was a board of managers of thirty-two members, to be elected annually, and each Annual Conference was to have the privilege of electing a vice-president

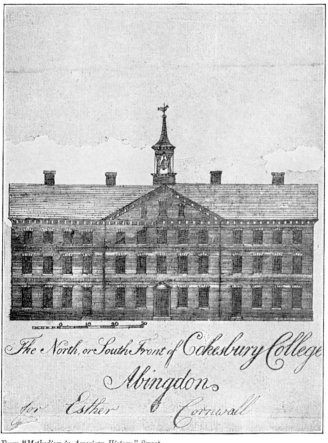

The North, or South Front of Cokesbury College
Abingdon
for Esther Cornwall

From *"Methodism in American History,"* Sweet.

COKESBURY COLLEGE

from its own body. Auxiliary societies were to be formed, which were to agree to turn over to the general society all monies above the amount to carry on their own work. The General Conference of 1820 indorsed the Society, and it thus became a part of the church.

The first year the total income of the Missionary and Bible Society, as it was called, was $823.04; while in the fourth year the society received $5,521.06½ and this year there were nineteen missionaries in the following places: one missionary was employed in the extreme southern part of the United States about Mobile and Pensacola; Jesse Walker was laboring in Saint Louis, recently Spanish territory, where he succeeded in forming a society of one hundred members; another missionary was traveling in Arkansas Territory; while a promising mission had been begun among the Cherokee Indians by the Tennessee Conference; James B. Finley and another missionary were in charge of the Wyandot Mission, where a church had been formed of 154 members, and a school with sixty scholars was in operation; William Capers, with two helpers, was in charge of a mission to the Creek Indians, while the South Carolina Conference was employing five additional missionaries in sections formerly destitute of the gospel. In the northeastern section of the country were several missionaries, one employed by the Genesee Conference, while two were at work within the bounds of the New England Conference.

This was a period of extensive missionary operations among the Indians, carried on by all the larger churches. No doubt the policy of the federal government begun in 1820,

193

of distributing annually several thousands of dollars among missionary societies engaged in Indian work, was partly responsible for this rapid expansion of Indian mission activity among all the churches, and perhaps at no period was more progress made toward civilizing and Christianizing the Indians than at this time.

Soon auxiliary societies were formed in many of the Conferences, while smaller auxiliary societies were numerously organized in many towns and cities. There were "Female" Societies; "Mite" Societies; "Young Men's Auxiliary" Societies; "Juvenile" Societies, all of them carrying on work of their own, but also contributing to the funds of the general Society. Thus Bishop McKendree reported in 1822 that the Philadelphia Conference society had authorized him as president of the general society to draw upon them for $500, which he divided between the Wyandot and the Creek missions.

From 1821 to 1826 James B. Finley was in charge of the mission among the Wyandots. The following is his summary of the progress made during the five years of his missionary labors:

In January, 1821, the first class was formed. Since that time two hundred and ninety-two have been received on trial, two hundred and fifty of whom now remain on our class paper—sixteen have died, I trust, in the Lord, and twenty-six have been expelled, discontinued, and have moved away. The two hundred and fifty now in the church are divided into ten classes, each having a leader of its own. There are four licensed exhorters, godly and zealous men, moving regularly in a circuit among their brethren, and doing much good. They all manifest a disposition to improve in the arts of civilized life; and as religion increases among them, so does industry, cleanliness, and all the fruits of good living. There are on our school list the names of sixty-five children, most of whom are now regular attendants, and are doing well, learning the English language and other useful knowledge.[4]

In the spring of 1826 Finley, with two of the Wyandot Indian chiefs and an interpreter, made a trip to the East, at the invitation of Nathan Bangs, to attend the anniversary of the Missionary Society. The trip was made on horseback from the mission to the shores of Lake Erie, thence by steamboat to Buffalo, where they took a canal boat over the Erie Canal, just completed the year before, to Schenectady, thence to Albany by stage and from Albany down the river by steamboat to New York. Finley and his party visited, besides New York, Philadelphia, Baltimore, and Washington. Everywhere the two chiefs, Between-the-Logs and Mononcue, attracted popular interest, and the journey was a great help to the missionary cause.

In 1843 the Wyandots sold their lands in Ohio and moved to the forks of the Missouri and Kansas Rivers, where they settled on lands purchased from the Delawares, in what is now Wyandot County, Kansas. Their church organization was continued, though feebly, after their removal to Kansas, and their church records may now be found in the archives of the Kansas State Historical Society.

The ninth annual Report of the Methodist Missionary Society (1828) lists five missions among the aborigines in the United States, and six missions among the Indians of Upper Canada. The Indian missions in the United States were the Wyandot, the mission among the Cherokees, the Pottawattamie

---

[4] Report of the Missionary Society for 1825 found in the *Methodist Magazine* (1826), Vol. IX, p. 275.

Mission in the state of Illinois, the Asbury Mission among the Creeks of western Georgia, and the Choctaw Mission in the state of Mississippi. The six Canadian missions were the Grand River, the mission to the Muncy towns on the River Thames, the Credit Mission on the river of that name emptying into Lake Ontario, the Bellville Mission in the Bay of Quinte, the Rice Lake Mission, and the Lake Simco Mission. Besides the Indian missions there were nine domestic missions, maintained in those regions where there were new settlements, or where there was little support for the gospel. In 1830 and 1831 missions were formed among the Oneidas in central New York, and among the Shawnees in what later became the Territory of Kansas. In 1828 the Society expended $8,106, while five years later (1833) the amount expended was in excess of $22,000.

A Methodist missionary enterprise of great romantic interest and importance was that of Jason Lee and his party to the Oregon country, which set out on the long overland journey across the plains and the Rocky Mountains in the spring of 1834. In March, 1833, there appeared in *The Christian Advocate and Journal,* New York, an article by the president of the newly founded Wesleyan University, Willbur Fisk, headed, *A Great Proclamation, Missionary Intelligence, Hear! Hear!*

"Who will respond to the call from beyond the Rocky Mountains?"

The reason for this excitement was the story first printed in the *Christian Advocate and Journal* that had become current throughout the country that a delegation of Indians from the far Northwest had visited Saint Louis and had appealed to General Clark, asking that the "white man's Book of Heaven" be brought to them. Fisk, in his ringing *Proclamation,* states:

We are for having a mission established there at once. . . .

Money will be forthcoming. I will be bondsman for the church. All we want is the men. Who will go? Who? I know one young man who, I think, will go, and of whom I can say, I know of none like him for the enterprise. If he will go (and I have written to him on the subject), we only want another, and the mission will be commenced the coming season. Were I young and unencumbered, how joyfully would I go! But this honor is reserved for another. Bright will be his crown. Glorious his reward.

The young man to whom Fisk had written was Jason Lee, who had been a student under Fisk at Wilbraham Academy. Lee was six feet three, "frank and affable in his intercourse with men," "sincere and sound to the core." Lee accepted the call as missionary to the Oregon Indians as providential, was admitted to the New England Conference and ordained. For a year after his acceptance of the mission Lee stayed in the East, addressing churches, and during this period visited Washington and secured the indorsement of President Jackson and the secretaries of state and war to the founding of the mission in territory then under the joint occupation of the United States and Great Britain. Meanwhile four other missionaries and teachers were added to the expedition, and in the latter part of April, 1834, the party set out from Saint Louis with another party under Captain Wyeth, going west to establish a fur company. The story of that journey has been told recently in great detail in

METHODISM IN AMERICAN HISTORY

Pilgrim and Pioneer, by John M. Canse, based largely upon the *Journals* of Lee and Professor Townshend, a distinguished botanist, accompanying the Wyeth party. The most adequate account of Jason Lee's mission is that by Brosnan, C. J., *Jason Lee: Prophet of the New Oregon,* New York, 1932. On June 15, 1834, the missionary travelers reached the summit of the Rockies, and soon afterward left the Wyeth Company and joined another under the leadership of Captain McKay.

The original intention of the missionaries had been to establish a mission among the Flathead Indians, but on arrival in the country of the Flatheads, on the upper Columbia, they found them to be so few in number and so scattered that they concluded to select another location for their mission. After much consultation with traders, trappers, Indian chieftains, and finally with Doctor McLoughlin, of the Hudson Bay Company, Lee and his associates finally decided to open their mission in the valley of the Willamette, the chief southern tributary of the Columbia.

On October 6, 1834, the missionary party arrived at the place selected for the mission. The hardships of the long journey were past, but the task of building the mission buildings and founding the mission colony was herculean. Before spring a large log mission building had been erected, and preparations were made to plant crops the following spring. Lee and his company were also kept busy gathering Indian children for a school, while he found numerous members of Hudson Bay Company who had not heard the gospel for years.

Lee soon saw that successful missionary work

among the Indians must consist largely of applied Christianity, and in carrying out this policy he had purchased cattle for the mission and had introduced the teaching of practical arts to the Indian children. Lee had gained the statesman's outlook soon after reaching Oregon, and he became active in encouraging white settlement, and had an important part in setting up a provisional government. In 1838 Lee returned to the East to explain the changing conditions in the Oregon country to the Missionary Society and the church. He also carried a memorial from Oregon to the United States government, and in a letter to Caleb Cushing, chairman of the House Committee of Foreign Relations, who had received the memorial, Lee stated, "It may be thought that Oregon is of little importance; but, rely upon it, there is the germ of a great state." There is abundant evidence that Lee's representations of the Oregon situation greatly influenced the federal government in the policies later pursued in reference to the great Northwest.[5] Though interested in these large projects, Lee's chief interest remained that of promoting Christianity among the Indians.

In 1840 Lee returned to Oregon with a party of fifty-two persons, of whom five were ministers. He also had the society's authorization to purchase farm machinery, iron works for a sawmill and grist mill, and all kinds of merchandise. The Missionary Society granted to Lee for his various needs the sum of $42,000, the largest grant ever made, up to that

---

[5] Bashford, J. W., *The Oregon Missions*. New York: The Abingdon Press, 1918, especially Chaps. II, IX, X, XIII. Also Bancroft, H. H., *History of Oregon*, San Francisco, 1886.

time, to a single missionary enterprise. On Lee's return to his mission he found conditions had changed materially. The Indians of the Willamette Valley were dying off rapidly of smallpox and other diseases, contracted from the whites, while the Indian Farm Mission had proved a failure, due to Indian indolence. An attempt was made to save the whole Indian situation by establishing a Manual Labor Boarding School on the present site of Salem, Oregon, where the largest building then on the Pacific Coast was erected at a cost of $10,000. "Here the Indians of both sexes were gathered in 1842-43, and the missionaries here made their last and most heroic struggle to save a dying race." Two years later (1844) the building, with a block of land in what is now the heart of Salem, Oregon, was sold by Lee's successor for the sum of $4,000.

These seeming failures, together with the shock to the missionaries when Lee returned from the East with a second wife, his first wife having died in childbirth in his absence—though his second marriage was largely due to the advice of friends, and did not take place until fifteen months after the death of the first Mrs. Lee—aroused a spirit of criticism among the missionaries, and in 1843 Lee was superseded. He was on his way East a second time to explain again the changed situation in the mission, when he learned of his removal. Meanwhile his second wife had died, and overwhelmed with sorrow, he quickly succumbed to tuberculosis and died March 12, 1845—"one of the most statesmanlike and heroic figures in missionary annals."

We must not suppose that the Methodists were the only missionary force working in the Northwest in these early years, though they were first in the field. The American Board of Commissioners for Foreign Missions sent out their first representatives the year following the arrival of the Lee party, and in 1836 a mission was established in what is now western Washington at Walla Walla. The outstanding leader of this mission enterprise was Marcus Whitman. Whitman, like Lee, became interested in saving the Oregon country to the United States, but the importance of his part in the final decision of the United States in regard to its Oregon policy has long been in dispute and is now generally conceded to have been considerably less than his earlier partisans claimed. Whitman, however, did induce some settlers to come to the Oregon country and performed heroic service for the Indians. On November 29, 1847, both Whitman and his wife were murdered by the very Indians for whose welfare they felt the tenderest solicitude.

Two Catholic missionaries also came into the Oregon country in 1838 at the request of the Canadian employees of the Hudson Bay Company. Their coming led to conflict between the Catholic and Protestant missionaries, and the Catholics won back to the Catholic fold numerous converts to Protestantism, among them Doctor McLoughlin, of the Hudson Bay Company. In 1843 the Oregon country was erected into an apostolic vicarate, and Father Blanchet became the first archbishop. Large funds were raised in Europe for the Catholic mission in Oregon, and by 1847, the year of the destruction of the American Board's mission, the Catholics had three bishops and thirty-one priests, besides thirteen sisters and lay brethren at work in the re-

gion. The Catholic missionaries have been accused
of large responsibility in the massacre of the Protestant missionaries at Walla Walla, but perhaps
cooler judgment can lay no greater charge against
them than that of unheroic conduct and cowardice.[6]

The first foreign missionary sent out by the
Methodist Episcopal Church was Melville Bever-
idge Cox,[7] a young but frail minister of the Virginia
Conference, "who was burning for zeal to do something for Christ in a foreign land." As early as
1825 the Missionary Society had requested the bishops to send a man to Liberia, but evidently because
of the lack of suitable candidates, no one was sent
until the General Conference of 1832. This scarcity
of suitable missionary material in the Methodist
Episcopal Church was at least partially due to the
fact that there were at that time no Methodist colleges. The first American foreign missionaries came
from Williams College, and Andover Theological
Seminary, and through the years colleges have been
the most "fruitful centers of missionary contagion."

Through the work of the American Colonization
Society, organized in 1816, the new Negro republic
of Liberia was established on the west coast of Africa,

[6] See Bancroft's *History of Oregon*, Vol. I, p. 663; also Bashford's
The Oregon Missions, pp. 72-78.
[7] Melville B. Cox was a native of Maine, born November 9, 1799.
He joined the New England Conference in 1822, and for three years
preached on circuits in his native state. A severe illness in 1825
caused him to seek a better climate in the South, and for a time he
was in charge of a local church paper, called *The Itinerant*, in Baltimore. In 1828 he married Ellen Cromwell Lee, a young lady residing
near the city of Baltimore, but in less than two years his wife died in
childbirth. He was appointed to a circuit in the Virginia Conference in 1831, but the feeble state of his health compelled him to
relinquish it. Sprague, *Annals of the American Pulpit*, Vol. VII, pp.
656-661.

and attracted large attention in the United States.
Cox at first had his thoughts centered upon South
America as a field of missionary labor, but Bishop
Hedding had turned his attention to Liberia, and
soon, we are told, Liberia was "swallowing up all
his thoughts." To us of this day, accustomed to the
careful physical examinations which all missionary
candidates must undergo before receiving their appointments, the appointment of Cox, whose health
was already undermined, to a region having one of
the worst climates in the world, seems strange pro-
cedure. Yet his devotion and willingness to give
his life for a great cause have left a great heritage to
the church, and his early death four months after
his arrival in Liberia was one of the influences which
soon raised up others to take his place. In many
respects the life of Melville Cox reminds one of
David Brainerd. Both gave themselves to the cause
of missions in the face of ill health, facing the prospect of an early death; both died soon after beginning their missionary labors, and both, though dead,
exercised a powerful influence in arousing their
churches to their missionary task.

Cox died July 21, 1833. To a student at the
newly established college at Middletown, Connecticut, he had said, "If I die in Africa, you must come
over and write my epitaph." "I will," said the
youth, "but what shall I write?" "Write," said Cox,
"Let a thousand fall before Africa be given up."

And Africa was not given up. Within the first
three years eleven missionaries were appointed,
while in the first fifty years thirty-three missionaries
were sent to Liberia. Fifty years later Methodism
spread to other parts of Africa, and the names Tay-

lor and Hartzell are associated by Methodists with that of Melville B. Cox, whenever the name "Africa" is spoken.

The second foreign mission attempted by the Methodist Episcopal Church was to South America. In 1835 an advance agent was sent to Rio de Janeiro, Buenos Aires and other places to survey the field, and a year later Justin Spaulding and John Dempster began missions in Brazil and Argentina. Daniel P. Kidder came to Brazil in 1837, and was soon preaching in Portuguese and translating books and tracts, as well as circulating Bibles. The mission promised immediate success and permanence, but unfortunately the great financial crisis, which held the United States in its grip from 1837 onward for a number of years, caused the recall of the three missionaries in 1841. Later the work was renewed, though Dempster and Kidder came home to render pioneer service in the establishment of theological education in the Methodist Episcopal Church.

There was a large and growing interest in South and Central America on the part of the American people in the opening years of the nineteenth century due to their long struggle for independence, then under way. This was evidenced not only by the fact that the United States was the first government to recognize the independence of several of the South American states but also by the promulgation of the Monroe Doctrine in 1823. The recurrence of "Brazil," "Peru," "Mexico," and "Bolivar" as names of towns then being established in the United States, is further evidence of the popular interest in our Hispanic-American neighbors. The attempt to establish Methodist missions in these lands was stimulated by the same feelings of interest.

Protestant missions began in China with the work of Robert Morrison, who was sent out by the London Missionary Society in 1807. After nearly thirty years of devoted work, he had seen only ten converts baptized, but he had laid a permanent foundation for future work by his translation of the New Testament and his Chinese dictionary.

New England merchants and shipowners had long carried on a profitable trade with the Far East. In the years immediately following the Revolution, during the period when the trade in the old channels was largely cut off, American vessels found their way in increasing numbers to distant ports. One of the pioneers in this distant trade was "Captain Robert Gray, of Boston, who, in his ship, Columbia, doubled the Cape of Good Hope and completed the first American voyage around the world" (1789-90). Soon the Yankee clipper ships were to be seen in every Eastern port, while the New England ship captains brought home as souvenirs porcelain, brocade, and lacquer-ware from China, some of which may still be seen in many a New England homestead.

In 1842-44 five Chinese ports were opened to foreign trade, while Hong-Kong was ceded outright to Great Britain as a result of what is known to history as the Opium War, one of the most discreditable in the whole history of the English people. Whatever may have been the provocation which finally led the British to declare war on China, the fact remains that the root of the trouble was the attempt of China to destroy the nefarious opium traffic, while the British authorities objected, because the growth and sale of the drug formed one of the chief sources of revenue of India. Yet the opening of these "Treaty Ports" to Western trade was considered by many good Christian people of that time as a providential event, thereby enabling Christian missionaries to establish missions in China. And, as a matter of fact, up to 1860 a large proportion of the Protestant missions were in these treaty ports.[8]

The first Methodist Episcopal mission in China was in Foochow, one of the treaty ports, and was established in 1847. By this time the Missionary Society had learned not to expect immediate results, and provision was made at the start for the support of the missionaries over a period of ten years. In 1855 a church was erected, though a school had been organized within a few months after the arrival of the missionaries. It was not, however, until 1857 that the first convert was baptized.

In 1848 the Methodist Episcopal Church, South, established a mission in China.

From 1820 to 1854 the Missionary Society of the Methodist Episcopal Church had raised $2,481,-794.38; while in addition to this great sum the Missionary Society of the Methodist Episcopal Church, South, which had been formed in 1846, had raised $927,203. In this year (1854) the two Episcopal Methodisms were maintaining 11 missions in Africa with 22 missionaries; 2 missions in China with 11 missionaries; and 43 missions among the American Indians with 57 missionaries.

---

[8] Latourette, K. S., *A History of Christian Missions in China*, p. 407. New York, 1929.

CHAPTER XI

BEGINS HER EDUCATIONAL TASK

THE small church college has been essentially a frontier institution. The reason for the multiplication of small colleges in newly settled regions becomes clear when we examine the general situation presented by the typical American frontier. The people who lived in newly settled regions were uniformly poor, and the sending of their sons to older established institutions in the East was out of the question, therefore education was brought to the frontier as the only means of training frontier youth. Since the disappearance of the frontier the founding of the small church college has practically ceased, and the educational effort of the church in recent years has been in the direction of amalgamating small colleges and strengthening institutions already in existence.

A very large proportion of the better-known educational institutions in America were, in their origin, frontier institutions. Harvard was established but eight years after the foundation of Massachusetts Bay Colony; New Haven was a frontier village when Yale was established; William and Mary College was built in the midst of a forest, while Dartmouth was located at Hanover, New Hampshire, in order that it might be in close proximity to the Indian country, since its founding was mainly for the purpose of training missionaries to work among the Indians. Most of the present-day Methodist colleges in the Middle West were frontier colleges in their origin. McKendree College was established in Illinois soon after the admission of that state to the Union; Indiana Asbury, now DePauw, began its long history in 1837; Baker University was founded while Kansas was still a territory (1858), and these are but typical of many others.

The first attempts of the Methodist Episcopal Church to establish a college in the East, where there was competition with older established institutions, failed. We have already noticed the founding of Cokesbury, which was opened with appropriate religious exercises and a dedication sermon by Bishop Asbury on the 8th, 9th, and 10th days of December, 1787. In 1792 the college had seventy students, and in 1794 it was incorporated and authorized to confer degrees, but the next year, as already recorded, a fire completely destroyed the building. Asbury seems to have experienced a feeling of relief when the news reached him at Charleston, South Carolina, that the college was destroyed, for he wrote in his *Journal:*

"We have now a second and confirmed account that Cokesbury College is consumed to ashes, a sacrifice of about ten thousand pounds in about ten years. Its enemies may rejoice, and its friends need not mourn. Would any man give me ten thousand pounds a year to do and suffer again what I have done for that house, I would not do it." And then he proceeds: "The Lord called not Mr. Whitefield or the Methodists to build colleges." But he observes, "I feel distressed at the loss of the library."

During the period of the life of Cokesbury, Asbury spent a good portion of his time begging funds. Often he donated a large portion of his meager sal-

From *Wesleyan's First Century*, Carl F. Price

WESLEYAN UNIVERSITY IN 1831

The oldest Methodist institution of higher learning in America

ary to help the school, and it is no wonder that when the news reached him of its destruction, a sigh of relief escaped him.

Cokesbury College had been established in the very center of Methodist influence, for at least one third of the total Methodist membership in the United States was at that time in the state of Maryland, and an even larger proportion was in the state of Virginia. Abingdon was located on the main stage route between Philadelphia and Baltimore and was thus easy of access. The brick building erected for the college, 40x100 feet and three stories high, was the equal of, if not superior to, any other college building in the country. Cokesbury also had the strictest of regulations. Rising time for students was five o'clock, summer and winter; at six they assembled for prayer; breakfast came at seven, and from eight to twelve they "were closely kept" to their respective studies; dinner came at one; after dinner until three was a time for recreation, but the recreation was to consist of gardening, walking, riding, and bathing, without doors; and the carpenter's, joiner's, cabinetmaker's, or turner's business, within doors. "There were three acres set aside for students' gardens, where students might cultivate vegetables or flowers as their taste directed." The students were not to indulge in anything "which the world calls play," nor were they to be permitted to sleep on feather beds.

The Methodist Episcopal Church at that time contained few, if any, well-educated ministers, and accordingly the first teacher employed at Cokesbury was a Quaker, Freeman Marsh, who was reputed "to be a good Latin scholar" and what was perhaps more important, "an excellent disciplinarian." An appeal to John Wesley to recommend a man for the presidency resulted in the coming of a Rev. Mr. Heath, a former master of an English grammar school, who with his wife and "two lovely daughters" took charge of Cokesbury at its dedication, when twenty-five students were entered. With Heath came also Patrick McCloskey as an additional teacher.

A second attempt was made to establish Cokesbury College in Baltimore, the college being located in a brick building adjoining the Light Street Church. In December, 1796, this enterprise met the same fate as the first Cokesbury, when it was burned to the ground, together with the neighboring church. Commenting on this disaster Asbury says in his *Journal:* "I conclude God loveth the people of Baltimore, and will keep them poor in order to keep them pure."

A third unsuccessful attempt to establish a Methodist college was made in 1816, when a group of Baltimore Methodists opened Asbury College in that city. Dr. Samuel K. Jennings, a local preacher and a successful physician, was placed at its head, and for a few years the institution seemed to prosper. In the first volume of the *Methodist Magazine* (1818) is a laudatory notice of the college, and in that year a charter was secured. How long the college lasted is not known, but its life was short, and it died "for want of money and of a mongrel religion," as few of its teachers were Methodists.

These disasters having convinced Asbury that God did not intend that the Methodists should establish colleges, he now began to urge the founding of schools of lower grade in various sections of the country. As early as 1792 Asbury drew up a plan for district schools "which," he says, "with little alteration, will form a general rule for any part of the continent." As a consequence such schools as Ebenezer Academy in Brunswick County, Virginia, Bethel Academy in Jessamine County, Kentucky, Cokesbury School in western North Carolina in the Yadkin country, Wesley and Whitefield School in Georgia, and Union Seminary at Uniontown, Pennsylvania, were established. But not a single one of the schools which Asbury had a hand in establishing became permanent institutions. The schools were generally located in out-of-the-way places in order that the students might be shielded from the temptations of crowded centers, and this fact made the problem of their support difficult. Added to this was the indifference of Methodist people to the need of education and the general poverty which prevailed.

The General Conference of 1820, as we have already noticed, recommended to the Annual Conferences the establishment, as soon as practicable, of literary institutions under their control. This General Conference also changed the *Discipline* so as to permit the bishops to appoint traveling preachers as officers and teachers in colleges. Previously the church had frowned upon a preacher leaving the active itineracy to engage in teaching. These several actions resulted in numerous attempts of Annual Conferences to establish colleges, and the great college-building era in the Methodist Episcopal Church was the twenty years between 1820 and 1840.

First on the list stands Augusta College, Kentucky, the joint child of the Ohio and the Kentucky Conferences. At the 1820 session of the Ohio Conference a resolution was adopted providing that every presiding elder "take the sentiments of every Quarterly Conference under his charge with regard to the establishment of a seminary within the bounds and under the direction of this Conference." The next year a committee of three was appointed to consider the information furnished, and at the same session made their report, advising the establishment of a seminary in or near the state of Ohio. Augusta, on the Kentucky side of the Ohio River, was the site suggested, and since it was within the bounds of the Kentucky Conference a committee was appointed to confer with a similar committee from the Kentucky brethren looking toward the joint support of the new institution. The following year (1822) Augusta College was established by the joint action of the two Conferences, and in 1825 a three-story brick building was completed, and the work of the college begun.

The first president was John P. Finley, the brother of James B. Finley, who received his education through the instruction of his father, an alumnus of the College of New Jersey. On Finley's death in 1825 he was succeeded by Martin Ruter, the founder of The Methodist Book Concern in Cincinnati and one of the first men in Methodism to receive the degree of Doctor of Divinity. John P. Durbin, later to become famous in Methodism as the great secretary of the Missionary Society, was the professor of languages, and in 1831 Henry B. Bascom, then a brilliant young preacher in the

West, became professor of "moral science and belles-lettres." In 1841 Transylvania University at Lexington, Kentucky, was tendered to the Methodist Episcopal Church, and the Kentucky Conference accepted the offer. The next year several members of the Augusta College faculty, including Dr. H. B. Bascom, who had accepted the presidency of Transylvania University, joined the Transylvania faculty, thus greatly weakening the college at Augusta. The slavery controversy was becoming more and more acute, and the Kentucky Conference desired to withdraw from Augusta College and pledged its support to the newly acquired institution at Lexington. This brought on a series of lawsuits, and after the schism in the church over slavery in 1844 a college in Kentucky under Ohio Conference patronage could not continue, and as a result Augusta College closed its doors in 1849. Though the life of Augusta College was short, yet it gave to the church one of its bishops, Randolph S. Foster, and two of its greatest teachers, Dr. John Miley and Professor W. G. Williams, the first for many years professor of systematic theology at Drew, the latter professor of Greek for more than fifty years at Ohio Wesleyan University.

The Pittsburgh Conference at its session in 1826 made plans to establish a college at Uniontown, Pennsylvania, to be called Madison College. Henry B. Bascom became the president, and the college was opened in 1827 with six teachers and sixty-three scholars. The college was named in honor of ex-President James Madison, who, replying to a letter from President Bascom informing him of that fact, stated, "I feel that my name is greatly honored by such an association as has been made of it." President Bascom was extremely active in promoting the college and carried on an interesting correspondence with ex-President Madison and other prominent men, among them Charles Carroll, John Marshall, Henry Clay, DeWitt Clinton, and John Quincy Adams, regarding his plans. Among his proposals was the establishment in connection with the college of an Institute of Agriculture to be called Carroll Institute. The aged Charles Carroll, though a Roman Catholic, wrote to President Bascom that he considered the proposed "Carroll Institute of Agriculture to be established in Madison College as a distinguished honor conferred" upon him.[1] All these fine plans, however, soon came to naught, for money was not forthcoming, a faculty could not be adequately supported, while patronage was too limited to warrant continuance of the college. In 1829 Bascom resigned the presidency, and the college soon afterward closed its doors.

The first permanent educational institutions established by the Methodists in America were seminaries or academies. The first in the long list of such institutions was Wesleyan Academy, first established in Newmarket, New Hampshire, in 1817, but removed to Wilbraham, Massachusetts, in 1825. The proposition to establish an academy was brought before the New England Conference at its session in 1816, but the real inception of the academy dates from a meeting of several preachers at Newmarket, New Hampshire, the year previous.

---

[1] For Bascom's activities and plans for Madison College, see *The Life of Henry Biddleman Bascom*, by M. M. Henkle, pp. 183-197. Louisville, 1854.

The new enterprise was adopted by the Conference, and a subscription taken to erect a building, the cost of which when completed was $755. The school opened in September, 1817, with ten scholars—five boys and five girls. The next year Martin Ruter was chosen principal. It was soon found that the academy was badly located, and in 1825 it was relocated at Wilbraham, Massachusetts, and Willbur Fisk, a young and energetic member of the Conference, was chosen principal. Fisk remained at the head of the institution until 1831, resigning to accept the presidency of Wesleyan University.

Other seminaries now came into existence 'in rapid succession. Cazenovia was established by the Genesee Conference in 1824 as a school for both sexes, then an experiment in education. In 1821 a farmer in the state of Maine established a school on Kent's Hill for "better education of persons designing to enter the Methodist Ministry." The school began as a manual training school, and in 1825 the charter was amended, and the name changed to Maine Wesleyan Seminary. In 1832 Genesee Wesleyan Seminary was opened under the presidency of the Rev. John Dempster at Lima, New York. By 1840 there were at least twenty-eight academies, seminaries, and manual-labor schools in operation under Methodist auspices, each of them sponsored by an Annual Conference. These institutions were well distributed throughout the country and were by no means confined to the North. The Mississippi Conference in 1840 was sponsoring Elizabeth Female College, Emory Academy, Vicksburg Academy, and Woodville Female Academy; the Georgia Conference had under its control Emory College, Georgia Female College, Georgia Conference Manual Training School, Collingsworth Institute, and Wesley Manual Labor School, while the North Carolina Conference was aiding in the support of Randolph-Macon College, a female college at Greensboro, and two academies.

The successful operation of the several seminaries was one of the factors which led to the founding of the first permanent Methodist colleges. During the eighteen thirties the following colleges were established: Wesleyan University, Connecticut; Randolph-Macon College, Virginia; Dickinson and Allegheny Colleges in Pennsylvania, McKendree College in Illinois, Indiana Asbury University in Indiana, Emory College in Georgia, and Emory and Henry College in southwestern Virginia.

Dickinson and Allegheny Colleges were the continuation of older institutions, which had been begun under other auspices, while Wesleyan University began its work in a building formerly occupied by a military academy. The decision of the New York and New England Conferences to locate their institution at Middletown, Connecticut, was, no doubt, due to the offer of the trustees of the military academy to convey their property to the Methodist Episcopal Church on condition that $40,000 be raised as an endowment, and that the property should be used in perpetuity for a college. This offer was accepted, and the trustees held their first meeting on August 24, 1830, when Willbur Fisk, the principal of Wilbraham Academy, was chosen the first president. The Middletown Preparatory School opened in the college building in October, 1830, under W. C. Larrabee, an alumnus of Bowdoin College, and the college began operations the following September with five teachers, including the president, and forty-eight students.

The charter of Dickinson College dates from 1783 and was named in honor of John Dickinson, who was the first president of the board of trustees and donated seven hundred acres of land and $500. Among the early trustees was Dr. Benjamin Rush, and the first president was Dr. Charles Nisbet, who came from Scotland to assume that office in 1785. The present site of the college was purchased from the Penn family for $150 in 1798. The college continued under Presbyterian control until 1832, though the college had been closed for a time in 1816 because of conflict and misunderstanding between the trustees and the faculty. Due to the continued discord and poverty of support negotiations to transfer the college to the Baltimore and Philadelphia Conferences of the Methodist Church were begun, and the two Conferences assumed control in 1833. An amended charter was secured lessening the right of the trustees to act in the internal government of the college, and a new board of trustees was chosen. The first president under the new management was John P. Durbin, and the college was opened as a Methodist institution in September, 1834. Durbin was president for twelve years and was succeeded by Robert Emory, and he, in turn, by Jesse T. Peck.

Allegheny College, like Dickinson College, had been established under Presbyterian auspices in 1815. The first president, Timothy Alden, traveled through the East raising money for the college, securing subscriptions from numerous famous men, among them ex-Presidents John Adams and Thomas Jefferson. The first building was erected in 1820. President Alden was indefatigable in his labors for the college, and a valuable library was collected. The college as a Presbyterian institution, however, was doomed to failure because of the rivalry of two other Presbyterian institutions in western Pennsylvania—Jefferson and Washington Colleges. All three institutions were located within the bounds of the Pittsburgh Synod, and competition for students was therefore keen and the number too few to support three colleges. The result was that on the resignation of President Alden in 1831 the college was closed, and two years later (1833) opened as a Methodist institution, supported by the Erie and Pittsburgh Conferences, with Martin Ruter as the first Methodist president.

The oldest Methodist institution of college grade in the South is Randolph-Macon College, which was first located at Boydtown, in Mecklenburg County, near the Virginia-North Carolina line, since it was intended to serve Methodists in both Virginia and the Carolinas. The institution opened as an academy in January, 1832, college work beginning, however, the following fall. The Rev. John Emory, afterward bishop, was chosen president, but did not accept, when the Rev. Stephen Olin, later to achieve larger fame as the president of Wesleyan University, was elected president and served until 1839. Next in point of priority among the Southern colleges is Emory College at Oxford, Georgia, established by the Georgia Conference in 1836 and opened under the presidency of Dr. Ignatius Few the following year.

In the year 1828 the Rev. Edward R. Ames, later Bishop Ames, opened a Methodist academy at Lebanon, Saint Clair County, in western Illinois. Two years later (1830), Bishop McKendree having donated 480 acres of land, the institution became McKendree College. In 1834 three Illinois colleges were granted charters by a reluctant General Assembly—Illinois College, the Congregational-Presbyterian institution at Jacksonville; Shurtleff College, the Baptist school at Upper Alton, and McKendree at Lebanon. In 1841, due to the terrible financial panic and the failure of a scheme of the trustees to raise endowment by selling scholarships on credit, the college was compelled to close its doors. For five years the institution ceased operations, when in 1846, through the devotion of a local preacher, Davis Goheen, at that time living in Lebanon, a plan was proposed to reopen the college and save it to the church. The plan was to secure the promise of every class leader in Illinois to pledge his class to pay to the college twenty-five cents quarterly. In spite of the extreme poverty of the people enough money was thus collected, added to that from tuition, to keep the college alive. In 1852 Peter Akers became the president and continued in that office until 1857.

At their first session in 1832 the Indiana Conference appointed a committee on education and in their report state: "We therefore think that seminaries and colleges under good literary and moral regulations are of incalculable benefit to our country, and that a good Conference seminary would be of great and growing utility to our people." They further urged the establishment of a Methodist institution in the state of Indiana because the State College at Bloomington was at that time largely under Presbyterian influence, and they advocated having an institution under Methodist control, where all doctrines deemed dangerous might be excluded, though they would not advocate an institution so sectarian as to repel the sons of their fellow citizens. Before proceeding to found a Methodist institution in Indiana, the Indiana Conference, however, made an effort to amend the charter of the State College, whereby there might be a possibility of getting Methodists on the board of trustees and in the faculty. Petitions were prepared and largely signed and presented to the state Legislature, but it was to no avail.

The Methodists of Indiana had four complaints against the State College: 1. The institution was regarded as belonging to the Presbyterian Church and was actually listed among Presbyterian colleges. 2. The religious beliefs of Methodist students were not respected. 3. The trustees seemed to presume that none but Presbyterians were competent to teach in higher institutions of learning. 4. Under the existing system no Methodist could be represented on the board of trustees, although at that time there were more Methodists in Indiana than any other religious body. Finally, at the session of the Conference in 1835 it was definitely determined to establish a Methodist college in Indiana, and a plan was drawn up to raise endowments for professorships, and steps were taken to find a suitable location. At the Conference of 1836 a number of Indiana towns bid for the new college, the choice finally falling upon the village of Greencastle, since its citizens had offered the largest sum, $25,000. At the previous session of the Conference the name Indiana Asbury University had been selected as the name of the new institution.

Instruction began in the preparatory department in June, 1837, and in the fall the college proper began operations, with the Rev. Cyrus Nutt as acting president. Two years later the Rev. Matthew Simpson was chosen the first president. In 1840 W. C. Larrabee became a member of the faculty of Indiana Asbury University, he having been the first actual teacher at the opening of Wesleyan University in Connecticut.

Although the Methodist Episcopal Church was busy founding academies and colleges from 1820 onward, yet there continued to be for many years a strong prejudice against college-bred ministers, especially in the West. The first college graduate to join the Indiana Conference was Thomas A. Goodwin, and he states that the presiding elders were afraid to show too much favor to a college man, and on several occasions he was actually demoted for no other reason than that he was a college graduate. One of Goodwin's colleagues on a certain Indiana circuit was a man very deficient in training and education, but he was more popular on the circuit because he could outshout Goodwin. Goodwin states: "He got all the socks, but he generally divided with me, for he got more than twice as many as he could possibly wear out. He would put up for the night or for a week, as the demands of the appointment would allow, and smoke his pipe, and talk gossip, but read, never, beyond the *Western Christian Advocate*. I met his praise everywhere I went. He kissed all the babies and had several namesakes before the year was half out."[2] The jealousy and prejudice against college graduates finally drove Goodwin from the active ministry, and he became the editor of a newspaper, established to fight the saloon and slavery. William Capers was the first college-trained man to join the South Carolina Conference, and his experience was much the same as was that of T. A. Goodwin. His presiding elder advised against further literary preparation and warned him, "If you are called to preach, and sinners are falling daily into hell, take care lest the blood of some of them be found on your skirts."

While the years from 1820 to 1840 were the most active in the history of the church in the establishment of educational institutions, yet the period following 1840 to the Civil War saw the beginnings of several important educational ventures. Perhaps the most important in the North was the establishment of Ohio Wesleyan University, 1844; Northwestern University in 1851; Iowa Wesleyan, 1854; Baker University, 1858; and the beginnings of theological education in New England, and at Evanston, Illinois. In the South the chief educational institutions founded during these years were Trinity College, now Duke University, in 1851; Wofford College at Spartanburg, South Carolina, in 1854; and Central College, at Fayette, Missouri, in 1855.

Ohio Wesleyan University succeeded Augusta College as the educational child of Ohio Methodism. It was located at Delaware, Ohio, as the result of an offer of the citizens of that town to transfer

---

[2] Tarkington, Joseph, *Autobiography*. Introduction by T. A. Goodwin. Cincinnati, 1899.

to the Ohio and North Ohio Conferences a property known as the Mansion House, built as a hotel, together with $10,000 in cash. The offer was accepted, and a charter obtained in 1842 conferring university powers. A preparatory school was put in operation at once, but the college proper did not open until 1844 under the presidency of Edward Thomson, with a faculty of four teachers, and a student body of twenty-nine young men. Northwestern University was projected at a "meeting of persons favorable to the establishment of a university in Chicago under the patronage of the Methodist Episcopal Church, held in Chicago on May 31, 1850." The next year a charter was obtained, and the new institution opened at Evanston, Illinois.

For many years the leaders in the Methodist Episcopal Church were opposed to theological education. The committee of the Indiana Conference on the establishment of Indiana Asbury University repudiated the idea that they were founding "a manufactory in which preachers are to be made." The early Methodist leaders felt much as did the Baptists that when God called a man to preach, it was sinful for him to waste time getting ready, for God would not have called an unprepared man. The *Discipline* of 1784 advised preachers not to permit study and learning to interfere with soul-saving: "If you can do but one, let your studies alone. We would throw by all the libraries in the world rather than be guilty of the loss of one soul." Peter Cartwright compared educated preachers to "lettuce growing under the shade of a peach tree" or to "a gosling that has got the straddles by wading in the dew," while Alfred Brunson explained his opposition to theological schools on the ground that they turned out "learned dunces and second- and third-rate preachers."

The growing number of Methodist colleges and academies throughout the country were soon turning out an ever-increasing body of educated laymen, who were no longer content to sit under the preaching of uncouth and untrained preachers. Before the middle of the century advocates of a better educated ministry were becoming numerous and vocal. Leading laymen were asking for ministers as well trained as those in other denominations, while others contended that Methodism needed men prepared to defend her against her opponents, both in the press and on the platform. Even Alfred Brunson, before his death, had come over to the necessity of theological seminaries, and said: "In view of all the circumstances of the case, the change from the circuit to the station system—each young preacher being alone, instead of having an elder brother with him to teach him, the elevated state of society, and the wish of our good people to have educated men, . . . and in view of the influence mere tinsel of this kind has upon outsiders in attracting them to our places of worship, it is probably best to have such institutions. . . ."[3]

John Dempster was the father of theological education in the Methodist Episcopal Church. Dempster, while a presiding elder in the Oneida Conference, appealed to Bishop Hedding to appoint better trained men to his district, as he had discovered that

---

[3] Brunson, Alfred, *A Western Pioneer: or, Incidents of the Life and Times of Rev. Alfred Brunson*, 2 volumes, Vol. II, pp. 330-331. Cincinnati: Hitchcock and Walden, 1879.

From *Harper's Weekly*, August 10, 1872.   Reproduced by permission

NEGRO CAMP MEETING IN THE SOUTH

while educated people were converted under Methodist preaching, they generally joined other churches where they could be under better educated ministers. The bishop replied that "We have no such men to spare." This incident made Dempster a tireless advocate of theological schools, and from this time to the end of his life this remained his chief interest.

Beginning with the founding of Andover Theological Seminary in 1808 many theological seminaries had come into existence. In fact, every leading denomination in the United States had established at least one theological seminary before the Methodists opened their first institution of this sort. This includes the Episcopalians, the Congregationalists, the Unitarians, the Baptists, the German Reformed, the Dutch Reformed, the Lutherans, the Free Will Baptists, and the Catholics, while the Presbyterians had no less than nine. Seemingly it was high time the Methodists were stirring themselves in the matter of better ministerial training.

It was but natural that the New England Conference should take the lead in this matter, since here were to be found the oldest theological institutions in the country. The first step was the calling of a convention of ministers and members of New England Methodists on April 24, 1839, in Boston, to consider the "expediency of establishing a Methodist theological institution." The result of this meeting was the decision to open a school at Newbury, Vermont, where a Methodist academy was already in operation. In November, 1840, a board of trustees was elected, financial agents were appointed, and a faculty chosen. But still no school was opened, for funds were lacking. The next year, however, theological instruction was begun under the presidency of Osman C. Baker, the principal of the Newbury Academy, and one other professor. In 1844 Baker resigned his post and the Rev. John Dempster was elected his successor. Dempster's first task was to raise funds, and he traveled far and wide—he even went to Scotland—but only meager success attended his efforts. In 1846 the North Congregational Society of Concord, New Hampshire, came to the rescue and tendered the use of their old church to the Methodists for a theological school, with the provision that the seminary was to remain at Concord for twenty years. This offer was accepted and the school lasted out the twenty years though its existence was always precarious.

When the twenty years were up, a movement was begun, furthered by influential ministers and laymen, to move the Biblical Institute to Boston, and in 1867 it was opened as the Boston Theological Seminary.

To Dr. John Dempster is due the credit for raising a large share of the funds which kept alive the Methodist Biblical Institute at Concord. He remained with the Institute until 1853, when he resigned to help found a biblical institute in the West. When Dempster reached Chicago, he learned that Mrs. Eliza Garrett, who by death of her husband had become possessed of large properties in Chicago, was desirous of helping to establish such an institution. With Mrs. Garrett's promise of help, Dempster proceeded at once to open a theological school, and in January, 1854, Garrett Biblical Institute opened at Evanston, Illinois, in a wooden building, with four students and a faculty of three. At the end of seven years' service at Garrett Biblical Institute Dempster resigned, and was on his way to the Pacific Coast to urge the establishment of a theological seminary in the far West when death stepped in and removed the father of Methodist theological education. The cause he advocated "from an overwhelming sense of duty" was fiercely opposed by at least two thirds of the ministry of the church, and some of the highest church dignitaries "exerted their influence to embarrass and subvert the enterprise."

At the General Conference of 1824 it was made the duty of each traveling preacher to encourage the establishment and progress of Sunday schools, and arrangements were made for the publication of a catechism for Sunday schools and for the instruction of children. The book agents were also instructed to provide books suitable for children. Three years later (1827) the Methodist Sunday School Union was established, and by 1830 more than 150,000 scholars were reported as enrolled in Methodist Sunday schools throughout the land. While in a sense this is the official beginning of Methodist Sunday schools, as a matter of fact Methodist instruction of children dates back to 1748, when the Methodist Conference meeting at Gloucester, England, provided for the formation of children's societies for religious instruction. As early as 1786 there are traces of Sunday schools among the American Methodists, and at the Conference of 1790 action was taken to establish Sunday schools for white and black.

With the election of John H. Vincent in 1868 as secretary of the Methodist Sunday School Union and editor of the Sunday-school literature of the church, a period of rapid change and improvement was begun, which was to have far-reaching results. For twenty years Vincent held this office, and with his genius for popular education he influenced all denominations and revolutionized Sunday-school teaching. Among the many new features introduced by Doctor Vincent were teacher-training classes, teacher's institutes, and regular training courses for teachers, while his introduction of the Uniform Lesson system, which was approved by International Sunday School Convention in 1872, soon popularized Bible study as nothing else had ever done. Another important development in the general field of popular education, very largely brought about through Methodist influence, was the rise of the Chautauqua Assemblies. John H. Vincent is the founder of the original Chautauqua Assembly on the beautiful lake of that name in western New York, which was originally a Methodist camp meeting ground. The Chautauqua began as a Sunday-school teacher's assembly, gradually developing into an elaborate institution, with regular courses of study covering many fields, and a highly trained corps of instructors.

CHAPTER XII

SLAVERY CONTROVERSY AND SCHISM

AMERICAN Methodism came in contact with Negro slavery from its beginning, and no other church has been so largely influenced by the presence of the Negro in American life. As has already been pointed out, Methodism in its early history in America was very largely a movement confined to the colonies south of Pennsylvania. During the Revolution every preacher received into the ministry was from the South, and all the Conferences from 1776 to 1787 were held in what came to be known as the slave states. For many years after the formation of the Methodist Episcopal Church Methodism continued to expand much more rapidly in the South than in the North. Every General Conference from 1784 to 1824, with the exception of that of 1812, met in the city of Baltimore, for the simple reason that Baltimore remained during all that period the center of American Methodism.

Throughout the entire colonial period Negro slavery was a recognized, legal institution in every one of the thirteen colonies. New England ports, and especially Newport and Providence, Rhode Island, were the most active American centers for the carrying on of the slave trade. The slaves, brought from Africa in New England ships, were, of course, sold mostly to Southern planters, but there were slaves in every New England colony, and at the opening of the Revolution Massachusetts alone had more than six thousand. In the middle colonies slaves were more numerous than in New England, though even here plantation life never developed, largely because of climatic conditions. Nine tenths of the Negro population in 1754, however, was to be found in the Southern colonies. At this date there were in round numbers about four hundred thousand people in the Southern colonies, and about half of this number were Negroes.

Practically all the larger colonial churches accepted the institution of slavery without question. The Established Church, through its great missionary organization, the Society for the Propagation of the Gospel in Foreign Parts, instructed its missionaries to give attention to the instruction and conversion of the Negroes, but nowhere do we find them opposing the institution of slavery itself. Some of the New England ministers held slaves as house servants, while some of the most respectable New England citizens invested in the slave traffic. The only colonial churches which took an active anti-slavery position were the several small German sects, such as the Mennonites, and Dunkers, and the Quakers. By the opening of the American Revolution the Quakers had largely eliminated slaveholders from membership in the middle and northern colonies, and by 1787 all the Yearly Meetings in America had passed legislation completely ridding their churches of slaveholders.

By the end of the eighteenth century there were two forces at work, particularly among English-speaking people, which soon were to exercise large influence in regard to the institution of slavery. One was the increased humanitarian impulse coming out of the great eighteenth-century revivals. It is interesting to bear in mind that the group of men in England who were back of the growing opposition to the slave trade, such as Thomas Clarkson, William Wilberforce, and Granville Sharpe, were all *evangelicals* and were the friends of John Wesley. The last letter written by Wesley, February 24, 1791, was addressed to Wilberforce, who was then in the midst of his great fight in Parliament to abolish the slave trade. In that letter occur these words:

"O, be not weary in well-doing! Go on, in the name of God and in the power of His might, till even American slavery (the vilest that ever saw the sun) shall vanish before it." In 1774 Wesley had written a notable pamphlet against the slave trade, and the rules of the early Conferences held in America show a strong anti-slavery attitude. Thus the Conference of 1780 asks:

Does this Conference acknowledge that slavery is contrary to the laws of God, man, and nature, and hurtful to society; contrary to the dictates of conscience and pure religion, and doing that which we would not others should do to us or ours? Do we pass our disapprobation on all our friends who keep slaves, and advise their freedom?

To this question the answer is an emphatic "Yes."

Another anti-slavery influence, particularly powerful in America, was the so-called Revolutionary philosophy. Such statements as "All men are by nature free and independent," and that all men have the "right to life, liberty, and the pursuit of happiness," were not only frequently heard but generally believed. These expressions, as is well known, found a place in the Declaration of Independence, and the Virginia Declaration of Rights, while this philosophy found among its followers Thomas Jefferson, Patrick Henry, and George Washington, and all the other outstanding Revolutionary leaders.

The combined effect of these two influences produced the first anti-slavery movement in America, and brought into existence the first anti-slavery societies. During the latter eighteenth and early nineteenth centuries anti-slavery opinion was commonly held by the leaders throughout the entire nation, and slavery found no defenders of any prominence, either in church or state. Jefferson denounced slavery as a system endangering the very principle of liberty; Patrick Henry wrote, "I will not—I cannot justify it!" while Washington declared in 1786 that one of his chief wishes was that some plan might be devised whereby slavery might be abolished.

By the beginning of the nineteenth century all the states north of Delaware had either abolished slavery or had made provisions for gradual emancipation, and at the adoption of the federal constitution all the Southern states had prohibited the slave trade. As might be expected, during these years in which anti-slavery opinion was commonly held throughout the nation, the churches likewise were taking strong anti-slavery action. The strongest anti-slavery resolutions passed by the Presbyterians, from their nationalization in 1788 to the Civil War, were adopted by the General Assembly of 1818. So likewise the strongest anti-slavery position taken by the Methodists occurred at this time, when general opinion was favorable to such action. Generally speaking, I think it is true that the church does not lead public opinion on such matters as the slavery issue, but, rather, tends to follow public opinion.

The Christmas Conference (1784) passed stringent rules regarding slaveholding church members. They provided that every slaveholding member must within a year execute a legal instrument, agreeing to free his slaves, and the preachers were required to keep a record of all such transactions in their circuits. Those who had not complied with this rule within the year were to withdraw from the church. Exceptions, however, had to be made at once for those residing in states where manumission was prohibited by law, and a special exception was made for the Virginia brethren, because of their special situation, and they were given two years to accept or reject the provision. And within six months it was recommended "to all our brethren to suspend the execution of the minute on slavery till the deliberation of a future Conference." The rule, however, was undoubtedly responsible for the manumitting of numerous slaves. Among the Methodist slaveholders who freed their slaves at this time was Andrew Barrett, of Delaware, who in his deed of manumission states that, "being persuaded that liberty is the natural birthright of all mankind, and keeping any in perpetual slavery is contrary to the injunctions of Christ," therefore, he "did manumit and set absolutely free all his Negroes, thirteen in all, so that henceforth they shall be deemed, adjudged, and taken as free people."

Both Bishops Asbury and Coke were bitter opponents of slavery, and Coke, in April, 1785, because of his open denunciation, barely escaped bodily harm at the hands of a hostile Virginia mob. On another occasion he was indicted by a grand jury because of his anti-slavery activity. Asbury, while equally opposed to slavery, was more cautious in his public statements. Later Coke also tempered his utterances to the rising tide of pro-slavery opinion in the South. Soon both Coke and Asbury learned that by advising slaves to obey their masters, the masters were then willing to listen to what they had to say regarding their duties.

A society which found hearty support among Methodists, as well as among the other churches in every section of the country, was the American Colonization Society, which was formed in 1816. The plan of the organization was to transport free Negroes out of the country and colonize them in Africa. During the early years of this organization it was generally thought that the net influence of colonization would be in the direction of the ultimate abolition of slavery. Annual Conferences year by year, in both North and South, indorsed the activities of the Colonization Society, and many men, who later became leaders in the abolition movement, after 1830, supported whole-heartedly the colonization scheme. After about 1840, however, the Northern churches and Conferences began to grow more and more suspicious of the colonization idea, and the society was accused of being a pro-slavery organization, whose prime purpose was to get rid of the free Negroes, whose presence in the South, particularly, was considered by the slave-owners as a growing menace, and a cause for discontent and possible slave insurrection.

The first phase of anti-slavery agitation had come

to an end by about 1830, and a new and more aggressive phase began. From the beginning of the century certain influences were exerted which made it increasingly difficult for the churches to take an aggressive stand on the question of slavery. The early anti-slavery movement had been largely negative. Its leaders were no doubt sincere in their desire to promote abolition of slavery, but to most of them abolition was a theory to be held, rather than a fact to be accomplished. Thus slave-owners often belonged to the early anti-slavery societies, and slave-owning church members who had no notion of seeing their own slaves actually freed, voted for resolutions condemning the institution.

A new situation was created largely by two factors; first, was the revolution taking place in Southern agriculture known as the rise of cotton culture; the second was the new aggressive anti-slavery leadership arising in the North, producing what is usually termed the abolition movement.

The invention of spinning and weaving machinery created an increasing market for raw cotton in England, while the invention of the cotton gin (1792) made possible the profitable growing of the short staple cotton in the South, and thus greatly increased the total output. Between the years 1791 and 1795 the total production of cotton in the South was 5,200,000 pounds; between 1826 and 1831 the South produced 307,244,400 pounds. Cotton soon became the most important single crop of the nation, and in 1860 it constituted fifty-seven per cent of the total exports of the United States. The economic revolution going on in the South is also reflected in the rising value of slaves. In 1790 good

Negroes could be purchased for $300; the same Negro in 1830 brought $1,200, and in 1860 from $1,500 to $2,000. Thus cotton became the "King" crop of the nation, and since it was generally considered by Southerners that cotton could not be raised without slave labor, slavery became to them an indispensable institution.

While the institution of slavery was becoming increasingly important in the eyes of the South, a new and aggressive anti-slavery movement was arising in the North. This new type of anti-slavery agitation is typified by William Lloyd Garrison and his *Liberator;* by Wendell Phillips with his eloquent appeals for the downtrodden slave; and by John Greenleaf Whittier with his anti-slavery poems. This new gospel of abolitionism was very different from the older negative anti-slavery doctrine and called for immediate and uncompensated emancipation. Garrison announced in his *Liberator* that he would be "as harsh as truth and as uncompromising as justice" on the subject and that he did "not wish to think, or speak, or write with moderation." Soon there were many abolition propagandists as radical as Garrison, and anti-slavery papers and societies sprang up numerously, especially throughout New England, in central New York, northern Ohio and Michigan. Such is the background of the slavery controversy which now arose in all the great democratic churches in the country.

This rabid anti-slavery movement found many supporters among Northern church people, and slavery by the latter eighteen thirties had become the issue of chief importance in the churches. Methodist Conferences in the North and other religious bodies began to pass anti-slavery resolutions, and Methodist anti-slavery societies and Methodist anti-slavery papers soon made their appearance. One of the principal Methodist anti-slavery agitators was Orange Scott, a member of the New England Conference. He subscribed for a hundred copies of the *Liberator* and had them sent to the members of the New England Conference, and when *Zion's Herald* opened its columns to discussions of slavery, Scott became one of the principal contributors. The first Methodist Anti-Slavery Society was formed in New York City in 1834, at which LeRoy Sunderland, another radical champion of the cause, presided. In 1835 both the New England and the New Hampshire Conferences formed anti-slavery societies, and Methodist pulpits began to be opened to abolition speakers.

Naturally, as the agitation continued, the bishops and the other general officials of the Methodist Episcopal Church were increasingly concerned for the unity of the church. The bitter Northern attacks upon slavery brought out pro-slavery defenders in the South, and Southern ministers were not long in finding arguments, based upon the Scriptures, which confirmed their pro-slavery position. The Southern brethren, of course, wanted the extreme anti-slavery agitation stopped, and in the General Conferences from 1832 to 1840 the moderates, combining with the Southern delegates, succeeded in pretty thoroughly muzzling the abolition radicals.

At the General Conference of 1832 there was no action on slavery. The General Conference of 1836, which met at Cincinnati, censured two New England delegates for attending a meeting of the Cincinnati anti-slavery society, and one of the Southern delegates wanted the names of the two members included in the resolutions, in order that they might "be brought forth in all the length and breadth of their damning iniquity." The pastoral address issued by this General Conference to the church at large set forth the hostility of the church to all radical movements and urged that the brethren wholly "refrain from the agitating subject" of abolitionism and "from patronizing any of the abolition publications." Some of the Conferences, as the Philadelphia, contained both free and slavery territory, and to avoid conflict, every man applying for admission to the Conference after 1837 was asked, "Are you an abolitionist?" and if he replied in the affirmative, he was not admitted. In 1837 the Georgia Conference declared slavery not a moral wrong, and an institution with which the church had nothing to do, while the next year the South Carolina Conference passed a similar resolution. The New England Conferences were equally emphatic in expressing their abolition views. At the New England Conference in 1837 an attempt was made to take some action against slavery, but Bishop Waugh refused to allow the resolutions to be introduced, stating that it was not Conference business, and that such action would unchristianize the South. He made a fervid appeal to the Conference and asked: "Will you brethren hazard the unity of the Methodist Episcopal Church . . . by agitating those fearfully exciting topics, and that too, in opposition to the solemn decision and deliberate conclusion of the General Conference?" The preachers, however, were not convinced by the bishop's argument and demanded that they be permitted to express their views, as had the other Conferences.

This "gag" policy, as might have been expected, instead of allaying agitation, only increased it. Unable to introduce their resolutions and express their opinions in their own church Conferences, the abolition ministers began the publication of anti-slavery papers and called anti-slavery conventions. Such conventions were held at Lynn and Lowell, Massachusetts, and at Utica and Cazenovia in New York, while the *Wesleyan Journal,* published in Hallowell, Maine, *The American Wesleyan Observer,* Lowell, Massachusetts, edited by Orange Scott, and *Zion's Watchman,* published in New York, spread far and wide the abolition gospel. LeRoy Sunderland, the editor of *Zion's Watchman,* was brought to trial on two occasions before his Conference on charges of slander and misrepresentation. Nathan Bangs brought the first charges in 1836, which were not sustained, but in 1840 Sunderland was convicted of having slandered Bishop Soule. These bitter experiences finally drove Sunderland from the church and in later life he repudiated orthodox Christianity entirely.

At the General Conference of 1840, which met at Baltimore, the question of slavery received chief consideration. There were many petitions presented, asking for anti-slavery action, and many protesting against any anti-slavery action, but the great question before the Conference, "insistent, transcendent, threatening, on the decision of which hung the future unity of the church, was the question of Conference rights." Would the General Conference confirm the practice of bishops and presiding

METHODISM IN AMERICAN HISTORY

elders in refusing to put a question which in their judgment did not relate to the proper business of Annual or Quarterly Conferences? Such had been the practice for the past four years in numerous instances. The anti-slavery delegates claimed that by so doing the privileges of the Conferences had been curtailed. The bishops asked that the Conference make an authoritative ruling on the question for their future guidance. This the Conference did, stating that the president of a Conference "had the right to decline putting a question, which, in his judgment, did not relate to the proper business of an Annual Conference," but, if requested, his refusal and the reasons therefor must be inserted in the *Journal*. It was also decided that he might adjourn a Conference, when, in his opinion, the proper business of the Conference had been transacted. In other words, it was now decided that the presiding officers were to control fully the activities of all local Conferences, which to the Methodist anti-slavery advocates meant the defeat of their cause.

There is no doubt that the General Conference of 1840 attempted, as it stated, to serve "the best interests of the whole family of American Methodists," but its task was an impossible one. The difficulty of the situation was thus summed up by the Conference itself: The United States was composed of some states where slavery was prohibited; in others slavery was allowed, but the majority of the people are favorable to emancipation; while in still others slavery existed universally and was so interwoven with the civil institutions that the laws disallowed emancipation, and the great majority of the

From *Harper's Weekly*, August 20, 1864. Reproduced by permission

THE CHRISTIAN COMMISSION IN THE FIELD

people considered it treasonable to set forth "anything by word or deed tending that way." The Methodist Episcopal Church extended throughout all these states; therefore, it was utterly impossible to frame a law on slavery that could be satisfactory to all. The report on slavery made by this Conference was noncommittal, and the Conference would not allow a minority report to be presented. Orange Scott, however, was permitted to oppose the adoption of the report, and in a speech which lasted two hours, spoke with dignity, courage, and in a conciliatory manner. But the report was adopted, and the anti-slavery delegates went home disappointed and discouraged.

During the next four years (1840-1844) many things happened to change the situation completely when the General Conference of 1844 convened in New York. Until 1842 it seemed, as Bishop Hedding stated, that the radical excitement in the church was at an end. The Methodist abolitionists were all discouraged, and even the anti-slavery press seemed to have lost its spirit. Numerous individual Methodists withdrew and joined other denominations, while in May, 1841, a small group in Michigan formed themselves into a connection and took the name Wesleyan Methodists, and in two years reported more than a thousand members and seventeen preachers. In the East Scott and Sunderland, with other Methodist abolition leaders, were corresponding as to what had best be the next move. In one letter Scott proposed the formation of a church organization advocating anti-slavery, anti-intemperance and anti-everything-wrong. This correspondence finally resulted in the calling of a convention at Albany in November, 1842, at which it was definitely decided to withdraw from the Methodist Episcopal Church. A paper, *The True Wesleyan*, was established, and in the first issue the reasons for the forming of a new connection were given as follows: (1) The Methodist Episcopal Church having no rule forbidding slaveholding by private members; and by declaring that slaveholding is in harmony with the Golden Rule, and by allowing Annual Conferences to say that it is not a moral wrong, makes itself responsible for slavery; (2) the government of the church is aristocratic; and (3) its attitude toward dissenting brethren is uncharitable.

In May, 1843, a convention was held at Utica, and there the Wesleyan Connection was formally organized. The *Discipline* adopted prohibited slaveholding and the use of intoxicating liquors; it provided for lay representation in the Conferences and permitted Conferences to elect their own presidents, the stationing of the preachers being performed by a committee of six, whose duty it was to confirm as far as possible the arrangements already made between pastors and congregations. The new church was divided into six Conferences, extending from Maine to Michigan, and began with a membership of six thousand members; within eighteen months its membership had increased to fifteen thousand.

Meanwhile how were these happenings being received by the leaders in the Methodist Episcopal Church? *The Christian Advocate and Journal* for November 30, 1842, headed a sarcastic editorial "The Denouement. Wonderful Explosion. Sunderland, Scott & Co. Again," in which occurred the statement "the truth is, this ultra abolitionism is only the mask, the thin disguise, which has been made to hide an ulterior purpose for a long time past." The actual aim of these radical leaders, according to this conservative editor, was to "make a place for themselves," and he predicts the fall of the building they are erecting. While some waxed sarcastic, others considered the movement with great apprehension. The moderates saw that while they had been attempting to avoid a Southern pro-slavery secession, they had precipitated a Northern anti-slavery split, which might become even more serious. This tended to develop the anti-slavery spirit among loyal Methodists in order to stem the exodus already begun.

A series of Methodist anti-slavery conventions were held in 1843 in New England, the purpose of which was to preserve the unity and harmony of the church. One convention, held in New Market, New Hampshire, declared in favor of complete separation from the South and slavery, if necessary, in order to prevent the destruction of the Methodist Episcopal Church in New England. An influence, increasing anti-slavery opinion within the church, was the action of a slaveholders' convention in Maryland in January, 1842, asking that the Legislature pass a law which would result in driving every free Negro from that state or reduce them to bondage. This action aroused even the conservative editor of *The Christian Advocate and Journal*, Dr. Thomas E. Bond, who was himself from Maryland, and for a time the chief Methodist organ became mildly anti-slavery in tone, though very soon the editor assured his Southern constituency that he had returned to "safety and sanity."

The net result of the changing sentiment in the church during the years 1842 to 1844 was that in the General Conference of the latter year anti-slavery delegates for the first time held the balance of power. The past four years had increased the radicalism of both sections, while the moderates were leaning toward the position of the abolitionists. The Conference met on May 1, 1844, in the Greene Street Methodist Episcopal Church, New York City. There were 180 delegates. All parties were ably led. In the Northern moderate group were Stephen Olin, president of Wesleyan University, who had lived in the South and sympathized with both sections; Nathan Bangs, one of the founders of the Missionary Society and historian of the church; Peter Cartwright, the famous backwoods preacher from Illinois; and Charles Elliott, who was to become the official historian of the schism. The Southern delegates were led by Henry B. Bascom, of Kentucky; William Capers, of South Carolina, who had taken the leadership in promoting missions among the slaves; William Winans, now of Mississippi, who had begun his ministry in the old Western Conference; and the two Pierces, father and son, of Georgia, both able representatives of their section. From Virginia was William A. Smith, a stickler for the letter of the constitution, while James Porter and Phineas Crandall were perhaps the outstanding abolition leaders, both from New England.

The question of slavery came up early and occupied the center of the stage throughout the long session, for the Conference did not adjourn until

June 11. The Episcopal Address, read by Bishop Soule, made no reference to slavery, but dwelt at length upon missions to colored people, as much as to say, "Let us occupy ourselves with converting the colored people and cease concerning ourselves regarding their enslavement." An attempt was made to divert the mind of the Conference from the dangerous subject, but it was to no avail, and a standing committee on slavery was raised to consist of one member from each Annual Conference. On May 7 an appeal of Francis A. Harding, of the Baltimore Conference, was made the order of the day, and from that time on slavery had the right of way. Harding had been suspended from his Conference for refusing to manumit certain slaves, that had come into his possession by marriage. The discussion of this case lasted five days, and when finally a vote was taken, the action of the Baltimore Conference was sustained by a vote of 117 to 56. The significant fact of this case is that it revealed the clash "between the two irreconcilable views on slavery represented in the Conference. It revealed also that the opponents of slavery were in the majority, and that they were willing to use their power."

The great discussion over slavery, however, came up in connection with the Report of the Committee on Episcopacy on May 21. Bishop James O. Andrew, a modest, quiet man, "who had never felt quite at home in his elevated position," had, by indirection, become a slave-owner. An old lady, of Augusta, Georgia, had left a slave girl to him, on condition that he should liberate her and send her to Liberia, when the girl reached the required age. The girl refused to go to Liberia, and legally she remained the property of the bishop. He had also inherited from his first wife a slave boy, which the laws of Georgia prohibited him from setting free, and on his second marriage, he had married a lady who had inherited slaves from her first husband's estate. When Bishop Andrew reached Baltimore on the way to the Conference, he learned that his connection with slavery was causing great excitement in the church, and that his affairs would probably be investigated. This disquieting news, added to his natural inclinations, determined him to resign, for he thought this action might allay the excitement and prevent a dangerous situation from arising. This intention he communicated to his Southern brethren, but the Southern delegates objected to his resignation and assured him that his resignation would most certainly lead to the withdrawal of the Southern churches. On the other hand, a large majority of the Northern delegates were determined that slavery should never be connected in any way with episcopacy.

The committee on episcopacy fully investigated the affairs of Bishop Andrew, and when the matter was presented to the Conference, a resolution was introduced in which he was affectionately requested to resign. Later James B. Finley offered a milder substitute, and instead of asking the bishop to resign, requested him to "desist from the exercise of this office so long as this impediment remains." There now followed a remarkable debate, which lasted eleven days and fills about a hundred pages of the official record of the Conference. In the course of the debate the real issue, slavery, fell into the background, while its legal and constitutional phases became prominent. The Southern delegates took the position that the episcopacy was a co-ordinate body with the General Conference, and therefore, the Conference had no constitutional right to suspend a bishop. They contended that Bishop Andrew had violated no rule of the church, since a resolution had been passed in 1840 legalizing slaveholding in all grades of the ministry. This view the Northern brethren denied. They claimed that a bishop was simply an officer of the General Conference and was amenable to it in every respect. Still others argued that the question was not one of law, or the constitution, but of expediency. Bishop Andrew could never preside over a Northern Conference as long as he was a slaveholder, therefore he should resign. To this the Southerners replied that if continuing a slaveholding bishop in office would work disaster in the North, his suspension from his office for that reason would work ruin in the South.

On May 30 the bishops took a hand at trying to find some compromise and proposed that no afternoon session be held. The next day they brought in a proposal that the whole question be postponed for four years, suggesting that Bishop Andrew's embarrassment might, by that time, be removed. To this proposition all the bishops attached their names. Bishop Hedding, among the several bishops, was the only one who leaned in the direction of the abolitionists. So far the Northern radicals had taken little part in the debate, since in both the Harding case and in the debate over Bishop Andrew the moderates had become the defenders of the radical viewpoint, and things were, therefore, going to their satisfaction. The bishops' suggestion to postpone the whole question for four years now aroused the abolitionists, and on presenting their case to Bishop Hedding, he was persuaded to withdraw his name from the bishops' report. Since the bishops were now no longer unanimous, the suggested plan was laid on the table. The New Englanders felt that the adoption of such a plan would work disaster to their section, though postponement was undoubtedly acceptable to the Southerners, and perhaps to a majority of others. On June 1 the question of the virtual suspension of Bishop Andrew came to a vote and was carried, 111 ayes to 60 nays. Only one of the affirmative votes came from the slaveholding section of the church, while 17 of the negative votes came from non-slaveholding Conferences.

The church had now come to the parting of the ways. To preserve its unity everything possible had been done by sincere men, representing all sections; and the long debates had been carried on in fine spirit. No one can read the reports of the discussion without a feeling that able Christian men were bending every effort to see eye to eye. But it was an impossible situation, and division was now inevitable.

When the vote was taken, showing beyond any doubt that the anti-slavery party had won, a spirit of concession became manifest at once. On June 3 Doctor Capers brought in a series of resolutions proposing the formation of two equal and co-ordinate General Conferences, divided by the line between the slave and free states. Foreign missions and publishing interests were to be carried on jointly. This plan was referred to a committee of nine. Before action could be taken on this proposal, a resolution was presented calling upon the Conference "to devise, if possible, a constitutional plan for a mutual and friendly division of the church." This was followed by the presentation of another document, signed by fifty-two delegates, declaring that "the continued agitation on the subject of slavery and abolition" and the frequent action on the subject in the General Conference, together with "the extra-judicial proceedings against Bishop Andrew," produced a situation in the South which made the continuance of the jurisdiction of the General Conference over the Southern Conferences "inconsistent with the success of the ministry in the slaveholding states." This was also referred to a second committee of nine. Three days later the Southern delegates entered their protest against the action of the Conference in the case of Bishop Andrew, closing with an expression of hope that if the minority found it necessary to separate, that it could be done with justice to all sections. The next day, June 7, the report of the committee of nine was presented, which has come to be known as the Plan of Separation.

The following is a summary of this Plan:

In the event of separation, which was considered not improbable, the General Conference was to proceed with Christian kindness and strictest equity.

If the Annual Conferences in the slaveholding states found it necessary to unite in a distinct ecclesiastical connection, the Northern boundary should be determined by the following rule:

All the societies, stations, and Conferences adhering to the Church in the South, by a vote of the majority of the members of said societies, stations, and Conferences, shall remain under the unmolested pastoral care of the Southern

Church; and the ministers of the Methodist Episcopal Church shall in no wise attempt to organize churches or societies within the limits of the Church, South, nor shall they attempt to exercise any pastoral oversight therein; it being understood that the ministers of the South reciprocally observe the same rule in relation to stations, societies, and Conferences adhering by vote of a majority to the Methodist Episcopal Church, *Provided* also that this rule shall apply only to societies, stations, and Conferences bordering on the line of division, and not to interior charges, which shall in all cases be left to the care of that church within whose territory they are situated.

Other resolutions provided that ministers had the privilege of choosing between the two churches; recommended that the Annual Conferences repeal the restrictive rule regulating the proceeds of The Methodist Book Concern; provided for the transfer to the Church South of all Book Concern property located there, as well as accounts owed to the Concern by ministers and citizens of the South; made arrangements for the division of the Book Concern property and all other general funds, and requested that the bishops bring before the Annual Conferences such matters as required their action.

An interesting debate now followed in which various views were expressed. Charles Elliott, of the Ohio Conference, favored the plan because he had felt for some time that the church was too large and would soon need to be divided in some way in any case. The Southern delegates, as a rule, favored the plan. Several from the border Conferences opposed it, as did Peter Cartwright, of Illinois, and Dr. T. E. Bond,[1] of Baltimore, on the ground that

---

[1] Bond was not a member of the Conference, but as editor of *The Christian Advocate and Journal* had great influence.

it would create war and strife along the border. But an overwhelming majority, North and South, voted on June 8 to adopt the Plan of Separation, the vote standing 136 ayes to but 15 nays. Three days later the Conference adjourned.

While the lawmaking body of the church had been considering the momentous question for nearly a month and a half, the church throughout the country was watching the outcome with growing agitation. All over the South meetings were being held and resolutions passed denouncing the alleged tyranny of the Northern majority. *The Richmond Christian Advocate* printed "at least sixty-seven sets of resolutions passed by such meetings" between July 4, 1844, and March 1, 1845. The resolutions eulogized Bishops Soule and Andrew and denounced abolitionism as a "foul spirit of the pit whose mildew breath" would blast the Church of God. Most were violent in their denunciation of foes, and fulsome in their praise of friends. All this, of course, found response and resentment in the North, and the gulf of misunderstanding was thereby made wider.

The day following the adjournment of the General Conference the Southern delegates convened in New York and drew up an address to the members of the Southern Conferences. After reviewing what had taken place at the Conference, especially in regard to the Plan of Separation, they suggested the calling of a convention to meet in Louisville, Kentucky, on May 1, 1845, to be composed of delegates from the Southern Conferences, one for every seven members. The Southern Annual Conferences, with practically complete unanimity, indorsed the calling of the convention and elected delegates. Some of the Conferences were still in favor of one more effort to prevent division, while the Virginia Conference suggested that the Southern Conferences should not dissolve their connection with the Methodist Episcopal Church, but only with the General Conference. But these suggested compromises had no effect in delaying the formation of a separate Southern church.

The Southern convention met at Louisville at the appointed time; it was made up of delegates from thirteen Conferences. The three bishops present— Soule, Andrew, and Morris—were invited to preside. Soule and Andrew consented, while Morris declined. The work of the convention moved quickly, a committee made up of two from each Conference carrying on the real work, while the other members occupied their time making speeches, some of which, even in the eyes of the Southerners, misrepresented the Northern brethren. On May 15 the Committee on Organization made its report. This included a declaration of independence of the Southern portion of the church from the jurisdiction of the General Conference; and a statement that it was "right, expedient, and necessary to erect the Annual Conferences represented in this convention into a distinct ecclesiastical connection." They declared their desire "to maintain Christian union and fraternal relations with their Northern brethren and expressed their willingness" "to consider any proposition or plan having for its object the union of the two great bodies in the North and South." Bishops Soule and Andrew were invited to become their bishops. On June 17 the report of the committee was adopted, 95 to 2, and the Methodist Episcopal Church, South, thus became a fact.

A year later, May, 1846, the first General Conference of the Methodist Episcopal Church, South, convened at Petersburg, Virginia. The new church had adopted the old *Discipline* with only a few verbal changes, since the South had always contended that the fundamental law, when correctly understood and interpreted, fully protected their rights. At the first General Conference attempts were made to change the sections in the *Discipline* on slavery, but the majority were hostile to any change. Later attempts to change the ruling on slavery were made in other General Conferences before the Civil War, but they too were unsuccessful, and thus, strange as it may appear, the two branches of American Methodism continued to have the same rules on slavery until 1860.

CHAPTER XIII

TWO EPISCOPAL METHODISMS—1845-1861

THE period from the organization of the Methodist Episcopal Church, South, to the opening of the Civil War may well be termed the tragic era in the history of American Methodism, for these were years of gathering storm, of widening abyss.

The Church South, at the Petersburg General Conference, had elected, in addition to Andrew and Soule, two bishops—William Capers and Robert Paine. Editors for the three *Christian Advocates* within their bounds, at Richmond, Charleston, and Louisville, were chosen; H. B. Bascom was made editor of a new *Quarterly Review;* a missionary secretary was elected; a commission of three was appointed to meet with a similar commission from "the other church," to look after their interests in the Book Concern, and the last important action was the selection by a rising and unanimous vote of Dr. Lovick Pierce to visit the next General Conference of the Methodist Episcopal Church to be held in Pittsburgh in 1848 "to tender to that body the Christian regards and fraternal salutations of the General Conference of the Methodist Episcopal Church, South."

Meanwhile changes were rapidly taking place within the Methodist Episcopal Church. The Northern delegates to the General Conference of 1844 returned to their homes to meet a rising tide of disapproval of what they had done in New York. Immediately there broke forth a heated newspaper controversy over the expediency and constitutionality of the Plan of Separation. Did the General Conference possess the powers which were assumed in the drawing up of such a plan? Many thought the General Conference a "body of delegated and limited powers," but it had proceeded as though it could do whatever it pleased. Others claimed that the Conference had infringed upon the fifth restrictive rule, "which prohibited the Conference from abridging the rights of trial and appeal"; some said the third restrictive rule had been violated in modifying the general superintendency, so as to hinder the bishops from traveling freely over all the connection. Doctor Bangs, arguing for the validity of the Plan, stated that the General Conference was the sole judge of the validity of its own acts, though some of the Annual Conferences declared that they had the right to pass on the constitutionality of General Conference action, and straightway proceeded to declare the Plan null and void. Some of the stanchest supporters of the Plan on the floor of the General Conference of 1844, Dr. Charles Elliott, for example, turned complete somersaults, and soon were numbered among its most bitter opponents.

The Northern Annual Conferences which voted earliest on the recommendation to change the sixth restrictive rule, permitting the dividing of the Book Concern properties, were found to be overwhelmingly in favor of the change. When, however, the later Conferences convened, it was found that a strong wave of opposition had developed, and the recommendation was defeated, in spite of the fact that the Southern Conferences had voted unanimously in the affirmative.[1]

This change in Northern sentiment was due to several factors. One was the hostile action of the Southern Conferences, and the violent language which they had employed in denouncing the North. Another was the fear, especially on the part of the radical abolitionists, that the Southern church would serve to perpetuate slavery, while perhaps the most general reason was the revulsion of feeling which came with the thought of a divided church. But whatever the causes, when the General Conference of the Methodist Episcopal Church convened in Pittsburgh in 1848, the great majority of the delegates were found to be in opposition to the Plan of Separation, upon which the Southern Conferences had proceeded to set up a new church.

Few of the members of the General Conference of 1844 were chosen to the Conference of 1848. In some Annual Conferences only those who were pledged to vote against the Plan of Separation were elected as delegates, and when the Pittsburgh Conference assembled, its temper was soon manifest.[2]

On the third day of the Conference Dr. Lovick Pierce presented his credentials, stating that he was the delegate appointed to bear the Christian saluta-

[1] For a discussion of the action of Annual Conferences regarding the sixth restrictive rule, see Norwood, J. N., *The Schism in the Methodist Church, 1844*, pp. 117-118.

[2] Myers, E. H., *The Disruption of the Methodist Episcopal Church 1844-1846*. Nashville, Tennessee, & Macon, Georgia, 1875. A very bitter Southern account of the events of these years. Myers states that only forty-one who voted in the General Conference of 1844 were delegates in 1848. Of these forty-one, eleven had voted against the Plan, and of the thirty remaining, five voted against repudiation in 1848.

From a photograph furnished by Duke University

THE CHAPEL OF DUKE UNIVERSITY

tions of the Church South to the Northern brethren, assuring them that his church desired to maintain "at all times a warm, confiding, and fraternal relation to each other." This communication was referred to a committee, which, after due deliberation, reported:

That, while we tender to the Rev. Dr. Pierce all personal courtesies, and invite him to attend our sessions, this General Conference does not consider it proper at present to enter into fraternal relations with the Methodist Episcopal Church, South.

An amendment was added, stating that nothing in the resolution was to be so construed as to hinder Doctor Pierce or any other representative of his church from making any proposition looking toward the settlement of the difficulties between the two bodies.

Doctor Pierce naturally declined the invitation to a seat within the bar of the Conference, stating that his church could never renew the offer of fraternal relations between the two great bodies of Wesleyan Methodists. "But," he said, "the proposition can be renewed at any time, either now or hereafter, by the Methodist Episcopal Church; and if ever made on the basis of the Plan of Separation, as adopted by the General Conference of 1844, the Church South will cordially entertain the proposition."

The commissioners from the Southern church were also present to adjust all matters pertaining to the Book Concern properties and all general funds, but, of course, their mission likewise was futile.

The whole question of the validity of the Plan of Separation was referred to a committee "On the

State of the Church,"[3] of which Dr. George Peck was chairman. On May 24 this committee made its report, and after several days of discussion a vote was taken on its several parts, in which the opponents of the action of the General Conference of 1844 were overwhelmingly in the majority. Thus the General Conference of 1848 completely repudiated what the Conference of 1844 had done for the following reasons: (1) there was no necessity for division; (2) the Southern church had violated the Plan by crossing the line of division; (3) the Annual Conferences had failed to authorize a division of the church property. Because of these and other violations, the Methodist Episcopal Church, South, they declare, have themselves overthrown the Plan, "and have left none of it remaining for us to overthrow; and now, in pronouncing it null and void, the South have compelled us to this action."

A recent and capable student of this great controversy, and a non-Methodist, looking at the issues involved with an impartial eye, has come to this conclusion:

While it is easy to explain the action of the Conference of 1848, it is not easy to justify it. True, the church loved its unity and power. It was a pity to disrupt a mighty aggregation of Christians. True, the patience of Northern Methodists had been sorely tried by the bitterness of Southern partisans. True, some in the South adopted too selfish an interpretation of the boundary provisions of the Plan. It may be true in the long run repudiation worked good rather than harm in simplifying the situation for both branches of American Episcopal Methodists. Nay, even

[3] *Journal of the General Conference of the Methodist Episcopal Church,* held in Pittsburgh, Pennsylvania, 1848. New York: Lane and Scott, 1848. See pp. 68; 73-78; 80-85; 86-89. See also full report of the Committee on the State of the Church, Appendix, pp. 154-171.

while we admit for the sake of argument that the Conference of 1848 had a strict legal right to nullify the Plan, still we find it impossible to contemplate its acts with complete approval. The Plan was a wonderful exhibition of Christian charity, manifested in a situation as baffling as any that ever confronted a great religious assembly. In that sense the Plan was the glory of a self-sacrificing church. In agreeing to it the church followed closely in the footsteps of its Head. When removed from the mellowing influences of that trying session, the North took a more cold-blooded view of the issue; Northern Methodists concluded that their delegates had gone too far. Repudiation was born and grew lustily. If the Southerners wished to leave, let them leave as seceders. This feeling marked a violent reaction from the noble expressions and acts of the General Conference of 1844. Then in 1848, when the partner most vitally interested in the Plan was unrepresented, the other half of the supposedly dissolved partnership, assuming to act as judge in its own case, declared the act sanctioning dissolution unconstitutional, null and void from the start. Admitting the difficulties of the problem, and speaking in all charity, we cannot help feeling that it was a mistake to repudiate the Plan of Separation.[4]

Whether or not the Northern Methodists acted unwisely in the General Conference of 1848, their repudiation of the Plan of Separation created a situation out of which was soon to come increased contention and bitterness. Those who had predicted conflict along the border now saw their predictions come true. Immediately each church began to make great efforts to retain the border Conferences and churches, and there was constant conflict between them in such regions as Missouri, Kentucky,

---

[4] The author of this statement is Professor J. N. Norwood, of Alfred University, Alfred, New York, in his *Schism in the Methodist Church, 1844*, pp. 124-125. This study was a dissertation presented at Cornell University in partial fulfillment for the degree of Doctor of Philosophy. Professor Norwood's study is a triumph of impartiality.

western Virginia, and Maryland, up to the outbreak of the Civil War. It was not an uncommon
occurrence for a church service, conducted by one
side of the controversy, to be broken up by a mob
representing the other. One form which the border
conflict took was disputes over church property. In
Maysville, Kentucky, the Methodist congregation
was divided, one faction adhering to the Northern
church, the other to the Southern, the dispute finally
getting into the courts, and eventually reaching the
Court of Appeals, where the Church South finally
won. In Missouri a small minority of the Missouri
Conference attempted to keep that Conference with
the North, though only fourteen members voted to
remain with the anti-slavery church. In Saint Louis
several congregations were in hopeless confusion,
and everywhere Northern minorities were urged to
stand firm, and a new church paper, the *Central
Christian Advocate,* was established in Saint Louis
to help bolster up the Northern cause.

Attempts were made to stop the circulation of
Northern church papers in western Virginia and
Missouri. A grand jury in Wood County, Virginia,
declared that the *Western Christian Advocate* was
an "incendiary publication printed with the intent
to make insurrection within the commonwealth of
Virginia," and to read or even to receive it was
deemed an act of felony to be punished with imprisonment up to five years. Even the Wyandot Indians, then living at the forks of the Missouri and
Kansas Rivers, in what is now eastern Kansas,
and among whom the Methodist Episcopal
Church had begun its missionary work, were divided over the question of their church allegiance.

In 1848 the Indian congregation voted on the question, and a majority favored the Church South. The minority was not satisfied with the decision, however, and attempts were made to reverse it, and they asked the Northern church to send them a missionary. Finally the majority appealed to the Indian Agent, requesting that "he keep out of our territory those reverend disturbers of the nation," while the non-Christian Indians, disgusted with the whole squabble, decided that the missionaries of both churches should be expelled from their tribe.[5]

The conflict in Missouri was the most bitter, and with the passage of the Kansas-Nebraska Bill in 1854 opening up Kansas Territory for settlement, the churches soon became more than ever involved, as the settlers passed through Missouri on the way to Kansas. With the introduction and final passage of the Kansas-Nebraska Bill, which specifically repealed the Missouri Compromise, moral and religious sentiment throughout the nation was greatly stirred. Three thousand New England clergymen of all denominations signed a protest, while all the Northern church papers took an active part in the discussion of the measure. *Zion's Herald* proclaimed that the passage of the bill was a "treacherous deed, disgraceful alike to the Senate and the nation." The papers of the Church South, on the other hand, severely criticized the Northern church editors for taking part in political discussion. One Southern editor declared: "We most sincerely wish that he"—the editor of *The Christian Advocate and Journal*—"and all the religious editors in this land would

[5] *Kansas State Historical Collections*, Vol. IX, pp. 217-219. See also Swaney, p. 166.

261

attend to their appropriate work, and leave great national questions and state politics to the people as citizens. . . . Better preach repentance and holiness than to meddle with the organizations of states and territories."[6] Another Southern editor urged "Southern Methodist preachers, as such," to "stick to their work of great moral reform and allow the people who are competent to attend to the affairs of the nation and the state."

While this bitter border conflict between the two Episcopal Methodisms was in progress, the controversy over slavery was by no means at an end within the Methodist Episcopal Church itself. In 1856 there were six Annual Conferences of the Methodist Episcopal Church which were wholly or in part in slave territory. This fact, the bishops in their address to the General Conference of 1856 stated, did "not tend to extend or perpetuate slavery." On the other hand, there was a growing party within the church which refused to agree with the bishops and favored the complete withdrawal from slave territory and urged the passage of a rule entirely prohibiting slaveholding by church members. This course was opposed by the Methodists living in or adjacent to slave territory. The several church papers lined up on each side of the issue; the *Northwestern* of Chicago, the *Northern* of Auburn, New York, and *Zion's Herald* favored withdrawal from slave territory, while the *Central* of Saint Louis, the *Western* of Cincinnati, the *Pittsburgh* and the New York *Advocates* argued for the continuance of the church in slave territory and opposed any change in the rule on slavery. The *Northwestern* warned

---

[6] *Nashville and Louisville Christian Advocate,* April 6, 1854.

the border Conferences that they were "on the road to the Church South, by a philosophical necessity." To this warning the *Central* replied that there was no such danger, for there was a radical difference in the spirit of the two churches, which will forever prevent any affiliation. and the brethren in the free states could always exercise watchful care over the church in slave territory.

As time went on, the radical party gradually gained in numbers and influence, and at the General Conference of 1860 a new rule on slavery was adopted which read: "We believe that the buying, selling, or holding human beings as chattels is contrary to the laws of God and nature; inconsistent with the Golden Rule, and with that rule in our *Discipline* which requires all who desire to remain among us to do no harm, and to avoid evil of every kind; we, therefore, affectionately admonish all our preachers and people to keep themselves pure from this great evil, and to seek its extirpation by all lawful and Christian means." The passage of this "New Chapter on Slavery" aroused protests from the border Conferences and resulted in the withdrawal from the church of numerous ministers and members, many of whom went over to the Church South. The Baltimore Conference was divided over the new rule and a majority of its ministers voted for an immediate separation from the church.

Another issue which tended to widen the breach between the two churches was the contest which ensued over the division of the Book Concern properties. As we have seen, the Annual Conferences had failed to pass by the required three-fourths majority the recommendation to change the sixth restrictive rule, to permit the division of the Book Concern. When the Southern commissioners presented themselves at Pittsburgh in 1848 to adjust the property question the Northern body faced a strange dilemma. Some argued that the General Conference did not possess the power to divide the Book Concerns, and since the Annual Conferences had voted against the suspension of the sixth restrictive rule, the authority of the commissioners was thereby vetoed. Elliott stated that if the funds were divided with the South, then earlier seceders would put in their claims and future divisions would be encouraged, and if the South were given the funds, it would only use them to promote unscriptural division in the church.

Some, be it said, were anxious to adjust amicably the property matter, among them the editor of *The Christian Advocate and Journal*, Dr. T. E. Bond, who, though an enemy of the Plan of Separation, had strong convictions on the justice of the Southern claim to its share of the Book Concern. Many of the arguments advanced against any division were little more than mere quibbling, and in the clear light of history seem unworthy of Christian men, and one could well wish that such arguments had not been used. Handicapped by the vote of the Annual Conferences the General Conference of 1848 proposed the following scheme, after stating that they wished to go as far as their constitutional powers permitted: 1. The book agents at Cincinnati should submit the dispute to voluntary arbitration, if they should find that they had a legal right to do so. 2. If this proved impossible and the South began a legal suit, they might propose an arbitration under the authority of the court. 3. In case neither of these plans materialized, the Annual Conferences should again be appealed to, to suspend the sixth restrictive rule.

It was soon found that the agents had no legal power to offer voluntary arbitration, and in December, 1848, they so informed the Southern commissioners. Since the South had not yet brought suit, it became the duty of the bishops to present the matter of suspending the sixth restrictive rule again to the Annual Conferences. Six Conferences had voted, two—the Baltimore and the Philadelphia—voting unanimously to suspend, while four—the New England, Troy, Black River, and Providence—to reject, when the voting was stopped by the commencement of a suit brought by the Southern commissioners. The Church South has been criticized for destroying the only peaceful means of settling the matter, but it is doubtful whether the Conferences would have changed their decision, and, besides, the voting in the Annual Conferences was stirring up the old arguments, and a whole crop of new ones were germinating, so that perhaps in the long run the bringing of the suit in the United States Court was best for all concerned.[7]

The story of the *Methodist Church Property Case*[8] is soon told. On August 20, 1849, the Church South gave notice that they had entered suit in the

---

[7] Norwood, J. N., *The Schism in the Methodist Church, 1844.* Chap. VII, "The Settlement of the Property Case," is the best discussion of this difficult question.

[8] Sutton, R., *The Methodist Church Property Case.* Richmond and Louisville: John Early for the Methodist Episcopal Church, South, 1851. This report was published with the common sanction of the book agents at New York and Richmond. Sutton was the special and Congressional reporter.

United States Circuit Court for New York, Pennsylvania, and Ohio, for the division of the New York Book Concern property. The suit over the Ohio property had been filed the previous month, but it was not argued until June 4, 1852. The suit brought in New York was tried in May, 1851, in the United States Circuit Court for the southern district of New York. Each side secured famous counsel. The Church South was represented by Daniel Lord and Reverdy Johnson, Sr., and his son Reverdy Johnson, Jr., while the famous jurist Rufus Choate headed the counsel for the defense. The New York case was decided in favor of the Church South, while the decision in the Ohio case was favorable to the Northern defendants. The South, having lost the suit in Ohio, appealed to the Supreme Court of the United States in April, 1854. The highest court in the land reversed the decision of the lower court and ordered a pro rata division of the Book Concern properties. The final decision of the court accepted the Plan of Separation as valid, and stated that the superannuated preachers in the Southern church were as much entitled to their share of the profits of the Book Concern as were the Northern preachers. One of the distinguished members of the Supreme Court at this time was Justice McLean, who was a stanch Methodist, and in the deliberations of the court in this case he took no part, but after the decision was made he proved a real peacemaker and succeeded in getting representatives of the two churches to agree to a final settlement. The South was awarded altogether $275,000 by the book agents in New York and about $100,000 by the settlement of the Cincinnati agents, and at the same time the

TWO EPISCOPAL METHODISMS—1845-1861

Chartered Fund was amicably divided, the South receiving $17,000.

The Southern church was, of course, jubilant at the outcome of the suits. Many in the North, however, denounced the decision as a political one, and felt that a great wrong had been done the church, but others were inclined to rejoice that the Plan of Separation had thus been validated, while the entire church breathed a sigh of relief that the whole miserable affair was at last at an end.

While both churches had been concerned with the affairs growing out of this long contest, they had not permitted it to completely absorb their attention. The fifteen years previous to the Civil War were active ones for both North and South.

In the five General Conferences between 1844 and 1860 the following bishops had been elected by the Methodist Episcopal Church: 1844, Leonidas L. Hamline and Edmund S. Janes; in 1848 there were no episcopal elections, but in 1852, at the seventeenth General Conference, meeting in Boston, four bishops were chosen all on the first ballot, Levi Scott, Matthew Simpson, Osmon C. Baker, and Edward R. Ames. There were no further episcopal elections until the General Conference of 1864. To the General Conference of 1852 Bishop Hamline had sent a letter tendering his resignation as bishop, accompanying it with his certificate of ordination. His reason for this action was ill health, which rendered him unfitted for the work. The General Conference, though reluctant to accept the resignation, finally did so, and by this action the Conference definitely established the position of the Methodist Episcopal Church in regard to the episcopal office.

Bishop Hamline had taken the position in the Bishop Andrew case that a bishop could be legally relieved of his office, and opposed the position that "once a bishop, always a bishop." Thus was established the right of a bishop to resign, and of the General Conference to accept, and repudiated the idea that the bishop's office constitutes a third order.[9]

The church periodicals during these years were becoming increasingly important. By 1860 there had come to be eight official *Advocates,* besides a German weekly, *The Christian Apologist (Der Christliche Apologete), The Methodist Quarterly Review,* a literary magazine; *The Ladies Repository,* a Missionary paper, and four Sunday-school publications. *Zion's Herald and Wesleyan Journal* was the most influential nonofficial paper, though several others were published. Of the editors of this period Thomas E. Bond, of the New York paper, followed by Abel Stevens (1856-1860), and Edward Thomson (1860-1864); Charles Elliott, first of the *Pittsburgh Advocate,* and later of the *Western* and *Central;* Matthew Simpson, of the *Western* (1848-1852), and John McClintock, of the *Quarterly Review,* were perhaps the most conspicuous. In 1860 the New York *Advocate* had 29,-000 subscribers, the *Western* 31,000, the *Northwestern* 13,300, and the *Sunday School Advocate* had a circulation of more than 200,000.

While the slavery controversy was occupying the main attention of the leaders in the church, momen-

---

[9] Hibbard, F. G., *Biography of Rev. Leonidas L. Hamline,* pp. 354, 368, 369. New York and Cincinnati: The Methodist Book Concern, 1880.

tous happenings were taking place in the nation. In 1836 Texas had achieved independence from Mexico, and twelve years later the treaty which brought to a close the War with Mexico had given the United States vast new territories in the Southwest. The discovery of gold in the far West started a rush of population to the Pacific Coast and California unequaled in the history of America, and California was soon applying for admission into the Union. The beginning of the movement of population into the Oregon country has already been noted, and with the settlement of the northern boundary dispute with Great Britain, from the Rocky Mountains to the Pacific, increasing numbers of settlers were attracted to the fertile regions west of the Cascade range.

By order of the General Conference of 1848 the Oregon and California Mission Conference was formed, and Isaac Owen, of Indiana, was the first missionary to California, receiving his appointment in the spring of 1849. Owen made his way across the plains in wagons drawn by oxen. William Taylor, of Baltimore, later to become a bishop, was the second California missionary. Taylor purchased a church and shipped it by way of Cape Horn to San Francisco, where he arrived in 1849, and soon achieved fame as a street preacher.[10] Three other missionaries arrived in 1850, and the following year the *California Christian Advocate* began publication. In 1852 the Oregon country was set apart as a separate Conference, and in 1856 the *Pacific Christian Advocate* began publication at Portland, Ore-

[10] Taylor, William, *Seven Years' Street Preaching in San Francisco, California.* New York: Phillips and Hunt, 1856.

gon. As early as 1844 a Methodist college, known as Willamette University, had been started at Salem, Oregon, while in 1851 an institution was chartered as California Wesleyan College, located near San José, which later took the more ambitious name, University of the Pacific.

Bad political and economic conditions in western Europe sent a flood of German immigrants to seek their fortunes in America during the years from 1830 to 1860. This immigration became particularly large during the forties, and in 1847 alone more than fifty thousand entered the United States. In the early years of the Methodist Episcopal Church a great opportunity had been lost when Asbury and his colaborers failed to provide for Methodist work among the Germans of Pennsylvania and adjoining states, with the result that two German Methodistic bodies were formed, the United Brethren in Christ (1800) and the Evangelical Association (1803). In the early thirties the editor of the *Western Christian Advocate* began to urge that work be begun among the rapidly increasing new German population, and to this work William Nast, a young German, who had come to the United States in 1828, was appointed and began his work in Cincinnati in 1835.

German work now developed in many Conferences, and in 1839 a German religious weekly, *Der Christliche Apologete,* began publication at Cincinnati with Nast as the editor. This position Nast held for more than fifty years, and at the same time busied himself with extensive writing and translating and was the founder of German Methodist literature in America. Nast was also one of the founders of German-Wallace College at Berea, Ohio (1864), and for many years was its nominal president. This institution grew out of a German department which had been established at Baldwin University, designed to educate German candidates for the ministry. By the opening of the Civil War more than a million Germans, nineteenth-century immigrants, had entered the United States, and Methodist work among them prospered accordingly. At first the German work[11] in the Conference was placed under one or more German presiding elders, but this plan proved distasteful to the Germans, and they petitioned the General Conference (1864) for separate Annual Conferences. Accordingly, at this General Conference three German Conferences were formed, and provision was made for the eventual formation of a fourth.

During these years a beginning was also made in the introduction of Methodism among Scandinavian immigrants. The founder of this work was Olof Gustaf Hedström, a Swedish sailor, who was stranded in New York in 1825, by the disbanding of the crew of his ship. Soon after this he married an American woman and professed conversion to Methodism. In 1835 he was admitted to membership in the New York Conference, serving English congregations for a number of years. In 1845 he began his work for Scandinavian immigrants in an old ship in New York harbor, and here for thirty years he conducted a place of refuge and spiritual consolation for be-

---

[11] *Geschichte der Zentral Deutschen Konferenz, Einschliezlich der Anfangsgeschichte des deutschen Methodismus*, von C. Golder, J. H. Horst, J. B. Schall (Cincinnati: n.d.), is the best source for an understanding of the early German work.

wildered immigrants of his native land. His brother, Jonas J. Hedström, became the founder of Swedish Methodism in the West.[12]

After the slavery schism each branch of the Methodist Episcopal Church became denominationally conscious to an exaggerated degree, and as a result carried on its work with an increased aggressiveness. The Methodist Episcopal Church, South, was especially active in its work among the Negroes and Indians and soon had missionaries working in California, Oregon, Idaho, and Washington territories, as well as in the new regions of the Southwest. The Southern church also sent out its first foreign missionaries to China in 1848.

The Church South, however, up to the time of the Civil War confined its missionary work principally to the slave population. From the beginning of Methodism in America Negroes had been admitted into church membership, and in the *Minutes* for 1786, the first in which Negroes are listed separately, there were 1,890 Negro members. But there was little or no attempt to reach the slaves on isolated plantations, especially in the further South, until 1828. The early stringent rules against slave-holding naturally caused suspicion on the part of slave-owners against Methodist preachers, and access to their slaves was often denied. With the toning down of General Conference legislation, and the fact that an increasing number of Methodists became slave-owners, opposition to Methodist work

[12] Stephenson, G. M., *The Religious Aspects of Swedish Immigration.* Minneapolis: The University of Minnesota Press, 1932. Chaps. VIII and XVIII contain materials relating to the beginning of Swedish Methodism both in Sweden and America.

272

among the slaves largely ceased. By 1844 there were at least 200 traveling preachers owning 1,600 slaves; a thousand local preachers held 10,000; while there were at least 25,000 Methodist laymen holding more than two hundred thousand slaves. It has been estimated that there were twice as many slaves held by Methodists than were owned by Southern Baptists. The very fact that there were so many slaves held by Methodists would naturally give rise to a feeling of responsibility for slaves in general, on the part of the Southern Methodist Church. The attitude of the Southern Methodists toward the religious work among the slaves is well summed up in the following statement:

Originally brought from Western Africa, the most ignorant and degraded portion of the realm of paganism; enslaved, many of them, in their fatherland; victims of debasing superstitions; what recuperative element was there to be found in their condition? That inscrutable providence of God, whose march through the centuries is apparently slow but with unerring tread and in the right direction, seems to have overruled the cupidity of the British slave-traders, and allowed an exodus of hundreds of thousands of Africa's children to the shores of this country, where, under the mild form of servitude known in the Southern states, they contribute to the feeding and clothing of the world, and at the same time are environed with the light and saving influence of Christian civilization. Unfit for political freedom, unable to govern themselves; put by color and cast, as well as by intellectual inferiority, beyond the possibility of any future absorption into the dominant white race, their condition requires but one additional element to render it, in their present circumstances, in the South, the best that appears attainable by them—and that is religious instruction, adapted to their mental capabilities. Much has been said or "shrieked" by traders in philanthropy, concerning the "chattel" into which the Negro has been transformed by Southern legislation. The fact, however, remains unaltered, that the Southern law considers the slave a *person*, treats him as possessed of *ethical* character, and protects him as fully in his place, as it does his master in his. And public opinion freely concedes that moral capabilities and an immortal destiny righteously demand moral cultivation, religious opportunities—in a word, the gospel, which is the chartered right of the poor, and the precious boon of the "bond" as well as the free. The master is under obligation to have his servant taught the duties he owes to God and man. This is one of the responsibilities involved in the relation between the parties; and from this responsibility there is no escape while the relation exists and while the sanction of the New Testament is claimed for it.[13]

From 1829 onward work among plantation Negroes advanced rapidly, and within ten years there were seventeen missionaries working under three superintendents on two hundred and thirty-four plantations. William Capers became the first superintendent of these missions, while "some of the best preachers in Southern Methodism spent their best days in this work." In 1850 there were 135,594 colored members of the Methodist Church, South, while by 1858 the number had increased to 188,036.

The second General Conference of the Methodist Episcopal Church, South, convened in Saint Louis in 1850 and elected H. B. Bascom to the episcopacy, but he was permitted to preside at but one Annual Conference, dying within a month of his election. The third General Conference of the Southern church convened at Columbus, Georgia, in 1854, and decided to strengthen the episcopacy

---

[13] Wightman, W. M., *Life of William Capers, D.D.,* . . . *including an Autobiography,* pp. 293-294. Nashville, Tennessee: Barbee & Smith, 1902.

by the election of three additional superintendents, as only one of the bishops, Paine, was in the prime of his manhood, while Soule was in his seventies, and Andrew and Capers were approaching old age. The three men elected were George F. Pierce, of Georgia; John Early, of Virginia; and H. H. Kavanaugh, of Kentucky. The next General Conference (1858) convened in Nashville, Tennessee, in which city the new publishing house of the church had been located by the action of the previous General Conference. A new building had been completed, and the publishing house was in operation. New Orleans was selected as the seat for the Conference of 1862, but it was destined never to meet, for New Orleans was captured by the Union forces in April of that year.

CHAPTER XIV

METHODISM NORTH AND SOUTH AND THE CIVIL WAR

IN the great debate in Congress over Henry Clay's Compromise measure of 1850 the slavery schism in the churches received attention in the speeches of John C. Calhoun and Daniel Webster. Calhoun, opposing the Compromise and speaking of the cords binding the states together, said: "Some are spiritual or ecclesiastical; some political, others social. . . . The strongest of those of a spiritual and ecclesiastical nature is the unity of the great religious denominations, all of which originally embraced the whole Union." These organizations contributed greatly to strengthen the bonds of union; they formed a strong cord binding the nation together, but as powerful as they were, they have not been able to resist the explosive effects of the slavery agitation. The first of these cords to snap under its explosive force was that of the powerful Methodist Episcopal Church. "The numerous ties which held it together are all broken and its unity gone. They now form separate churches, and instead of that feeling of attachment and devotion to the interests of the whole church which was formerly felt, they are now arrayed into two hostile bodies, engaged in litigation about what was formerly their common property." Referring to the other churches, he continued: "The next cord that snapped was that of the Baptists, one of the largest and most respectable of the denominations. That of the Presbyterians is not entirely snapped, but some of its strands have given way. That of the Episcopal Church is the only one of the four great Protestant denominations which remains unbroken and entire."[1]

In his reply to Calhoun, Daniel Webster, in perhaps the greatest speech of his long career (March 7, 1850), referred to the slavery schism in the churches thus: "The honorable senator from South Carolina the other day alluded to the separation of that great religious community, the Methodist Episcopal Church. That separation was brought about by differences of opinion upon this particular subject of slavery. I felt great concern, as that dispute went on, about the result. I was in hopes that the differences of opinion might be adjusted, because I looked on that religious denomination as one of the great props of religion and morals throughout the whole country, from Maine to Georgia, and westward to our utmost western boundary. The result was against my wishes and against my hopes. I have read all their proceedings and all their arguments, but I have never yet been able to come to the conclusion that there was any real ground for that separation," but it was brought about by lack of "candor and charity."[2]

That the snapping of the ecclesiastical cords binding North and South together had a powerful influence in bringing about the final breach between the sections, there can be no doubt. Indeed, it has been claimed that the division in the churches was not

[1] *Congressional Globe*, Vol. XXI, Pt. 1., p. 453.
[2] *Webster's Works*, Vol. V, p. 331.

only the first break between the North and the South, but that it was the chief cause of the final break. Of all classes of men Protestant ministers, and especially Methodist ministers, are least liable to compromise on questions which they consider moral, and a majority of the Northern Methodist preachers having made up their minds that slavery was a sin, no amount of argument could induce them to consent to any compromise. On the other hand, the Southern Methodist preachers being equally convinced that slavery was not a sin, no amount of argument could persuade them to change their views. Compromise between good men is always possible when they believe the issue is not that of absolute right and wrong. But when, in their opinion, right meets wrong at right angles, no compromise is possible.

The long contest between the two branches of Episcopal Methodism over the question of slavery prepared each of them to take a definite stand with their sections when the Civil War began. In spite of the fact that there were still some slaveholders in the Methodist Episcopal Church at the opening of the war, the question as to the attitude of the church toward slavery was settled, and a great majority of Northern Methodists were ready to identify themselves with any political movement which might rid the nation of that institution. Southern Methodist leaders, on the other hand, were undoubtedly in full sympathy with their political leaders in the movement toward secession following the election of Abraham Lincoln.

With the opening of the Civil War the immediate problem of the Lincoln administration was to keep the border states in the Union, and it is a significant fact that all the border Conferences except the Baltimore passed resolutions in 1861 expressive of loyalty to the national government and the new administration. The governor of Maryland at this time was Thomas H. Hicks, a stanch member of the Methodist Episcopal Church, and likewise thoroughly union in his sentiments. His refusal to call a special session of the Maryland Legislature was largely responsible for saving Maryland to the Union. A section of the Baltimore Conference lay in Virginia, and at the session of that Conference in 1862, sixty-six ministers were reported as having withdrawn, together with more than twenty thousand members. Later several other ministers organized three independent Methodist churches in Baltimore, and during the course of the war these congregations, with their ministers, were suspected of disloyalty.[3]

The Philadelphia Conference likewise lay partly in slave territory and at its session in 1861 passed resolutions calling for the repeal of the "New Chapter" on slavery which had been adopted at the previous General Conference. At every subsequent session, however, throughout the war, its loyalty to the Union cause was unmistakable. At its session in 1862 it required that every candidate for admission to the Conference must answer the question, "Are you in favor of sustaining the Union, the Government, and the Constitution of the United States

---

[3] One of the Baltimore Methodist ministers suspected of disloyalty was John H. Dashiel, who was arrested and imprisoned by the military authorities in 1863. See McPherson, E., *History of the Rebellion*, pp. 524-532.

against the present Rebellion?" and every member of the Conference was required to vote on the resolutions affirming loyalty, and even those absent when the vote was taken were asked to record their vote sometime during the session.

The situation in western Virginia, Kentucky, and Missouri was particularly trying to both branches of Methodism during the war. In Kentucky and Missouri the membership of the Church South was larger than that of the Methodist Episcopal Church, while in western Virginia the Northern body was more numerous. The Methodist Episcopal preachers in western Virginia stanchly championed the cause of the Union, and preached boldly against all disunionists. "Tell them" (the members of the Methodist Episcopal Church, South), said one preacher, "that the Methodist Episcopal Church shall exist on slave territory to the end of time, and that as a heaven-appointed instrumentality . . . we shall aid in preserving the integrity of the Union." It has been claimed that the Methodist Episcopal Church was chiefly responsible for the dismemberment of Virginia and for the formation of the new state of West Virginia in 1862. The entire accuracy of this statement may be questioned, but it is significant that the Union and Southern "strength of western Virginia in 1861 could have been measured and located by determining the membership and location of the various churches of the Methodist Episcopal and Methodist Episcopal Church, South, respectively."[4]

---

[4] On this point see article in the *Am. Hist. Review*, July, 1910, p. 771, by C. H. Ambler, "Cleavage Between Eastern and Western Virginia."

METHODISM AND THE CIVIL WAR

In Kentucky, where the Methodist Episcopal Church was greatly outnumbered, some of the ministers were fanatical in their loyalty. One preacher at Newport, across the river from Cincinnati, on a certain Sabbath morning in 1861 had his church decorated with flags and brass eagles; the hymns sung were "Star-Spangled Banner," the "Red, White, and Blue," and "Hail, Columbia." In his prayer he prayed that the Union may be preserved, "even though blood may come out of the wine-press, even unto the horses' bridles, by the space of a thousand and six hundred furlongs." In his sermon he said: "I trust our troops will rally and wipe out the disgrace of Manassas, though it cost the life of every rebel under arms. Let Davis and Beauregard be captured, to meet the fate of Haman. Hang them upon Mason's and Dixon's line, that traitors of both sections may be warned. Let them hang until vultures shall eat their rotten flesh from their bones; let them hang until the crows shall build their filthy nests in their skeletons; let them hang until the rope rots, and let their dismembered bones fall so deep into the earth that God Almighty can't find them in the day of resurrection."[5]

The Church South in Kentucky, however, contained some strong Union men. In 1862 thirty-six preachers of the Louisville Conference of that church intimated that if their state seceded they would return to the Methodist Episcopal Church. The Kentucky Conference (Church South) passed resolutions in 1864 declaring the Conference practically independent of the Church South, and stated

[5] Moore, Frank, *The Rebellion Record—a Diary of American Events*, Vol. IV, p. 22.

that they were and always had been loyal to the government of the United States. In the spring of 1865 eighteen of the ministers of this Conference withdrew from the Southern church and joined the Methodist Episcopal Church.[6]

The story of the happenings in Missouri throughout the entire war, as far as the relationship of the two branches of Methodism is concerned, contains little of which either side can be proud. Nowhere were the churches more bitterly opposed to one another, and nowhere were greater barbarities practiced in the name of the church and religion. In the spring and summer of 1861, while the contest was going on to determine whether Missouri should remain in the Union, the services of the Methodist Episcopal Church were suspended throughout the state outside of Saint Louis. The Church South was in the large majority in the state, and in several instances Methodist Episcopal ministers were compelled to leave their circuits for safety. On one occasion the Rev. N. Shumate, while holding a Quarterly Conference at Leasburg, where the preacher had already been driven away, was threatened by a mob, but he and his congregation armed themselves, placed pickets around the house and proceeded with the service by singing:

"Though troubles assail
And dangers affright,
Though friends should all fail
And foes all unite"—

___

[6] Manuscript Journal of the Rev. Daniel Stevenson. Stevenson was one of the eighteen ministers to withdraw from the Church South. He was the secretary of the Kentucky Conference of the Church South.

and after this the presiding elder went the rounds of his district carrying two revolvers.

The affairs of the Northern church in Missouri, however, began to improve as soon as the Confederate forces were driven from the state, and then the Methodist Church, South, came in for its share of persecution. Dr. Charles Elliott, editor of the *Central Christian Advocate* in Saint Louis, was accused of seizing "every event that could be tortured into an occasion for an inflammatory article against the ministers and members of the Methodist Episcopal Church, South." The *Saint Louis Christian Advocate,* the organ of the Church South, advised their people "to remain at home, cultivate their lands, and pursue their avocations of peace and piety, in the fear of God." The editor of the Southern paper claimed that his church was unsectional, unpolitical, and loyal to the government and Constitution of the United States, but he had difficulty in persuading the authorities to believe it, and the Methodist Episcopal Church used every opportunity to increase these suspicions.[7]

More or less throughout the nation, North and South alike, patriotism crowded religion in all of the churches. In New England political sermons were commonly preached throughout the war, and, indeed, for twenty-five years previously abolition and slavery had been common pulpit themes. All the New England Conferences passed patriotic res-

---

[7] The story of the persecutions experienced by the Methodist Church, South, in Missouri during the war has been set forth by W. M. Leftwich, *Martyrdom in Missouri*, 2 Vols. Saint Louis, 1870. For experiences of the Methodist Episcopal Church in Missouri during the same period, see Elliott, Charles, *Southwestern Methodism*. Cincinnati, 1868.

olutions at their several sessions, while in the Boston Preacher's Meeting the theme for discussion was often one relating to the national crisis. At the session of the New York East Conference in 1863 it was voted to have the oath of allegiance administered to the whole body, and a judge of the United States District Court and a major general of the army were called in to administer it, and were given "seats within the altar near the bishop." The *Minutes* state that: "It would be impossible to convey, in any terms, . . . a truthful view of the most impressive occasion; the vast audience was moved by emotions of moral sublimity, which nothing besides this happy union of religion and patriotism could have aroused."

Patriotic orators representing various causes appeared before the Annual Conferences in every section of the country. The minister of the church at Lawrence, Kansas, made numerous addresses before church gatherings, describing Quantrell's raid on that town, arousing his audiences to righteous indignation at the barbarities practiced by the raiders, and incidentally collecting money for the erection of a new church.

The Conferences in the central and northwestern states were no less patriotic than were those in New England and the East. During the course of the war every Conference had a committee on "The State of the Country," which brought in resolutions pledging support to the government. Thus the Cincinnati Conference in 1862 declares that it will "besiege the Throne of God in behalf of the cause of liberty and good order, and will continue our efforts publicly and privately as ministers and as citizens in behalf of our government." The Central Ohio Conference in 1863 declared that "loyalty to our government is our motto; that we hate treason, under whatever garb it may appear." Indiana Methodists were no less patriotic, and the four Indiana Conferences passed patriotic resolutions promising support to the government in putting down the rebellion, and condemning "copperheadism." The members of the Rock River (Illinois) Conference in 1861 declare that "as Christians, as Christian ministers, we can only say this rebellion must be subdued; this constitution must be maintained."

Often ministers took an active part in encouraging enlistments, which was particularly true in rural districts. Sometimes recruiting took place in churches, the minister and recruiting officer standing behind the altar, while the preacher urged the young men to come forward and place their names upon the roll; and in not a few cases the first name on the list was the minister's. In some of the larger churches military companies were organized, made up largely of members of the congregation. The women of the churches formed themselves into sewing societies, where soldier's underwear was made, socks knitted, and lint pulled for use in hospitals.

In 1862 it was reported that there were sixty-three Methodist preachers holding commissions in the Union armies, as follows: four colonels, two lieutenant-colonels, one major, thirty-six captains, and twenty other commissioned officers. General Clinton B. Fisk stated in 1862 that fifteen per cent of the composition of the Union armies were Methodists, and if this proportion holds true for the entire period of the war, it would mean that there were

300,000 Methodist soldiers in the Union armies during the four years. Church statistics for 1862 show a loss of 45,617 in membership from 1861; in 1863 there was a decrease of 19,512, though for the years 1864 and 1865 there were small increases. At the opening of the war there was a total membership in the Methodist Episcopal Church of 990,447; when the war closed there was a membership of 929,259, or a net loss of 61,188.

At the opening of the war an order was issued by the War Department stating that one chaplain would be allowed to each regiment, to be appointed by the regimental commander. In August, 1861, Congress passed an act stating that none but regularly ordained ministers of some Christian denomination shall be eligible for chaplains, and that the method of their appointment was to be left to the President. Later a further act was passed providing for hospital chaplains. The pay of chaplains was fixed at $100 per month and two rations a day. It was not long until there were reports that certain unworthy persons were serving as chaplains in the Union armies. In one instance it is said that an actor bore the name and received the pay of a chaplain, and in another regiment a French cook was mustered in as a chaplain in order to meet the expense of keeping him. Certain local preachers of the Methodist Episcopal Church obtained ordination at the hands of an independent Congregational Church for the purpose of gaining chaplaincies, but such cases were few and when discovered were condemned by church bodies.

Numerous Methodist preachers were soon to be found acting as chaplains in the armies and navies of the Union. It is stated that Gilbert Haven, of the New England Conference, was the first chaplain commissioned in the war. The bishops uniformly agreed to relieve ministers from their churches and to appoint them regularly as chaplains. Altogether the Methodist Episcopal Church furnished at least five hundred chaplains to the Union armies and navies, while several loyal ministers of the Church South also served as chaplains in the Union armies. Four Annual Conferences which furnished twenty or more chaplains were the Cincinnati, Illinois, Indiana, and Philadelphia, while five Conferences —East Baltimore, Iowa, Pittsburgh, Ohio, and Southern Illinois—furnished fifteen or more.

In many instances a regimental church was formed by the chaplain, and when a regiment remained long in camp the Methodist chaplain usually improved the time by conducting a revival service. At the close of such a meeting in an Indiana regiment forty-eight joined the regimental church. In a New York regiment a revival meeting was kept up for thirty nights, and one hundred and twenty-five soldiers professed conversion. A Methodist preacher, the Rev. Granville Moody, was the colonel of an Ohio regiment, which he formed into a church, known as the "Church of the Living God." The chaplains also served as distributing agents for the American Bible and Tract Societies, wrote letters to the church papers, comforted homesick and discouraged soldier-boys, attended the sick and buried the dead.

Religious activities in the Confederate armies were even more pronounced than among Northern soldiers. Generals Lee and Jackson were particularly hospitable to the activities of chaplains. In General Jackson's corps log chapels were built and regular services held, while General William Pendleton, Lee's chief of artillery, held services and preached every Sunday, whenever the army was not fighting or marching. "Prayer meetings and revivals were common in camps, and at these generals were as active and conspicuous as in a battle." Itinerant preachers and "circuit riders" were always welcome in the camps and were better treated than any other visitors.

The Methodist Church, South, furnished many chaplains to the Confederate armies, besides numerous missionaries, who performed duties similar to those of the regular chaplain. Many Southern preachers were also found among the commissioned officers or as ordinary soldiers, perhaps an even larger number in proportion than was furnished by the Northern church to the Union armies.[8]

In 1863 the Holston Conference of the Methodist Episcopal Church, South, expelled five of its members for disloyalty to the Confederacy. Later these members, having joined the Methodist Episcopal Church, had the satisfaction of voting their rebel brothers guilty of "a crime sufficient to exclude them from the kingdom of grace and glory," and that they "had forfeited all claims to Christian confidence and fellowship." Southern preachers were considered no fit apostles to loyal Union people, and were arrested for treason on a wholesale scale in Nashville and other sections occupied by federal

[8] For a partial list of Methodist chaplains and missionaries found in the Confederate armies, see Sweet, W. W., *The Methodist Episcopal Church and the Civil War*, Appendix E., pp. 219-225. Cincinnati, 1912.

armies. Federal generals declared them more dangerous than a company of the rebel army, for Southern preachers were considered the best recruiting officers in the South.

The Methodist Episcopal Church, South, naturally suffered much more during the four years of Civil War than did the Methodists at the North. In 1860 there were 542,489 white members; in 1866 there were 429,233—a loss in membership of more than 100,000. In 1860 there were 2,458 effective traveling preachers; in 1866 there were 2,116, or a loss of 342. Their publishing house at Nashville, Tennessee, had been seized by the federal authorities and was used as a United States printing office at great damage to the property. Southern missionaries in China were cut off from all communication from the home land, though for a time their drafts were honored by the treasurer of the Missionary Society of the Methodist Episcopal Church, in New York, one of the few acts of Christian generosity during the war. Indian missions in the South were almost destroyed, since their country had been overrun by federal forces, and some of their chiefs had enlisted with their warriors under the Confederate flag.

Interdenominational organizations, to which Methodists gave generous co-operation, such as the American Bible and Tract Societies, were particularly active during the course of the war, distributing tracts and Testaments to the soldiers on both sides. Grants of Bibles and tracts were made all through the war to Southern Bible Societies. In 1863 alone 30,000 Bibles were given to the Virginia Bible Society, and in the same year 25,000 Testaments were granted to the Southern Baptist Sunday School Board for use in the South. Other large grants were made directly to Northern and Southern armies, as well as to Union and Confederate prisoners, and hospitals. The Methodists also cooperated with the American Temperance Union in furnishing temperance tracts to soldiers and sailors.

The total circulation of the official publications of the Methodist Episcopal Church during the Civil War was at least 400,000 weekly, while a number of independent Methodist publications rivaled in importance and influence the best of the official family. The two outstanding nonofficial papers were *Zion's Herald* of Boston, and *The Methodist* of New York. The latter paper began publication in 1860 and was established by an association of influential ministers and laymen. Its editor was George R. Crooks, assisted by an able staff of contributing editors. Indeed, no Methodist publication was ever more ably conducted. The chief object of *The Methodist* was to promote lay representation in the General Conference. It took, at first, a conservative position on the slavery question, but with the opening of the Civil War it dropped the slavery issue and became a stanch supporter of the government.

In all the *Advocates* war news occupied large space. Letters from chaplains and soldiers appeared in almost every issue, while in their columns were appeals from various societies, such as the *United States Christian Commission* and other war organizations, asking support of church people. The President of the United States found loyal backing in most instances in the editorials of the church press. Thus the New York *Advocate* stated editorially in its issue the week after Lincoln's inauguration:

The incoming Executive will have of necessity a difficult task to perform. Called to the head of the nation at the most critical time in our history, confronted at once by a most extraordinary state of affairs, such as none of his predecessors have had to contend with, and having no precedence or lights to guide him in the perilous path of duty; embarrassed by the most complicated difficulties and beset on every hand by dangers the most imminent, with but limited experience in public life and thousands anxious to defeat every well-meant effort he shall make to adjust the measures of his administration to the state of things existing, he is justly entitled to the sympathy and support of every friend of the Union. . . . Under ordinary circumstances men may perhaps be excused for nursing their opposition and hostility to a political opponent. . . . But here is a totally changed condition of things. . . . He who loves his party better than his country is a traitor.

The Western Christian Advocate, edited by Calvin Kingsley, and the *Central* at Saint Louis, with Charles Elliott as editor, contained frequent articles and editorials of the "fire-eating" kind, urging that the war be pushed with all vigor. An editorial in the *Western* (August 6, 1862), entitled "Attention! Young Men," is typical of many which appeared in its columns.

The index finger on the great dial-plate that counts and reveals the movement of ages, to-day points to the hour in which your nation's doom for the next thousand years is cast; and it is for you, young man, to say what that doom shall be. Shall it be Union, Peace, Brotherhood, Liberty, Freedom, and equalizing, humanizing Christianity? Or shall it be disunion, war, selfishness, slavery, and a besotted, barbarous, brutalizing, bastard corruption and perversion of our holy religion? You, young men, must decide it.

In 1863 a conference of ministers, representing most of the important Protestant churches in the Confederacy, drew up a long address to Christians throughout the world. This address is signed by three Southern Methodist bishops—Andrew, Early, and Pierce; the presidents of Randolph-Macon and Trinity Colleges; the editors of the *Richmond* and *Southern Christian Advocates,* besides several influential ministers. The address stressed the following points: First, the purpose of the war as waged by the North, to restore the Union, is impossible of achievement; second, the Confederate States' government is a fixed fact, promising in no respect a restoration of the Union; third, the Emancipation Proclamation of the President of the United States is in their judgment "a suitable occasion for solemn protest on the part of the people of God throughout the world," since it conduces to slave insurrection, making necessary the slaughter of tens of thousands of "poor deluded insurrectionists." They further contend that the war has accomplished no good results, while hundreds of thousands of lives have been lost, and not a single county or section of the seceded States has returned to the Union. And, finally, the moral and religious interests of the South have not been benefited by the war. They realize that they suffer undeserved reproach because of their attitude on slavery, but they "testify in the sight of God, that the relation of master and slave among us, however we may deplore abuses in this, as in other relations of mankind, is not incompatible with our holy Christianity, and that the presence of the Africans in our land is an occasion of gratitude on their behalf before God." And in closing they appeal for an enlightened Christian sentiment going forth "against war, against persecution for conscience sake, against the ravaging of the Church of God by fanatical invasion."[9]

Soon after the opening of the Civil War a voluntary organization was formed in the North called the *United States Christian Commission,* the purpose of which was to provide supplies and comforts to the soldiers. During the four years of the war the commission received more than two and a half millions of dollars, largely collected through the churches. The commission published no periodical of its own, so its appeals were sent out through the columns of the church papers. Collections for the commission were taken in the churches on fast days and Thanksgiving days, while special agents went about the country raising money for its work. The Rev. C. C. McCabe, later to become a Methodist bishop, was its most successful agent, and on one occasion secured $10,000 from an Illinois farmer, the largest single gift received. The churches also co-operated with the commission in sending "delegates" to serve in hospitals, in the camps and on the battlefields, where they distributed stores, circulated religious publications, helped soldiers to communicate with their friends, discouraged vice, and in other ways helped to raise the tone of the soldiers. These delegates volunteered their services and worked without pay. Among them were large numbers of ministers of all denominations. The total number of "delegates" who served in this way dur-

---

[9] McPherson, Edward, *The Political History of the United States of America during the Great Rebellion,* Appendix, pp. 517-520. Washington, D. C., James J. Chapman, 1882, 4th ed.

ing the course of the war was 4,119, and of this number there were at least 458 Methodist ministers, besides numerous laymen.

Of the six Methodist Episcopal Civil War bishops, Matthew Simpson and Edward R. Ames were the best known for their patriotic activities. Bishop Ames during the war lived in the city of Indianapolis and was the friend of Indiana's war governor, Oliver P. Morton. In 1862 Bishop Ames was appointed on a commission by the War Department to visit the Union prisoners in Richmond and elsewhere "to relieve their necessities and provide for their comfort at the expense of the United States." His appointment on this commission aroused some protest in the South and led an ex-minister of the Methodist Episcopal Church to write a letter to Jefferson Davis warning him against allowing "this astute politician, who in the garb of a Christian minister and with the specious plea of 'Humanity' upon his lips, would insinuate himself into the very heart of that government whose very foundation he would most gladly destroy." Bishop Simpson, through his gift of eloquent speech, was soon a nationally known figure. His lectures on patriotic themes were given throughout the North and always created a tremendous effect. Bishop Simpson was a close friend of Mr. Lincoln's, and it was arranged that he give his lecture, "Our Country," just before the Presidential election of 1864, in the Academy of Music in New York, which, according to newspaper reports, was filled from pit to dome long before the time announced for the lecture. *Harper's Weekly* states that the lecture produced a scene that Demosthenes might have envied.[10]

METHODISM AND THE CIVIL WAR

A type of religious activity in the South during the war which has been largely forgotten on the part of the victorious North was the attempt of Northern churches to push into the South following the invading armies of the Union. In November, 1862, the secretary of war issued an order to Union commanders in the Departments of Missouri, Tennessee, and the Gulf, instructing them to turn over to Bishop E. R. Ames "all houses of worship belonging to the Methodist Episcopal Church, South," in which a loyal minister "who has been appointed by a loyal Bishop" does not officiate.

Later in the year a similar order was issued for three other military Departments, instructing the commanders to turn over Southern church property to Bishops Baker, Janes, and Simpson. Bishop Ames soon after these orders were issued journeyed into the South to investigate conditions, and during the last two years of the war a number of Northern preachers were sent into the South to work as missionaries.

In 1864 the Missionary Board at New York appropriated $35,000 for this Southern work. Perhaps the best known of the Northern Methodist missionaries in the South was John P. Newman, later a bishop, who came to New Orleans in 1864 to have charge of Methodist work in that city, and the first Methodist Episcopal Church formed in that city was called Ames Church.

The ministers in the South strongly objected to

---

[10] Crooks, G. R., *The Life of Bishop Matthew Simpson of the Methodist Episcopal Church*. New York: Harper, 1891. Chap. XVII deals with the activities of Bishop Simpson during the Civil War and his relation with President Lincoln.

such a policy and at a convention of Southern Methodist preachers, held in Louisville, Kentucky, in
1864, at which eight Annual Conferences were represented, a series of resolutions in protest were
adopted. "There is nothing in this whole wretched
war, more astonishing, or more to be deplored,"
writes one Southern Methodist editor (March 8,
1864), "than the course pursued by the professing
Christians of the North." The invasion of Bishop
Ames "caps the climax of Yankee despotism and
meanness." "As the United States is trying to reduce the Southern States to territories, so the Methodist Church, North, is trying to reduce the Methodist Church, South, to the status of missions." The
Northern preachers were denounced as church rob-
bers, while the Northern churches justified their
action on the ground that they were simply occupying vacant pulpits and were following the scriptural
injunction to "go into all the South and preach the
gospel to every creature." One is tempted to express the opinion that the zeal manifested by the
Northern churches, in forcing themselves into the
South in this manner and at this time, was ill calculated to further either the cause of the union or of
religion. Unfortunately, though perhaps inevitably,[11] patriotism in both North and South too often
became the only consideration, and as a result Christian forgiveness and the Golden Rule gave way to
bitter vindictiveness.

The Civil War period saw the development of char-

[11] Sweet, W. W., *The Methodist Episcopal Church and the Civil War*. Chap. V, "Methodist Missions in the South During the War," pp. 96-110. See also Nicolay, J. G., and Hay, John, *Abraham Lincoln, A History*, New York, 1890, Vol. VI, pp. 333-338.

ities on a larger scale than ever before existed in the United States. Patriotism loosens the purse strings as does nothing else, and people of moderate means, as well as men of wealth, vied with one another in their generosity to every good cause. All benevolent enterprises of the Methodist Episcopal Church showed a steady increase throughout the years of the war. In 1860 $258,000 was contributed for home and foreign missions; in 1865 the amount given was in round numbers $602,000. In 1860 the total amount contributed by the Methodist Episcopal Church to the American Bible Society was $39,903 and to the Tract Society, $16,239; in 1865 the sums were $101,743 and $22,322, respectively. There was not, however, a corresponding increase in preachers' salaries as a result, and the rising cost of living bore heavily upon the preachers and their families. One preacher, writing to the *Western Christian Advocate* in 1863, complains "that a great many of our preachers are working for the same salaries they received two years ago. Then flour was $4.00 a barrel; pork, 3 cents a pound; sugar, 6 cents; coffee, 12; calico, 10; corn, 25, and other articles in proportion. Now we pay 80 cents for corn . . . ; 18 cents for sugar, 10 cents for pork. . . . Prices have gone up nearly fourfold, and farmers are coining money, but preachers must do with the old salary or starve." In 1862 the highest salary paid any preacher in the North Indiana Conference was $800, but by 1865 eight preachers and presiding elders were receiving $1,000 to $1,200.

Generally speaking, war is always detrimental to the cause of religion and morals, and the Civil War in this respect was no different than others. Most of the ministers throughout the country, North and South, could have subscribed to the following complaint: "The sound of the drum calling for volunteers, the training of soldiers, companies leaving for the war, are but scenes of every day's occurrence. Amid the excitement consequent upon such a state of things, you can readily understand the difficulty of sustaining the institutions of religion. In fact, the pastor and his church are continually in danger of having their feelings more deeply interested in the fearful conflict between the North and South than in their own growth in grace, or in the winning of soldiers for Christ."[12] When war becomes the all-engrossing subject of thought and conversation, the higher interests are thrown into the background. Toward the close of the war a larger religious interest began to be manifest throughout the country and reports of revivals are found with increasing frequency in the church papers. But the four bloody years of war left their brutalizing effect upon society; increased drunkenness and human selfishness and exercised a blighting effect upon the life of the nation for the years that were to follow.

The General Conference of 1864 met in the city of Philadelphia and the "atmosphere of the national conflict pervaded the assembly." Charles Elliott, the editor of the *Central Christian Advocate*, had brought with him a flag which had been made by the loyal women of Saint Louis, and by a unanimous vote of the Conference this flag was displayed over the building where the Conference convened. The rule on slavery was amended so as to prohibit "slave-

[12] Fite, E. D., *Social and Industrial Conditions During the Civil War*, pp. 304-310. New York: Macmillan, 1910.

METHODISM AND THE CIVIL WAR

holding, buying or selling slaves," and a committee was sent to Washington to bear to the President of the United States the sympathy and approbation of the church. In reply to the committee's address President Lincoln read the following response:

Gentlemen: In response to your address, allow me to attest the accuracy of its historical statements, indorse the sentiments it expresses, and thank you in the nation's name for the sure promise it gives.

Nobly sustained as the government has been by all the churches, I would utter nothing which might in the least appear invidious against any. Yet without this it may be fairly said that the Methodist Episcopal Church, not less devoted than the best, is by its greater numbers the most important of all. It is no fault in others that the Methodist Church sends more soldiers to the field, more nurses to the hospitals, and more prayers to heaven than any. God bless the Methodist Church! bless all the churches! and blessed be God, who in this our great trial giveth us the churches.

(Signed) A. LINCOLN.

The agitation for lay representation in the General Conference was becoming increasingly insistent, especially since the ably edited independent periodical, *The Methodist,* began publication. To this General Conference a strong committee of laymen, deputed by a lay convention held in Philadelphia just previous to the General Conference, presented an able address. They urged a more adequate method of ascertaining the attitude of the laity upon the subject and insisted that lay representation stood firmly on Methodist, Christian, and scriptural grounds. Strong prejudice prevailed among some of the ministers against lay participation, which is illustrated by an incident which took

299

place in the Philadelphia Conference in 1847. An applicant for admission into the Conference was under discussion, when one of the members of the Conference arose and stated: "Mr. President, I am opposed to the admission of this brother. I am told that he is a lay-delegation man, and I had as lief travel with the devil as with a lay-delegation man." For a number of years following the formation of the Methodist Protestant Church, which introduced lay representation, for a Methodist Episcopal preacher to be known as favorable to lay delegation was as much as his ecclesiastical life was worth. Those who favored it were called radicals, and radicalism became synonymous with "destructivism."

After 1830 the undemocratic Methodist system of church polity became the target for attacks from outsiders, especially from Congregationalists and Baptists. It was with difficulty that the societies of the Methodist Episcopal Church in Massachusetts secured incorporation by the state legislature, the chief objection being the absence of lay representation. This convinced the editor of *Zion's Herald* that a change must eventually come, and the columns of his paper from this time forward were opened for the discussion of the question.

The most severe arraignment of Methodism at this period came from a Baptist preacher of Tennessee, R. J. Graves, the editor of the *Tennessee Baptist*. In a book entitled *The Great Iron Wheel, or Republicanism Backwards and Christianity Reversed*,[13] which passed through at least thirty edi-

---

[13] Graves, R. J., *The Great Iron Wheel, or Republicanism Backwards and Christianity Reversed*. Nashville: Southwestern Publishing House, 1853, 30th ed., 1860. To this book W. G. Brownlow, a Ten-

tions, the author attacks Methodism on many grounds, but especially because of its "clerical despotism," which he pictured as a great iron wheel. He calls Methodism the "Popery of Protestantism—as absolute and all-controlling as Jesuitism." Elder Graves was answered by "Parson" (W. G.) Brownlow, an eccentric Methodist preacher, editor of the *Knoxville Whig,* in *The Great Iron Wheel Examined; or, Its False Spokes Extracted and an Exhibition of Elder Graves, Its Builder.* To what extent such controversial writings furthered the cause of democratizing the Methodist Episcopal Church, it is probably impossible to discover, but to a certain degree they served to put the system of complete clerical control on the defensive.

The most important legislation passed by the General Conference of 1864 was the establishment of the *Church Extension Society,* to be located at Philadelphia. The purpose of this society was to aid in the erection of churches, especially in the newer sections of the country, and for three decades following the Civil War it was a factor of great, if not chief importance, in planting Methodism in the prairie and Rocky Mountain states. Population had continued to move westward throughout the Civil War and new Conferences had been formed in Kansas, Nebraska, and Colorado.

This General Conference also made plans for the celebration of the centennial of American Methodism in 1866, and a committee of twelve ministers and an equal number of laymen was appointed to

nessee Methodist preacher, replied in a book called *The Great Iron Wheel Examined; or, Its False Spokes Extracted and an Exhibition of Elder Graves, Its Builder.* Nashville, Tennessee, 1856.

direct the special activities. All branches of Methodism were invited to unite with the Methodist Episcopal Church in this celebration.

It is significant that the three additional bishops chosen by this General Conference were all war editors of church periodicals. Edward Thomson was chosen from the editorship of the New York *Advocate,* Calvin Kingsley from the *Western Christian Advocate* at Cincinnati, while D. W. Clark had been editor of *The Ladies Repository* for twelve years.

On Good Friday, April 14, 1865, Abraham Lincoln was shot in the back of the head by a half-deranged actor and on the following morning at twenty-one minutes after seven o'clock he breathed his last. "Now he belongs to the ages," said Secretary Stanton, as he stood with streaming eyes. Six days previous General Lee had surrendered to General Grant at Appomattox, and the bloody Civil War was at last at an end. The greatest blow suffered by the South was not the surrender of their armies, but, rather, the death of the kindly President, who on March 4 had delivered his second inaugural address, which breathed a Christian magnanimity and a longing for a just and lasting peace for his war-torn country, "with malice toward none, with charity for all."

Who should be asked to say the last words over the bier of the dead President? Mr. Lincoln had been a member of no church, but both at Springfield and in Washington he had regularly attended worship in the Presbyterian church. It was finally decided, however, by the official family that Bishop Matthew Simpson, the dead President's friend and close adviser, should perform that duty. And so

METHODISM AND THE CIVIL WAR

it was that when Abraham Lincoln's body was taken
to its last resting place at Oak Ridge Cemetery, at
Springfield, Illinois, Bishop Matthew Simpson stood
beside the coffin and pronounced an eloquent and
pathetic address, closing with the words:[14]

Chieftain, farewell! The nation mourns thee. . . . Statesmen shall study thy record and from it learn lessons of
wisdom. Mute though thy lips be, yet they still speak.
Hushed is thy voice, but echoes of liberty are ringing
through the world, and the sons of bondage listen with
joy. Thou didst fall not for thyself. The assassin had
no hate for thee. Our hearts were aimed at; our national
life was sought. We crown thee as our martyr, and humanity enthrones thee as her triumphant son. Hero,
Martyr, Friend, farewell!

[14] *Bishop Simpson and the Funeral of Abraham Lincoln,* by W. W.
Sweet. (Journal of the Illinois State Historical Society.)

CHAPTER XV

THE TRYING YEARS OF RECONSTRUC-
TION, 1865-1880

FOR half a generation following the Civil War
the political, economic and social reconstruction of the South occupied the chief attention of the nation. So likewise the churches were
occupied with problems created because of changed
conditions following upon the war.

Before the close of the Civil War, as has already
been seen, the Methodist Episcopal Church had
entered the South with the two-fold mission—first
to carry the work of their church to those localities
from which ministers of the Methodist Church,
South, had fled on the approach of the Union
armies; and, second, to share in the task of caring
for the freedmen, whose helpless condition appealed
strongly to Christian people of every denomination.

Both of these missions concerned intimately the
Methodist Episcopal Church, South, and it was not
long until the two churches were in contact and
conflict. The Southern policy of the representatives from the North brought forth protests at once
from Southern Methodist leaders, especially when
they came to take possession of their churches which
had been turned over to their Northern brethren
during the course of the war. In eastern Tennessee, "there was much trouble," writes a minister of
the Church South, "where our houses of worship
had been taken from us by force and our preachers

threatened with all sorts of violence if they should dare come into the country to preach." The Southern bishops, at their first meeting after the close of the war, drew up a pastoral letter, in which they declare: "The conduct of certain Northern Methodist bishops and preachers in taking advantage of the confusion incident to a state of war, to intrude themselves into several of our houses of worship, and in continuing to hold these places against the wishes and protests of the congregations and rightful owners," causes us pain, "not only as working an injury to us, but as presenting to the world a spectacle ill calculated to make an impression favorable to Christianity." Again in 1869 the bishops of the Church South, when approached upon the question of union by the Northern bishops, assert "that the conduct of some of your missionaries and agents who have been sent into that portion of our common country occupied by us, and their avowed purpose to disintegrate and absorb our societies, that otherwise dwelt quietly, have been very prejudicial to that charity which we desire our people to cultivate toward all Christians, and especially those who are called by the endeared name Methodists." There were doubtless many in the South who felt that it was the deliberate policy of the "Northern" church to press the Southern church to the wall, and finally absorb and exterminate it.

The church papers of both branches of Methodism, for a number of years following the close of the war, were filled with discussions relating to reconstruction of Methodism in the South. In the North there was some agitation for a reunion of the two branches of Methodism, since the cause which had created the division was now forever gone. The Union was now restored, why should not there be a reunited Methodism? "The authorities of our church should make overtures for a reunion to the Methodist Episcopal Church, South, on two general conditions," wrote J. P. Newman, and these conditions were loyalty to the government and acceptance of the anti-slavery doctrine. Northern opinion in regard to union with the Southern church was by no means unanimous in its favor. The New England Conference at its session in 1866 stated that to "regard even a seeming recognition of that Southern organization as a branch of the Methodist Episcopal Church" was impolitic and contrary to every act of justice and piety. The Wisconsin Conference was opposed to reunion *en masse,* since the leaders of the Church South had not shown evidence of penitence and reformation, while *The Christian Advocate and Journal* asks: "Shall we unite with the men who led the great slaveholders' rebellion? Take them to our bosoms, that they may wound us near the seat of life? Shall their so-called loyal episcopacy lay 'hands episcopal' upon our young men who come to fill up our decimated itinerant ranks from the gory battlefields of contested liberty?" A New England correspondent to the New York *Advocate* (September 21, 1865) stated that he had opposed fraternization in 1848 and that he was still opposed to it, for the Church South, to his mind, was just as guilty as ever, and her hands still unwashed. "The Methodist Episcopal Church, South, is dead," wrote another correspondent from Michigan, "stung in its vitals by the treason it was instrumental in originating, and withered by the power of God," and therefore the Methodist Episcopal Church has a great work to do "in the sunny lands of the South."

"We will, the whole Southern church, will entertain any proposition coming from the North for fraternal relations, when that proposition comes from a proper source, and with reasonable and Christian conditions and suggestions," writes a Southern Methodist, while still another Southerner declared, "The South is ready for conciliation."[1] On the other hand, there was considerable fear expressed on the part of some of the Southern church leaders that their church was in danger of being "swallowed" by their more powerful Northern rivals, and in order to help prevent such an unwelcome assimilation, it was proposed to change the name of the Southern church to *Episcopal Methodist Church*. This proposed change was passed by the General Conference of the Church South at its session in 1866, but failed to receive the concurrence of a three-fourths majority of their Annual Conferences and thereby failed of final adoption.

Many in the North did not concur in the Southern policy of their church. One minister refused to accept the pastorate at Norfolk, when he learned that the church had been taken by force, while Daniel Curry, the editor of the New York *Advocate*, stated before the New York Preacher's Meeting that "wherever we have taken churches the policy has proved bad." In 1870 L. C. Matlack, in an article

---

[1] *Journal of the Illinois State Historical Society.* Vol. VII, No. 3, pp. 147-165. *The Methodist Episcopal Church and Reconstruction*, by W. W. Sweet. See also *The Mississippi Valley Historical Review.* Vol. I, March, 1915. No. 4. *Methodist Church Influence in Southern Politics*, by William Warren Sweet.

in the *Central Christian Advocate* (March 15, 1870), deplored the policy and asked: "Did we not wrong our brethren in this? Is not a confession of wrong better than defense of wrong? Can we ignore our duty and be guiltless before God and the Church of Christ? Our attitude as a church toward the South, both ecclesiastically and politically, needs to be examined." In 1865 a Southern Methodist minister from New Orleans went to Washington and made a formal application to the President and the secretary of war for the restoration of the churches in Louisiana to their rightful owners. After four months President Johnson finally issued the order restoring the property.

The aggressive Southern policy of the Northern church immediately following the war resulted by 1869 in the formation of ten new Annual Conferences in the South as follows: Holston Conference was organized in eastern Tennessee on June 1, 1865, in territory the majority of whose population had been strongly Union throughout the war. In December, 1865, the Mississippi Conference was formed at New Orleans as a result of the activities of such Northern preachers as J. P. Newman and J. C. Hartzell, who had come to New Orleans soon after its capture by the Union army in April, 1862. At its formation this Conference had five white and twelve colored members. In October, 1866, the Tennessee Conference was organized; in 1867 the Texas, the Virginia, the Georgia, and Alabama Conferences were formed; while in 1869 the Louisiana and North Carolina Conferences were organized. By 1871 the Southern Conferences of the Methodist Episcopal churches had 135,442 members and 630 preachers. Of the preachers 260 were white and 370 were colored; of the membership 47,017 were white and 88,425 were colored.

Northern activity in the South undoubtedly acted as a stimulus to the Southern Methodists, and the rehabilitation of their disordered and depleted churches went forward rapidly in spite of confusion and poverty. The first General Conference of the Church South following the war met at New Orleans in May, 1866, and of the one hundred and fifty-three elected delegates one hundred and forty-nine were present. The Conference was forward-looking to an extraordinary degree, for even conservative men having become accustomed to great changes now gave their support to what they would have considered a few years before as radical legislation. The rigid probationary period for church membership was abolished; the pastoral term was lengthened from two to four years; but most important of all was the passage of resolutions for the admission of laymen to the General and Annual Conferences. These measures were later ratified by the requisite three-fourths vote of the Annual Conferences, and for the first time laymen took their seats as delegates in the General Conference of 1870. The plan provided for equal representation of laymen in the General Conference and for four lay delegates for each district in the Annual Conferences. Four additional bishops were elected, W. M. Wightman, Enoch M. Marvin, D. S. Doggett and H. N. McTyeire; "the Publishing House and Missionary Society were patched up and sent forth . . . to sink or swim;" the *Advocates* one by one began to appear; the colleges and schools were reopened, and thus the Church South courageously arose from its humiliation and defeat to help rebuild Southern society.

The Southern General Conference of 1866 authorized the formation of five new Annual Conferences; one, the Illinois, crossed the line into the North. This Conference was formed as a result of an amalgamation with the Church South of the Christian Union Church, a small body mostly found in Ohio, Indiana, and Illinois, a secession from the Methodist Episcopal Church during the war. The editor of the *Western Christian Advocate,* commenting on this affiliation, says: "We invite the Church South to any field in the North they can occupy. The people they propose to serve in Illinois, as God knows, need all possible moral influences. Their preachers may be compelled to go on short rations, but we will not duck them, or hang them. We will stand by them against all violence. We give them a free North, and we demand for ourselves a free South." The Church South also received at this General Conference that part of the Baltimore Conference which had withdrawn from the Northern church at the opening of the war, so that both Methodist bodies displayed no hesitancy in furthering aggressive movements, or occupying territory formerly unoccupied.

The second reason which called the Methodist Episcopal Church into the South at the close of the war was the great mass of ignorant and needy freedmen. This work had already begun before the close of the war, and the Northern churches of all denominations were largely supporting the numerous Freedmen's Associations which had sprung up in almost every city in the North. Christian people generally urged upon the federal government the creation of a *Freedmen's Bureau,* and among the resolutions of the General Conference of 1864 was one stating "that the best interests of the freedmen and of the country demand legislation that shall foster and protect this people," and they urge upon Congress the necessity of establishing a bureau of freedmen's relief. On the passage of such a measure by the federal Congress and the formation of the *Bureau* the Methodist Episcopal Church became a stanch defender of its work, and numerous Methodist ministers and laymen found employment in it, among them being General Clinton B. Fisk, who became assistant commissioner for Kentucky. In 1866 the Freedmen's Aid Society of the Methodist Episcopal Church was formed in Cincinnati, and by 1867 had received the cordial approval of the Annual Conferences. The following year the General Conference sanctioned its organization and approved its objects, and recommended that it receive the support of the church. Its first secretary was Richard S. Rust, and at the end of its first year the society had received more than $37,000.

Meanwhile the Church South was also concerning itself with the problems of the Negro. One Southern editor says: (September 21, 1865) "As the father would tenderly nurture the child, and stimulate, encourage, and direct his labor to bring it to the productive point, so a wise political economy would impel Southern people to do the same by the Negro." Again, the same editor urges upon his readers that the duty of bringing the gospel to the Negro "is no less ours than it was before the slaves were emancipated. It is as much our duty to look after their spiritual interests as it is to send missionaries to the Indians or to China." Another Southern Methodist editor declared that he would rejoice if the "Northern Christians" did half as much as they declared they intended to do, and claims a genuine regard for the colored race.

It was but natural that the newly emancipated Negroes should be suspicious of the church of their former masters, while the action of their Northern friends contributed to increase that suspicion. There was much foolish sentiment regarding the Negro expressed by many good people in the North at this period. The Negro was idealized, his virtues exaggerated, and his weaknesses, his ignorance, and his faults were overlooked. Methodist Conferences in the North passed resolutions demanding that the Negro be given the suffrage at once, declaring that he was fully capable of assuming all the responsibilities of citizenship. Thus the Negro soon came to believe that the North was more friendly to him than was the South, and that Northern churches were better for him than were the Southern churches, hence the large exodus of Negro membership from the old Southern white churches into independent Negro and Northern white churches. In 1860 there had been 207,766 Negro members of the Methodist Episcopal Church, South; in 1866 there were but 78,742 remaining. The Church South at its General Conference in 1866 directed that if the colored membership desired it and the bishops approved, the Negro members should be formed into an independent ecclesiastical body. Four years later this was done at Jackson, Tennessee, when two colored bishops were ordained by Bishops Paine and McTyeire, and the name adopted by the new body was the Colored Methodist Episcopal Church in America. From that time, therefore, there has been no Negro membership in the Methodist Episcopal Church, South.

The Northern churches which reaped the largest benefit from the Negro withdrawals from Southern churches were the independent Northern Negro churches, the African Methodist Episcopal and the African Methodist Episcopal, Zion. Both of these organizations had been formed in the North in the early years of the century, as a result of the resentment felt by Negro members of Methodist churches in New York and Philadelphia because of discrimination against them. The African Methodist Episcopal Church was formed in Philadelphia in 1816 under the leadership of Richard Allen, who became their first bishop; while the African Methodist Episcopal, Zion, Church was formed in New York in 1820 when James Varick was chosen their first bishop. Previous to the Civil War these Negro churches had no Southern membership, but when the war was over, both churches began a vigorous and successful campaign for the winning of the Southern Negro. The rapid growth of these two Negro churches is shown by the following figures: In 1866 the African Methodist Church had in round numbers about 70,000 members, and about 500 preachers; ten years later (1876) the traveling preachers had increased to 1,832, the number of local preachers had reached the astounding number of 7,928, while the membership totaled 391,044. In 1866 the African Zion Church had some 42,000 members, which had increased by 1868 to 164,000, while their ministers numbered 694. Large numbers of Negroes formerly members of Southern white Presbyterian churches also went into independent Methodist or Baptist churches.[2]

Unfortunately, these independent Negro churches came to be much involved with the carpetbag and Negro politics, and their church buildings were frequently used for political meetings, while their leaders in numbers of instances during this period obtained political offices. This fact led the Colored Methodist Episcopal Church to place in its *Discipline* a rule forbidding the use of their church houses for political speeches or meetings. The other Negro churches called the Colored Methodists the "rebel church"[3] or the "Democratic church" and in some instances even refused to enter into social relations with those connected in any way with the Colored Methodist Church. On the other hand, the Northern Negro churches openly professed their sympathy with the Republican party. In a series of resolutions passed by the American Methodists at a convention in Florida in 1871 they declared a boycott on all "steamers, railroad companies, merchants, and others who treat" the Negro disgracefully, and

---

[2] In 1865 Bishop Payne, of the African Methodist Episcopal Church, made arrangements with the American Missionary Association, the Congregational organization working among the freedmen, whereby that organization agreed to assume the partial support of African Methodist missionaries in South Carolina (Smith, C. S., *History of the African Methodist Episcopal Church*, p. 60).

[3] For a fuller discussion of the Negro churches and their political activities, see Sweet, W. W., *Methodist Church Influence in Southern Politics*. The *Mississippi Valley Hist. Rev.*, Vol. I, No. 4, pp. 547-560. See also *Negro Churches in the South: A Phase of Reconstruction*, by W. W. Sweet. The *Methodist Review*, 1921 (Fifth Series, Vol. XXXVII, No. 3), pp. 405-418.

declared that the minister "cannot do his whole duty" except he look out for the political interests of his people. Such activity caused the Ku Klux Klan to vent its wrath upon the Negroes who had joined the Northern churches by burning their churches and school buildings and by intimidating their preachers and teachers.

Thus there came to be four Methodist bodies competing for the Southern Negro: the Methodist Episcopal Church; the African Methodist; the African Methodist, Zion; and the Colored Methodist. At first the Negroes flocked to the churches of the Methodist Episcopal missionaries, but when the great wave of African Methodist preachers swept southward preaching, "I seek my brethren," they left their white missionary pastors for the more entreating call of the colored leader.

Nor were the Negro churches alone in their interest in reconstruction politics. The loyal support of the cause of the union by the Methodist Episcopal Church during the Civil War had created a political-mindedness among them which was to continue throughout the period of reconstruction and beyond. In some quarters the Methodist Episcopal Church was considered a sort of adjunct to the Republican party, and too often even the missionaries of the freedmen became involved in party politics and were elected to political office, and must, therefore, share the blame for the unspeakable corruption which attended carpetbag and Negro rule.

Generally speaking, the Northern Methodist press took an attitude of criticism and open hostility to President Andrew Johnson and his policy of reconstruction. As the contest between President Johnson and Congress became more and more bitter the Methodist press lined up openly against the President and in favor of his impeachment. The General Conference of 1868, which convened in Chicago, during the impeachment trial of President Johnson, set aside an hour of prayer that the country might be delivered from the "corrupt influences" which were being exerted to prevent the conviction of Andrew Johnson, which is a commentary on the fallibility of ministerial judgment. All this does not mean that the motives of all the missionaries and teachers from the North who came into the South during this period were mean and selfish. Some, it is true, did disgrace the church and their calling, but the motives of the majority were as high and as unselfish as were those of any missionary to China or Africa.

The primary issue before the General Conference of the Methodist Episcopal Church of 1868, which met in Chicago, was that of lay representation. Many prominent laymen of the church were now actively back of the movement, and it was soon evident that a large majority of the delegates to this General Conference were favorable to it. There were some, however, who doubted the constitutional right of the Conference to admit laymen because of the second restrictive rule. Finally resolutions were adopted with only three negative votes, declaring the General Conference ready to admit lay delegates, and recommending that the matter be voted upon by the Annual Conferences, and also that the laymen be given a chance to an expression of opinion during the month of June, 1869. The Conference further resolved that:

TRYING YEARS OF RECONSTRUCTION

Should a majority of the votes cast by the people be in favor of lay delegation, and should three quarters of the Annual Conferences vote in favor of the proposed change in the constitution of the church, then the General Conference of 1872, by the requisite two-thirds vote, can complete the change, and lay delegates previously elected may then be admitted.

After a period of uncertainty as to the outcome of the balloting, it was finally decided in favor of the resolution, and the General Conference of 1872 was the first to admit lay members. This did not provide for equal lay representation, however, but only for two lay delegates from each Annual Conference. Thus was begun after so long delay the Americanization of Methodism. The idea that the ministry has a divine right to control has no place in Protestantism, and it is strange that American Methodism was so slow in adopting this thoroughly Protestant and American principle. The final step in giving laymen equality in all the church's councils was taken by the General Conference of 1932, when that body completed the constitutional process of admitting them to membership in the Annual Conferences. The period immediately following the Civil War was one of remarkable educational development in the church. The program of the Centennial celebration (1866) called for the establishment of a Centenary Educational Fund; the strengthening of the two biblical institutions already in existence and the founding of new biblical institutes in the Eastern Middle States, in Cincinnati or vicinity, and on the Pacific Coast. Daniel Drew, a wealthy New York layman, gave $600,000 for the establishment of a theological seminary at Madison, New Jersey, and the beautiful Gibbons estate was purchased for the institution. Drew Theological Seminary opened its doors in 1867 under the presidency of Dr. John McClintock, the "most universally accomplished man American Methodism had produced." In 1869 Boston University was chartered; three prominent laymen of Boston co-operating in its establishment— Isaac Rich, Lee Claflin, and Jacob Sleeper. Sleeper had been mayor of Boston and for twelve years was a member of the board of overseers of Harvard University. In 1870 Syracuse University was chartered and began operation the following year. The new university opened with an endowment of $300,000.

The Church South was also educationally active during these years. In 1872 an attempt was made on the part of several Southern Annual Conferences to establish a real university, which would meet more adequately the demands of the church. The institution was not to be opened until a sum of $500,000 was obtained. The attempt to raise this large sum was unsuccessful and its promoters were about to admit failure when Cornelius Vanderbilt, of New York, gave $500,000, which he later increased to $1,000,000; and subsequently his son, William H. Vanderbilt, added $250,000. The opening of Vanderbilt University in 1875 was a notable event in the history of Southern Methodism. In a sense it was the first real university in the South and began operations with six departments, among them a school of theology, the first theological school of the Southern church. Some years later George I. Seney, a Methodist layman of New York, gave $260,-000 to Emory College and Wesleyan Female College of Georgia, greatly strengthening those institutions.

TRYING YEARS OF RECONSTRUCTION

In connection with the Centennial celebration in 1866 the church raised nearly $9,000,000 for many objects, but a large proportion of the money went to local enterprises. Out of the Centennial also came the Board of Education, and the institution of Children's Day, which has been almost universally observed throughout the church since that time.

The years of reconstruction have been characterized by a recent interpreter as a period of moral collapse in both government and business. The country's wealth was increasing with almost incredible rapidity, while the men in public office were too often not only incapable, but were woefully lacking in moral and ethical perceptions. War, as a rule, brings to prominence a class of rough and unscrupulous men with low standards of personal conduct, and such a class was now largely in control of the nation's government and business. These were the years when the notorious Tweed ring was in complete control of the government of New York City and to a large degree of the government of the Empire State as well. This gang of thieves "scooped in the rewards of their unholy labors, multiplying the debt of the city tenfold in a decade and putting no small part of the proceeds into their own pockets." Bribery was everywhere rampant, not alone in the great cities of the East but in Kansas, Iowa, and other states, and in every section of the land men of low moral standards robbed the public. The session of the Legislature of Illinois in 1867-1868 "was a veritable orgy of boodle legislation"; in Iowa the funds of the State Agricultural College were stolen; the state treasurer of Minnesota was impeached and removed for dishonesty; in Missouri a senatorial candidate attempted to buy his way into the United States Senate with a bribe of fifteen thousand dollars; while in Kansas Senator Pomeroy was found to have paid a member of the Legislature seven thousand dollars for his vote. These are not isolated cases, but are typical of the general situation in state and city governments throughout the land. Nor was the federal government immune from corruption, and officials of high rank, including well-known Congressmen, Cabinet members, and even the Vice-President of the United States, were not beyond suspicion of receiving bribes.

Nor was commercial morality ever so debased. The public was looked upon as fair prey, and nationally known men, some in high public office, lent the prestige of their names to all kinds of dishonest schemes. Stocks were sold in railroads which were never intended to be built, while mines, oil wells, and railroads were pawns in the game of dishonest speculators. Many men, like Daniel Drew and Cornelius Vanderbilt, and others, gave money lavishly to good causes, and at the same time were carrying on business transactions which can only be characterized as unscrupulous plundering.[4]

It is not strange that in the face of the general scramble for wealth, with dishonest business practices on every hand, some of the servants of the church should have fallen into pitfalls. By this time the publishing business of the church, both in New York and Cincinnati, had reached large

---

[4] For an excellent account of the political and business corruption of the period, see Allan Nevins, *The Emergence of Modern America,* 1868-1878. Vol. VIII, *A History of American Life,* New York: Macmillan, 1927. Especially Chap. VII.

proportions. From 1844 to 1848 the sales of the Book Concern totaled $612,625. In the years following there was a steady rise in the volume of business, so that in the quadrennium from 1884 to 1888, which marked the end of the first one hundred years of the life of the Book Concern, the total sales reached the impressive figure of $6,920,743. Each Concern was entirely under the control of an agent and an assistant agent, and a Book Committee made up of fifteen traveling ministers, elected by the General Conference. At the General Conference of 1868 the Rev. John Lanahan, of the Baltimore Conference, was elected assistant agent of the New York Book Concern, and soon after taking up his duties he discovered serious irregularities in the management of several of the departments. Among the things discovered was the fact that the son of the former assistant agent for some reason was permitted to sell to the Book Concern practically all the paper used, amounting to at least $100,000 a year. The various paper firms sold at a low price to Porter, and he, in turn, charged the Book Concern what he pleased. Lanahan found that in 1868 he had put into his pocket from nine to eleven thousand dollars from this particular "racket." All the paper concerns stated that they would have much preferred to have sold the paper directly to the Concern and would have given them the same price as was allowed Porter. This was known by the senior agent, but the practice continued until Lanahan, in the face of great opposition, stopped it. Glaring frauds were also found in the bindery department. Other frauds were discovered in the payment of wages, in inventories, in the purchase of ink and leather, covering a relatively long period of time, the losses totaling at least $300,000.

Having made these discoveries of dishonesty in the conduct of the publishing business of the church, Lanahan sought the co-operation of the senior agent in putting a stop to them. But instead of co-operation he found evasion and active opposition. At least four of the official papers of the church held up Lanahan to public reproach because of his activities, and the New York *Christian Advocate* even published a supplement to refute his charges. Finally the Book Committee was convened and the assistant agent submitted his evidence of fraud. The Committee at once divided, the majority supporting the senior agent, while the minority approved the work of the assistant agent. Both reports were presented to the Annual Conferences, where in most cases the report of the majority was approved, while the minority report was laid on the table. Lanahan was now suspended and placed on trial before the Book Committee and the bishops, whose concurrent action was necessary to convict. The charges against Lanahan were five in number: official misconduct; neglect of official duty; untruthfulness, irascibility, and other objectionable characteristics; insubordination, and finally want of business qualifications. Before the completion of the trial the charges were dismissed,[5] largely through the action of the bishops, who disapproved of the manner in which the charges were made, and of the nature of the charges themselves. The whole pro-

---

[5] For a detailed account of the trial, see Lanahan, John, *The Era of Frauds in The Methodist Book Concern at New York*. Baltimore: Methodist Book Depository, 1896.

cedure of the Book Committee seemed to be dictated by their desire to cover up and conceal the wrongdoing rather than to bring the actual wrongdoers to light.

There now arose a strange controversy between the senior and assistant book agents. When the assistant agent attempted to gain access to the books to permit their examination by experts for further evidence of fraud, the senior agent refused. This led Lanahan to appeal to the Supreme Court of New York for an injunction to compel him to do so. This the court finally refused to do, though the judge who gave the decision was soon after impeached and removed. Meanwhile Lanahan was again suspended by the Book Committee for taking the affairs of the church into the civil courts.

The result of the second trial was that the majority of the committee found Lanahan guilty of taking the affairs of the church into the civil courts and decided that he should be removed from office. The two bishops, Janes and Ames, whose concurrence was necessary to remove the assistant agent, divided over the matter, Ames declining to concur, with the result that the assistant agent was left in the possession of his office. Later Lanahan was arrested for slander, and although he desired the case to come to trial, that he might prove in the court that serious frauds had been perpetrated in the Book Concern, the case was finally dropped.

The revelations brought out by this long and bitter controversy were influential in determining the vote on lay representation in the General Conference. Many felt that the business interests of the church had become so large and the possibility of evil so great that assistance of laymen had become a necessity. The case is also an example of the tendency of ministers to palliate wrongdoing among their number under the mistaken idea that bringing it to light and punishing the wrongdoers somehow injures the church. Here lies a large share of the danger of complete clerical control.

At the ensuing General Conference (1872) a special committee on the affairs of the Book Concern was ordered, made up of one member from each delegation. On this committee were numerous distinguished business men and several lawyers. The committee reported that there had been repeated frauds practiced in the management of the Book Concern, particularly in the bindery department, but that the losses were not so great as to endanger the financial strength of the business. They condemned the manner in which the paper of the Concern had been purchased, as well as certain other transactions.

While not satisfactory to Dr. John Lanahan, who had unearthed the frauds, the report of the committee impressed the Conference with the necessity of a change in the management of the Book Concern, and the following changes were authorized: Hereafter the two agents were to have equal authority. Three laymen residing in the vicinity of New York, and three residing in the vicinity of Cincinnati were to constitute a Local Committee, with whom the agents were to confer at least once a month. The Local Committee were also to have power to suspend an agent or editor, but a two-thirds vote of the General Conference was necessary for removal of the said agent or editor.

TRYING YEARS OF RECONSTRUCTION

The General Conference of 1872 convened in the city of Brooklyn with 292 ministerial delegates and 129 lay delegates, representing seventy-six Annual Conferences. The important legislation enacted was the recognition of the newly formed Woman's Foreign Missionary Society, which had been organized in 1869 through the efforts of two ladies, Mrs. E. W. Parker, and Mrs. William Butler; the recognition of the Freedmen's Aid Society; the adoption of a plan for the forming of District Conferences; the adoption of a rule on amusements, which specifically condemned the buying, selling, or using intoxicating liquors; dancing, playing at games of chance, attending theaters, horse-races, circuses, dancing parties, or patronizing dancing schools. A new court of appeals from the decisions of Annual Conferences was created, made up of seven elders of each Annual Conference, who were to be known as triers of appeals. The bishops, who heretofore had lived where they chose, were now assigned specific residences. This Conference elected eight new bishops: Thomas Bowman, William L. Harris, Randolph S. Foster, Isaac W. Wiley, Stephen M. Merrill, Edward G. Andrews, Gilbert Haven, and Jesse T. Peck, the largest number elected up to that time at any one General Conference.

The question of union among the several Methodist bodies in the United States was considerably agitated during the years of reconstruction. There was a gesture of union between two Southern Conferences of the Methodist Protestant Church and the Methodist Episcopal Church, South, in 1866 and 1867, and commissions representing each body met, but no terms of agreement were reached. At the

same time there was a movement set on foot to unite
the non-Episcopal Methodist bodies: the Methodist
Protestant, the Wesleyan Methodist, the Independent Methodist, and the Free Methodist, at a convention in Cincinnati in 1866. A new church to
be known as the Methodist Church was projected
and a committee was appointed to draw up a form
of *Discipline,* but at a General Conference in Cleveland the next year (1867) it was found that the
Northern Conferences of the Methodist Protestant
Church were practically the only ones to send representatives. The Southern Conferences continued
under the old name. Thus instead of uniting four
independent churches—a fifth was added. In 1874,
however, negotiations for reunion of the Northern
or Methodist Church with the Southern Methodist
Protestant Church were begun, and a basis of union
was formed by a joint commission the following
year. In 1877 the two bodies met in their conventions in Baltimore, and there the union was happily
consummated. At this time the reunited church
contained a membership of 113,405, with 1,314 ministers.

A ray of fraternal sunshine also began to break
through the clouds of suspicion surrounding the two
great bodies of Episcopal Methodists. The New
York East Annual Conference at its session in 1866
sent its Christian salutations to the General Conference of the Church South at New Orleans, and
invited the Southern Conference to make Sunday,
April 8, 1866, a day of special prayer for the peace
and unity of the country and a restoration of full
Christian sympathy between the churches, especially between the two branches of Methodism. To

this invitation the Southern General Conference returned a hearty response. At a meeting of the bishops of the Methodist Episcopal Church, in the spring of 1869, at Meadville, Pennsylvania, two of their number were sent to the annual meeting of the Southern Bishops at Saint Louis where the question of a possible reunion was broached, "since," as they stated, "the cause of the separation has been removed." To this the Southern Bishops replied that slavery was not the cause but only the occasion of separation, and they reminded their Northern brethren that "we separated from you in no sense in which you did not separate from us," and reminded them that "nearer approaches to each other can be conducted, with hope of successful issue, only on this basis." A delegation from the Methodist Episcopal Church was also sent to the Southern General Conference of 1870, convening at Memphis, Tennessee. The delegation was cordially received and presented an address urging the Church South to appoint a commission to consider the subject of union. The Northern delegation's commission was, however, unfortunately worded in that it was not specifically authorized to treat with the Church South, but with the African Methodist Episcopal, Zion, Church, or any other church which came knocking at the door of the Methodist Episcopal Church. Naturally, the Church South wanted it distinctly understood that they were not knocking at the doors of the Methodist Episcopal Church and passed resolutions stating that: "the true interests of the Church of Christ require and demand the maintenance of our separate and distinct organization."

The General Conference of 1872 (Methodist

Episcopal) took up the matter of fraternal relations with the Church South and recommended the appointment of a delegation to bear fraternal greetings to its next General Conference. A delegation of three was chosen, the Rev. A. S. Hunt, the Rev. C. H. Fowler, and General Clinton B. Fisk. Each delegate gave a short address before the Southern General Conference at its session in Louisville in 1874, and later the Conference appointed a large committee to take action on the question of fraternity. This committee brought in a long report, pointing out the differences between the two churches which rendered union both difficult and impractical. The report closes, however, with an expression of pleasure at the visit of the fraternal delegates from the North and authorized the Southern bishops to send a similar delegation to the next General Conference of their sister church. Also the report suggested a commission to meet with a similar one from the Methodist Episcopal Church to adjust all existing difficulties.

The next step in the direction of better understanding was taken at the Baltimore General Conference (1876) of the Methodist Episcopal Church, where Southern fraternal delegates were cordially received. The Conference then appointed a commission to meet that of the Church South. This resulted in what is known as the Cape May Conference, which met at Cape May, New Jersey, in August, 1876, where a *Declaration and Basis of Fraternity* was unanimously adopted. This declaration declares:

Each of the said churches is a legitimate branch of Episcopal Methodism in the United States, having a common origin in the Methodist Episcopal Church organized in

TRYING YEARS OF RECONSTRUCTION

1784. Since the organization of the Methodist Episcopal Church, South, was consummated in 1845 by the voluntary exercise of the right of the Southern Annual Conferences, ministers, and members to adhere to that communion, it has been an evangelical church, reared on scriptural foundations, and her ministers and members, with those of the Methodist Episcopal Church, have constituted one Methodist family, though in distinct ecclesiastical connections.

By this action the "irritating discussion of the Plan of Separation was officially closed," which was a distinct gain for closer relationships between the two great Methodist Episcopal bodies.

The first decade following the Civil War saw the rapid expansion of foreign missions. The mission to India established in 1856 by Dr. William Butler and his wife, after consultation with missionaries of other churches already in India, began its work in the territory between the Ganges River and the Himalayas. The Sepoy Rebellion (1857) compelled the infant mission to abandon its station at Bareilly, but the work was soon resumed, and in 1864 the India Mission Conference was organized at Lucknow. In 1872 the American Methodists began work in Italy and headquarters were established at Rome, where valuable properties were acquired. Although the work in point of numbers was disappointing, yet through its educational institutions especially, the mission has exercised a wide influence outside its actual membership. Doctor and Mrs. William Butler, who had been the founders of the Indian mission, were also the first missionaries to begin work in Mexico. They arrived in Mexico City in 1873. The ancient palace of Montezuma, which for three hundred years had

329

been a Catholic monastery, was purchased and became the Methodist headquarters. Soon Methodist work was being carried on successfully in Pueblo and in numerous other centers, and in 1885 the Mexican Missions were organized into an Annual Conference. The same year Methodist work began in Mexico (1873) Robert S. Maclay arrived in Yokohama to start Methodist work in Japan. Other missionaries soon came, sent by the Woman's Foreign Missionary Society, as well as by the general Board; schools were opened and many stations established, and in 1884 an Annual Conference was organized.

The most spectacular missionary figure in American Methodism in this period of vigorous missionary expansion was William Taylor. His pioneer work in California has already been noticed, where he was the second Methodist missionary on the scene. Having become personally responsible for the debts of a church that had burned, he spent the next seven years "evangelizing" through the Eastern states and Canada. In 1862 he began an extensive foreign evangelizing tour, visiting Australia, Tasmania, southern Africa, Ceylon, and India. In southern India he founded several self-supporting mission churches composed of Englishmen, Eurasians, and English-speaking natives, which under other laborers grew into two Annual Conferences. In 1879 Taylor planted several self-supporting missions in the republic of Chile in South America, making the center of each station a school, the fees being the chief support of the missionary teacher. While in South America the South India Conference requested him to represent them as a lay delegate at the General Conference of 1884, and that Conference made him missionary bishop for Africa. The self-supporting-mission idea was far more difficult to work out in Africa than in the other lands where it had been attempted. Here Taylor introduced such industries as were best suited to the various parts of the continent where missions were opened, though in most instances subsidies were required until these industries were developed to the point of adequate returns.

In 1890 the foreign missionary work of the Methodist Episcopal Church carried on by the Woman's Foreign and the general Missionary Societies reported 2,208 missionaries and other workers; 1,237 local preachers, colporteurs, Bible readers, etc.; 1,319 teachers, native and foreign; and 74,731 members and probationers, and 63,763 regular adherents. There were in the foreign fields no less than 18 theological schools for the education of native preachers, with 52 teachers and 326 students; 1,072 regular day schools with more than three hundred teachers and 33,518 pupils; the total property of the missions, including churches, chapels, hospitals, orphanages, and parsonages, amounted to $2,964,158.

The Methodist Episcopal Church, South, was likewise fully alive to the call of foreign fields during the very years in which they were facing their most difficult domestic situation. In 1874 they established a mission in Brazil which grew into a Conference in 1886. In 1873 Mexican work was begun, which likewise, in 1886, was formed into a Mission Conference. Later missions were established in Japan (1886), in Korea (1897), in Cuba (1898), and in Africa (1914).

CHAPTER XVI

METHODISM IN THE GILDED AGE, 1880-1900

IF FRANCIS ASBURY could have returned to life in the year 1880, he would have contemplated American Methodism with mixed emotions. He would have witnessed in Methodism the most evenly distributed church in the land and would have recognized in that fact the triumph of the circuit system for which he in so large a measure was responsible. From Ohio westward to the Pacific Coast, and from the Great Lakes to the Gulf of Mexico he would have found a Methodist church established in almost every county seat town, as well as in every considerable village and at innumerable country crossroads. He would have seen preachers in the newer sections of the land still riding large circuits, much as they had done in his day, but, on the other hand, he would have found in the cities and larger towns an increasing number of stationed preachers. There were now many "splendid" churches, in which, according to Alfred Brunson, "the people praised God by proxy, having quartets, choirs, and musical machines to do it for them, instead of doing it directly themselves." In such churches the class meeting was rapidly dying out, for with the coming of the stationed preacher and weekly services such an official as the class leader was soon found to be in a large degree superfluous. Many of the older members, however, still clung to the time-honored institution and held class meetings after the morning preaching, though with a rapidly declining attendance. The gradual dying out of the class meeting was naturally attended by the sorrowful complaints of the older generation, who saw in its disappearance not only an indication of a decline in vital religion but also a sure sign that Methodism itself was rapidly approaching the "rocks."

Many of the old camp-meeting grounds, with which the pioneer bishop was so familiar, were still in use, but the rows of tents were rapidly giving place to streets of frame cottages, and instead of the old-time camp-meeting revival, the religious services were now interspersed with lectures on semi-religious and even secular subjects. If there was less evidence of the old-time religious fervor, fewer shouts and hallelujahs, there was also less rowdyism. In fact, many of the old-time camp-meeting grounds were rapidly being transformed into respectable middle-class summer resorts with only a tinge of religion.

Perhaps nothing would have astonished the good bishop more than the long list of Methodist institutions of learning, many of them bearing the name "university," which were to be found in every section of the land. At his death sixty-four years before there had not been a single institution above the grade of academy under Methodist patronage. There were under the control of the Methodist Episcopal Church alone in 1880, 11 theological seminaries and institutes; 44 colleges and universities and 130 seminaries and women's schools, with a total enrollment of 21,000 students and property valued at $11,560,100. In Bishop Asbury's day there was no Methodist Missionary Society, no foreign or home missions, nor were there any church periodicals, while Sunday schools, now designated "church schools," were just beginning to be formed here and there among the circuits and stations. In 1880 there were twenty periodicals published under the authority of the General Conference of the Methodist Episcopal Church, besides many other periodicals published in the interests of the church. In 1816 there were 11 Annual Conferences and a total membership of 224,853; in 1880 there were in the Methodist Episcopal Church alone 89 Annual Conferences in the United States, besides 7 Mission Conferences and 15 Missions, with a total membership of 1,742,922; in the Methodist Episcopal Church, South, there were 39 Annual Conferences in the United States, and 4 Mission Conferences, with a total membership of 832,175; in the Methodist Protestant Church there were 44 Conferences with a membership of 130,000; while in the three large Negro Methodist Episcopal Churches there were at least 600,000 members, or a total of nearly 4,000,-000 Methodists in the United States alone.

It is safe to say that no Christian organization had ever shown such spectacular growth in so short a time. And yet in the face of these statistics indicating the rapid growth of the church, there was an increasing number of both ministers and the more serious-minded laymen who beheld certain changes taking place within the church with grave misgivings. Methodism, they proclaimed, was on the retreat, not because of any change in the constitution of the church, but, rather, because of administration. The Methodist Church had been a living organism, and it was now becoming more and more a mere mechanism. Christian fellowship was formerly the conserving principle, kept alive by the class meeting and the circuit system. It was not then a matter "of architecture, æsthetics, or pulpit talent." An ominous change has transpired, "when highest authority asserts the necessity of putting a quarter million dollars into church property to save certain families to a city's Methodism." Is "a preacher, a building, a voice, a distinguished name" sufficient to compact the membership together? This was not Wesley's answer, nor Coke's, nor Asbury's, nor Paul's. Other symptoms of the serious decline of Methodism, more manifest in some places than others, were the rise of the trustee and the decline of the leader and the steward, the drying up of the local ministry, the widespread and increasing laxity of discipline, the toning down of the visible lines between the church and the world, the uneasy doubt concerning positive conversion, the loss of the grip on the masses, especially in the "best appointments," and the growth of professional evangelism. To some these changes represented progress, but it really meant the discarding of the apostolic principle, which gave organic life to the church. It meant that the machinery of Methodism was ungeared "from the great shaft over which Mr. Wesley placed its bands; therefore its wheels revolve less frequently; therefore the thing slows down; and if we mistake not it is running down."

But such changes as were taking place in American Methodism were inevitable, for the church could not stand apart from the social, educational, and economic changes which were taking place in the nation. In the very nature of the case Methodists were bound to become economically prosperous. The emphasis upon personal redemption, individual worth, cleanness of life and all the common virtues, such as sobriety, faithfulness, and frugality, will eventually bring their economic rewards. John Wesley saw this clearly enough when he said: "Religion must necessarily produce both industry and frugality, and these cannot but produce riches. But as riches increase so will pride, anger, and love of the world in all its branches." How is this dilemma to be met? "We ought not," he says, "to prevent people from being diligent and frugal; we must exhort all Christians to gain all they can, and to save all they can—that is, in effect, to grow rich. What way, then, can we take, that our money may not sink us into the nethermost hell? There is one way, and there is no other way under heaven. If those who gain all they can, and save all they can, will likewise give all they can, then the more they gain, the more they will grow in grace, and the more treasure they will lay up in heaven."

It was just this problem, which Wesley so clearly perceived, that an increasing number of American Methodists began to face in the last two decades of the nineteenth century. In fact, it can be said that the most serious problem faced by American Methodism as a whole at this time was its rapidly increasing wealth. It was this, together with the growing luxury of urban life, which was responsible for the many disturbing changes taking place in the church, which to an increasing number of earnest people seemed to be sapping Methodist vitality. In rare instances Mr. Wesley's formula of gaining all you can, saving all you can, and giving all you can, doubtless worked, but many Methodists with newly gained riches forgot to apply the third part of the formula and failed, therefore, to lay up treasures in heaven.

No longer were Methodists drawn from the lower and humbler economic and social groups, but rather represented the great middle class, and, as Mr. Roosevelt asserted, constituted "the most representative church in America." "Though members of its upper ranges, fired by the ostentatious display of the plutocracy, crowded the hotels at Saratoga Springs and Long Branch, attended the opera, and made 'the grand tour' of Europe, the large majority was composed of people who possessed only moderate incomes or were, in fact, struggling along on the margin of subsistence to maintain appearances—hard-working husbands and pinching wives fighting desperately to keep their heads above water, support their sons in college, and marry their daughters into a better class."[1] Though these are the words of a rather unfriendly critic, they are not greatly different from the statement of a contemporary Methodist correspondent who blames "European travel, increasing culture and wealth, the evolutionary philosophy, and 'French flats'" as the influences which were destroying what he felt to be the cardinal principles of Methodism.

The period from 1880 onward was one of voracious money-getting in the United States. To many persons the accumulation of wealth became the one

[1] Beard and Beard, *Rise of American Civilization*, Vol. IV, p. 400. By permission of The Macmillan Company, publishers.

all-absorbing and all-important object in life, and it was in this period that the foundations of many of the great American fortunes were laid. As Doctor Beard has pointed out, most of those enrolled as the leaders of the new industrial age were members of churches, in good and regular standing. Few of them were Methodists, but the ideal of business efficiency, system, and organization began to exercise a powerful influence in the councils of the church. This is reflected in the rising scale of ministers' salaries, the building of larger and more costly churches, the introduction of pipe organs and paid choirs, while with increasing frequency the complaint was heard that in the local church the business meeting was taking the place of the prayer meeting.

To an increasing degree the business of the church fell more and more into the hands of laymen. The growing influence of laymen is especially apparent in the administration of the Methodist colleges. Prior to the Civil War Methodist colleges were controlled almost without exception by Annual Conferences. The presidents were always ministers, as were a majority of the members of the faculties. But as the number of wealthy laymen increased, more and more they began to take the places on boards of trustees formerly held by ministers, and not infrequently wealthy laymen who were without church affiliation were urged to accept such positions with the hope, no doubt, that they might be induced to contribute liberally to the institution. With boards of trustees controlled by business men, the business and administration end of the colleges began to receive greater attention. Before 1890 the Methodist college president taught at least one subject, but more and more they began to give their entire attention to administration, and new administrative officials increased with alarming rapidity, until the administration budget often equaled the amount spent for instruction.

Such exaltation of administration was likewise reflected throughout the church. The change of the title "presiding elder," in spite of its long and honorable use in the church, to that of "district superintendent" in 1908 indicates the changing functions of that official from those of an inspirational leader to those of a business and administrative officer. To an increasing degree also the office of a bishop has become an administrative one. Episcopal headquarters, almost without exception, are in great city office buildings. The great boards of the church, such as that of World Service, Foreign Missions, Home Missions, and Education, likewise called for administrative efficiency, whose secretaries could not be distinguished, on the street or in their offices, from the usual type of American business man. The pastors of the larger churches also to an increasing degree became of necessity largely administrative officials, giving a major share of their time and energy to attending business meetings, caring for the social and athletic program of the local church, and in promoting the great connectional interests of the church.

Another influence of wealth upon the institutions of the church is well illustrated by the withdrawal of Vanderbilt University from the control of the Methodist Episcopal Church, South. This institution had been established by six of the Annual Conferences of the Church South in 1873, and was controlled by these Conferences until 1898, when, at their request, the university was transferred to the control of the General Conference, thus becoming an institution for the entire church. The Board of Trust recognized that control and "rejoiced in the ownership of the university" until 1905. In this year an attempt was made by a majority of the trustees and the chancellor to end that control in order to bring about an alliance between Vanderbilt University and the funds under the control of the Peabody Foundation. The bishops, who were *ex officio* members of the Board of Trust, brought an action in the Chancery Court to restrain the majority of the Board of Trust from carrying out their purpose. This the court did, when the majority of the Board appealed the case to the Supreme Court of the State of Tennessee. While this case was pending, the chancellor approached Andrew Carnegie with a request for a million dollars for the medical school of the University. This request was favorably received by Mr. Carnegie, but he suggested that unless the Board of Trust won its appeal, he would hesitate to give the money, since he did not believe it wise "for any sect to control educational institutions, such as universities, whether the organization be a Methodist Conference or a Presbyterian Assembly or a Catholic order." The next year (1914) the Supreme Court handed down its decision completely reversing the findings of the Chancery Court, and confirming the action of the Board of Trust. The General Conference of 1914 accepted the decision of the Supreme Court of Tennessee after entering their "solemn protest," and immediately took action authorizing the establishment of two new universities and a school of theology. The church almost at once accepted Southern Methodist University at Dallas, Texas, as its university west of the Mississippi, and made Emory College at Oxford, Georgia, a university, adding several professional schools in the city of Atlanta, among them the Candler School of Theology and the Atlanta Medical School, and planned the establishment of Lamar School of Law. A theological school was also established at the Southern Methodist University.

An important feature of the history of American Methodism in the eighties and nineties was the rise of protest groups, especially in the South and Middle West, against the tendencies we have noted. As the church became more and more dominated by men of wealth and controlled by business methods, and as the services became more formal, and the preaching less fervid, complaints were raised that "heart religion" was disappearing. Beginning about 1880 and continuing until the close of the century and beyond, the so-called "holiness" question agitated the Methodist Episcopal and the Methodist Episcopal Church, South, and the other churches of the Methodist family.

In the two decades previous to the Civil War Wesley's doctrine of Christian perfection was largely neglected and had become little more than a creedal matter among the main Methodist bodies. In 1860 the Free Methodist Church had been organized in western New York by a group of members of the Genesee Conference, who had formed an association for mutual protection against discrimination on the part of the appointing officials. When the leader of the movement, Benjamin T. Roberts, was expelled for attacking members of the Conference, others withdrew and a separate church was organized. The new church attempted to revive all the old Methodist forms and techniques, such as class meetings and believers' meetings, opposed the wearing of gold and costly apparel and emphasized the cultivation of the perfect life. The Wesleyan Methodists and a small imported body, the Primitive Methodists, introduced into the United States in 1844, also emphasized the doctrine of Christian perfection, but the great "holiness" revival came, however, after 1880.

In the years immediately following the Civil War the Church South was visited by a general religious awakening, and "a sound of revival was heard from one border to the other." In the North revivals occurred here and there, which soon merged into a nation-wide movement for the restoration of "holiness" to a place of central importance. The national holiness movement began as an interdenominational emphasis, but under Methodist leadership. In 1867 the first general holiness camp meeting was held at Vineland, New Jersey, resulting in the formation of the "National Camp-Meeting Association for the Promotion of Holiness." This organization drew practically all of its support from Methodistic churches. Periodicals emphasizing the doctrine of holiness were soon enjoying wide circulation among Methodist people, and organizations were formed, made up of those professing to have received the second blessing. Soon many churches throughout the South and the Middle West especially contained holiness parties, which were often critical of those whom they thought did not possess heart religion.

The holiness movement came to a crisis between 1890 and 1894. Up to this time it had been carried forward largely within the regular churches through loose organizations. But in the middle nineties a number of influences operated in the formation of separate holiness sects. One of these influences was the growing estrangement between the two extreme wings in the churches; another, the growing tendency of Methodist leaders to accept modernistic views, convinced the holiness leaders that "true religion" could only be preserved by separating from the older communions and the organizing of their own churches.

The Bishops' address at the General Conference of the Church South in 1894 thus summarizes the situation in that body:[2]

There has sprung up among us a party with holiness as a watchword; they have holiness associations, holiness meetings, holiness preachers, holiness evangelists, and holiness property. Religious experience is represented as if it consists of only two steps, the first step out of condemnation into peace and the next step into Christian perfection. . . . We do not question the sincerity and zeal of their brethren; we desire the church to profit by their earnest preaching and godly example; but we deplore their teaching and methods in so far as they claim a monopoly of the experience, practice, and advocacy of holiness, and separate themselves from the body of ministers and disciples.

The matter took on a more serious aspect in the minds of the Methodist administrative officials when the movement for separation began. In some sec-

---

[2] For an excellent treatment of this whole subject see Gaddis, M. E., *Christian Perfectionism in America* (Ph.D. Thesis, The University of Chicago, 1929), especially Chap. XI, "The National Holiness Movement and the Small Holiness Sects."

tions entire Annual Conferences were permeated with the doctrine, and many churches, large and small, were divided into conflicting groups. The bishops and presiding elders hastened to assure the holiness advocates that the church had always held to the Wesleyan doctrine of entire sanctification and attempted to hold these people in the church by persuading them that there had been no deviation from the Wesleyan teaching. In some instances such tactics were mildly successful, but through the latter nineties and beyond the turn of the century many small holiness and pentecostal bodies came into existence, most numerously in the Central West and in the South, where their chief feeders, the Methodistic churches, were the most numerous. As a whole these sects were largely made up of the poorer and less educated classes, while their membership has been largely drawn from rural and small urban communities.

The most important of the twenty-five or more holiness bodies is the Church of the Nazarene, which came into existence in the period following 1894. This church represents the merging of at least eight smaller sects, two of which originated in Tennessee, one each in New York, New England, and Los Angeles, two in Texas and one in Scotland. It took its present name in 1919 and according to the census of 1926 has a membership of 63,558. Both in doctrine and polity it is patterned after the Methodist Episcopal Church with certain modifications emphasizing its holiness character and insuring a wider democracy. With the rapid growth of the denomination there are indications that the holiness emphasis is being somewhat modified, illustrated by the changes in the names of its several schools. The Texas Holiness University has become Peniel College; Pentecostal Collegiate Institute has become Eastern Nazarene College; and Illinois Holiness University has become Olivet College. As a matter of fact, the Church of the Nazarene now seems the right wing of the holiness movement, and occupies a position midway between Methodism and the more radical holiness sects.

The twenty years following the Civil War were ones of feverish railroad construction. In 1869 the Union Pacific, the first transcontinental line, was completed; the work of building the Northern Pacific began in 1870, and by 1883 its tracks had reached the western slope of the Rocky Mountains, while other lines—the Sante Fe, the Southern Pacific, the Great Northern, and the Burlington—were soon carrying settlers into the trans-Missouri, the Rocky Mountain and southwestern sections of the great West. Two years following the close of the war Nebraska became a state and during the latter sixties and seventies the great mining boom brought an increasing number of people into the Rocky Mountain region. Between 1876 and 1896 the two Dakotas, and five Rocky Mountain states were admitted to the Union, while population in this territory had increased from less than 200,000 to more than 3,000,000.

Perhaps the organization which did most to extend Methodism into the great trans-Missouri region was the Church Extension Society. With the passage of the Homestead Act (1862), by which a quarter-section of land was given to the settler who would live on his claim for a given period of time, the movement of population into the prairie region was greatly enhanced. But the prairie regions presented a peculiar problem to the churches. In the heavily timbered regions such as Ohio, Kentucky, and Indiana the building of a church was a simple and cheap matter. But suitable timber was lacking in western Kansas, Nebraska, and the Dakotas. Here the rude sod building could serve a temporary purpose but for a more or less permanent building lumber would need to be brought in from a distance, which involved a much larger expense than the average new prairie community could meet. Hence the forming of a society intended to meet just this situation was a great boon to these new regions. The purpose of the society was to "secure suitable houses of public worship and such other church property" as may assist in the carrying forward of the work of the church. In 1872 the society became the Board of Church Extension. Within the first ten years the Extension society collected $3,000,000, of which $555,000 became a permanent loan fund. In 1916 a Board of Home Missions and Church Extension was authorized by the General Conference with five departments—Church Extension, City Work, Rural Work, Frontier Work, and Evangelism. This Board now carries on its work in the territories of Hawaii and Alaska as well as in Porto Rico and Santo Domingo; among the Indians of North America, among Negroes in all sections of the country, among recent immigrants and foreign-language groups, in agricultural communities, and among industrial workers.

Working alongside of the Home Mission and Church Extension organizations of the church was the Woman's Home Missionary Society, which was formed in Cincinnati in 1880. Though organized primarily to assist in the Freedmen's work in the South, it was soon assisting the needy and destitute women in all sections of the land. It conducts many kinds of institutions, but specializes in orphanages; homes for girls, known as Esther and Friendship Homes; nurseries, kindergartens and day schools for under-privileged children; and training schools for those preparing for Christian life service in either the home or foreign fields. In the last number of years it has raised more than a million and a half dollars annually and employs more than a thousand workers.

A work in the South following the Civil War of which the Methodist Episcopal Church may legitimately feel proud is that which has been carried on among the poor whites and the Negroes. The Southern leaders as well as those at the North fully recognized the appalling need among these under-privileged people. For a decade following the war their prevailing poverty made it impossible for the Southern people to do for these classes what many of them were anxious to do. The census of 1870 showed that Massachusetts had $1,463 for every man, woman and child in the state; Alabama had but $202; Georgia, $226; North Carolina, $243. In Kentucky there were twenty counties in which more than half the people were unable to read and write, and half of the people in six counties lived in houses without windows. In the year 1870 a leading minister of the Methodist Episcopal Church, South, Doctor Haywood, speaking before the students of Emory College, Oxford, Georgia, expressed devout thanksgiving for the abolition of slavery and recognized the fact that the South was in great need of education, stating that: "We are a hundred years behind the Eastern and Middle States. We are also behind many of the new states of the West."

It was to help meet this need that the Freedmen's Aid Society of the Methodist Episcopal Church entered the South at the close of the war, and has remained there, an effective force for economic, social, moral and religious uplift, through more than sixty-five years. At the end of the first thirteen years of its work the Society had collected and disbursed $893,918. In 1889 the total receipts for the year were $221,438. In that year the Society was maintaining twenty-nine colleges, professional and industrial schools, besides twelve academies for Negroes; eight colleges and professional schools and sixteen academies for whites. More than 200,000 Negroes have received instruction in these schools and their graduates have gone into every honorable occupation. One third of the Negro physicians, pharmacists and dentists practicing in the United States have graduated from the Meharry Medical College in Nashville, Tennessee. From Claflin College, a typical institution maintained by the Society, have gone out eighteen lawyers, seventy-eight ministers, six foreign missionaries, four hundred and thirty school teachers, fifty-three doctors, besides more than five hundred tradesmen and business men. At the present time the work in the South is carried on under the Board of Education for Negroes, a division of The Board of Education of the Methodist Episcopal Church.

The Epworth League is the living testimony of

American Methodism's interest in her younger sons and daughters. Sometime previous to 1872 young people's societies began to appear here and there in local churches. One of the earliest was the Church Lyceum, originating in the Fifty-First Street Methodist Episcopal Church in Philadelphia, of which the Rev. T. B. Neely was the pastor. Soon other churches in Philadelphia formed Lyceums and a union organization was proposed and eventually effected. A memorial was presented to the General Conference of 1872 asking that the Church Lyceum be authorized by that body, but press of business before the Conference prevented action at this time. In 1880, however, the General Conference adopted the society. In 1884 another young people's organization, known as the Oxford League, was formed which largely absorbed the Lyceums. Still another society, the Young People's Methodist Alliance, originated at the Des Plaines Camp Ground, near Chicago, in 1883. The Young People's Christian League came from a movement begun in Boston in 1887, while the Methodist Young People's Union was cradled in Detroit the same year.

In 1881 the Christian Endeavor Society had been founded in Portland, Maine, by Francis E. Clark as an interdenominational young people's organization, and numerous Endeavor Societies were formed in Methodist churches. Within the next few years young people's societies were established by most of the evangelical churches.

In 1889 the five Methodist young people's societies mentioned above, sent delegates to a convention which met in Central Church (now Epworth-Euclid), Cleveland, and there agreed to consolidate, and adopted the name Epworth League.[3] Within seven months charters had been granted to 1,480 chapters, and at its seventh anniversary there were 16,302 local societies. At its session in 1892 the General Conference gave the Epworth League its official approval. One of the early leaders of outstanding importance was Dr. Jesse L. Hurlbut. He had been associated with Dr. John H. Vincent in the Chautauqua as well as in the Oxford League and became the first corresponding secretary of the Epworth League.

Organized under four departments—Spiritual Work, Mercy and Help, Literary, and Social Work—with four vice-presidents, the Epworth League proved a great stimulus in the religious training of Methodist youth.

Much the same influences that had created the young people's societies in the Methodist Episcopal Church were being felt among the young people in the Church South, and in May, 1890, the General Conference, meeting at Saint Louis, authorized the formation of Epworth Leagues, for the "promotion of piety and loyalty to our church among the young people, their education in the Bible and Christian literature and in the missionary work of the church."

An outstanding tendency in the United States since the Civil War has been consolidation of political and economic institutions. This is illustrated in politics by the steadily growing power of the federal authority at the expense of the states; in busi-

---

[3] Helmers, John, *History of the Epworth League.* (M.A. thesis manuscript, University of Chicago, 1923.) Also Hutchinson, Paul, *The Story of the Epworth League.* New York: The Methodist Book Concern, 1927.

ness by the rise of the trusts and the consolidation of management at the expense of the individual operator. At the same time there was a growing emphasis upon organization and efficiency, while responsibility was delegated more and more to boards and committees. Nor was the church long in feeling this influence and in responding to it. The period since 1880, in both branches of Episcopal Methodism, has witnessed the rise of many new boards and connectional officials. At the head of these boards are secretaries elected by the General Conference, who direct the management of their particular board, and are responsible to the General Conference.[4]

With the rise of these great boards with their secretaries the Methodist bishops have found their field correspondingly narrowed. Thus in a sense we no longer have in the Methodist Episcopal Church real "general superintendents," for no Methodist bishop to-day exercises the wide control over every activity of the church as did Asbury. In fact, the bishop has become an administrative office of the General Conference with quite limited functions, while the great boards are administered by other executives. "In short, the bishops as bishops are no longer charged with direct responsibility in any of the specific fields of church work"[5] which are placed under the direction of a secretary.

[4] The following are the principal boards of the Methodist Episcopal Church as provided for by the General Conference of 1932: Board of Foreign Missions; Board of Home Missions and Church Extension; Board of Education; Board of Pensions and Relief; Board of Temperance, Prohibition, and Public Morals; Board of Hospitals, Homes, and Deaconess work.

[5] See Goodloe, R. W., *The Office of Bishop in the Methodist Church.* Manuscript Ph.D. Thesis, The University of Chicago, 1929.

This change has come about not because present-day Methodist bishops are less capable than were those of an earlier day, but, rather, because the work to be done is vastly more complicated.

From 1880 to 1900 seventeen general superintendents were elected; while the number chosen from 1904 to 1932 was fifty-one. In 1884, with the selection of William Taylor as bishop for Africa, the question arose as to the status of the missionary bishop. The General Conference of 1888 determined that since the missionary bishop was limited in his field of jurisdiction he was not, therefore, a general superintendent. He was not, however, considered subordinate to the general superintendents, but co-ordinate with them in authority in the field to which he had been assigned. From 1884 to 1916 nine missionary bishops were elected. Among them, besides Bishop Taylor, were, J. M. Thoburn for India; E. W. Parker, F. W. Warne, and J. C. Hartzell for Africa. In 1920 the General Conference adopted the policy of sending general superintendents to foreign fields, but the office of missionary bishop was not abolished.

A still further change in episcopal supervision of mission fields was authorized by the General Conference of 1928, by which Central Conferences were set up in Eastern Asia, Southern Asia, and Latin America, with power to elect one or more bishops, to fix their tenure of office, the amount of their salary and residence. Within the next quadrennium four bishops were elected by Central Conferences, two for Eastern Asia, and one each for Southern Asia and Latin America.

The growing nationalistic feeling among native

Christians on mission fields has led also to the establishment of independent Methodist Churches in Japan, in Mexico and in Korea. In Japan the presence of competing Methodist bodies, the two American Methodist Episcopal Churches and the Canadian Methodist Church, was an additional factor in creating an independent Japanese Methodist Church. This was accomplished in 1907. Among the distinctive features of the Japanese Church are, elective district superintendents, laymen as full members of the Annual Conferences, and laymen in equal numbers with district superintendents in the bishops' cabinet, women evangelists, and a term general superintendency. The Mexican Church was formed in 1930. According to Mexican law all ministers of Mexican churches must be citizens of that republic, and for that reason all ministers and officers in the new church are native Mexicans. At the first General Conference a bishop was chosen for four years with eligibility for re-election. The Korean Methodist Church was likewise formed in 1930 and maintains friendly relationship with the Methodist Episcopal and Methodist Episcopal Church, South. The ministry of the Korean Church has but one order, that of elder, to which women are eligible. The Annual Conference is composed of an equal number of men and women; the appointments are made by a committee; the general superintendency is a term office for four years with one possible re-election for another term of four years.

To the office of bishop in Episcopal Methodism many different types of men have been called. Some have been primarily preachers, others have given chief attention to administration. Up to 1900 few bishops were chosen directly from the pastorate; they came to their office generally through a secretaryship of one of the great boards of the church, or from a college or university presidency. So far the episcopacy has been considered a life office, though within the last eight years agitation has increased to limit the term. By a law passed in 1932 the bishop must now retire from active service at the General Conference nearest his seventieth birthday. In 1912 the General Conference adopted the Area system[6] of episcopal supervision. By this plan the church is divided into episcopal areas over each of which a bishop is made responsible. A bishop may preside at Conferences outside his area, but his chief responsibility is the area to which he is assigned; since

[6] In 1932 the following were the official residences of the bishops of the Methodist Episcopal Church:

In the United States: Atlanta, Frederick T. Keeney; Boston, Charles Wesley Burns; Chattanooga, Wallace E. Brown; Chicago, Ernest Lynn Waldorf; Cincinnati, H. Lester Smith; Covington, M. W. Clair; Denver, Ralph S. Cushman; Detroit, Edgar Blake; Kansas City, Charles L. Mead; New Orleans, R. E. Jones; New York, F. J. McConnell; Omaha, F. D. Leete; Philadelphia, E. G. Richardson; Pittsburgh, A. W. Leonard; Portland, Titus Lowe; St. Paul, J. Ralph Magee; San Francisco, James C. Baker; Washington, Edwin H. Hughes.

Outside the United States: Cape Town, Eben S. Johnson; Shanghai, Herbert Welch; Bombay, Brenton T. Badley; Delhi, John W. Robinson; Stockholm, Raymond J. Wade; Zurich, John L. Nuelsen; Santiago, Chile, George A. Miller; Singapore-Manila, Edwin F. Lee.

The Methodist Episcopal Church, South, has not as yet adopted the Area system, but their bishops are assigned to definite episcopal residences. The assignments for 1930 were as follows:

Atlanta, W. A. Candler; Richmond, Va., Collins Denny; Charlotte, N. C., E. D. Mouzon; Dallas, Texas, J. M. Moore; Fayette, Mo., W. F. McMurry; Huntington, W. Va., U. V. W. Darlington; Nashville, H. M. Du Bose; Birmingham, Ala., W. N. Ainsworth; Washington, D. C., James Cannon, Jr.; San Antonio, Texas, S. R. Hay; Shreveport, La., H. M. Dobbs; Houston, Texas, H. A. Boaz; San Francisco, A. J. Moore; Shanghai, China, P. V. Kern; Houston, Texas, A. F. Smith. (General Minutes and Yearbook, 1930-1931, Methodist Episcopal Church, South, p. 412.)

1928 a bishop may remain in one area longer than eight years—indeed, indefinitely.

The rapidly developing complexity of social and industrial life with its growing paganism and glaring injustices began to disturb greatly certain leaders among the Protestant churches. The last decade of the nineteenth century saw the inception of a movement directed toward some application of religion to the social and industrial problems of the time. Simultaneously a distinct line of cleavage was fast developing between the church and the masses. Following the Civil War a movement for the organization of labor culminated in the formation of the Knights of Labor at Philadelphia in 1869. All branches of labor were included in this organization, whose object was to improve the moral, social, educational, and economic condition of its members. After 1890 the Knights of Labor gradually was supplanted, in large measure, by the American Federation of Labor. With such organizations labor soon became class conscious and accusations began to be heard that the church was an institution allied to capitalism, and was composed of, or at least controlled by, those who were in sympathy with the capitalistic classes. The wage-earning classes to a large extent came to believe that the church was untrue to its ideals, and was permitting itself to become an organ of capitalism. Thus Mr. Gompers, the president of the American Federation of Labor, stated:

My associates have come to look upon the church and the ministry as the apologists and defenders of the wrong committed against the interests of the people, simply because the perpetrators are possessors of wealth. . . . whose real God is the almighty dollar, and who contribute a few of their idols to suborn the intellect and eloquence of the divines, and make even their otherwise generous hearts callous to the sufferings of the poor and the struggling workers, so that they may use their exalted positions to discourage and discountenance all practical efforts of the toilers to lift themselves out of the slough of despondency and despair.[7]

The latter seventies and the eighties were a period of industrial strife throughout the United States characterized by many labor disturbances, riots, and strikes with their revelations of social injustice. In the year 1886 alone there were more than fifteen hundred labor disputes involving at least 600,000 men and causing an estimated loss of more than thirty millions of dollars. The early nineties likewise witnessed much economic distress, caused by falling wages and general unemployment, accompanied by violent strikes, such as that at Homestead, Pennsylvania, in 1892, among the steel workers, and that in Chicago two years later among the employees of the Pullman Palace Car Company. In 1894 an army of unemployed men known as "Coxey's army" started for Washington to lay before Congress their demands for relief. Such was the immediate economic background out of which came an increased emphasis upon the social teachings of Jesus among the evangelical churches in America.

The Methodists, like all the other evangelical groups, had through the years laid chief emphasis upon the salvation of the individual. The church leaders thought that the business of the church and

---

[7] Mathews, Shailer, *The Church and the Changing Order.* New York, The Macmillan Company, 1907, especially Chaps. V and VI.

of religion was to deliver individual men from sin and spiritual death. But as the conception of religion broadened, many saw that there needed to be a change in the concept of salvation. An increasing number began to feel that to bring about needed reforms in the social and industrial world something more than a revival of religion in the old sense was necessary. Not only must individual sins be forgiven, but something must be done about the sins of society. "Poverty, intemperance, extortion, irresponsible use of wealth, unhealthful and indecent conditions of life, ignorance, social ostracism, despair, lust, cruelty, laziness, dishonesty, untruthfulness" were social evils which must concern the church. But there were still many who believed that "conversion will cure all ills; that if everybody were converted, this would solve the social and all other problems." But to this contention came the reply that "many slave-owners professed conversion, but did not give up their slaves."

Thus the reaction against an extreme individualism in religion gained momentum. The writings of such leaders as Washington Gladden, Josiah Strong, Charles R. Henderson, and Walter Rauschenbusch were widely read in Methodist circles and their teaching spread throughout the church. Gladden in his book, *Tools and Men* (1893), wrote: "The end of Christianity is twofold—a perfect man in a perfect society. These purposes are never separated; they cannot be separated. No man can be redeemed and saved alone; no community can be reformed and elevated save as the individuals of which it is composed are regenerated." Soon Methodist writers were echoing these sentiments, and from 1895 onward the pages of the *Methodist Review* and other Methodist publications abound in articles urging upon the church this wider conception of the duty of religion. "If society is to be saved by saved individuals, then having saved them it still remains to set them about saving society," wrote one Methodist contributor.

An important factor in the development of the social conception of religion was the discovery and reinterpretation of the social teachings of the Bible, especially of the prophets and of Jesus. It was found that the prophets were not primarily foretellers, but rather forthtellers of the eternal verities, who stood before the corrupt monarchs of their time and demanded reforms in the name of the Almighty. Jesus' conception of the Kingdom of God was interpreted as constituting a reorganized and thoroughly Christianized society here on earth, which must turn men's attention to a consideration of the construction of society here and now in order to fulfill Christ's plan and purpose. Professor Ely[8] insisted that young ministers should study social and economic problems along with theology in their seminaries, and young ministers were soon flocking to the universities to study sociology, and professorships of sociology were numerously established in the denominational colleges and the theological seminaries.

Another result of the new emphasis upon social questions was the appearance of the "institutional" church. The institutional church has been defined

---

[8] Barnhart, K. E., *The Evolution of the Social Consciousness in Methodism* (Ph.D. Thesis, manuscript. The University of Chicago, 1924).

as one "performing for portions of the community the functions not performed for them by the home and society at large." In a community of homes this type of church had little place, but among the poor, especially in the tenement districts of large cities, this new kind of church found a large work to do, and by 1900 there were hundreds of these churches to be found in the cities and larger towns throughout the country. In New York City alone in 1900 out of four hundred and eighty-eight Protestant churches, one hundred and twelve were carrying on direct institutional activities. During these same years the social-settlement movement was inaugurated. In 1889 Jane Addams opened Hull House "amid the dreary industrial wastes of Chicago," and within the next score of years numerous settlements were established in the large cities where students from the colleges and universities learned at first hand the new gospel of "social redemption."

From the beginning of this movement Methodist leaders were found among those interested in the new emphasis, and in 1907 the Methodist Federation for Social Service was formed, the first organization of the kind among the American churches. Those who had a large share in the founding of this significant organization were Herbert Welch, Francis J. McConnell, Frank Mason North, Harris Franklin Rall, Worth M. Tippy, and Harry F. Ward. Principally through this medium Methodism has exerted extensive influence upon other churches, fulfilling to a large degree the prophecy of Walter Rauschenbusch, who had written:

The Methodists are likely to play a very important part

in the social awakening of the American churches. . . .
They have rarely backed away from a fight when the issue
was clearly drawn between Jehovah and Diabolus. . . .
Their leaders are fully determined to form their battalions
on this new line of battle, and when they march, the ground
will shake.

Through the labor of this Federation for Social
Service the General Conference of 1908 formulated
a definite declaration on social questions, which
after slight modifications was adopted by the Federal Council of the Churches of Christ in America
as the Social Creed of the Churches.

It declared that the Methodist Episcopal Church
stands:

For equal rights and complete justice for all men in all
stations of life.

For the principle of conciliation and arbitration in industrial dissensions.

For the protection of the worker from dangerous machinery, occupational diseases, injuries, and mortality.

For the abolition of child labor.

For such regulation of the conditions of labor for women
as shall safeguard the physical and moral health of the
community.

For the suppression of the "sweating system."

For the gradual and reasonable reduction of the hours
of labor to the lowest practical point, with work for all;
and for that degree of leisure for all which is the condition
of the highest human life.

For release from employment one day in seven.

For a living wage in every industry.

For the highest wage that each industry can afford, and
for the most equitable division of the products of industry
that can ultimately be devised.

For the recognition of the Golden Rule and the mind of
Christ as the supreme law of society and the sure remedy
for all social ills.

That such a creed was not accepted by all the members of the church goes without saying. Many, in fact, opposed it bitterly. Some thought that the church was departing from its rightful function and was interfering with matters which rightfully belonged to the state. Others opposed it because they themselves were engaged in business enterprises where labor was exploited, or because their habits of thought were cast in conservative molds. Some withdrew from the church or stopped their support. But these relatively few opposers did not deter the Methodist Episcopal Church from going forward along the path indicated in 1908, and at every General Conference since that time other courageous declarations and appeals have been issued. The General Conference of 1928 declared that in addition to the former creed they stood for "a social order in which every child has the best opportunity for development"; for a program of religious and secular education designed to Christianize everyday life; for conservation of health; for free speech, freedom of the press and the right of peaceable assemblage; for Christian care of dependents; for a program of international education to promote "peace and good will and exposing the evils of war, intoxicants, illiteracy, and other social sins." Besides this they proposed a definite program for improving industrial and economic relationships; for assisting the agricultural communities in meeting their difficult problems; for applying Christian principles in race relations; and for Christianizing international relationships, and closing with the statement:

We believe it is the duty of every local church to investigate local, moral and economic conditions as well as to know world needs. We believe that it is only as our churches themselves follow the example and spirit of Jesus in the fullest sense—translating these social ideals into the daily life of the church and the community—that we can ever hope to build the kingdom of God on earth.

The Episcopal Address before the General Conference of 1932, meeting in the midst of the greatest economic depression of recent times, contains these courageous and biting words:

It cannot be denied that the industrial practices of past decades have given us the deplorable conditions of to-day. Industry has as a rule given labor a grudging, insufficient wage, keeping it down by child exploitation, by suppression of legitimate organizations, and by other expedients, while at the same time huge fortunes have been amassed for the favored owners of the resources of production. To-day the burden is without conscience shifted to the worker, who, after giving his labor for miserable financial results, is turned off to starve or beg. . . .

The worth of human life lies at the root of the social teachings of Jesus. When industry has violated that ideal it has been un-Christian. . . . We as a church stand ready to share the blame for these conditions. But we know now that the kingdom of God cannot be built on the poverty of the many and the absurd and cruel wealth of the few. From the viewpoint of citizenship we of America know that the democracy for which our fathers died may be destroyed by the inhuman and un-Christian monopoly of great wealth. Such a monopoly would destroy business itself. And if not corrected it would destroy society and the state. In no uncertain terms and with deep conviction we call upon the leaders of both capital and labor to remake the whole structure of industrial life upon the teachings of Christ. . . . Those who refuse to listen to the demands for such reconstruction constitute a most dangerous threat to the development of orderly civilization.

Perhaps the two most important questions occupying the attention of the church at the opening of the twentieth century were the problems presented by the country church and foreign mission expansion. During Mr. Roosevelt's administration the nation became aware for the first time of a whole series of problems growing out of changing conditions in the vast rural domain of the United States. This was brought to the attention of the public through a report of a Commission on Country Life appointed by the President. This disclosed that the natural resources of the country were rapidly declining, due to the extravagance and waste with which these vast resources had been used. The conservation policy of President Roosevelt led to the constructive reclaiming of soil, the reforestation of denuded areas, the prevention of forest fires and the creation of great forest preserves, the prevention of floods, and the reclaiming of vast mineral wealth and water power for the government, formerly leased at low cost to individual operators. Accompanying this economic conservation carried on by the federal and state governments, religious leaders began to see that they had a rural problem of growing importance to the well-being of the church.

The drain of rural population to the cities or to the West, especially from such sections as New England and the middle Atlantic states, the growing scarcity of farm labor and the resultant high cost of farming, immigration which displaced Protestants by Catholics, the coming of the automobile into popular use with the turn of the century, were some of the factors which were rapidly changing the character of rural communities. The larger churches in the cities and county-seat towns were naturally the ones to receive the largest amount of attention from the appointing officials. The bishops seldom, if ever, visited a country church, and in too many instances the immediately responsible officials were ignorant of or indifferent to the critical situation in rural communities.

During the last two decades of the nineteenth century the number of rural churches greatly decreased, and by the end of the century the larger Protestant denominations were fully alive to the seriousness of the situation. The Roosevelt Commission on Country Life stated in its report that the time had "arrived when the church must take a larger leadership, both as an institution and through its pastors, in the social reorganization of rural life." Soon the church began to create agencies both to study and meet the situation. Home missionary boards have given special attention to the rural problem. A literature giving the results of surveys and suggesting solutions appeared; professorships of rural sociology were established in the colleges and seminaries; summer schools for the training of rural leaders were conducted; the Federal Council (1910-1912) maintained a bureau of research, information, and promotion touching the church and country life interests, while state agricultural schools, the federal Department of Agriculture, and the Bureau of Education have co-operated in awakening the national consciousness to the importance of maintaining the country church as a conserving force in our civilization.[9]

---

[9] Some of the books dealing with the country-church problem are: Gill, C. O., and Pinchot, Gifford, *The Country Church: The Decline*

IN THE GILDED AGE—1880-1900

Throughout the last years of the nineteenth and the early years of the twentieth century interest in foreign missions greatly increased, and the church became thoroughly converted to the missionary enterprise. This was evidenced not alone by the greatly increased giving to the cause but also by the new promotion agencies which arose, mostly of an interdenominational character. One of the most effective of these new agencies was the Student Volunteer Movement, which grew out of a small meeting of individual workers assembled at Northfield, Massachusetts, in 1886. The movement at once caught the imagination of students throughout the country and Student Volunteer Bands were formed in all the church colleges and even in the state universities. In 1888 Mr. John R. Mott became the chairman of the Executive Committee of the movement, and it is in connection with this organization that Mr. Mott has done his greatest work. In 1895 to 1897 Mr. Mott toured the world in the interest of the Student Christian Movement. By 1914 this organization had furnished more than five thousand missionaries, and thus was created an ever increasing army of occupation to help Christianize the world.

Another foreign-missionary agency, interdenominational in scope, but having large influence in Methodism, was the Laymen's Missionary Movement, which grew out of the Student Volunteer

of Its Influence and the Remedy, New York: Macmillan, 1913. Vogt, Paul L., *The Country Church and Country Life,* New York: Missionary Education Movement, 1916. Earp, E. L., *The Country Church Movement,* New York: The Methodist Book Concern, 1914. Hooker, E. R., *Hinterlands of the Church: A Study of Areas with a Low Proportion of Church Members,* New York: Institute of Social and Religious Research, 1931.

Convention in Nashville, Tennessee, in 1906. A layman in attendance was struck with the idea that if "these young people can give their lives to the cause of God in the mission fields, surely the laymen of the churches can provide the money to send them." Some time later the Laymen's Missionary Movement was organized in New York. It has maintained an effective organization and has been the direct and indirect cause of greatly increased financial support for the missionary enterprise. In this connection must be mentioned also the Missionary Education Movement which was organized in 1902 to promote missionary education in all denominations. It maintains an editorial and educational department for the purpose of issuing missionary literature for the forty-seven co-operating denominations.

The Home Missionary forces of the evangelical churches working in the United States also formed what was known as the Home Mission Council, the purpose of which was "to promote fellowship, conference, and co-operation among Christian organizations doing missionary work in the United States and its dependencies."

One of the great weaknesses of American Protestantism is its inability to speak with a united voice on matters of moral and religious concern. A long step in the direction of overcoming this handicap was the formation in 1908 of the "Federal Council of the Churches of Christ in America." The beginnings of church federation go back to the formation of the Evangelical Alliance in London in 1846. One of the most influential delegates to this meeting was Dr. Stephen Olin, president of Wesleyan

University. Here fifty different evangelical bodies in Europe and America formed an organization to promote evangelical union, to promote the cause of religious freedom, and further the cause of Christ everywhere. At the World Evangelical Alliance meeting in Berlin in 1857 Bishop Matthew Simpson and Dr. John McClintock were delegates. During the course of the meeting Bishop Simpson preached a sermon on "Christian Unity" in the Emperor's Royal Garrison Church—in which he pleaded not for unity of belief or worship, but for unity in activities and labors. Due to the slavery controversy a branch Alliance was not formed in the United States until 1867. Through its influences many cooperative Christian enterprises were undertaken. Toward the end of the century this organization became less active and other interchurch organizations began to be formed, the most notable being the "Open and Institutional Church League." Among the most active promoters of this organization was Dr. Frank Mason North, at that time secretary of the New York City Church Extension and Missionary Society of the Methodist Episcopal Church. He, with several Presbyterian and Congregational ministers and laymen, was responsible for the vigorous promotion of the idea of a National Federation of all the Protestant denominations through their official heads. From 1900 to 1905 this idea was brewing. In the latter year the constitution of the Federal Council of the Churches of Christ in America was drawn up, and three years later (1908), after ratification by the thirty denominations constituting its first membership, the Federal Council began operations with Bishop E. R. Hendrix, of the Methodist Episcopal Church, South, as its first president.

The Methodist Episcopal, the Methodist Episcopal, South, the Methodist Protestant, and the three Negro Methodist Episcopal Churches were among the original members of the Federal Council and have co-operated actively in all its great endeavors. Within the several Methodist bodies the large majority of the leaders have always been "ready for any feasible co-operation, friendly to definite federation, responsive to the appeal for organic union, and sympathetic with the ideals of those who seek to promote it," but often "incredulous as to its practicability."[10]

---

[10] Sanford, E. B., *Origin and History of the Federal Council of the Churches of Christ in America.* Hartford, Conn., S. S. Scranton Co., 1916. Macfarland, C. S., *The Progress of Church Federation.* New York, Revell, 1921. See also Sanford, E. B. (Ed.), *Church Federation: Inter-Church Conference on Federation,* New York, November 15-21, 1905. New York, Revell, 1906.

CHAPTER XVII

FACES THE GREAT WAR AND ITS AFTER-
MATH

FROM the close of the Spanish American War to the outbreak of the World War agitation for international peace was especially energetic throughout the Western world. Among the most important peace agencies of the early years of the period were the Lake Mohonk Conferences, begun in 1895, to which clergymen of all denominations were invited. In 1899 the Interparliamentary Union was formed in Paris and began to spread propaganda for a permanent court of arbitration, and ten years later the first Hague Conference was held, to which twenty-six nations sent representatives, including the United States. Religious forces were soon enlisted in organizing the work for peace; peace committees were formed in many of the cities, composed of leading ministers. The American Peace Society, which had been formed in 1828, largely through Quaker influence, now became more active, and its publications and lecturers were in increasing demand. In the early years of the new century Andrew Carnegie began to devote a part of his great fortune to the promotion of world peace, and the most prominent leaders in both church and state were enlisted in the great cause. In 1890 the observance of the third Sunday in December as *Peace Sunday* was inaugurated and its observation urged upon churches and Sunday schools.

From 1905 to 1914 the peace movement in the
United States was especially prominent. In 1905
it was stated in the report of the National Department of Peace and Arbitration of the W. C. T. U.
that more peace sermons had been preached
that year than ever before. The W. C. T. U. was
one of the active agencies promoting the movement,
and in the above year its Peace Department published a course of study for Sunday schools and
boys', girls' and women's clubs, entitled "World
Peace," while part of its work was in keeping mili-
taristic teaching out of the Sunday schools. In 1907
the first National World's Peace Congress was held,
and a second conference met in Chicago two years
later. In the year 1909 the American Peace Society
doubled its membership, and throughout the country ministers were more outspoken on the question
of peace than at any other time. In 1910 "The Carnegie Endowment for International Peace" was established with $10,000,000, and while the charter
and constitution of this organization were not
couched in religious language, yet a high moral purpose was at the center of the enterprise. It was now
the height of respectability to condemn war as barbaric and to advocate peace as an enduring ideal,
and "great and good citizens all over the land came
to believe that humanity was finally nearing the
goal of universal peace."

The response of American Methodism to this
peace agitation may be summarized in the words of
the Episcopal Address before the General Conference of 1912:

It is for mammon, not for righteousness, that thrones and
parliaments are crowding the oceans with leviathans of

battle, even while the people are praying for an end of war and pleading for international arbitration; for they have balanced the ledgers of the centuries and they have found that the honors and spoils of war have never been equitably divided. Save in the wars of the people for freedom, the thrones and the honors have gone to the few, and thorns and horrors to the many. In the awful arithmetic of war it takes a thousand homes to build one palace, ten thousand lives of brave men to lift a pedestal for one man to occupy in lonely grandeur. The people are also learning the secrets of financial diplomacy, and the day is not far away when monarchs and plutocrats must shed their own blood in their own battles, or settle their accounts at The Hague. Ink is cheaper than blood. Law is better than force, and patience is a wiser diplomat than threat and bluster. But still the strategists are busy. Not content with drenching the soil and reddening the sea with blood, they are planning batteries that shall rain destruction from the clouds on helpless cities, and death on peoples who have no quarrel with each other until baited to battle by a painted lure labeled patriotism.

Even while the churches are calling upon rulers to submit all international disputes to arbitration, our own republic answers with more doves of peace made of steel, breathing fire and winged with death. If some suspect that treaties are held up at the signal of capital interested in steel plate for making more such doves, it cannot be denied that popular government has been perverted to such dastardly uses. The people can and must assert their nobler love of country by demanding that no American battleship shall disgrace its colors in a war for trade, or in any war, until every peaceful resort has been thoroughly tried. The high courage of our President in declaring that all disagreements, involving questions of whatever sort, should be submitted to an international court, is worthy the acclamations of all peoples who have escaped the brutal spirit of barbaric ages. Let every Methodist pulpit ring out clearly and insistently for Peace by Arbitration.[1]

---

[1] *General Conference Journal, 1912*, pp. 216-217. New York: The Methodist Book Concern, 1912.

There was an undoubted feeling of optimism regarding the coming of world peace when the Great War began, and at least theoretically the whole church believed enthusiastically in the cause of peace. From 1914 until the entrance of the United States into the war, the church, through its ministers and press, supported the President's policy of maintaining neutrality. At its session in 1915 the Illinois Conference thanked God "that after a year of a World War that has surpassed in deadly destructiveness all records of the past, we remain by the wise guidance of our President, Woodrow Wilson, and his advisers, at peace with the whole world."

"We urge our people to maintain the neutrality of the nation by supporting our beloved President in this trying hour of our nation's peril, so that when the time shall come we may be the better able to aid in matters of world-wide peace."

When Germany, on February 1, 1917, announced her policy of unrestricted submarine warfare, and President Wilson recommended to Congress that the United States break diplomatic relations with Germany, *The Christian Advocate,* New York, editorially stated that "It is peace which we desire—not war—and it is peace which we still expect. Whether war shall be forced upon us, or whether it shall be averted by tardy councils of sobriety and prudence, it will not alter the growing conviction of thinking people that only through such a peace as President Wilson outlined to the Senate two weeks ago (January 22, 1917) can the nations be guaranteed not to learn war any more." As a whole, the Methodist press supported President Wilson in his

policy during the months just preceding the declaration of a state of war, and all but *Der Christliche
Apologete* condemned the handful of "willful men"
in the Senate who defeated President Wilson's (February 26th) recommendation of an "armed neutrality."[2]

"How shall a Christian meet the call of the hour?"
was the question being asked in Christian homes,
in the churches, and in church assemblies. The
declaration of war undoubtedly was a tragic disappointment to many Christian people, who had hoped
against hope that war might be averted. But once
declared no class of citizens were more active or
self-sacrificing in the whole-hearted support of the
war than were the members of the Christian
churches, and soon the cause for which the nation
fought was seen by them to be a holy and righteous
one.

A storm "of passionate patriotism . . . swept
the New York Conference" at its session in April,
1917, produced under the eloquence of Chancellor
James R. Day, and in its session in 1918 the report
of the Committee on the State of the Country, read
by Chancellor James R. Day, declared: "The length
of the war is not on our calendars. . . . When will
the war close? When Germany is whipped out of
all semblances of militarism into Christian democracy! . . . Germany has reaped her materialistic
philosophy and is being destroyed by it. The voice
of Luther has been smothered by the voices of

---

[2] See *The Pittsburgh Christian Advocate*, March 8, 1917; *The Western Christian Advocate*, March 7, 1917; *The Central Christian Advocate*, March 7, 1917; *The Northwestern Christian Advocate*, March 7,
1917; *Zion's Herald*, March 7, 1917; *The Christian Advocate*, Nashville, Tennessee, March 9, 1917.

Nietzsche, Bernhardi, and Treitschke."[3] The long resolutions passed by the Troy Conference contain among others these impassioned words: "We see the trembling lines above which float the Tricolor and the Union Jack, as the hellish Hunnish hordes beat against them to seize the panting throat of the world. We hear the cry 'Hurry up, America,' and we go with fierce passion for world freedom to twine with Union Jack and Tricolor the Stars and Stripes and say to the sinister black eagle flag of Germany, 'You shall not pass.' We cannot do otherwise, God help us!" The Baltimore Conference at its session in 1918 adopted these eloquent resolutions:

Redemptive days, these. Days of torrential blood-streams, of deafening boom, of unutterable anguish—travail days, the like of which earth never knew before, nor dreamed, yet days of redemption. This redemptive quality that justifies the agony and gilds the crimson tide. The earth for which Jesus gave his life is having a supplemental ransom price paid by the lives of a host of his brethren. Men in khaki and blue and white are filling up the measure of the suffering of Christ.

But 'tis a morning storm, preluding a new day for man. And we are grateful for the honor of a part in this air-clearing tempest of war. Shuddering at its rack, and bleeding inwardly, we are unashamed and unafraid. . . . Earth's acres are not broad enough to tenant both brotherhood and autocracy. And if in the process of waging our fight, and in the sure and fine reaction thereof, we find our own land purged of the materialism which threatened its security and mocked its mission, we shall the more eagerly declare warranted our prodigal investment.

In that faith, then, we steady our hearts and set our wills.

[3] See resolutions on the State of the Country passed by the New York Conference, *Minutes*, 1918, pp. 59-62; Illinois Conference, *Minutes*, 1917, pp. 82-84; Baltimore Conference, *Minutes*, 1918, pp. 70-71; North Indiana Conference, *Minutes*, 1918, pp. 301-302; Troy Conference, *Minutes*, 1918, pp. 74-75.

Not in personal hate, but in clean, white anger against a malignancy which can so threaten the peace of the world, we pledge our prayers, our purses, and our boys.

To the Methodist preachers assembled in their Conferences during these years of warfare the issues seemed "clearly drawn." To them it was "a struggle for fundamental human rights, a war to determine whether or not the race shall revert to the unbridled and unblushing paganism of force." "We have unsheathed the sword," declared the Ohio Conference in 1917, "in defense of faith, honor, and justice, and we must not falter in our task till these ends are attained." As Americans they saw their duty, "august and imperative," was to support with all means at their command the policy of the President and Congress.

The just and noble cause of the Allies in contrast with the greedy and unholy ambition of Germany to conquer the world and to grind the vanished peoples under the iron heel of despotism was the theme of many a sermon in those days of war extravagance and excitement. All the exaggerated stories of German cruelty were generally believed, and outlines for war sermons, sent out by the various war agencies of the federal and state governments, were eagerly accepted and used. Church parlors became the headquarters for Red Cross activities, while ministers and church leaders were prominent members of local committees to sell government bonds or help raise the communities' apportionment in the many drives for the various kinds of war relief.

With the United States' declaration of war against Germany the Methodist Episcopal Church sent word to the President of the United States that the church was ready to help to the full extent of her resources. *A National War Council of the Methodist Episcopal Church* was immediately formed, and incongruous as it may now seem, it was placed under the Department of Evangelism of the Board of Home Missions and Church Extension. A drive for $250,-000 was at once begun, and it was soon realized that this sum would be entirely inadequate and the sum sought was increased to $1,000,000.

The activities of the War Council were divided into four divisions: visiting clergymen, activities near camps, war industry work, and chaplains. The Methodist Episcopal Church was among the first to send ministers into the camps to look after the spiritual welfare of the soldiers. In most cases these visiting clergymen were the ministers of churches near the camps. The Council supplemented the salaries of such ministers, and in some instances made possible the employment of an assistant minister to aid the activities. The work of the War Council in the centers where thousands of men and women were brought together in war industries was perhaps the greatest service rendered. Housing and health situations which vitally affected the efficiency of the workers were in many instances cleaned up, and the general welfare of the workers was given attention. Each Methodist chaplain was equipped with a communion service and $250, and where chaplains were so situated as to make necessary considerable travel, motorcycles with side cars were provided. The Methodist chaplains at the Training School for Chaplains, maintained at Louisville, Kentucky, were equipped as soon as they had received their commissions. The number of Methodist Episcopal chaplains who served "with the colors" was approximately three hundred and twenty-five, while at least five hundred Methodist ministers were engaged in Y. M. C. A. work at home and overseas.[4]

After the signing of the armistice a Department of War Emergency and Reconstruction was organized as a part of the Centenary campaign which took over the duties of the National War Council. Two committees, one on reconstruction abroad and a second on reconstruction at home, were formed. The committee on home reconstruction gave special attention to effects of the influenza epidemic, especially in relation to the emergency situations in Methodist hospitals and orphanages. It assisted the disbanded soldiers to return to their schools and colleges; it gave attention to the problems created by the great Northern migration of Negroes.

The War-Work Commission of the Methodist Episcopal Church, South, performed a similar work. They gave special attention to the distribution of Bibles, service-books, songbooks, and Sunday-school lesson books among enlisted men and encouraged the study of the Bible among the soldiers through soldier-pastors and chaplains. They also looked after the personal equipment of their own chaplains and also of the chaplains of the Colored Methodist Episcopal Church. Special attention was given to the colored troops in France; and an agreement was made to house, clothe, and educate forty French

---

[4] Renton, Margaret (Ed.), *War-Time Agencies of the Churches: Directory and Handbook.* New York, General War-Time Commission of the Churches: Federal Council of the Churches of Christ in America, 1919. See chapters on the War-Time Commission of the African Methodist Episcopal Church; the War-Work Commission of the Methodist Episcopal Church, South; and the National War Council of the Methodist Episcopal Church.

orphans in Paris. Through its Centenary drive the Church South made provision to raise $5,000,000 to further its reconstruction work, both at home and in Europe.

The Methodist Protestant Church, through its War-Work Commission, co-operated with all the interdenominational agencies and gave direct assistance to the Committees for Armenian and Syrian Relief; to Near East Relief; to the suffering Christians in the war zone; to the Y. M. and Y. W. C. A., and contributed its full share of chaplains, Red Cross, and Y. M. C. A. workers. Like the other churches, every church had its service flag conspicuously displayed, with a star for every member of the church and Sunday school in the service of the nation, and a gold star for each one who had lost his life while in such service.

The African Methodist Episcopal Church co-operated through its War-Time Commission with the other government and interdenominational agencies. It furnished twelve chaplains to colored troops, and gave attention to the needs of colored troops in American camps as well as those overseas.

Besides the several denominational agencies for carrying on war-time activities the several Methodist bodies co-operated heartily with the "General War-Time Commission of the Churches" created by the Federal Council. Among the important committees of this Commission were The Committee on Army and Navy Chaplains, of which Bishop W. F. McDowell was chairman; Committee on Camp Neighborhoods; Committee on Interchurch Buildings; Literature and Publicity; Joint Committee on War Production Communities; Committee on the Welfare of Negro Troops and Communities; Days of Prayer and the Devotional Life; on Interchange of Preachers and Speakers between the Churches of America, Great Britain, and France; on Employment of Returning Soldiers; Interned Allies; on Social Hygiene; on National Prohibition as a war measure; on war-time work in the local church and co-operation with the Red Cross; and the Committee on Conference with the Young Men's and Young Women's Christian Associations.

The Methodist Book Concern and the several church boards issued numerous special publications, books and pamphlets, bearing on many particular phases of the church and its relation to the war.

The Board of Home Missions and Church Extension sent out from time to time a multigraphed news sheet called *Methodist Episcopal War Camp News,* besides campaign material to help ministers raise the emergency relief fund. *Methodism Backs the Boys in Khaki and Blue, Will You Help Do It?* was an appeal for reconstruction funds, while the Sunday School Board prepared *Marshaling the Forces of Patriotism* for use in Sunday schools. The Church South was also active in sending out publications and multigraphed letters to the men in service, besides letters and pamphlets to the churches and pastors, suggesting ways of co-operation, methods of helping re-employment of returning soldiers and messages from chaplains and others engaged in war work.

How was the individual church affected by the many war activities? The selective draft reached into the ranks of the working forces of the churches, and drew out thousands of men upon which much of the responsibility for the carrying on of the church work had been resting. Many who were not touched by the draft were drawn into other kinds of service, while numbers of the most active women in the churches gave their time, energy, and substance to the numerous worthy causes closely connected with the carrying on of the war. As a result it became increasingly difficult for the local church to "carry on" after the usual fashion.

At the General Conference of 1916 there were three separate resolutions introduced looking toward the celebration of the centenary anniversary of the beginning of Methodist missions, and the establishment of the Missionary Society of the Methodist Episcopal Church. The General Conference was asked to set aside the years 1918 and 1919 as centennial thanksgiving years and suggested the securing of gifts so that the income of the mission boards might be doubled. The Methodist Episcopal Church, South, was invited to join in the celebration.

Speaking before the Board of Foreign Missions in New York on November 8, 1917, John R. Mott, the Christian statesman and world traveler, urged upon the church the launching of a World Program of Missions. In that address he said:

The history of Christianity shows that periods of suffering have for some reason always been creative moments with God. It was so in the period of the Napoleonic wars. Nearly every great Protestant missionary society was called into being in those tragic years of suffering and despair and pessimism. The church found her opportunity in men's extremity. . . .

It is a belief of mine that we have come to one of those

moments when, if there is adequate spiritual leadership, God may do his great creative works. I see those unend· ing graves. I see those countless homes that I have visited in Europe since the war began. I see the mutilated and the maimed, I see the fatherless children. It is an age of suffering and it is an hour of creation. May our board be easily in the hands of God in these creative hours.

And so it was in the midst of the most stupendous war which ever cursed and crushed mankind that the greatest program for the Christianization of the world ever planned was launched by the Methodist Episcopal Church. It was called the *Centenary* in commemoration of the beginning of Methodist Missions among the Wyandot Indians in the year 1819. A world program recommended by a committee of one hundred proposed ten great objectives:

1. That the Methodist Episcopal Church now take its full share in the evangelization of the world, according to the facts of need as definitely ascertained and presented.

2. That eight million dollars ($8,000,000) a year for five years be secured to cover askings of the foreign fields, to establish permanent funds to meet overhead expenses, retiring allowances for missionaries and relief for their widows and orphans. That this amount ($40,000,000) be put with the amounts needed for home missions.

3. That the Centenary Commission conduct a joint campaign (1918-19) under the auspices of Boards of Foreign and Home Missions.

4. That a powerful church-wide educational campaign be prosecuted, by means of press, picture, and pulpit.

5. That a vital missionary organization be carried from Area, Conference and District, down to the last church.

6. That every local church be made dominantly evangelistic at home and missionary in its outreach.

7. That the teaching of stewardship of life, character, and possessions (the tithe) be taught as fundamental to Christianity.

8. That the prayer life of the church be zealously cultivated.

9. That a denomination-wide celebration be held on the State Fair Grounds at Columbus, Ohio, in June, 1919, as the culmination of the Centenary, to be followed by echo meetings in every section.

10. When approved by the Board of Bishops and the Boards of Foreign and Home Missions, the authorities of the Methodist Episcopal Church, South, be asked to co-operate.

The rank and file in the church as a whole were in the proper mood to give hearty support to such a program, for the war compelled the average citizen to think in terms of world needs and world problems as never before. Then, too, the many war "drives" for funds had trained the common people in the art of giving as nothing else could have done.

Immediately new and elaborate, and perhaps extravagant, machinery was created to carry out this challenging world program. Each Episcopal Area was a unit with its offices and secretaries, and its definite quota to be raised. Attractive literature setting forth the Christian needs of every nook and corner of the world was distributed throughout the church and an educational program was carried forward with success. Numerous ministers were drawn from their pastorates and other regular church work to take over certain phases of the Centenary drive, and the spirit of the time perhaps was responsible for a more lavish expenditure of money than would have been thought necessary or wise under ordinary conditions.[5]

---

[5] *The World Service of the Methodist Episcopal Church,* edited by Ralph E. Diffendorfer, assisted by Paul Hutchinson and William F. McDermott, is an exceedingly useful and attractive volume published in 1923, setting forth the World Program of the Church as it had developed during the period of the Centenary.

The financial end of the movement was an astonishing success, and the grand total subscribed was
estimated at $115,000,000. The financial campaign
came to an end on May 31, 1919. The General
Conference of 1920 created the Council of Boards
of Benevolence with a Committee on Conservation
and Advance as its promotional agent and established its headquarters in Chicago. Up to April 1,
1923, a sum totaling $55,878,201 had actually been
collected and paid in to the various Centenary
causes.

During the period of the war there had been created on all sides an "enthralling idealism" which
found ready response among the church leaders.
It was a "war to end war" in which we were engaged, and we fought to "make the world safe for
democracy." But by the time of the Presidential
campaign of 1920 the idealism with which we had
entered the struggle was shattered. The grand crusade was at an end. Mr. Harding stated in one of
his campaign speeches that "we asked the sons of
this republic to defend our national rights," rather
than to "purge the Old World of the accumulated
ills of rivalry and greed"; we did not enter the war
"proclaiming democracy and humanity." The
change in American opinion regarding United
States' responsibility for the world is well illustrated
by a contemporary cartoon, picturing General
Pershing on a very large white elephant riding away
from the tomb of Lafayette and calling back over
his shoulder, "Lafayette, we've quit."

The victory in 1920 of the party opposed to the
League of Nations ushered in a period of return to
strong nationalism. One of the characteristics of

this period was the multiplication of organizations devoted to the creation of a larger loyalty to local communities and national enterprises. Business men dined once a week with their Rotary Clubs, Kiwanis Clubs and Lion's Clubs, where there was much hilarity and every member was addressed by his first name. They boosted local enterprises, did much good work for local charities, and supported boys' and girls' clubs and listened to speeches on every conceivable subject. Often the ministerial member of these clubs was the local Methodist preacher. Another organization of the post-war period, which for a time disturbed numerous churches, especially in the Middle West, was the Ku Klux Klan, a strongly nationalistic society, opposed to Catholics, Jews, and Negroes. "With its weird ritual and hooded regalia, its parades, and its outbursts of violence," it attracted wide attention and considerable concern. It appealed to many ministers and church members, some of whom became members, and not infrequently Methodist ministers became organizers and its active promoters.

"Gradually," to use the words of the resolutions of the Baltimore Conference of 1919, the objectives of interest were "shifting from Petrograd, London, and Paris, to Washington, New York, Chicago, and San Francisco." Many felt that we had been so engrossed with saving the world that we had overlooked our own legitimate needs and interests. This shift of interest from the world to America is manifest in the great number of church building programs launched in every section of the land, in the gathering of increased endowments for colleges and universities, and in the new emphasis upon the hospital

work of the church and its other home benevo-
lences. During these years new church buildings
costing in the neighborhood of a million dollars
each were erected in Chicago, New York, Minneapolis, Springfield, Massachusetts, and in many other
places. These years were also notable for advance
in educational foundations. Northwestern University projected a great development of its professional schools in the city of Chicago and began a
great building program reaching into many millions of dollars. In 1924 there was announced the
notable benefaction of Mr. James B. Duke, consisting of at least $40,000,000. The major portion
of this great endowment was to go toward the expansion of Trinity College into Duke University,
but other worthy causes were likewise to receive a
share of the benefaction. Another notable gift to
Methodist education in this period was the establishment of the Rector Scholarship Foundation,
made possible by the gift of more than $2,000,000
by Mr. Edward Rector, at DePauw University
in 1919, whereby at least four hundred carefully selected young men were to have all tuition and
fees paid during their college course, provided they
maintained the required standard of scholarship.
At Syracuse University a new foundation was established, known as the School of Citizenship, by Mr.
George H. Maxwell with a gift of $1,500,000, while
practically every Methodist college in the land materially increased its endowments and added to its
equipment.

During the very years in which the church was
engaged in this active building and promotional
advance at home there began to be a steady decline

in the giving for World Service. A study of missionary and benevolent contributions for the years 1918 to 1927 shows that the year 1920 marked the highest point in the church's benevolent giving.[6] The year 1928 showed a decrease in receipts over the previous year of $669,000, and since that time decreases have continued, which have compelled the making of drastic cuts in appropriations. These cuts have affected both foreign and home missions as well as every other benevolent enterprise of the church.

A movement, both in and out of the Christian Church, which has gained greater momentum than at any other time in the history of mankind, is that for World Peace. In contrast with the more or less negative peace movement before the outbreak of the World War the present movement is positive and increasingly aggressive. The Great War, with its trench fighting and its use of gas and submarines, largely destroyed the glamour of war. Also the fact that it produced no great heroes of high command is a significant factor in helping to destroy the popularity of modern war. The Methodist churches have gone on record in each of their General Conferences since the close of the war, favoring World Peace. They have pronounced war to be the supreme enemy of mankind, and its continuance, they believe, means the suicide of civilization. The General Conference Commission on World Peace has stressed particularly the necessity of an adequate educational program, especially in the Epworth Leagues and church schools, looking toward the

[6] *The Methodist Year Book, 1928.* O. S. Baketel, Ed. New York: The Methodist Book Concern, 1928. See chart on p. 130.

making of a new mind on this all-important subject among the rising generation.

An achievement for which the Methodists have perhaps received a larger share of credit—or odium—than they deserve, was the passage in the year 1917 of the Eighteenth Amendment to the constitution of the United States prohibiting the manufacture and sale of liquor as a beverage. This was ratified by the necessary number of states within two years and went into effect on January 16, 1920. Previous to the Civil War the cause of temperance had made great progress under such leaders as Neal Dow, John B. Gough, Father Mathew, and others, and numerous societies were formed, such as the Washingtonians, the Good Templars, and the Sons of Temperance, for the promotion of the cause. Legislation of the Civil War period by which the liquor business received the legal sanction of the federal government greatly strengthened the hold of the traffic upon the American people. Out of this situation the saloon quickly developed, and it was not long until the liquor interests had become a powerful factor in both local, state, and national politics.

The Civil War was hardly over, however, before the temperance forces began to rally. In 1865 the National Temperance Society was formed at a national temperance convention held in Saratoga, New York. In 1873 the Woman's Crusade against the saloon began in Hillsboro, Ohio, when seventy-five women gathered at a church, sang and prayed and then marched to the saloons of the town and appealed to the saloon-keepers to give up their business. This movement, however, soon gave way to more permanent and effective organizations. In 1872 the Prohibition Party nominated its first candidate for the Presidency, and two years later the Woman's Christian Temperance Union was formed, and Frances E. Willard soon became its recognized leader.

It was the founding of the Anti-Saloon League, often characterized as "the church in action against the saloon," at Oberlin, Ohio, in 1895, however, which marks the beginning of the most formidable attack upon the liquor interests in the nation. From the beginning a large proportion of the strong leaders of this organization were Methodists and Methodist contributors furnished a large share of its financial backing. The League refused to ally itself with any political party, and supported only those candidates who stood for the "dry" program. By 1907 a great wave of "dry" legislation began in the country, which by 1919 had resulted in outlawing the liquor traffic in thirty-three states and in the passage of the Eighteenth Amendment. When the Eighteenth Amendment went into operation, at least ninety per cent of the land area of the nation was at least theoretically dry and about seventy per cent of the population was living under a dry regimen. To say that this program was put over by a fanatical minority taking advantage of war psychology is manifestly absurd in the face of the above facts.

Since the General Conference of 1872 American Methodism has steadily maintained the necessity of "total legal prohibition." Since 1925, especially, the Temperance Boards of both the Methodist Episcopal and the Methodist Episcopal Church, South, have been the objects of most vicious attacks by "wet" congressmen and the so-called liberal press, displaying an astonishing disregard for the facts and a fanaticism, in most instances, surpassing anything that can be found among the advocates of Prohibition. So far, however, the vast majority of Methodists, both ministers and laymen, have remained loyal to their "dry" convictions, and in many instances attacks which have been made upon their traditional anti-liquor position have but strengthened their opposition to the return of legalized liquor. The present Methodist position is well summarized in the words of the Episcopal Address before the General Conference at Atlantic City in 1932:

As a church we can follow no course except the one that will reduce the consumption of beverage alcohol to the minimum. We are convinced that national prohibition is that method.

The Methodists have never been a heresy-hunting people, chiefly for the reason that there are no specifically Methodist doctrines. The sole requirement for admission to the early Methodist classes was a "desire to flee from the wrath to come and to be saved from their sins." When John Wesley was a very old man, he reaffirmed this position, saying:

They [the Methodists] do not impose, in order to their admission, any opinions whatsoever. Let them hold particular or general redemption, absolute or conditional decrees; let them be Churchmen or Dissenters, Presbyterians or Independents, it is no obstacle. Let them choose one mode of baptism or another, it is no bar to their admission. The Presbyterians may be Presbyterians still; the Independents and Anabaptists use his own mode of worship. So may the Quaker; and none will contend with him about it. They think and let think.

With such an example of liberality set by their great founder it would have been strange indeed for his spiritual children to set up rigid doctrinal tests. And yet toward the close of the last century, and especially since the Great War, doctrinal issues have in a number of instances arisen which for a time bid fair to disrupt the church.

The first such controversy arose in 1895, when Professor H. G. Mitchell, of the Department of Old Testament in Boston University School of Theology, was accused by certain of his students of having gone too far in accepting the so-called higher criticism. The authorities, however, decided in this instance that Professor Mitchell had not passed beyond the limits of legitimate freedom. Other attacks were made in 1900 and again in 1905. At that time it was necessary for professors in the theological institutions of the church to be confirmed by the bishops, and in 1905 the bishops refused their endorsement of Professor Mitchell. Mitchell now demanded that he be tried by his own Conference, the Central New York, but the Conference, instead of giving him a fair trial, appointed a committee to investigate Professor Mitchell, which advised that a reprimand be administered. The matter was next carried to the General Conference of 1908, which ruled that the action of the Central New York Conference had been a violation of the law of the church, and declared the action of the Conference in adopting the report of the committee null and void. The most important outcome of this unfortunate affair was the decision of the Judiciary Committee of the General Conference (1908) relieving the bishops of the duty of investigating and reporting upon charges of erroneous teaching in the theological schools.[7]

Professor Borden P. Bowne, for many years the outstanding figure in the faculty of Boston University, who had stanchly defended his colleague, Professor Mitchell, was likewise accused of heresy and was brought to trial before his Conference in 1904. The accusations against him were that he was teaching doctrines contrary to the Articles of Religion, as well as contrary to the other established standards of the Methodist Episcopal Church. The charges were given in five specifications and were tried before the body known as the Select Number of Fifteen of the New York East Conference. None of the five specifications were sustained, and the church as a whole breathed a sigh of relief at the favorable outcome.[8]

The Fundamentalist-Modernist controversy which gained increased momentum immediately following the Great War, due to the general conservative reaction, began during the early years of the century with the publication of a series of little books called *The Fundamentals: A Testimony to the Truth* (begun in 1910).[9] These publications professed to set forth the old-time gospel, and through generous funds,

[7] See *General Conference Journal*, 1908, pp. 482-483. This decision was *based on the fact that the bishops as* presidents of Annual Conferences and Judicial Conferences sitting to try accused persons would tend to prejudice the trial of such person "by reason of an opinion formed and expressed, founded upon an *ex parte* investigation made by a committee of the Board of Bishops, one of whom must, or may, preside at the trial."

[8] For the best account of this trial see the *Methodist Review*, Vol. CV, 1922, pp. 399-413; also McConnell, Francis J., *Borden Parker Bowne*, pp. 189-206. The Abingdon Press.

[9] Cole, Stewart G., *History of Fundamentalism*, Chap. IV, "The Rise of Fundamentalism." New York: Richard R. Smith, 1931.

provided by two wealthy laymen, were sent broadcast to ministers of all Protestant denominations, as well as to evangelists, missionaries, theological professors, Y. M. and Y. W. C. A. secretaries, Sunday-school superintendents and religious editors. These booklets undoubtedly had far-reaching influence and were welcomed by many thousands of loyal churchmen. Besides such publications, Fundamentalist Bible schools were established and frequent Bible conferences were conducted to fan the flame of religious reaction.

This movement found considerable response in the Methodist churches, manifesting itself particularly immediately following the Great War. The main centers of agitation in the Methodist Episcopal Church were the New Jersey, the Philadelphia, and the Baltimore Conferences. The program of the conservatives was twofold: first, to compel the Commission on Courses of Study for young ministers to choose only those books which the conservatives considered in harmony with Methodist doctrinal standards; second, they urged upon the General Conference to declare "the binding authority of our Articles of Religion and other established standards of doctrine." A third subject of controversy was the question of retaining in the *Discipline* the specific rule on amusements which had been adopted in 1872.

The controversy continued from the General Conference of 1916 through the next three quadrenniums. The special object of conservative attack in 1916, 1920, and 1924 was the Course of Study, and to the General Conference of 1920 more than thirty petitions were presented asking that the

Courses of Study be modified in order to protect the faith of young ministers. The same issue was before the 1924 General Conference, but by this time the conservative leaders had lost much of their former strength and instead of condemning the Course of Study, the commission, which had prepared it, were praised for their work, and practically no changes were made in its content. At the General Conference of 1928 the conservatives constituted a weak minority and failed to get a single issue before the delegates.

In 1925 the Methodist conservatives formed themselves into a *Methodist League for Faith and Life,* whose purpose, they described, was "to reaffirm the vital and eternal truths of the Christian religion, such as the inspiration of the Scriptures, the deity of Jesus, his virgin birth," etc. The league began the publication of a monthly paper called *The Call to the Colors.* Later their publicity organ was renamed *The Essentialist,* which carried on the propaganda activities of the League with considerable success, but by 1927 there were clear signs that the movement was waning. The premillennialist craze which swept the country in the post-war years, and won many followers among the Fundamentalists in other denominations, found little response among the Methodists.

Progress toward the unification of American Methodism since the first interchange of fraternal greetings following the Civil War has been disappointingly slow. One marked advance was the creation of a joint commission made up of representatives of the two great branches of the church, which in 1898 formulated a number of important recommendations. Among these recommendations were the preparation of a common catechism, a common hymn book, and a common order of public worship, and the co-ordination of missionary operations in the foreign fields. In due time these recommendations were carried out and a joint hymnal and order of worship has now been in use for a generation, and at the moment a joint commission, representing the Methodist Episcopal, the Methodist Episcopal, South, and the Methodist Protestant Churches, are at work on a new joint hymnal and order of worship, which is to serve the next generation.

Between the years 1906 and 1925 the movement for merging the three Methodist Churches—the Methodist Protestant, the Church South, and the Methodist Episcopal—went forward slowly but with seemingly every prospect of final success. The first definite proposal of a joint commission for unification was made in 1911, which suggested the creation of four quadrennial Conferences, the colored membership to constitute one of these Conferences. At their respective General Conferences of 1920 and 1922 the two Episcopal Methodist Churches again created commissions on unification and the plan of union worked out by these commissions was adopted by the two General Conferences and was then sent to the Annual Conferences for their ratification. This plan provided that the Methodist Episcopal, and the Methodist Episcopal Church, South, should compose separate jurisdictions, each with its Jurisdictional Conference having full General Conference powers except such as are vested in the General Conference; that a General Confer-

ence, composed of the same delegates voting by jurisdictions, should have certain specified powers over
all matters distinctly connectional. In other words,
the plan provided that the two churches were to go
along much as formerly, working together wherever
possible, hoping that in the course of the years the
two bodies would actually become one in spirit and
life, as well as in name.

Little opposition to this plan developed in the
Methodist Episcopal Church, for the simple reason
that the Northern brethren had little to forget, and
the plan was adopted in their Annual Conferences
by large majorities. In the Southern Church, however, conditions were greatly different. It was found
that the wounds of the Civil War and Reconstruction period were not yet healed, while the large
Negro membership in the Methodist Episcopal
Church, together with their Negro bishops, made it
impossible to secure the necessary three-fourths vote
in the Southern Annual Conferences. Many in both
churches were keenly disappointed at the outcome,
and some have expressed the feeling that the union
of the two Episcopal Methodisms is still a long way
off. There are undoubtedly many grave difficulties
still to be overcome. The two churches differ on
such questions as episcopal power. In the Southern
church since its organization the bishop has exercised larger power than in the Methodist Episcopal
Church, and even has the right to question a General Conference enactment, and may send it down
to the Annual Conferences for their decision. In
the Methodist Episcopal Church the bishop is as
much subject to the General Conference as any other
minister in the church.

The Northern church is also more liberal theologically than is the Southern church and has taken a more decided stand on such matters as the social gospel.

But these difficulties are by no means insuperable, and the fact that the two churches have a common ancestry, "hold a common faith, and live for a common purpose" is a sure indication that the question of unification will come up again. The Southern bishops in their Episcopal Address before the General Conference of 1930 stated:

> We believe . . . that this failure was only temporary, and we cherish the hope that at some future time we shall be wise enough to find a way whereby a united Methodism with undivided energies and unwasted resources may deliver her full strength upon the common task.

The commission of the Methodist Episcopal Church on Interdenominational Relations, created by the General Conference of 1928, was active in carrying on conversations with representatives of the Methodist Episcopal Church, South; the Methodist Protestant Church, the Presbyterian Church in the United States of America, and with the Protestant Episcopal Church. A definite plan of union between the Methodist Protestant and the Methodist Episcopal Churches was agreed upon by the committees of these two churches, but the Methodist Episcopal commission recommended that before this plan be consummated it would be best to appeal to the commissioners of the Church South to join in a consideration of such questions of comity as might arise out of the proposed merger.

CHAPTER XVIII

THROUGH TWO DECADES OF STORM
AND STRESS
1933-1953

IT is no exaggeration to say that the two decades
from 1933 to 1953 constitute one of the most
momentous periods in the history of civilized
man. A mere listing of the major events of these
years supports the validity of this statement. The
period opened with the most disastrous economic
depression of modern times, the effects of which
reached into every home and every life in the land.
Ten millions and more were unemployed; bank failures on a scale never before known precipitated
hardship and loss upon millions of people whose
life savings were swept away in the general crash.
These years saw the rise of Hitler to power in
Germany and witnessed the spread of Nazism over
Europe, with its threat of besmirching every decent
thing in our civilization. Then came World War
II, the most destructive, the most ruthless war in
the whole history of warfare. These years also saw
the end of the war and the attempts of the Allies to
create another world organization to preserve peace.
And now we find the world divided into two al-
legiances, the free world on the one hand and the
vast accumulation of people under the dominance
of Russia on the other. This period has witnessed
the development of atomic power with all its tre-

mendous potentialities both for good and evil. Its destructive power is beyond all calculation. Whether it will serve to advance human progress or destroy mankind, only the future can tell. It is the purpose of this chapter to appraise the part American Methodism has played in this era of world confusion.

Unification Completed

By the year 1934 the three Methodist bodies had set up machinery for the preparation of a plan for reunion. The plan as finally adopted by the commissioners appointed by the three churches provided, first, for a united Church to be called The Methodist Church. Second, the Articles of Religion were to be those historically held by all three of the uniting churches. Third, episcopacy was to continue, the Methodist Protestant Church being given the opportunity of electing two bishops. Fourth, there was to be one General Conference with legislative power over all church-wide interests, it being understood that the historic restrictive rules were to remain in force. Fifth, the United States was to be divided into five jurisdictions, each with its own Jurisdictional Conference; its principal function being the election of bishops, though each jurisdiction might elect a bishop or bishops outside its own jurisdictional boundaries. A sixth jurisdiction was to be composed of the Negro membership of the former Methodist Episcopal Church, a provision without which union could not have been accomplished. Seventh, there was to be equal lay and ministerial representation in all the conferences—annual, jurisdictional, and general. And, finally, the General Conference was to elect a Judicial Council to which was to be referred all questions of constitutionality and disputed matters of law.

This general framework of union met a favorable response in each of the three churches. The General Conference of the Methodist Protestant Church ratified it at once by a vote of 142 to 39; in the Annual Conferences there were only five negative votes. The Methodist Episcopal Church in its General Conference of 1936 voted 470 to 83 in favor of the plan, while its Annual Conferences voted 17,239 for and 1,862 against. The Annual Conferences of the Methodist Episcopal Church, South, voted 7,652 in favor of union and 1,247 against; in the General Conference of the Southern Church in 1938 only 26 votes were recorded against union with 434 in its favor. This largest unification movement in American Protestantism was consumated at a Uniting Conference, made up of some 900 delegates, which convened in Kansas City, Missouri, on April 25, 1939. The principal purpose of the conference was to make administrative adjustments, all of which were put into operation at once with a minimum of friction. The new Methodist Church started with a membership of more than eight million, the largest Protestant body in the United States.

What were the underlying factors which made the unification of American Methodism possible? In the first place, American Methodists—whether North, South, or Methodist Protestant—had never lost sight of their common historical heritage. John and Charles Wesley, Francis Asbury, William McKendree, and a host of other early Methodist worthies were held in equal reverence by them all, even throughout all the vicissitudes of controversy and division. The fact that the several Methodist churches had always had a substantial undergirding of unity was noted in one of the addresses given at the Methodist Ecumenical Conferences held in Washington in 1891. The address called attention to the substantial unity which continued to exist among the various Methodist churches in such matters as a common creed, a common theology, and a common mode of worship. Some sincere advocates of Methodist unity thought that the best way to promote union was to forget the past with all its controversies. But the past cannot be forgotten. The only way to deal with the past is neither to attempt to forget it nor to ignore it, but rather to come to a full understanding of it. It is a significant fact that the leaders in the three churches who led the unification movement in their respective bodies were among those who best understood all phases of the past differences.

A second factor in bringing about Methodist union was the effective leadership furnished by the bishops in the episcopal bodies and by the president of the Methodist Protestant body. This leadership may well be epitomized in the persons of Bishop Eugene R. Hendrix of the Church, South, Bishop Earl Cranston of the Methodist Episcopal Church, and Dr. Thomas H. Lewis of the Methodist Protestant Church—all of whom came to look upon the furthering of the unification of American Methodism as the most important interest of their lives.

A third factor which underlay the movement toward unity in American Methodism was the founding by the Methodist Episcopal Church, South, of four new universities—each with a well-manned theological seminary—which exercised a powerful liberalizing influence in Southern Methodism. Although Vanderbilt University was lost to the church in 1914, during the forty years in which it was the principal intellectual center of Southern Methodism it turned out an increasingly influential and able church leadership. The transforming of Emory College into Emory University, with its Candler School of Theology; Trinity College into Duke University, with its well-trained theological faculty; and the founding of Southern Methodist University at Dallas, also with its school of theology, now Perkins School of Theology, gave Southern Methodism the undoubted leadership in theological education in the South. All of these universities not only drew their faculties from all sections of the nation, but increasingly their student bodies as well. To a large extent Southern Methodist leadership working for union came either directly or indirectly out of these new university centers.

A growing historical mindedness, among Methodists both North and South, was another influence of significance in promoting union. Historical mindedness is the willingness to consider all sides of all the historic issues which caused division. This attitude led to the restudy of past controversies and the publication of books and articles setting forth with equal objectivity all sides of the old differences. Thus Methodists, both North and South, as well as Methodist Protestants, came more and more to accept the same interpretations of the past. Here is an example of the practical value of history, for the creation of historical mindedness among American

Methodists has been the accomplishment of the trained historian, who had no side to defend.

Methodist union has been in operation for a half generation, and with each passing year the cords which bind the three former churches together grow stronger and stronger. More and more former Southerners have gone north and Northerners have gone south, and the Methodist Protestants, with a few exceptions, are now thoroughly integrated into the united Methodist Church.[1]

The Depression

The situation in the country caused by the economic collapse was well summarized in the address issued by the Council of Bishops of the Methodist Episcopal Church in November, 1933:

Millions are jobless and wageless, without income of any kind dependent upon public and private charity for their sustenance. The demands for relief are beyond those of any previous winter. Our resources are reduced below anything we have hitherto experienced. The means of aid at our command are tragically depleted.

The coming of the New Deal and its attempts at a planned economy with its numerous new agencies —the CCC camps for unemployed young men, the NRA, and the WPA—met widespread approval at first, for the country as a whole had become convinced that prosperity would not return by waiting for it to come around the corner. This address of the Methodist Episcopal bishops gave expression to the public impatience for something to be done to

[1] For a comprehensive survey of the whole story of Methodist unification, see John M. Moore, *The Long Road to Methodist Union.*

meet the crisis. It stated that to depend on the old formulas was

to trifle with a terrible catastrophe. . . . The naïve faith in our present economic gods must go. . . . No system built upon poverty, suffering and injustice can no longer be allowed to go unchallenged.

The concentration of wealth and power in the hands of a steadily narrowing minority, the control of the means of production and distribution, the ownership of the resources of the nation by the privileged few threaten the economic freedom and security of the people as a whole.

Though disclaiming any desire to pass judgment on ways and means of dealing with the national crisis, the bishops' address insisted that "some way should and must be found, and if necessary, new principles of social justice be accepted and applied." Such sentiments in normal times would have seemed radical and dangerous; but when they were uttered in 1933 in the depth of the depression, they met the approval of the rank and file of Christian people throughout the land.

The depression affected American Methodism in many ways, direct and indirect. The great building programs which had been started in the prosperous years left overwhelming debts, at the very time when giving on the part of church members was at its lowest ebb due to greatly curtailed income on the part of the great proportion of average income people. The Episcopal Fund was so depleted that for some time the bishops' salaries were cut in half. Pastors' salaries in most instances were sharply reduced. Instructors in Methodist colleges were dismissed, while those who were retained were, in numerous cases, on half pay. World service giving declined, the decrease in 1932 in the Methodist Episcopal Church alone being $1,248,575.

It has often been assumed that religion revives in periods of economic distress; that men automatically turn to God when there is nowhere else to turn. But the depression of the nineteen-thirties, contrary to the expectation of many ministers and unlike other periods of economic distress in the past, did not drive men to God, as shown by membership statistics in the large evangelical churches.[2] The financial crash of 1857 produced a revival, led mostly by laymen in the urban centers of the North, which has been characterized as a modern Pentecost. Perhaps one of the reasons why a period of revival did not materialize among Methodists during and following the last depression was because the older revivalistic doctrines and methods had been gradually discarded and no new methods had been developed to take their place. To illustrate this fact nine of the large conferences of the Methodist Episcopal Church, South, reported a loss in 1931 over 1930 of 21,712 members. At the same time revivals were in progress among the Pentecostal and Holiness bodies, which were ministering to the people who were most in distress as a consequence of the general economic collapse. In the Church of the Nazarene, which had stemmed from Methodism, was built on Methodist models, and stressed the Methodist doctrines of conversion and holiness, the membership increase was more than a hundred per cent between the years

---

[2] See Samuel C. Kincheloe, *Research Memorandum on Religion in the Depression.* See also A. T. Boisen, *Religion and Hard Times,* a case study of the effects of the depression on a group of Pentacostal and Holiness sects in several counties in Indiana.

1927 and 1937. The Assemblies of God, likewise revivalistic in emphasis, reported 48,000 members in 1926; in 1937 they reported 3,470 churches and 175,-000 members. The two principal Churches of God reported similar increases during the depression years.

Another doctrinal emphasis stressed by these revivalistic sects during these years was millennialism. Seeing little chance for a better life in this world, the economically depressed were attracted by a gospel of a better world to come and the speedy return of the Lord to this world of sin and poverty to make all things new—doctrines which are appropriately called poor men's doctrines. Such doctrines were rarely heard from Methodist pulpits, for they had no appeal to upper and middle class people, such as the Methodists had now become.

The effects of the depression brought some changes which were, in the long run, beneficial to the church. One such change was in the realm of religious education. It was soon found that there was an oversupply of half-trained persons who had found places on the staffs of the larger churches in the area of religious education. These persons were strong on technique, but weak on content and common sense. As Shailer Mathews phrases it in his *New Faith for Old,* they tended "to minimize churches as institutions," hid "God behind a smoke screen of psychology," and made "inadequate use of the Bible." The result was that the church found itself with a generation of religious illiterates on its hands. The cutting down of church budgets as the result of the depression screened out from the churches many inadequately equipped religious edu-

405

cation directors and turned the attention of the Board of Education of the church to the necessity of reconstructing the whole emphasis in the training of children and youth. The discovery of the religious illiteracy among young people brought the whole matter of religion in education to the fore, and it became a major concern of the board to remedy that defect in the educational program of the church.

Changing Winds of Doctrine

The extreme optimism which characterized the years immediately following World War I and which continued until the sudden economic collapse in the autumn of 1929 was reflected in the kind of theology which had gained a large vogue in certain so-called liberal circles of all the principal Protestant churches, Methodists among them. There was much talk of the scientific approach to religion. Those were the days when every branch of learning sought some tie-up with "science," and scientific religion was much extolled from many a cultured pulpit. The extreme liberals called themselves humanists. They abolished the "existence of any God other than the God resident in the human-will-to-goodness." Professor Edwin E. Aubrey in his *Present Theological Tendencies* suggests that this extreme position grew out of "a certain healthy impatience" with the too easy cures for the pains of the world offered by the so-called orthodox. This antitheistic and antisupernatural emphasis seemed to be gaining wide acceptance among liberal ministers of all denominations; but even at the time of its greatest vogue, it failed to gain the allegiance of the great body of moderate liberal opinion. This bringing God down to man's size had its main chance in the prosperous nineteen-twenties. But it proved to be only a "fair-weather" theology which had nothing to offer when the black clouds of the depression began to darken the sky.

Theological ideas tend to swing back and forth between two extremes—the part God plays in salvation and the part man has. When times are good, man tends to overstress his own part; when times are hard and the going is rough, the natural tendency is to throw all the burden on the Lord. Thus theology swings from a complete confidence in man to a complete dependence upon God.

A theology which began to filter into American Protestantism during the early depression years was what is known as Neo-Calvinism or neo-orthodoxy. It had taken root in German Protestantism following the close of World War I and was first introduced into the United States with the appearance of Karl Barth's *The Word of God and the Word of Man* in English translation, now a developed theological system. The basic emphasis in this theology is the "unbridgeable crevasse between God and Man"; that God and man can have no direct relationship because God is "totally other" than man. Every human attempt to build bridges between God and man, or to bring together the divine and the human, is vain. Our knowledge of God comes from God and not from the religious nature in man. That God has not "revealed Himself once and for all, but from time to time He reveals Himself"; and "even in the revelation of Christ no general idea of God is revealed, no valid and demonstrable idea." This all boils down to mean that God and man cannot work together to make a better world. It means the complete rejection of the social gospel emphasis, for God alone can reform society. Yet God is not interested in society, but only concerns himself to attend and assist the individual soul "in its passage through time to eternity." God achieves his victory not "in history but beyond history," for the world is doomed to go to ruin, and there is no use in man's trying to save it.[3] As far as this world is concerned, here is a "do-nothing" theology. Its acceptance infers the entire rejection of Methodism from John Wesley until now. The Hard-Shell Baptists on the American frontier who rejected all man-made organizations, such as missionary societies and Sunday schools, justified their position by the statement, "If God wants to make a better world, He will bring it about in his own time and way," which would seem to harmonize with neo-orthodoxy.

Though most Methodist theologians pretty largely rejected this pessimistic European theology, it found able supporters and advocates in the several great interdenominational seminaries—such as Union Seminary in New York and Yale Divinity School—which were attracting an increasing number of Methodist students. Such distinguished theologians as Paul Tillich and Reinhold Niebuhr at Union and Richard Niebuhr at Yale have had a profound influence on large numbers of young men entering the Methodist ministry, some of whom have become members of the faculties of Methodist theological seminaries. Two Methodist theologians produced books in which neo-orthodox views are reflected. Two such volumes

[3] For a clear and concise statement of the neo-orthodox theology, see Adoph Keller, *Religion and the European Mind,* especially ch. iii, pp. 45-69.

were Edwin Lewis' *Christian Manifesto* and George Croft Cell's *The Rediscovery of John Wesley*. Professor Lewis of Drew Theological Seminary inveighed against the softness in religion which had crept in during the comfortable years, and displayed impatience with the "sentimental theism which the Fatherhood of God too often is supposed to mean." Professor Cell of Boston University School of Theology in his study of John Wesley attempts to make John Wesley a Calvinist without much success. Both of the above books grew out of a common conviction of their authors that unless something be done to check the sliding of Methodist teaching into humanistic paths, it was doubtful whether Methodism had a future. On the other hand other Methodist theologians, such as Harris Franklin Rall of Garrett Biblical Institute and Professor L. Harold DeWolf of Boston University School of Theology published important books defending the historic Methodist "common sense" theology, that to make a better world as well as a better life God and man must work together.[4]

The Repeal of the Eighteenth Amendment

A matter of no little importance to American Methodists was the repeal of the Eighteenth Amendment to the Constitution of the United States. It was ratified in 1919, just at the close of World War I, after many years of temperance agitation carried on by the W.C.T.U. and the Anti-Saloon League—both the creation of the great evangelical churches—to which the Methodists gave full support. The

---

[4] L. H. DeWolf, *The Religious Revolt Against Reason.*

amendment was repealed soon after the presidential election of 1932. It had been a major issue in the campaign of 1928. Indeed, Alfred E. Smith's defeat for the presidency that year was largely due to his advocacy of the return of liquor and plenty of it, together with the fact that he was Roman Catholic. Because of Methodist activity in behalf of retaining the Eighteenth Amendment, the Temperance Boards of both the Methodist Episcopal Church, South, and the Methodist Episcopal Church were the victims of vicious attacks on the part of the wet press and the so-called liberal congressmen, who displayed an astonishing disregard for facts and a fanaticism that rivaled the most extreme prohibition advocates. It became evident as the presidential campaign of 1932 neared its close that repeal of prohibition was inevitable no matter which party won.

The Volstead Act was passed in October, 1919, to provide the machinery for the enforcement of national prohibition, but the experiment proved a sad disappointment to those who had sponsored it. Respectable citizens "who would not have thought of breaking other laws, cooperated with racketeers to violate the prohibition statute." [5] Bootleggers and Speakeasies flourished in all the cities and many so-called respectable citizens openly boasted of their defiance of the prohibition laws. Due to such brazen lawlessness many Methodist laymen became convinced that the prohibition experiment was a failure and welcomed the repeal of the amendment.

Those advocating repeal promised that the old

---

[5] Harry J. Carman and Harold C. Syrett, *A History of the American People,* II, 578.

malodorous saloon was never to return; that the evils
of rum-running and bootlegging would automatically disappear, while the federal and state governments
would reap a rich harvest of liquor taxes which
would ease the tax burden of the common man.
Three years after repeal Harry Emerson Fosdick in
a widely quoted sermon thus summarized the liquor
situation:

> The repeal of prohibition did not solve our problem. It
> simply plunged us once more into the intolerable situation
> which our fathers faced two generations ago, when they
> rose up in indignation against the liquor traffic. Once more
> we face that traffic, everywhere anti-social, not to say crim-
> inal in its consequences. . . . This present tipsy, cocktail-
> party generation cannot be the last word in the history of
> alcoholism. As sure as history repeats itself a revolt is due,
> a change in public attitude born out of disgust with the
> fear of the intolerable estate we are now in.

In a series of articles in the *Christian Century*,
John Haynes Holmes made the following appraisal
of what was happening. He concluded that repeal
was a sad failure, for not only had all the evils of
the prohibition period continued, but the saloon
had come back with its name changed to "tavern";
and contrary to "wet" promises, drinking had not
diminished, but had greatly increased, while the toll
of traffic deaths due to drunken drivers had steadily
mounted. The years following repeal saw the proportion of steady drinkers in the nation's population
greatly increased, while the "disease" of alcoholism
has claimed more than a million victims and is still
growing.

Methodists throughout the nation, through their
press and pulpit, generally fought for the retention

of the Eighteenth Amendment, though perhaps not with the vigor or conviction of some of the former Methodist stalwarts like George R. Stuart. He often said he would fight rum until he wore his fists off; he would kick it until he wore his feet off; and then he would butt it until he wore his head off. But it needs to be said that such furious methods of fighting "rum" have little vogue among Methodist Church people today, while many of them have succumbed to the lure of the cocktail. Yet opposition to alcohol as a beverage is in Methodist blood, and any movement to fight the liquor traffic will find most Methodists among its chief supporters.

Modern Pacifism

Following World War I there arose among the younger ministers of Protestant churches a type of pacifism which found a relatively large following among Methodists. The older peace movement had been more or less passive; the newer movement was positive and aggressive. The strength of this movement was indicated when a questionnaire was sent out to more than fifty thousand clergymen of all denominations by *The World Tomorrow* in 1931, and more than nineteen thousand replies were received. Of this number 52 per cent believed that the church should neither sanction nor support any future war, while ten thousand stated that it was their purpose not only to refuse to sanction war but that they would have no part whatever in any armed conflict. This pacifist movement was strong in all universities and colleges, particularly in the denominational institutions. It was promoted by youth organizations of all sorts, not a few of them leaning

toward leftist opinions. Great youth conventions
were held in all parts of the country where flaming
antiwar resolutions were adopted. Feeding the
pacifist movement among students was the emphasis
placed upon the futility of war in the teaching of
modern European history. Pretty generally the
teachers of modern European history in the colleges
accepted what is known as the revisionist position in
regard to the causes of World War I. This position
tended to whitewash Germany and make Britain the
scapegoat. Indeed pacifist opinion previous to the
outbreak of World War II was almost a hundred
per cent anti-British and laid the blame for many of
the world's ills upon British imperialism.

Umphrey Lee in his *The Historic Church and
Modern Pacifism* [6] clearly shows that the type of
pacifism which gained such a large hold upon the
Christian youth of the nineteen-thirties, among
Methodists and other evangelical bodies particularly,
stemmed from the social gospel. This is indicated
by the fact that the outstanding social gospel
preachers, such as Ralph Sockman and Ernest Fre-
mont Tittle and Harry Emerson Fosdick, were recognized leaders in the modern pacifism movement.
As Lee points out, the type of pacifism with which
the church has long been familiar rejected all forms
of resistance, whereas the pacifism that gained such
a large following among Methodists, as well as among
the youth of other churches, between the two World
Wars urged nonresistance as its main strategy and
exalted Gandhi and Tolstoy as its models. But nonresistance is a form of resistance intended to secure

[6] See particularly ch. ix, "Modern Pacifism."

power and control, and would seem to have as little relation to the teaching of Jesus as any other form of resistance.

Between the outbreak of World War II in September, 1939, and the entrance of the United States into the war after Pearl Harbor in December, 1941, the social gospel pacifists lined up almost a hundred percent against American participation in the war. While many Methodists sympathized with this position, there were no official pronouncements on the part of the Methodist bodies, as was the case among some other churches. For instance the Disciples of Christ Convention meeting at St. Louis in May, 1941, voted two to one in support of a resolution addressed to President Roosevelt, urging him to take no step in aid of Great Britain which might carry us into the war. The editorial policy of the *Christian Century* urged this position. In March, 1939, one hundred prominent ministers signed an "Affirmation of Christian Pacifist Faith," which stated that "the gospel of God as revealed in Jesus Christ" left them no other choice "but to refuse to sanction or participate in war." Bishop Francis J. McConnell, however, declined to sign such a statement, declaring that he would not "be put on the spot as to what he should do" if he should come home and find a murderer attempting to kill members of his family.

The Methodists at their Uniting Conference in May, 1939, took the position that the church would stand by all conscientious objectors among its membership and claimed exemption from military service for all Methodists who took that position. At the same time the conference recognized the right of all individuals to answer the call of government "in any

414

emergency according to the dictates of his Christian conscience." The Federal Council of Churches, which had the full support of Methodist opinion, created a committee on conscientious objectors which was responsible for securing a change in the draft bill. This change would give recognition to all conscientious objectors, not only those of the well-known historical pacifist bodies, such as the Quakers, Mennonites, and Dunkers, but also those who were members of any well-recognized religious denomination. The Draft Act thus contains this statement:

Nothing contained in this act shall be construed to require any person to be subject to combatant training and service in the land and naval forces of the United States who, by reason of religious training and belief is conscientiously opposed to participation in war in any form.

This action, however, did not excuse such persons from registering, and in a number of instances conscientious objectors refused to register on the ground that even to register was to recognize war. Some students in Union Theological Seminary and a few ministers refused to register, and in every instance the court sentenced them to prison terms—though there were few if any cases where the court did not express reluctance and regret at the necessity of imposing the sentences. Numerous polls taken in all the churches from September, 1939, to December 7, 1941, revealed the fact that there were probably more Methodist pacifists than in any other of the so-called nonpacifist churches.

American Methodism in World War II

Although the Methodist social gospel pacifists were undoubtedly sincere in maintaining their anti-interventionist position, the brutal Japanese attack on Pearl Harbor on December 7, 1941, transformed many, if not a majority of them, into reluctant participants. The Christian interventionist point of view as presented by Reinhold Niebuhr in *Christianity and Crisis* pretty generally represented the mood of most American Methodists toward the war. War, Niebuhr states, is basically sinful, and we stand in need of repentance for participating in it; yet, relatively speaking, in this particular conflict one side is right and the other wrong. The triumph of wrong can only be prevented by the defeat of the German and Italian Axis and the victory of the United Nations. This would not, to be sure, ensure all the ideal ends for which our Christianity stands, but, on the other hand, a victory of the Axis powers would make achievement of Christian ends absolutely impossible. He held that to say, as did some pacifists, both sides in the conflict were equally guilty, since the war was nothing more nor less than a conflict between two rival imperialisms, shows ignorance as well as moral confusion. Niebuhr pointed out further the basic distinctions between the two civilizations in conflict. One was a civilization "in which justice and freedom are still realities"; the other is one in which justice and freedom have been displaced by ruthless tyranny. For this reason Christians in countries such as ours cannot evade the ethical issues at stake.

This position, however, did not mean that American Methodists with other Christians were prepared to bless war and make it a holy cause. Rather they came to believe in the necessity of the defeat of the

416

Axis powers as the only possibility for a just peace. Most Methodists, both lay and clerical, agreed with Daniel Poling of the Philadelphia Baptist Temple when he refused to call the war holy, though he believed that the cause for which the Allies fought was holy. Professor John C. Bennett, now of Union Theological Seminary, called the war just but not holy. Dean Sperry of Harvard Divinity School in an article in *Christendom* entitled "The Feel of the War" noted the lack of the emotional response to the war on the part of the American people, as compared to the response in World War I. To Christian people in general and to Methodists in particular there was nothing glorious about the war; it was simply a grim business that had to be done and most Americans could join with Dean Sperry in this prayer: "Save us, O Lord, from letting our righteous anger ever become unrighteous hate, and from all presumptuous desire to take upon ourselves the office of that vengeance which is thine alone."

A significant contribution made by the American churches during the war was the furnishing of chaplains for the armed forces. The government announced in the fall of 1940 that there was to be one chaplain for every twelve hundred men in the armed forces. These chaplains would be in full charge of all spiritual interests in the camps and posts. In World War I the Young Men's Christian Association and the Knights of Columbus had a prominent part in carrying on religious and recreational work among the troops, but both of these organizations were barred from erecting special buildings for their work in the camps. In other words, the work of the chaplain's post was greatly enlarged, since all religious work was to be channeled through his office. The government established training schools for chaplains where every chaplain was trained to minister to soldiers, sailors, and airmen of every faith—Protestants, Catholics, and Jews. The various churches, the Methodist among the rest, set up their own commissions for the selection of chaplains, though they all were to conform to uniform requirements laid down by the Chief of Chaplains' office. And it is significant that the Chief of Chaplains was a fair-minded and highly respected Roman Catholic, William R. Arnold, who won the confidence of all groups. Each religious body was assigned its quota of chaplains, but unfortunately the Methodists were never able to secure a sufficient number to fill their quota. An A.B. degree was the minimum educational requirement and, in addition, from one to three years of pastoral experience. The age limit for Army chaplains was first fixed at forty-two, but later was lowered to forty; the Navy required both college and theological degrees, while the age limit was from twenty-four to thirty-three.

The co-operation of all religious bodies in the nation in serving the spiritual needs of those in the armed services is an example of how essential unity can come out of diversity. Though the most divided in the world in religious affiliations, the American chaplains of all faiths worked together with an astonishing minimum of friction in serving a common end. In pursuing this policy the government made it clear that it was not antireligious, but that a friendly relation between church and state could be carried on without violating the principle of the separation of church and state, and that the government could do much to promote the cause of religion entirely apart from any sectarian participation as such.

Another example of government concern for promoting religion in the armed forces was in the building of chapels on Army posts, camps, and other places where American troops were stationed. In the spring of 1941 Congress appropriated more than $12,-000,000 for the building of 604 chapels designed to serve all faiths—Protestants, Catholics, and Jews. Each chapel was equipped for all the various types of worship. Thus these chapels had reversible altars which could be easily adjusted for the holding of a Roman Catholic Mass or a Methodist preaching service.

The government also sponsored an agency called the United Service Organization (USO). Its board of directors consisted of five representatives—one each from the Young Men's Christian Association, the Salvation Army, the Jewish Welfare Board, the National Catholic Community Service, and the Travelers Aid Societies. Clubs and lounges were established all over the nation in such places as railroad stations and hotel lobbies. Each unit was managed by the co-operation of local agencies, chief among them being the churches. These USO clubs were open to all persons in the armed services, regardless of race, color, or creed. The government furnished the equipment, while the cost of conducting the clubs was raised by popular subscription.[7]

---

[7] See Ray H. Abrams, "The Churches and Clergy in World War II" in *Organized Religion in the United States*, pp. 110-19.

A Just and Durable Peace

Never before have the American churches exercised so large an influence upon public opinion as they did during the latter years of World War II in shaping our government's peace program. Soon after the United States became involved in the war, the Federal Council of the Churches of Christ in America appointed a Commission to Study the Bases of a Just and Durable Peace, and their report was considered and approved at a National Study Conference of the Federal Council held at Ohio Wesleyan University in Delaware, Ohio, in March, 1942. This report was circulated widely throughout the nation, was published in both the church and secular press, and exercised a powerful influence in preparing the American mind to face the problems of a post-war world. The report came to be known as the "Six Pillars of Peace." Leading Methodists, both lay and clerical, participated in these war meetings of the Federal Council, and Methodist opinion was a unit together with other American churchmen in supporting the principles set forth in the "Six Pillars":

1. The peace must provide the political framework for a continuing collaboration of the United Nations, and, in due course, of neutral and enemy nations.

2. The peace must make provision for bringing within the scope of international agreement those economic and financial acts of national governments which have widespread international repercussions.

3. The peace must make provision for an organization to adapt the treaty structure of the world to changing underlying conditions.

4. The peace must proclaim the goal of autonomy for subject peoples, and it must establish international organiza-

tion to assure and to supervise the realization of that end.

5. The peace must establish procedures for controlling military establishments everywhere.

6. The peace must establish in principle, and seek to achieve in practice, the right of individuals everywhere to religious and intellectual liberty.

The Roman Catholics also went on record, some months later, through their National Catholic Welfare Conference, which issued a notable statement in every respect in full harmony with the Federal Council's "Six Pillars of Peace." This statement called for "an international order in which the spirit of Christ shall rule the hearts of men and of nations." It deprecated any program of exploitation of the defeated nations; called for a peace that would repudiate totalitarianism of every sort; and demanded a lasting peace based upon the spirit of Christianity which would bring justice to all nations, "even those not Christian." The statement closes with this noble statement: "In the epochal revolution through which the world is passing, it is very necessary for us to realize that every man is a brother of Christ."

Thus the Christian mind of America, Protestant and Catholic alike, gave expression to a set of ideals which, it may be truthfully stated, our statesmen made every effort to implement Never before was the federal government more willing to listen to and to heed what the churches had to say on international affairs.

Growing Protestant-Catholic Tension

The United States has now become the principal Roman Catholic nation in the world, since there is no longer a first-rate Roman Catholic power in Europe. As a result of this fact, the Roman Church in the United States has become increasingly aggressive and is no longer hesitant in making its demands known. Although only about one sixth of our population is Catholic, yet the Catholic Church's control over the thought and action of loyal Catholic people is so potent that any program it supports, such as the demand for government assistance to its parochial schools, is sure to have the support of a great majority of Catholic citizens.

A generation ago such great American Catholic leaders as Cardinal Gibbons[8] and Archbishop Ireland were in full accord with all the great American freedoms, and openly supported what was known as Americanism, which included the great principle of separation of church and state. It was then quite generally assumed that American Catholicism was different from that of the Old World and the Latin American types. But all this has changed in the last generation and American Catholics have become increasingly a separated group. There is, of course, a mingling of Catholics and Protestants in business and in nonreligious community activities; but when the Catholic crosses the threshold of his church, he puts an impassable barrier between himself and his Protestant neighbors. In many instances Catholics are forbidden to enter a Protestant church. Thus there is being created a growing religious cleavage in

---

[8] Cardinal James Gibbons is the best example of an American Roman Catholic prelate upholding the American principle of separation of church and state. See *The Life of James Cardinal Gibbons, 1834-1921*, by John Tracy Ellis. 2 Vols. See especially ch. xvi, Vol. II, "Americanism."

American society which tends to create suspicion and often enmity.

The recent attempts of Roman Catholics to obtain government support for their growing parochial school system, the cost of which is undoubtedly becoming too great for Catholic people to bear, is the principal reason for the Catholic insistence that public funds either directly or indirectly be made available for their support. The agitation over the parochial school issue came to a climax with the introduction of the Barden Bill in the United States Congress in 1948. This bill provided for a federal grant of $300,000,000 to be used for the assistance of the public schools only in the most needy states. The Catholic leaders denounced the bill as anti-Catholic; and when Mrs. Franklin D. Roosevelt stated in her column that she favored the Barden Bill, Cardinal Spellman, recognized as the most influential Catholic official in the nation, issued a most astonishing blast in *The New York Times* denouncing Mrs. Roosevelt as misinformed, ignorant, and prejudiced. He further stated that he would not again publicly acknowledge her. It soon became evident that the cardinal's heated denunciation of the former first lady of the land had backfired. Immediately both Catholics as well as non-Catholics publicly deplored the cardinal's uncalled-for accusations. Among those coming to Mrs. Roosevelt's defense was Herbert Lehman, ex-governor of New York and later United States senator. He issued a long statement in *The New York Times* in which he stated that the real issue was "not whether one agrees or disagrees with Mrs. Roosevelt on this or any other public question—the issue is whether Americans are entitled freely to express their views on public questions without being villified or accused of religious bias." The cardinal was soon eating "humble pie." He telephoned Mrs. Roosevelt and asked that they issue a joint statement, to which Mrs. Roosevelt agreed. In her statement Mrs. Roosevelt simply reiterated her opposition to the granting of public funds for sectarian schools, while the humbled cardinal stated that he was only asking for what he called auxiliary aid to parochial schools.

This exchange between Mrs. Roosevelt and Cardinal Spellman simply highlighted a controversy that has continued ever since. Among the results is the publication of numerous books on both sides of the question. Among the books opposing the Catholic position are Paul Blanshard's *American Freedom and Catholic Power* and a later one, still more irritating to the Catholics, comparing the Roman Catholic methods with those of Communism. Among the most important books of recent publication defending the Catholic position are J. M. O'Neill, *Religion and Education Under the Constitution* and Wilfrid Parsons, S. J., *The First Freedom*. Two recent Supreme Court decisions bearing on the school question—the New Jersey School Bus case and the Champaign, Illinois, case, having to do with the machinery of teaching sectarianism in public school buildings —have caused widespread attention. The Catholic books noted above advance the argument that the First Amendment of the Constitution does not prohibit government support of the churches, but only prohibits the government from assisting one church. Accordingly these Catholic authors have advanced what they call multiple establishment, which would permit public funds to be distributed proportionally among all the churches.

The issue which caused the greatest storm of protest from American Protestantism was President Truman's announcement of his intention of appointing a regular United States ambassador to the Vatican in the place of the personal representative, Mr. Myron Taylor, who had been appointed by President Roosevelt. The announced reason for such an appointment was that it would tend to promote peace and combat Communism, while an embassy at the Vatican would be a valuable "listening post" for world trends. The United States maintained a regular representative to the Papal States from 1848 to 1867, but the representative was definitely instructed to have no relationship to the pope as the head of a church, but only as a temporal ruler of some three millions of people. With the unification of Italy and the creation of the Italian nation the United States representative was withdrawn, since the pope no longer was a temporal ruler in any real sense. The opposition to Truman's announced intention quickly reached nation-wide proportions and had overwhelming support from most Protestant church leaders of all denominations. The opposition held that such an appointment violated two great constitutional principles: first, the principle of the separation of church and state; and second, the principle of the equality of all religious bodies under the law. Another reason for opposing such an appointment was that it would inevitably create increased tension between Catholics and Protestants in the United States, since it would mean that the Catholics had been granted special recognition by the government. Mr. Truman's administration ended without achieving his announced purpose, and the administration of President Eisenhower seemingly sidetracked the issue by naming a leading American Roman Catholic as United States minister to Italy.

An agency to combat the growing Roman Catholic threat to the American principle of separation of church and state took shape in 1948 with the formation of "Protestants and Other Americans United for Separation of Church and State," which was spearheaded by some of the most influential Protestant leaders in the country, including a number of prominent Methodists. With headquarters in Washington its objective is not to combat Roman Catholicism as a religion, nor is it motivated by anti-Catholic bias, but its sole purpose is to preserve the foundations of the great American freedom by combating any attempt to break down the wall that separates church and state. It is particularly concerned in keeping public funds from being granted to sectarian schools and in the protection of public schools from sectarian domination.

American Methodism and the Ecumenical Movement

It can be fairly stated that no religious body in American is more ecumenically-minded than the Methodist. John Wesley on many occasions called attention to the fact that no doctrinal tests were ever laid down for membership in Methodist societies. The test of a Christian in the mind of Wesley was not the acceptance of a formal creed or the practice of certain modes of worship or the adoption of any particular type of church government, but rather the acceptance of Christ as a personal Lord and the manner of his daily walk. As Umphrey Lee has stated, Wesley's doctrine was "the doctrine that few doctrines are essential." [9] "This liberty of spirit and breadth of doctrinal tolerance has made Methodism," in the words of Bishop Paul B. Kern, "a willing ally of all those who wish to build the broader and Unisersal Church of Christ in the world." "Methodism," he states, "is ecumenical by nature, and Methodism has fostered the growth of the ecumenical movement from the beginning. We have no doctrinal claims staked off with No Trespassing signs on the gate. We are ready to unite with all Christ's children everywhere in the building of his Church and the bringing of the Kingdom of God on earth." [10]

We have already noticed the origin of the Federal Council of the Churches of Christ in America, and the important part Methodist leadership played in its formation (pp. 366-67). World War II brought home to all Christian people throughout the world the fact that no longer can we isolate ourselves on the basis of race or creed. We have become suddenly aware that we are all citizens of one world, and that the world has become one neighborhood. The vast destruction—physical, spiritual, and moral— wrought by World War II has created in American Protestantism a sense of world mission such as it has never known before, and Methodism in America shares with all the great sister churches a world task which demands, as never before, a united Prot-

---

[9] "Freedom from Rigid Creed," pp. 128-38 in W. K. Anderson, *Methodism.*

[10] *Proceedings of the Seventh Ecumenical Methodist Conference; Springfield, Massachusetts, U.S.A., September 24–October 2, 1947,* p. 6.

estantism. American Protestantism has become increasingly aware that the factors which have caused division have been matters of secondary importance and that there is agreement upon the basic principles of our common Christianity. It is a sad fact, as Harry Emerson Fosdick has so well pointed out, that instead of centering our convictions and loyalties upon the great universals of the Christian faith, too many Protestant bodies have been pledging their loyalties to petty and not infrequently trifling matters. And he asks the pertinent question, "Did Jesus bring a conception of God too big for us?" As a Jewish scholar has stated, the reason why the Jews rejected Jesus was because his conception of God was too big for his contemporaries. Increasingly the great Protestant bodies of the world, the Methodists among the rest, are realizing as never before that now is the time for greatness in religion in this needy and groping world.

In the summer of 1948 there gathered at Amsterdam representatives of 135 church bodies from forty nations to form a World Council of Churches. Every major religious body in America, except two, was represented. The outstanding world Christian, John R. Mott, who had done more than any other individual to prepare the world for Christian unity, was chosen honorary president. That he was a Methodist was only incidental. Vice-presidents were chosen from England, France, and the United States. The purpose behind this world-wide Christian agency has been clearly stated by the general secretary, Dr. Visser 't Hooft, of the Dutch Reformed Church of the Netherlands, as follows:

The World Council is not to be a new ecclesiastical power to compete with those already in existence. There is no plan to form a unified world church. There will be no centralized authority to speak and act in its name. The intention is much simpler than that. The Council is to provide a means of continuing relationship between the member bodies throughout the world so as to be able to collaborate regularly in matters of concern, and to render a common concern, and to render a common witness wherever possible.

It has been pointed out by Professor Latourette that the movement for Christian world unity had its origin in the most divided branches of Christianity —Protestantism; while the most divided branch of Protestantism—that of the United States—has played the largest role in its promotion. In this fact lies one of the most hopeful reasons for the success of Christian world unity, since Protestantism is the most flexible branch of the Christian world. As has been stated above, the principal motive back of the movement was not to achieve doctrinal unity or organization amalgamation, but rather to devise more effective ways of proclaiming the gospel throughout the world. In other words the World Council of Churches is simply an effort to bring together the Christian forces of the world for joint planning and action.[11]

The building of a world Christian community has stemmed from two nineteenth-century forces: one was the vast missionary expansion of Christianity into every corner of the world; the second was the migration of Christian people into the great unoccupied

[11] Kenneth S. Latourette, *The Emergence of a World Christian Community*, pp. 1-29.

areas of the South Pacific and the great trans-Alleghenian areas of North America. In both instances the movement of Occidental people into these new areas was largely a Protestant movement. Thus there came to be large islands of Protestant people throughout the world living in relatively close contact with non-Christian peoples. This is illustrated today by the way Methodism has spread throughout the world. American Methodism has expanded into Mexico and Brazil and throughout Latin America; while British Methodism has found firm rootage in the South Pacific; independent Methodist Churches have been formed in Australia, New Zealand, the Fiji Islands, South Africa, Mexico, and Brazil.

The great Protestant communions of the world have also created world organizations. The Anglicans since 1867 have held their Lambeth Conferences at stated periods at which Anglicans throughout the world have assembled. The Lutherans have now a world agency, as have also the Baptists, the Congregationalists, and the Reformed or Presbyterian bodies. Since 1881 the Methodists of the world have assembled every ten years in a great Ecumenical Conference, the last being held at Oxford, England, in the early autumn of 1951. Thus the whole world of Protestantism is drawing together. These great world denominational gatherings are not in conflict with the World Council of Churches, but are important steps toward the building of a world community.

The World Council of Churches, to use Professor Latourette's words, "is the most inclusive body that Christianity has ever possessed," for "it officially represents a larger number and a wider confessional and geographic range of Christians than any other organization which the centuries have known."

After World War II American Methodism moved forward in unprecedented growth, and at the same time attempted to do its part in binding up the wounds left by the holocaust of war. In 1941 a special fund for overseas relief was set up, and by 1943 it had reached the sum of $1,250,000; but lest American Methodists think too well of their generosity, let it be said that fifty times that amount would have been too small. In the face of all the want and suffering across the sea American Methodism grew richer and richer. Never before was church indebtedness paid off in such staggering amounts; never had gifts and endowments to Methodist institutions—colleges, universities, hospitals, and homes— mounted so high. In 1944 the $3,000,000 indebtedness of the Board of Missions was paid to the last dollar. In 1947 and in succeeding years The Methodist Publishing House did the largest business and had the largest sales in its long history, while the *Christian Advocate* reached its largest circulation since its founding in 1826. In 1944 The Methodist Church inaugurated a "Crusade for Christ," the first objective of which was to raise $25,000,000 for world rehabilitation and relief. This was oversubscribed by more than two million. The last phase of the Crusade was an evangelistic campaign to cover the entire nation, and more than a million members were added to the church rolls. In the face of all these mounting numbers American Methodists need to bear constantly in mind that mere bigness is not an end in itself, but a potential opportunity for greater service in a confused and groping world.

APPENDIX

Organizational Structure of The Methodist Church

Methodism from John Wesley onward has been notable for its organizational efficiency, and the basic features of its organizational structure have persisted through the years. The functions exercised by John Wesley in the Methodist Societies of Great Britain were taken over by Francis Asbury and his successors in American Methodism. Although Wesley objected to the title of bishop assumed by Asbury and Coke, both the title and the office persisted in American Methodism. After the division in 1844-46 in Episcopal Methodism the bishop in the Church, South, gained the right to pass on the constitutionality of conference action, a power which the bishops in the Methodist Episcopal Church never possessed. In 1934, however, the Church, South, created a Judicial Council whose function was to review all questions of constitutionality. Thus when unification came in 1939 the episcopal office in both Episcopal Methodisms had become identical as far as the power of bishops was concerned. Although the Methodist Protestants had abolished episcopacy as well as the presiding eldership, their main objection had not been so much to episcopacy as to the undemocratic appointment system. When the appointment power of the bishop was limited by the plan of unification, the Methodist Protestants were willing to accept the episcopal office, since the presidents of their conferences had exercised functions quite after the pattern of bishops.

The major change in the episcopal system made by the Uniting Conference in 1939 was the creation of a jurisdictional episcopacy. This provided that bishops were to be chosen by Jurisdictional Conferences, and their supervisory powers were limited to the area of the jurisdictions electing them. The Jurisdictional Conference was also given the

432

power to fix episcopal areas and residences. The bishop, however, could function throughout the church in their ordaining capacity, but not in their administrative capacity.

I

Like the episcopal system the conference system dates from the beginnings of organized Methodism, the first conference being called by John Wesley in England in 1744 while the first conference in America met in Philadelphia in 1773. The conference system as it had developed by 1952 consisted of the following conferences: the General Conference, the Central Conference, the Jurisdictional Conference, the Annual Conference, the District Conference, the Quarterly Conference, and the Annual Church Conference. The District Conference and the Annual Church Conference are optional, but all of the others are essential to the Methodist system. Each conference has its own rights and duties and each is dependent upon the others. The tendency has been for the conference system to grow in importance with a resultant decline in the power of the episcopacy.

Central Conferences are autonomous bodies formed in former missionary areas with certain large powers granted them by the General Conference, including the right to elect their own bishops, constitute conference boards, fix boundaries of Annual Conferences within their bounds, and to manage their own internal affairs—subject to the powers granted them by the General Conference. The Annual Church Conference had developed in the Methodist Church, South, as a promotional agency within each individual church which met once a year. Made up of all members of the church over eighteen years of age it meets at the end of the conference year to review the work of the year, hear reports, and elect officers for the local church. The functions of the General, Annual, District, and Quarterly Conference are the same as they have developed through the years.

II

The Judicial Council created by the Uniting Conference of 1939 is constituted of nine members—five ministers and four laymen—and must meet at least once each year. Its functions are to judge the constitutionality of any act of the several conferences and to hear and pass upon appeals from episcopal decisions. It is also empowered to issue declaratory decisions.

III

In putting the vast program of The Methodist Church into effect the General Conference has created certain agencies, which in 1952 numbered sixteen in all. These agencies function continuously under the direction of permanent staffs.

The Board of Missions superintends Methodist mission work at home and throughout the world and is divided into three divisions: World Missions, National Missions, and the Woman's Division of Christian Service. The first two divisions are financed by funds secured from pastoral charges throughout the church; the Woman's Division receives its support from the Woman's Societies of Christian Service in local churches.

The Board of Education, another of the major boards, is also divided into three divisions: the Division of Educational Institutions acts in an advisory capacity to all educational institutions which have an official relationship with the church—universities, colleges, theological schools, and Wesley Foundations; the Division of the Local Church concerns itself with church schools and youth and fellowship groups; while a third division—the Editorial—works in conjunction with the Board of Publication in the preparation of church-school publications of all kinds. Closely related to the Board of Education is the University Senate, composed of twenty-one persons not members of the Board of Education; all of the members must have had training and experience to enable them to set up standards and evaluate institutions.

Another great agency is the Board of Publication. Made up of an equal number of laymen and ministers it supervises the largest publishing interests of any church in the world. It elects two publishing agents, a book editor, and the editor of the *Christian Advocate*. While church-school

APPENDIX

publications make up a large share of the publications of the board, these publications are under the editorial control of the Board of Education.

Among the twelve other agencies the Board of Pensions was created by the Uniting Conference as an overhead agency to co-ordinate the several ministerial pension organizations that had previously arisen in the three uniting bodies. The Board of Evangelism was created to awaken the church to the need of carrying the gospel aggressively to all people, which it does largely through its literature. *The Upper Room* is the most successful of its projects through its immense circulation in many languages. The Board of Lay Activities, as its name indicates, encourages lay activities in local churches, such as lay personal evangelism, lay speaking, and the promotion of the circulation of church literature. The Council on World Service and Finance is a central agency for receiving, administering, and disbursing the general funds of the entire church. The Commission on Promotion and Cultivation is an agency made up of representatives of the several boards and commissions to co-ordinate all the promotion activities of the church. The increasing numbers of hospitals and homes under Methodist auspices called for an overhead agency— the Board of Hospitals and Homes—to make surveys, disseminate information, and assist in the promotion of new institutions. The Board of Temperance, the Board of World Peace, the Board of Social and Economic Relations, the Commission on Chaplains, the Co-ordinating Council, and the Commission on Public Relations and Methodist Information complete the list of executive agencies, whose names sufficiently indicate their functions.

The above paragraphs are largely based on Nolan B. Harmon, *The Organization of The Methodist Church* (rev. ed.).

BIBLIOGRAPHY

SUGGESTIONS FOR FURTHER READING

Chapter I

Abrams, Ray H. (Ed.), *Organized Religion in the United States*. Philadelphia: Annals of the American Academy of Political and Social Science, 1948.

Belden, A. D., *George Whitefield—The Awakener*. Nashville, Tenn.: Cokesbury Press, 1930.

Brydon, George M., *Virginia's Mother Church; 1727-1814*. Philadelphia: Church Historical Society, 1952. Vol. II.

Gewehr, W. M., *The Great Awakening in Virginia*. Durham, N. C.: Duke University Press, 1930.

Maxson, C. H., *The Great Awakening in the Middle Colonies*. Chicago: The University of Chicago Press, 1920.

McGiffert, A. C., Jr., *Jonathan Edwards*. New York: Harper & Brothers, 1932.

Hall, Thomas C., *The Religious Background of American Culture*. Boston: Little, Brown & Company, 1930.

Schneider, Herbert W., *The Puritan Mind*. New York: Henry Holt and Company, 1930.

Sweet, William Warren, *The Story of Religion in America*. New York: Harper & Brothers, 1950.

———, *Religion in Colonial America*. New York: Charles Scribner's Sons, 1942.

———, *Religion in the Development of American Culture*. New York: Charles Scribner's Sons, 1952.

Tracy, Joseph, *The Great Awakening: A History of the Revival of Religion in the Time of Edwards and Whitefield*. Boston, 1842.

BIBLIOGRAPHY

Chapter II

Curnock, Nehemiah (Ed.), *The Journal of the Rev. John Wesley, A.M., enlarged from original MSS., with notes from unpublished diaries, annotations, maps, and illustrations.* 8 vols. London: Robert Cully, 1909-1916.

Fitchett, W. H., *Wesley and His Century.* London: John Murray, 1925.

Lunn, Arnold, *John Wesley.* New York: The Dial Press, 1929.

Piette, Maximen, *La Réaction de John Wesley dans l'Evolution du Protestantisme. Etude d'Histoire Religieuse.* Universitas Catholica Lovaniensis. Dissertationes ad gradum magistri in Facultate Theologica consequendum conscriptæ. Series II. Tomus 16. 2d ed. revue et augmentée. Bruxelles, 1927.

Simon, J. S., *John Wesley and the Religious Societies.* London: The Epworth Press, 1921.

———, *John Wesley and the Methodist Societies.* London: The Epworth Press, 1923.

———, *John Wesley and the Advance of Methodism.* London: The Epworth Press, 1925.

———, *John Wesley the Master Builder.* London: The Epworth Press, 1927.

Telford, John (Ed.), *The Letters of the Rev. John Wesley, A.M.* 8 vols. London: The Epworth Press, 1931.

Tyerman, Luke, *John Wesley.* 3 vols. London: Hodder and Stoughton, 1878. 4th ed.

Vulliamy, C. E., *John Wesley.* New York: Charles Scribner's Sons, 1932.

Chapter III

Asbury, Francis, *Journal.* 3 vols. New York: Lane & Scott, 1852. Vol. I.

Barclay, Wade Crawford, *History of Methodist Missions.* Part One, *Early American Methodism, 1769-1844.* Vol. I, *Missionary Motivation and Expansion;* Vol. II *To Reform the Nation.* New York: The Board of Missions and Church Extension of The Methodist Church, 1949, 1950.

METHODISM IN AMERICAN HISTORY

Buckley, James M., *A History of Methodists in the United States.* (American Church History Series, Vol. V.) New York: The Christian Literature Co., 1896. Chapters I-V.

Bangs, Nathan, *A History of the Methodist Episcopal Church.* 4 vols. New York: J. Collord, Printer, 1839. Vol. I, Book I.

Faulkner, John Alfred, *The Methodists.* (The Story of the Churches.) New York: Baker & Taylor Co., 1903. Chapter III.

Lee, Jesse, *A Short History of the Methodists in the United States of America; beginning in 1766, and continued till 1809. To which is prefixed, A Brief Account of Their Rise in New England,* etc. Baltimore: Magill & Clime, Book-Sellers, 1810. Chapter II.

Lednum, John, *A History of the Rise of Methodism in America. Containing Sketches of Methodist Itinerant Preachers, from 1736 to 1785,* etc. Philadelphia: Published by the Author, 1859. Chapters I to XV.

Methodist Review, New York. Articles: July, 1856, Hamilton, W., "Early Methodism in Maryland, Especially in Baltimore"; Jan.-Feb., 1928, Cell, George E., "The First Foundation of American Methodism"; May-June, 1928, Porter, F. G., "Strawbridge and American Methodism"; 1929, Jan.-Feb., Streeter, L. R., "Methodism in Maryland"; May-June, Watson, E. L., "Maryland and American Methodism."

Wakeley, J. B., *Lost Chapters Recovered from the Early History of American Methodism.* New York: Published by the Author, 1858.

Watters, D. A., *First American Itinerant of Methodism, William Watters.* Cincinnati: Curts and Jennings, 1898.

Chapter IV

Asbury, Francis, *Journal,* Vol. I.

Bangs, Nathan, *History of the Methodist Episcopal Church.* Vol. I, Book II, Chapter I.

Gewehr, W. M., *The Great Awakening in Virginia, 1740-1790.* Especially Chapter VI.

BIBLIOGRAPHY

Jackson, Thomas (Ed.), *The Lives of Early Methodist Preachers, chiefly written by themselves.* Vols. V and VI contain the lives of Thomas Rankin and George Shadford.

Jarratt, Devereux, *Life of Devereux Jarratt.* Baltimore, 1806. An Autobiography written in a series of letters to a friend.

Lednum, John, *A History of the Rise of Methodism in America,* etc. Chapters XV to XXVII.

Lee, Jesse, *A Short History of the Methodists in the United States.* Chapter III.

Lee, Leroy M., *The Life and Times of the Rev. Jesse Lee.* Louisville, Kentucky, 1848.

Moore, M. H., *Pioneers of Methodism in North Carolina and Virginia.*

Stevens, Abel, *History of the Methodist Episcopal Church in the United States of America.* 4 Vols. New York: Carlton & Porter, 1864-1867. Vol. I, Book I, Chapters IV-X.

Sweet, William Warren, *Men of Zeal; The Romance of American Methodist Beginnings.* New York and Cincinnati: The Abingdon Press, 1935.

Chapter V

Baldwin, Alice M., *The New England Clergy and the American Revolution.* Durham, N. C.: Duke University Press, 1929.

Buckley, James M., *A History of the Methodists in the United States.* Chapter VII, "In the Throes of Revolution."

Humphrey, E. F., *Nationalism and Religion in America.* Boston: Chipman, 1924. Especially Part I, Chapter V.

Hurst, John Fletcher, *The History of Methodism.* 7 Vols. New York: Eaton & Mains, 1893. Vols. IV, V, and VI, devoted to American Methodism. See Vol. IV, Chapters XV-XXIV.

Jameson, J. F., *The American Revolution Considered as a Social Movement.* Princeton: Princeton University Press, 1926. Especially Chapter IV, "Thought and Feeling."

Lednum, John, *A History of the Rise of Methodism in America,* etc.   Chapters XXV-LV.

M'Lean, John, *Sketch of Rev. Philip Gatch.*   Cincinnati: Swormstedt & Poe, 1854.

Stevens, Abel, *History of the Methodist Episcopal Church in the United States of America.*   Vol. I, Book II, From the Beginning of the Revolutionary War, to the Episcopal Organization of Methodism, 1775-1784.

Sweet, William Warren, *John Wesley: Tory. Methodist Quarterly Review,* Nashville, Tenn., 1922, pp. 255-268.

Trevelyan, G. O., *The American Revolution.*   4 Vols.   New York and London: Longmans, Green & Co., 1905.   Vols. II and III.

Wakeley, J. B., *Lost Chapters Recovered from the Early History of American Methodism.*   Chapters XXX-XXXII.

Chapter VI

Bangs, Nathan, *A History of the Methodist Episcopal Church.*   Vol. I, Book II, Chapter III, *"An Account of the Organization of the Methodist Episcopal Church with some arguments in its defense."*

Buckley, James M., *A History of the Methodists in the United States.*   Chapters IX and X.

Faulkner, John Alfred, *Burning Questions in Historic Christianity.*   Chapter IX, "Did Wesley Intend to Found the Methodist Episcopal Church?"   New York: The Abingdon Press, 1930.

Humphrey, E. F., *Nationalism and Religion in America, 1774-1789.*   Chapter VII.

Lee, Jesse, *A Short History of the Methodists in the United States of America.*   Chapters V and VI.

Stevens, Abel, *History of the Methodist Episcopal Church in the United States of America.*   Vol. II, Book III.

Tigert, John J., *Constitutional History of American Episcopal Methodism.*   Nashville, Tenn.: Publishing House of the M. E. Church, South, 1904.   Book III, Chapters VII, X, and XI.

BIBLIOGRAPHY

Chapter VII

Asbury, Francis, *Journal,* Vols. II and III.

Bangs, Nathan, *The Life of Freeborn Garrettson: compiled from his printed and manuscript Journals and other authentic documents.* 3rd ed. New York: Emory & Waugh, 1832.

Buckley, James M., *A History of the Methodists in the United States.* Chapters X-XIII.

Hurst, John Fletcher, *The History of Methodism.* Vol. V. (American Methodism, Vol. II.) Chapters LXIV and LXX.

Lee, Leroy M., *The Life and Times of the Rev. Jesse Lee.* Louisville, Ky.: John Early, 1848.

Lee, Jesse, *A Short History of the Methodists in the United States of America,* etc. Chapters VII and VIII.

Sanderson, J. E., *The First Century of Methodism in Canada.* Toronto: William Briggs, 1908.

Stephenson, Mrs. Frederick G., *One Hundred Years of Canadian Methodist Missions, 1824-1924.* Toronto: Ryerson Press, 1925.

Stevens, Abel, *Memorials of the Early Progress of Methodism in the eastern states: comprising biographical notices of its preachers, sketches of its primitive churches, and reminiscences of its early struggles and successes.* Boston: C. H. Peirce and Co., 1852.

——, *History of the Methodist Episcopal Church in the United States of America.* Vol. III, Chapters VII, XVI and XVII.

Ware, Thomas, *Sketches of the Life and Travels of Rev. Thomas Ware,* etc., New York: Mason and Lane, 1839.

Chapter VIII

Barker, J. M., *History of Ohio Methodism.* Cincinnati: Curts and Jennings, 1898.

Brunson, Alfred, *A Western Pioneer: or Incidents of the Life and Times of Rev. Alfred Brunson.* 2 Vols. Cincinnati and New York: The Methodist Book Concern, 1872.

Cartwright, Peter, *Autobiography of Peter Cartwright the*

Backwoods Preacher. Edited by W. P. Strickland. Cincinnati and New York: The Methodist Book Concern, 1856.

Cleveland, Catherine C., *The Great Revival in the West, 1795-1805.* Chicago: The University of Chicago Press, 1916.

Finley, J. B., *Sketches of Western Methodism. Biographical, Historical and Miscellaneous; Illustrative of Pioneer Life.* Edited by W. P. Strickland. New York: The Methodist Book Concern, 1854.

————, *Autobiography of James B. Finley, of Pioneer Life in the West.* Edited by W. P. Strickland. New York: The Methodist Book Concern, 1857.

Gewehr, W. M., *Some Factors in the Expansion of Frontier Methodism. Journal of Religion,* Vol. VIII, No. 1, January, 1928, pp. 98-120.

Johnson, Charles A., *The Camp-Meeting; Methodist Harvest Time.* Doctor's dissertation, Northwestern University, 1949.

Jones, John G., *A Complete History of Methodism as connected with the Mississippi Conference of the Methodist Episcopal Church, South.* 2 Vols. Nashville, Tenn.: Publishing House of the M. E. Church, South, 1908. Vol. I. 1799-1817.

McFerrin, J. B., *History of Methodism in Tennessee.* 3 Vols. Nashville, Tenn.: Publishing House of the M. E. Church, South, 1888.

Mode, P. G., *The Frontier Spirit in American Christianity.* New York: The Macmillan Company, 1923.

Redford, A. H., *The History of Methodism in Kentucky.* 3 Vols. Nashville: Southern Methodist Publishing House, 1868.

Riegel, Robert E., *America Moves West.* New York: Henry Holt and Company, 1930.

Sweet, William Warren, *The Rise of Methodism in the West.* New York: The Methodist Book Concern, 1920.

————, *Circuit-Rider Days Along the Ohio.* New York: The Methodist Book Concern, 1923.

————, *Circuit-Rider Days in Indiana.* Indianapolis: W. K. Stewart & Co., 1916.

BIBLIOGRAPHY

———, *Religion on the American Frontier: The Methodists.* Chicago: University of Chicago Press, 1946. Vol. IV.

Tipple, Ezra Squier, *Francis Asbury, the Prophet of the Long Road.* New York: The Methodist Book Concern, 1916.

———, *The Heart of Asbury's Journal.* New York: The Methodist Book Concern, 1904.

Young, Jacob, *Autobiography of a Pioneer.* Cincinnati: The Methodist Book Concern, 1857.

Chapter IX

In addition to the references under Chapter VIII the following are added:

Drinkhouse, E. J., *History of Methodist Reform: Synoptical of General Methodism 1773 to 1898.* 2 Vols. Baltimore and Pittsburgh: Board of Publication, Methodist Protestant Church, 1899.

Elliott, Charles, *The Life of Bishop Robert R. Roberts.* Cincinnati: 1844.

Emory, Robert, *The Life of the Rev. John Emory.* New York: The Methodist Book Concern, 1841.

Nottingham, Elizabeth K., *Methodism and the Frontier: Indiana Proving Ground.* New York: Columbia University Press, 1941.

Paine, Robert, *Life and Times of William McKendree.* Nashville, Tenn.: Lamar & Barton, 1922.

Wright, John F., *Sketches of the Life and Labors of James Quinn.* Cincinnati: The Methodist Book Concern, 1851.

Chapter X

Atwood, A., *The Conquerors: Historical Sketches of the American Settlement of the Oregon Country.* Cincinnati: Jennings & Graham, 1907.

Bangs, Nathan, *An Authentic History of the Missions Under the Care of the Missionary Society of the Methodist Episcopal Church.* New York: The Methodist Book Concern, 1832.

Bashford, James W., *The Oregon Missions.* New York: The Abingdon Press, 1918.

METHODISM IN AMERICAN HISTORY

Brosnan, C. J., *Jason Lee: Prophet of the New Oregon.* New York: The Macmillan Company, 1932.

Cannon, James, III, *History of Southern Methodist Missions.* Nashville: Cokesbury Press, 1926.

Canse, John M., *Pilgrim and Pioneer.* New York: The Abingdon Press, 1930.

Drew, Samuel, *The Life of the Rev. Thomas Coke, Including in Detail His Various Travels and Extraordinary Missionary Exertions,* etc. London: Thomas Cordeux, Agent, 1817.

Elsbree, O. W., *The Rise of the Missionary Spirit in America.* Williamsport, Pa.: 1928.

Luccock, Halford E., and Hutchinson, Paul, *The Story of Methodism.* New York: The Methodist Book Concern, 1923. Especially Chapter IV.

Mitchell, Joseph (Printer), *The Missionary Pioneer, or a Brief Memoir of the Life, Labors and Death of John Stewart (Man of Colour). Founder under God of the Mission among the Wyandotts at Upper Sandusky, Ohio.* New York: 1827.

Reid, J. M., *Missions and Missionary Society of the Methodist Episcopal Church.* Revised and Extended by J. T. Gracey. 3 Vols. New York and Cincinnati: The Methodist Book Concern, 1895.

Sweet, William Warren, *Circuit-Rider Days Along the Ohio.* New York: The Methodist Book Concern, 1923. Especially Chapter IV, "The Wyandot Mission."

Chapter XI

Bangs, Nathan, *A History of the Methodist Episcopal Church.* Vol. I, Book III, Chapter I, contains a full account of the founding of Cokesbury College.

Cummings, A. W., *The Early Schools of Methodism.* New York: Phillips & Hunt, 1886.

Du Bose, H. M., *A History of Methodism.* Nashville: Smith & Lamar, Agents, 1916. Especially Chapter XXI, "Schools of Southern Methodism."

Garber, Paul N., *The Romance of American Methodism.* Greensboro, N. C.: The Piedmont Press, 1931. Especially Chapters VIII, "Educational Contributions";

BIBLIOGRAPHY

and IX, "Training the Preachers."

Hurst, John Fletcher, *The History of Methodism*. Vol. IV, Chapter XXXIX, "The First Methodist College"; Vol. VI, Chapter CVI, "The Higher Education."

Mode, Peter G., *The Frontier Spirit in American Christianity*. Especially Chapter IV, "The Small College."

Sweet, William Warren, *Indiana Asbury-DePauw University, 1837-1937*. New York and Chicago: The Abingdon Press, 1937.

Chapter XII

Alexander, Gross, *A History of the Methodist Church, South*. (Part of Vol. XI. American Church History Series.) New York: Christian Literature Co., 1894. Chapter II, "The General Conference of 1844."

Bascom, H. B., *Methodism and Slavery*. Louisville: Hodges, Todd, and Pruett, 1845.

Buckley, James M., *A History of the Methodists in the United States*. Chapter XVII, "Bisection of the Methodist Episcopal Church."

———, *Constitutional and Parliamentary History of the Methodist Episcopal Church*. New York: The Methodist Book Concern, 1909.

Clark, D. W., *Life and Times of Rev. Elijah Hedding*. New York: Carlton & Phillips, 1855.

Dodd, William E., *The Cotton Kingdom: A Chronicle of the Old South*. (The Chronicles of America Series, Vol. XXVII.) New Haven: Yale University Press, 1921.

Elliott, Charles, *History of the Great Secession from the Methodist Episcopal Church in the Year 1845, Eventuating in the Organization of the New Church Entitled the Methodist Episcopal Church, South*. Cincinnati: Swormstedt & Poe, 1855.

Hart, A. B., *Slavery and Abolition, 1831-1841*. (The American Nation: A History, Vol. 16.) New York: Harper & Brothers, 1906.

History of the Organization of the Methodist Episcopal Church, South, With the Journal of Its First General Conference. Nashville: Publishing House of the M. E. Church, South, 1925. (Reprint.)

Matlack, L. C., *Anti-Slavery Struggle and Triumphs in the Methodist Episcopal Church.* New York: Phillips & Hunt, 1881.

McTyeire, H. N., *A History of Methodism,* etc., Nashville: Publishing House of the M. E. Church, South, 1884; 1924. Chapters XLI to XLIV.

Norwood, J. N., *The Schism in the Methodist Episcopal Church, 1884: A Study of Slavery and Ecclesiastical Politics.* Alfred N. Y. Alfred University Press, 1923.

Phillips, U. B., *American Negro Slavery,* etc., New York: D. Appleton & Company, 1927.

Redford, A. H., *History of the Organization of the Methodist Episcopal Church, South.* Nashville: Southern Methodist Publishing House, 1879.

Swaney, C. B., *Episcopal Methodism and Slavery.* Boston: The Gorham Press, 1926.

Chapter XIII

Alexander, Gross, *A History of the Methodist Church, South.* Chapters III to VII.

Buckley, James M., *A History of the Methodists in the United States.* Chapter XIX.

Deems, C. F., *Annals of Southern Methodism,* 1855. Nashville: Stevens & Owen, 1856. Also for 1856.

McTyeire, H. N., *A History of Methodism.* Chapters XLIV and XLV.

Norwood, J. N., *The Schism in the Methodist Episcopal Church,* 1844. Chapters V, VI, and VII.

Sutton, R., *The Methodist Church Property Case.* Richmond and Louisville: John Early, for the Methodist Episcopal Church, South, 1851.

Swaney, C. B., *Episcopal Methodism and Slavery.* Parts III and IV.

Wightman, W. M., *Life of William Capers. . . . including an Autobiography.* Nashville: Barbee & Smith, 1902.

Chapter XIV

Buckley, James M., *A History of Methodists in the United States.* Chapter XX.

BIBLIOGRAPHY

Crooks, George R., *The Life of Bishop Matthew Simpson.*
New York: Harper & Brothers, 1891.

McPherson, Edward, *The Political History of the United
States of America during the Great Rebellion,* etc.
Washington, D. C.: James J. Chapman, 1882. Appendix, "The Church and the Rebellion," pp. 461-554,
is of great value for an understanding of the activities
of the churches during the Civil War.

McTyeire, H. N., *A History of Methodism.* Chapter XLVI.

Smith, G. G., *The Life and Letters of James Osgood Andrew.* Nashville: Publishing House of the M. E.
Church, South, 1883.

Swaney, C. B., *Episcopal Methodism and Slavery,* etc. Part
V, Chapters XXV to XXVII.

Sweet, William Warren, *The Methodist Episcopal Church
and the Civil War.* Cincinnati: The Methodist Book
Concern, 1912.

Chapter XV

Hood, J. W., *History of the African Methodist Episcopal,
Zion, Church.* Charlotte, N. C.: A. M. E. Zion Publication House, n. d.

Janifer, J. T., *History of the African Methodist Episcopal
Church,* Nashville, n. d.

Lanahan, John, *The Era of Frauds in The Methodist Book
Concern at New York.* Baltimore: Methodist Book
Depository, 1896.

Luccock, Halford E., and Hutchinson, Paul, *The Story of
Methodism.* New York: The Methodist Book Concern,
1926. Especially Chapters XX to XXIV.

Nevins, Allan, *The Emergence of Modern America,* 1865-
1878. (A History of American Life, Vol. VIII.) New
York: The Macmillan Company, 1927.

Northwestern University, *A Working Conference on the
Union of American Methodism.* February 15, 16, 17,
1916. New York: The Methodist Book Concern, 1916.

Phillips, C. H., *History of the Colored Methodist Episcopal
Church.* 2 (1) Vols. Jackson, Tennessee: Publishing
House C. M. E. Church, 1925.

Singleton, George, *The Romance of African Methodism; a*

Study of the African Methodist Episcopal Church.
New York: Exposition Press, 1952.

Sweet, William Warren, *Methodist Church Influence in Southern Politics.* (*Mississippi Valley Historical Review.* Vol. I, March, 1915, pp. 546-560.)

————, *Negro Churches in the South: A Phase of Reconstruction.* (*Methodist Review,* Fifth Series, Vol. XXXVII, No. 3, pp. 405-418.)

————, *The Methodist Episcopal Church and Reconstruction.* (*Journal of the Illinois State Historical Society,* Vol. VII, pp. 147-165.)

Chapter XVI

Beard, Charles A. and Mary R., *The Rise of American Civilization.* New York: The Macmillan Company, 1930. Especially Vol. II, Chapters XXV to XXVII.

Du Bose, H. M., *A History of Methodism with special references to the History of the Methodist Episcopal Church, South, down to the year 1916.* Nashville, Tenn.: Publishing House of the M. E. Church, South, 1916.

Faulkner, Harold U., *The Quest for Social Justice, 1898-1914.* (A History of American Life, Vol. XI.) New York: The Macmillan Company, 1931.

Gill, C. O., and Pinchot, Gifford, *The Country Church; The Decline of Its Influence and the Remedy.* New York: The Macmillan Company, 1913.

Hooker, Elizabeth R., *Hinterlands of the Church.* New York: Institute of Social and Religious Research, 1931.

Hutchinson, Paul, *The Story of the Epworth League.* New York: The Methodist Book Concern, 1927.

Luccock, Halford E., Hutchinson, Paul, and Goodloe, Robert W., *The Story of Methodism.* New York and Nashville: Abingdon-Cokesbury Press, 1949. Especially Chapters XXIV and XXV.

Mathews, Shailer, *The Church and the Changing Order.* New York: The Macmillan Company, 1907.

Niebuhr, H. Richard, *The Social Sources of Denominationalism.* New York: Henry Holt and Company, 1929.

BIBLIOGRAPHY

Especially Chapter IV. "The Churches of the Middle Class."

Sanford, E. B., *Origin and History of the Federal Council of the Churches of Christ in America*. Hartford, Conn.: Scranton Co., 1916.

Slosser, Gaius J., *Christian Unity: Its History and Challenge in All Communions, in All Laws*. London: Kegan, Paul, Trench, Trubner and Company, Ltd., 1929.

Sweet, William Warren, *The Story of Religion in America*. New York, Harper, 1950. Chapter XXI, "The American Churches in the Age of Big Business."

Chapter XVII

Brown, William Adams, *The Church in America: A Study of Present Conditions and Future Prospects of American Protestantism*. New York: The Macmillan Company, 1922.

Cherrington, Ernest H., *The Evolution of Prohibition in the United States of America: A Chronological History of the Liquor Problem and the Temperance Reform in the United States*, etc. Westerville, Ohio: The American Issue Press, 1920.

Cole, Stewart G., *History of Fundamentalism*. New York: Richard R. Smith, 1931.

Colvin, D. Leigh, *Prohibition in the United States: A History of the Prohibition Party and the Prohibition Movement*. New York: George H. Doran Company, 1926.

Diffendorfer, R. E., and others, *The World Service of the Methodist Episcopal Church*. New York: The Methodist Book Concern, 1923.

Garber, Paul N., *The Methodist Are One People*. Nashville: Cokesbury Press, 1939.

Gulick, Sidney L., *The Christian Crusade for a Warless World*. New York: Federal Council of the Churches of Christ in America, 1923.

Krout, J. A., *The Origins of Prohibition*. New York: A. A. Knopf, 1925.

Luccock, Halford E., Hutchinson, Paul, and Goodloe, Robert W., *The Story of Methodism*. New York and

Nashville: Abingdon-Cokesbury Press, 1949. Chapters XXV and XXVI.

McConnell, Francis J., *Borden Parker Bowne*. New York: The Abingdon Press, 1929.

Mecklin, J. M., *The Ku Klux Klan*. New York: Harcourt, Brace and Company, 1924.

Moore, John M., *The Long Road to Methodist Union*. New York and Nashville: Abingdon-Cokesbury Press, 1943.

Renton, Margaret, Editor, *War-Time Agencies of the Churches*. New York: Published by the War-Time Commission of the Churches, Federal Council of the Churches of Christ in America, 1919.

Chapter XVIII

Abrams, Ray H. (Ed.), *Organized Religion in the United States*. Philadelphia: Annals of the American Academy of Political and Social Science, 1948. Pages 110-19.

Bates, M. Searle, *Religious Liberty; an Inquiry*. New York: Harper & Brothers, 1945.

Blanshard, Paul, *American Freedom and Catholic Power*. Boston: Beacon Press, 1949.

DeWolf, L. Harold, *The Religious Revolt Against Reason*. New York: Harper & Brothers, 1949.

Fisher, Irving, *Prohibition at Its Worst*. New York: The author, 1927.

Harmon, Nolan B., *The Organization of The Methodist Church: Historic Development and Present Working Structure* (rev. ed.). Nashville: The Methodist Publishing House, 1953.

Latourette, Kenneth S., *The Emergence of a World Christian Community*. New Haven: Yale University Press 1949.

Lee, Umphrey, *The Historic Church and Modern Pacifism*. New York and Nashville: Abingdon-Cokesbury Press, 1943.

Lewis, Edwin, *A Christian Manifesto*. New York: Abingdon Press, 1934.

Keller, Adolph, *Religion and the European Mind*. London: Religious Tract Society, 1934.

BIBLIOGRAPHY

Kincheloe, Samuel C., *Research Memorandum on Religion in the Depression*. New York: Social Science Research Council, 1937.

Poling, Daniel, *A Preacher Looks at War*. New York: The Macmillan Co., 1943.

Proceedings of the Seventh Methodist Ecumenical Conference. Nashville, 1931.

Stokes, Anson Phelps, *Church and State in the United States*. 3 Vols. New York: Harper & Brothers, 1950.

Visser 't Hooft, W. A. (Ed.), *World Council of Churches, 1st Assembly, Amsterdam, August 22nd to September 4th, 1948. Official Report*. New York: Harper & Brothers, 1949.

INDEX

Abingdon, Maryland, 112, 209

Adams, John, quoted, 55, 218

Adams, John Quincy, 214

Addams, Jane, 359

Africa, Missions in, 202-4; visited by William Taylor, 330; Missions of Church, South, in, 331; Methodist Episcopal bishops for, 352

African Methodist Episcopal Church, 313, 327, 378

African Methodist Episcopal Zion Church, 313, 327

Akers, Peter, 219

Alabama Conference, 169; of the Church South, 308

Alaska, 346

Albany, District, 126; city of, 195; New York Convention of 1842, in, 242

Alcohol, historic Methodist attitude toward, 412

Alden, President Timothy, 217, 218

Allegheny College, 216, 217-18

Allen, Richard, founder of African Methodist Episcopal Church, 313

Amelia Circuit (Va.), 119

American Bible Society, 297

American Board of Commissioners for Foreign Missions, 187, 201

American Colonization Society, 202, 234

American Federation of Labor, 355

American Methodism, growth of since World War II, 431

American Peace Society, 369

American Temperance Union, 290

American Tract Society, 297

American Wesleyan Observer, 239

Ames, Edward R., 219; Bishop, 267, 294, 295, 323

Amherst College, 155

Amusements, General Conference rule on (1872), 325; controversy about, 392

Andover Theological Seminary, 202, 225

Andrew, Bishop James O., 183, 245 ff., 251, 252, 254, 268, 275, 292

Andrews, Edward G., Bishop, 325

Anglicans, in the colonies, 9, 18, 19, 20, 23, 26; attitude toward John Wesley, 45, 46; attitude of Wesley's missionaries toward, 62, 69, 73; attitude of Virginia Methodists toward, 101; their liturgy highly regarded by Wesley, 106

Antigua, Methodist circuit in, 114

Anti-Saloon League, 388

Anti-Slavery movement, 231, 232, 234 ff.

Arkansas territory, 193

Asbury, Francis, 52, 59, 187, 188; appointed a missionary to America by Wesley, 64; organizes circuit around New York, 67; organizes Maryland Circuit, 68; appointed to Baltimore, 68, 77; attitude toward Wesley in politics, 88; forced into hiding, 91; becomes head of American Methodists, 94 ff.; in Virginia and North Carolina, 96, 97, 99; attitude toward Established Church, 100, 101, 102; appointed joint superintendent for America by Wesley, 106; meets Coke, 108; at Christmas Conference of 1784, 110 ff.; attitude toward a Methodist college, 112;

INDEX

Capers, William, 183, 193, 222; General Conference delegate, 244, 248; elected bishop by Church South, 254, 275; superintendent of Negro missions, 274

Carey, William, early English Baptist missionary, 187

Carnegie, Andrew, 340, 369

Carolinas, 19, 22

Carroll, Charles, and his interest in Madison College, 214

Cartwright, Peter, 157 ff., 167, 170, 171, 173, 244, 250; opposes theological education, 223

Catholic Church, 26; missions in Oregon, 201, 202

Cazenovia, New York, anti-slavery convention at, 239

Cazenovia Seminary, established, 215

Cell, George Croft, quoted, 409

Centenary, The, 380 ff.

Centenary celebration (1866), 317, 319

Centenary Education fund, 317

Central Christian Advocate, established, 185, 260; opposes withdrawal of Methodist Episcopal Church from slave states, 263; Charles Elliott editor of, 268; flays Church South during Civil War, 283; rabid support given North by, 291

Central College, Missouri, established, 222

Central New York Conference, Professor Mitchell tried by, 390

Central Ohio Conference, 285

Chaplains, Civil War, 286; World War I, 376 ff.; World War II, 417-18

Charterhouse School (England), 29

Chautauqua Assembly, 228

Cherokee Indians, missions among, 193, 195

Chicago, 223

Children's Day, inaugurated, 319

Chile, Methodist missions in, 330

China, missions begun in, 205, 206; ports opened, 205, 206

Choate, Rufus, jurist, 266

Choctaw Indian mission, 196

Christian Advocate and Journal, established, 184, 196, 250; quoted, 242, 243, 261, 264, 268, 302, 304, 306, 322, 372, 373

Christian Advocate (Charleston, S. C.), 254

Christian Advocate, (Louisville, Kentucky), 254

Christian Endeavor Society, established, 349

Christian Union Church, 310

Christliche Apologete, Der, 268, 270

Christmas Conference (1784), 100-118, 233

Church building, 338, 384

Church of England. *See* Anglicans

Church Extension Society, 301, 345

Church of the Nazarene, founding of, 344

Cincinnati, circuit, 160; Conference, 287

Cincinnati, Ohio, General Conference (1836) meets in, 237; convention of non-Episcopal Methodists (1866) meets in, 326

Circuits, Methodist, 114, 119, 124, 144, 145, 160

Civil War, 222, 276 ff.; effect on public morals, and religion, 298

Claflin, Lee, founder of Boston University, 318

Claflin College, 348

Clark, D. W., bishop, 302

Clark, Francis E., founder of the Christian Endeavor Society, 349

Clark, Laban, assists in establishing missionary society, 192

Clark's Grant (Indiana), 163

455

INDEX

Cuba, missions of Church South in, 331
Cumberland District, 162
Curry, Daniel, editor, 307
Cushing, Caleb, 199
Cutler, Timothy, 19

Dakotas, 345
Dartmouth, Lord, 45, 82, 87-88
Dartmouth College, religious revival at, 155, 207
David, Christian, Moravian leader, 24
Davies, Samuel, leader of Presbyterian revival in Virginia, 18
Davis, Jefferson, 294
Day, James R., Chancellor Syracuse University, 373
"Declaration and Basis of Fraternity," 328
Deism, 123, 135
Delaware, colony, 15, 23; early Methodism in, 57; Asbury in, 89; Coke in, 107; Methodist growth in, 119
Delaware Indians, 195
Delaware, Ohio, 222; National Study Conference of Federal Council held in, 420-21
Dempster, James, 65
Dempster, John, father of Methodist theological education, 204, 215, 224-27
Department of Agriculture, U. S., interested in supporting the country church, 364
Department of Emergency and Reconstruction, Methodist Episcopal Church, 377
DePauw University; see also *Indiana Asbury University*, 208, 216, 385
Depression, the, 397, 402-6; effect upon American Methodism, 403; beneficial influences of, 405-6
Dickins, John, 107, 110, 120, 132
Dickinson College, founded, 216, 217

Dickinson, Jonathan, 17
Discipline, Methodist, 110 ff., 147; of Church South, 253
Dissenting churches in Middle and Southern Colonies, 10
District superintendent, 339
Doggett, D. S., bishop, Methodist Episcopal Church, South, 309
Dorsey, Dennis B., 181
Dow, Neal, temperance advocate, 387
Drew, Daniel, 317, 320
Drew Theological Seminary, 213, 318
Dromgoole, Edward, 77, 91
Duke, James B., 385
Duke University, 222, 385
Dunkers, 15, 24; attitude toward slavery of, 230
Durbin, John P., 184; college president, 212, 217
Dutch Reformed Church, 23, 26, 225

Early, John, 275, 292
East Baltimore Conference, 287
Eastern Asia, Methodist Episcopal Central Conference in, 352
Eastern Nazarene College, 345
Ebenezer Academy, 211
Ecumenical Movement, Methodism and the, 426-31
Education, 207-8, 317, 333 ff.
Edwards, Jonathan, 12, 13, 14, 16, 76
Eighteenth Amendment, repeal of, 409-12
Eliot, John, early Indian missionary, 186
Elizabethtown, 17
Elliott, Charles, 283
Embury, Philip, 51, 53 ff.
Emory Academy, 215
Emory College, Oxford, Georgia, 318, 341
Emory and Henry College, founded, 216
Emory, John, 182, 183-84, 218
Emory, Robert, 217

INDEX

General Conference, Methodist Episcopal Church, South, 1846 session of, 253; 1850 session of, 274; session of 1866, 312; 1870 session of, 327; 1894 session of, 343; 1930 session of, 396

"General War-Time Commission of the Churches," 378

Genesee Conference, 131, 168, 193, 341

George III, 87

George, Enoch, Bishop, 174, 191, 192

Georgia, 13, 31, 32, 33; Methodist growth in, 119, 183, 218

Georgia Conference, 169, 215, 216, 218; declaration on slavery, 238

German Reformed Church, 15, 17, 25, 26, 225

Germans, Methodist work among, 270, 271

Germany, missionary societies in, 187

Gibson, Tobias, 145, 154, 164

Gladden, Washington, 357

Gloucester (England), Whitefield at, 14; bishop of, 13

Gompers, Samuel, quoted, 355, 356

Good Templars, Temperance organization, 387

Goodwin, T. A., 221-22

Gough, John B., temperance advocate, 387

Gough, Henry Dorsey, of Perry Hall, Maryland, 109, 111

Graves, R. J., Southern Baptist editor, attacks Methodists, 300

Great Iron Wheel, The, 300

Hague Conference, for international peace, 369

Half-Way Covenant, 11

Hallowell, Maine, *Wesleyan Journal*, published in, 239

Hamline, Leonidas L., bishop, 267

Hancock, John, 84

Hanover County, Virginia, 18

Harding, Francis A., 245

Harding, Warren G., President, quoted, 383

Harper, Miles, 168

Harris, William L., bishop, 325

Hartley, Joseph, early Virginia preacher, 90

Hartzell, J. C., 308; missionary bishop, 352

Harvard College, religious liberalism at, 11, 12; Whitefield visits, 14, 207

Haskins, Thomas, 113, 138

Haven, Gilbert, Civil War chaplain, 287; Bishop, 325

Haw, James, early Kentucky preacher, 148

Hawaii, 346

Haygood, A. G., Dr., quoted, 348

Heck, Barbara, 54 ff.

Hedding, Elijah, Bishop, 179, 224, 241, 247

Hedström, Jonas J., Swedish Methodist missionary, 271

Hedström, Olof Gustaf, 271

Henderson, Charles R., 357

Hendrix, E. R., bishop Methodist Episcopal Church, South, 367

Henry, Patrick, 232

Herrnhut, Saxony, Moravian center, 25, 38

Hicks, Thomas H., Civil War Governor of Maryland, 279

Hillsboro, Ohio, Woman's crusade organized at, 387

Hockhocking Circuit, 160

Holiness "question," 341 ff.

Holmes, John Haynes, quoted on repeal of Eighteenth Amendment, 411

Holston, East Tennessee, circuit, 153; Conference, 169, 308; district, 162

Holy Club. See Oxford

Home Missions. See Board of Home Missions

Homestead, Pennsylvania, steel strike in, 356

459

INDEX

Kansas Territory, Slavery controversy in, 261
Kaskaskia, Illinois, 164
Kavanaugh, H. H., bishop of Church South, 275
Kentucky, Methodism in, 114, 119, 145, 148, 153 ff., 165, 211, 212; conflict of Methodist churches, North and South, in, 259, 260; Methodism during Civil War in, 280 ff.
Kentucky Conference, 169, 213
Kentucky District, 161, 162
Kidder, Daniel P., 204
King, John, 58, 59, 61, 63, 69
King's College (Columbia University), 19
Kingsley, Calvin, editor and bishop, 291, 302
Kingston Circuit (Canada), 130
Kingswood, Whitefield at, 39; Wesley's School at, 60
Kirkham, Betty, Wesley's friend, 29
Kirkham, Robert, member of Holy Club, Oxford, 29, 30
Knights of Labor, 355
Kobler, John, 148, 154
Korea, Missions of Methodist Episcopal Church, South, in, 331; independent Methodist Church established in, 353
Ku Klux Klan, 384

Ladies Repository, The, established, 185, 268; D. W. Clark, editor of, 302
Lake Mohonk Conference, 369
Lakin, Benjamin, early Western circuit-rider, 144, 168
Lamar School of Law, established, 341
Lanahan, John, assistant agent Methodist Book Concern, 321 ff.
Larrabee, W. C., first instructor Wesleyan University, 216; at Indiana Asbury University, 221
Latin America. See South America

Law, William, 29
Lawrence County, Indiana, home of Bishop Robert R. Roberts, 175
Lay preaching, development of, 42, 130
Lay representation, 299, 309, 316, 324, 338
Laymen's Missionary Movement, organized, 365 ff.
Lee, Jason, and the Oregon Mission, 196-201
Lee, Jesse, 58; quoted, 76, 97, 109, 112; appointed to Stamford Circuit, 123; activity in New England, 124 ff., 139; death of, 176
Lee, Umphrey, quoted, 413-14
Leeds (England), Conference in, 104
Lewis, Edwin, quoted, 409
Liberator, The, anti-slavery paper, 236
Liberia, 202, 203
Liberia Mission Conference, 169
Light Street Church, Baltimore, 210
Lincoln, Abraham, 147, 278, 291, 299, 302
Liturgy, Methodist, 106, 111
Local preachers, 147
"Log College," 16, 18
London, Methodist congregation formed in, 13; Whitefield at, 14
London Times, 185
Los Angeles, California, Holiness movement in, 344
Losee, William, 130
Louisiana, State of, 169
Louisiana Conference of Methodist Episcopal Church formed, 308
Louisiana Purchase, 164
Louis XIV, 53
Louisville, Kentucky, meeting of Southern Methodists in, 251 ff., 254, 296; training school of

461

INDEX

Methodism—*cont'd*
land, 126; its autocratic organization, 149; and missions, 187, 188; contact with slavery, 229; early expansion of, 229; schism over slavery, 242; in border states during Civil War, 278; movement after Civil War to unite, 305; and the Social Gospel, 359 ff.; attitude toward peace movement, 370 ff.; part in Temperance movement, 387 ff.

Methodist, The, independent Methodist paper (New York), 290, 299

Methodist Anti-Slavery Society, 237

Methodist Book Concern, 150, 177, 212, 250, 254, 255, 257, 263 ff., 320 ff., 379

"Methodist Church Property Case," 265

Methodist Episcopal Church, formed at Christmas Conference, 1784, 109-14; name suggested by John Dickins, 110; expansion, 1785-86, 114; in New England, 122 ff.; in the West, 165; its spread by 1844, 169; Jesse Lee first historian of, 176; membership in, 176, 177, 182, 254, 260, 262, 270, 272, 276, 280, 281, 285, 290, 296; policy during Civil War, 304; Southern membership of, 308, 309; connection with Southern reconstruction, 315; conditions in 1880, 333 ff.; missionary activity of, 352 ff.; attitude toward social reform, 361 ff.; one of original members of Federal Council of Churches, 368; supports President Wilson during Great War, 376; the "Centenary," 380 ff.

Methodist Episcopal Church, South, formed at Louisville, Kentucky, 1845, 252, 253; at-

Methodist Episcopal Church—*cont'd*
titude of Pittsburgh General Conference of Methodist Episcopal Church toward (1848), 257; sends first missionaries to China, 272; in Kentucky during Civil War, 281; effect of Civil War on, 289; attitude toward Southern policy of the Methodist Episcopal Church, 340 ff.; attitude toward reunion with Northern Church, 307; General Conference (1866) of, 309, 310; movement for union with Methodist Protestant Conferences, 325; missionary activity of, 331, 352 ff.; religious revival in, 342; one of original members of Federal Council of Churches, 368; World War activities of, 377; co-operation with other Methodist bodies, 394

Methodist Federation for Social Service, formed, 359

Methodist League for Faith and Life, 393

Methodist Magazine, 180, 210

Methodist Missionary Society, established, 191-93

Methodist Protestant Church, 144, 183, 200, 325 ff., 334, 378, 394

Methodist Quarterly Review, 268

Methodist Review, 358

Methodist unification, completed, 398-99

Methodist Young People's Union, 349

Mexico, 204; Methodist missions in, 329; Church South missions in, 331; independent Methodist Church established in, 353

Miami District (Ohio), 160, 165

Michigan, Methodist abolitionists in, 241

Middletown, Connecticut, 216

Miley, Professor John, 213

Missionary Enterprise among Methodists, 186-206

INDEX

INDEX

Prohibition. *See* Temperance

Prohibition Party, 388

Protestant Episcopal Church, 117; *see also* Anglicans

Protestant-Roman Catholic tensions, growing, 421-22; causes for, 423-26

Providence, Rhode Island, 20; center for slave trade, 229

Providence Conference, 265

Pueblo, Mexico, Methodist mission in established, 330

Puritans, 10, 12

Quakers, in the colonies, 9, 15, 17, 22, 23, 26; attitude toward slavery, 230

Quarterly Conference, first one held in America, 68

Quarterly Review, Methodist Church South organ, 254

Quebec, 130

Railroads, 345

Rall, Harris Franklin, 359, 409

Randolph-Macon College, 216, 218

Rankin, Thomas, 52, 65, 68, 69, 77, 88, 91, 93

Rauschenbusch, Walter, 357; quoted, 359, 360

Reconstruction, 304 ff.

Rector, Edward, 385

Rector Scholarship Foundation, 385

Red River, great revival on, 156; circuit, 168

"Reformers," 178, 179, 181, 183

Religious bodies, co-operate in serving the armed forces, 418-19

Religious education, 405

Republican Methodists, 134

Revival, in Virginia, 74 ff.; political significance of, 79; in 1787, 119; in Kentucky and the West, 1797-1805, 155

Revolution, American, 78, 100, 122, 229

Revolutionary Philosophy, as an anti-slavery influence, 231

Rhode Island, 15, 22; Methodists in, 126

Rich, Isaac, founder of Boston University, 318

Richmond Christian Advocate, 251, 254, 292

Rio de Janeiro, Brazil, 204

Roberts, Benjamin T., 34

Roberts, Robert R., Bishop, 146. 174 ff., 192

Rock River Conference, 285

Rodda, Martin, 65, 77, 89, 91

Roosevelt, Theodore, 363

Rousseau, Jean J., 135

Ruff, Daniel, 77

Rules of the United Societies, 44

Rush, Dr. Benjamin, 217

Rust, Richard S., first secretary of Freedmen's Aid Society, 311

Ruter, Martin, 178; first president of Augusta College, 212, 215, 218

Saint George's Church, Philadelphia, 62

Saint Louis, Missouri, 193, 197; division of Methodist congregations in, 260; General Conference (1850) of Church South meets in, 274

Salaries, preachers', 135, 136, 139, 297, 338

Sale, John, early Ohio circuit-rider, 163, 173

Salem, Oregon, 200; seat of Willamette University, 270

Sandy Creek Church (Baptist), North Carolina, 21

San José, seat of University of the Pacific, 270

Santo Domingo, 346

Saybrook Platform, 11

Scandinavians, Methodist work among, 271

Schlatter, Michael, father of German Reformed Church in America, 25

467

METHODISM IN AMERICAN HISTORY

Scioto Circuit, 160
Scotch-Irish, 15
Scotland, Methodism in, 44; missionary society in, 187; Holiness movement in, 344
Scott, Levi, Bishop, 267
Scott, Orange, Methodist antislavery agitator, 237; publisher *American Wesleyan Observer*, 239; opposes action of General Conference of 1840, 241, 242
Seabury, Bishop Samuel, first Protestant Episcopal bishop in America, 118
Seney, George I., 318
"Separates," 20, 21
Separatist Puritans, at Plymouth, 10
Sepoy Rebellion, 329
Shadford, George, 65, 68, 69, 74, 77, 91, 93
Sharpe, Granville, English humanitarian, 231
Shawnee Indian Mission (Kansas), 196
Shinn, Asa, 182
Shurtleff College, 219
Silver Creek Circuit (Indiana), 163
Simpson, Matthew, first president Indiana Asbury University, 221; editor, 268; bishop, 294, 295, 302, 303; delegate to World Evangelical Alliance (1857), 367
Slaveholders, Convention of (1842), 243
Slavery, 111, 120, 133, 136; contact with Methodism, 229; attitude of colonial churches toward, 230; churches follow public opinion in attitude toward, 232; rules passed by Christmas Conference (1784) regarding, 233; becomes issue of chief importance in churches, 236 ff.; General Conference of 1840 considers, 239; Methodist churches North and South until

Slavery—*cont'd*
1860 have same rule on, 253; Northern opinion about effect of Plan of Separation on, 256; Methodist Episcopal Church after 1844 still divided on, 262; New Rule on adopted by Methodist Episcopal Church in 1860, 263, 276 ff.
Sleeper, Jacob, one of founders of Boston University, 318
Smith, Henry, 144
Smith, William A., General Conference delegate (1844), 244
Snethen, Nicholas, 180
Social Creed of the Churches, 360
Social Religion, 356 ff.
Social Unrest, in the United States, 355 ff.
Society for the Propagation of the Gospel in Foreign Parts, 18, 19, 230
Sociology, 358
Sons of Temperance, 387
Soule, Bishop Joshua, 141, 175, 177, 179, 239, 244, 251, 252, 254, 275
South America, Methodist missions in, 204, 205, 330; Methodist Conference set up in, 352
South Carolina, Methodist circuits in, 114; growth of Methodism in, 119, 187, 222
South Carolina Conference, 129, 193
Southern Asia, Central General Conference set up in, 352
Southern Baptist Sunday School Board, 290
Southern Christian Advocate, 292
Southern Convention (Methodist) at Louisville, 252
Southern Illinois Conference, 287
Southern Methodist University, 341
Sperry, Willard L., on war, 417
Spragg, Samuel, 77, 93
Stamford Circuit, Connecticut, 123

468

INDEX

Stearns, Shubal, Baptist preacher in North Carolina, 21

Stevens, Abel, 55; quoted, 63, 268

Stewart, John, begins first Methodist mission among Wyandots, 190, 191

Stockton, William S., 179

Stone, Barton W., 134, 156

Strawbridge, Robert, 51 ff., 59, 61, 69

Strikes, 356

Strong, Josiah, 357

Stuart, George R., on rum, 412

Student Volunteer Movement, 365

Sunday schools, 227-28; publications, 268, 334; peace propaganda in, 370

Sunderland, LeRoy, Methodist anti-slavery leader, 237, 239, 241, 242

Supernumerary preacher, 135

Sussex Circuit (Virginia), 119

Syracuse University, chartered, 318; School of Citizenship at, 385

Tarkington, Joseph, early Indiana circuit rider, 172

Tasmania, visited by William Taylor, 330

Taylor, Jeremy, 29, 30

Taylor, William, missionary, 269, 330, 352

Temperance, 171-72, 241, 242, 325, 387 ff.; see also Intoxicating liquors

Tennent, Gilbert, 16, 17

Tennent, William, 16, 17

Tennessee, Methodism in, 153 ff., 165; conflict of Northern and Southern Methodist Churches in, 304; Holiness movement in, 344

Tennessee Baptist, periodical edited by R. J. Graves, 300

Tennessee Conference, 168, 193; organized following the Civil War, 308

Texas, achieves independence from Mexico, 269; Holiness movement in, 344

Texas Conference, organized following Civil War, 308

Theological Education, begun in Methodist Episcopal Church, 223-27

Theological trends, recent, 406-9

Thirty-nine Articles of Religion, 111

Thoburn, J. M., Missionary Bishop, 352

Thomson, Edward, first president of Ohio Wesleyan University, editor and bishop, 223, 268, 302

Tippy, Worth M., 359

"Tools and Men," 357

Toplady, Augustus, attacks Wesley, 82, 85

Training School for Chaplains in World War, 376

Transylvania University, 213

Trenton, New Jersey, *Wesleyan Repository* published in, 179, 180

Trinity College; see also Duke University, 222, 385

Troy Conference, 169; attitude toward Book Concern case, 265

True Wesleyan, The, 242

Tweed Ring, 319

Unification of American Methodism, factors making possible, 399-402

Uniform Lesson System for Sunday schools, 228

Union of Methodist bodies, movements for, 307, 325 ff., 393 ff.

Union Pacific Railroad, 345

Uniontown, Pennsylvania, seat of Madison College, 211, 213

Unitarians, 225

United Brethren Church, 110; formed, 270

United States Christian Commission, 290, 293

469

INDEX

Wesley, John—*cont'd*
47 ff.; licenses Captain Webb to preach, 56; sends Asbury and Wright to America, 63, 64; attitude toward American Revolution, 79 ff.; attitude toward Established Church, 100; American Methodists change attitude toward, 101 ff.; proposes to ordain Methodist preachers, 103 ff.; appoints Coke and Asbury joint superintendents for America, 105 ff.; writes concerning Cokesbury College, 112; attitude toward Methodist Episcopal Church, 115 ff., 116; attacked by Doctor Huntington, 127; death of, 132; attitude toward emotionalism, 159; intoxicating liquors, 170, 210; attitude toward slavery, 231; attitude toward wealth, 336; liberal attitude on doctrine, 389

Wesley and Whitefield School, 211

Wesley, Samuel, 28, 31

Wesley, Susanna, 28

Wesleyan Academy, 214

Wesleyan Connection, formed, 242

Wesleyan Female College, Georgia, 318

Wesleyan Journal, spreads abolition doctrine, 239

Wesleyan Methodists, 131, 241, 326, 342

Wesleyan Repository, 179

Wesleyan University, established, 215, 216, 221, 244, 366

Western Christian Advocate, The, 185, 221; barred from Wood County, Virginia, 260; opposes withdrawal of Methodist Episcopal Church from slave states, 263; circulation of, 268; supports Northern cause in Civil War, 291; quoted, 297; Calvin Kingsley, Civil War editor, 302

Western Conference, 129, 145, 161

West Virginia, Methodism in, 280

Whatcoat, Richard, 104, 106, 108, 109, 115, 139, 161, 165

White Water Circuit, early Indiana circuit, 160, 162

White, Judge William, 89, 93, 107, 117

Whitefield, George, 13 ff., 17, 37 ff., 45, 70 ff., 79, 123

Whitman, Marcus, 201

Whittier, John Greenleaf, poet, 236

Whitworth, Abraham, 69

Wightman, W. M., Bishop Methodist Episcopal Church, South, 309

Wilberforce, William, English anti-slavery leader, 133, 231

Wilbraham Academy, 197, 214, 215, 216

Wiley, Isaac W., bishop, 325

Willamette University, founded, 269

Willamette valley, 198

William and Mary College, 19, 207

Williams College, revival at, 155, 203

Williams, Robert, 58, 61, 63, 69, 72, 73, 75

Williams, Roger, 15

Williams, Professor William G., 213

Wills Creek Circuit, Kentucky, 222

Wilson, President Woodrow, 372

Winans, William, 244

Wisconsin Conference, opposes reunion with Church South, 306

Wofford College, founded, 222

Woman's Christian Temperance Union, peace activities of, 370, 388

Woman's Crusade, Temperance organization, 387

Woman's Foreign Missionary Society, 325, 330

Woman's Home Missionary Society, 347

471

DATE DUE